Adventure Guide to the

Bahamas

3rd Edition

Blair Howard

HUNTER

HUNTER PUBLISHING, INC.
130 Campus Drive, Edison NJ 08818
732-225-1900, 800-255-0343, fax 732-417-0482
comments@hunterpublishing.com

4176 Saint-Denis, Montréal, Québec
Canada H2W 2M5
514-843-9447; fax 515-843-9448; info@ulysses.com

The Boundary, Wheatley Road, Garsington
Oxford, OX44 9EJ England
01865-361122; fax 01865-361133
windsorbooks@compuserve.com

ISBN 1-58843-318-8

© 2003 Blair Howard

Maps by Kim André & Lissa Dailey,
© 2003 Hunter Publishing, Inc.

Cartoons by Joe Kohl

Cover photograph:
Bahamas market scene, eStock Photo/TPL/Harris
All others by Blair Howard or courtesy of Bahamas Tourist Board

For complete information about the hundreds of other travel guides
offered by Hunter Publishing, visit our Web site at:
www.hunterpublishing.com

4 3 2 1

Contents

Maps

Introduction

It's been many years since I began writing travel books. Over those years I've visited numerous exotic destinations: magnificent beaches, wild and remote mountain retreats, painted deserts, and bustling, historic cities, but of all those incredible places the islands of the Bahamas are my favorite. Time and again I return to Nassau, Freeport, Abaco, Eleuthera and Harbour Island, and I continue to be inspired by their beauty. There truly is no other place I'd rather spend a vacation. The Bahamas have everything, from bustling international cities – not too big, not too small – to tiny islets where it seems no human foot has ever stepped. The weather is sometimes wild, but not for long. The gentle sea breezes, the hot sun, and those great stretches of shallow, emerald water bounded by blinding white strips of sand are irresistible.

The Bahamas, some 700 islands and 2,000 islets, lie scattered like a broken string of pearls across the northern Caribbean and offer literally thousands of opportunities for adventure. In fact, they have provided a dozen or more generations of seafarers and travelers with more adventure than many of them might ever have imagined – or wanted.

In the earliest times, Spanish explorers headed west from Cadiz in search of riches and excitement. They found both – often to their detriment. The Spanish were followed by the Portuguese, then by the English, the French, the Dutch and then by anyone else who could find a craft seaworthy enough to endure the hazardous crossing.

In later years, the explorers were followed by adventurers of a different sort. Pirates, corsairs, brigands, ne'r-do-wells and privateers – all drawn by the promise of easy pickings and quick riches – flocked to the Bahamas in the thousands. Men such as the notorious Edward Teach (Blackbeard), "Calico" Jack Rakham, Henry Morgan, Major Bonnet, and nefarious women buccaneers such as Anne Bonney (Calico Jack's mistress), and Mary Reed scoured the seas in search of vulnerable merchant ships carrying gold, silver and jewels. Only slightly better were the so-called privateers, such as Francis Drake and John Hawkins, who pillaged and plundered in the name of whatever sovereign happened to be on the throne at the time.

Inhabited by Lucayan Indians, the islands were at first a haven for the tiny wooden ships, often at sea for several months, that headed westward to the New World. The Indians soon became the subject of mass exploitation and the few that didn't die of diseases brought from Europe were enslaved.

Today, the Lucayan Indians, the pirates and privateers are long gone. Today's adventurer, while still very much an explorer, is an outdoor enthusiast, a skin diver, an angler, a sailor, a hiker, a bird watcher, a gambler or even a shopper. All are looking for something different and all manage to find it one way or another in the Bahamas.

More than 3.5 million travelers come to the islands each year. They arrive sometimes by small boat, but more often by cruise ship or jet. Some are so taken with the magical beauty of the islands they stay for months.

Through the pages of this book, you will be able to find all the information you need quickly, no matter what place or activity appeals to you the most. This is not a book for bungee jumpers, sky divers, extreme skiers and those who live life on the edge. It's for the angler in search of the Big One, the honeymooner looking for the perfect beach, and those who've always wanted to dive to the depths of the ocean or explore ancient shipwrecks. No matter what your experience level, you can learn to dive in less than three hours and be swimming 30 feet beneath the waves in less than four hours.

You'll discover where the best fishing spots are and the best places to dive. I'll tell you the best places to eat, where to shop in the duty-free stores for magnificent emeralds, exotic perfumes and the unique hand-made crafts of the islands. And you'll find advice on where to stay: hotels, condominiums, and villas.

Whether you have only an hour or two ashore from a visiting cruise ship or are heading to the islands for a couple of weeks of fun in the sun, use this book to plan your visit, and take it with you as a reference guide. Above all, enjoy yourself. You are in for the experience of a lifetime.

Blair Howard

About the Bahamas

Geography

The Bahamas lie scattered across more than 100,000 square miles of the western Atlantic Ocean. From a point roughly 70 miles east of West Palm Beach, Florida, the great archipelago extends some 750 miles southward toward the northern Caribbean, almost to the island of Hispaniola.

The islands that make up the Bahamas are generally low and flat. The highest point in the entire archipelago, on Cat Island, is just 206 feet above sea level. Except on Andros, the largest island of the chain, there are no rivers or streams. Apart from New Providence – where fresh water is shipped in daily from Andros, pumped from wells dug into the underlying rocks – fresh water is abundant.

 DID YOU KNOW? *Because the islands are no more than the exposed top portions of the Great Bahama Bank, an extension of the North American continental shelf, there are only three deep-water channels suitable for the passage of large vessels.*

Of the 700 islands and 2,000 islets, called cays (keys), making up the archipelago, only about 30 are inhabited. Some are little more than boulders that appear and disappear with the rise and fall of the ocean. Some are long and thin and stretch for many miles. Still others are home to thousands of busy people. The vast majority of the islands, however, are deserted, with pristine beaches and tropical forests that are untouched by humans.

The Islands of the Bahamas

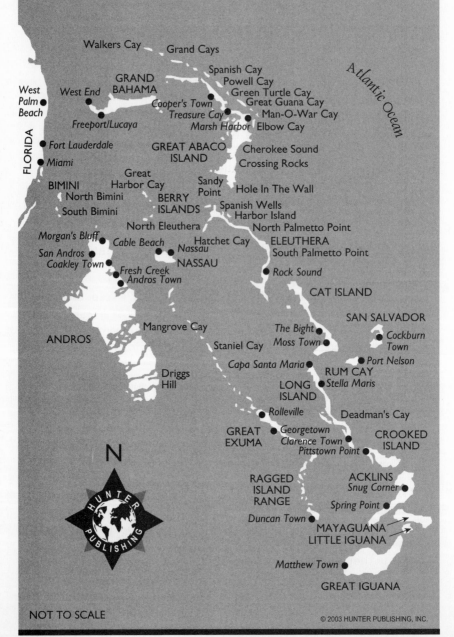

NOT TO SCALE

DID YOU KNOW? *With a total combined land mass of less than 5,400 square miles, the islands of the Bahamas constitute one of the smallest countries in the world.*

Tourism has brought prosperity to the Bahamas. But it hasn't spoiled the great natural beauty of the islands. In the early days, as in the coastal boom towns of Florida and California, little attention was given to the damage unrestricted exploitation was inflicting on Nassau and New Providence. Today, there's a new feeling in the islands. A feeling that the unique beauty of the archipelago must be preserved. Conservation is the new watchword of the Bahamas.

■ Nassau

The largest and best known city in the Bahamas is Nassau. Located on the island of **New Providence**, it boasts a population of more than 175,000 people. In times gone by, Nassau was an international playground for the rich. Today, the first city of the Bahamas attracts not only the affluent of the world, but vacationers of every class and culture, especially from America. The city has become a tax haven – Nassau has more than 400 banks – and is a popular location for international business conferences and meetings.

Nassau is also a microcosm of the nation's history. Visitors can explore its narrow streets, the old British forts, climb the Queen's Staircase and wander through outlying villages dating back to the days of slavery and beyond.

Throughout the Christmas and New Year's holidays, at the height of the Bahamian tourist season, **Junkanoo** – a spirited, Mardi Gras-style celebration born of slavery – explodes across the islands, but nowhere is it quite as exciting as in Nassau.

■ Paradise Island

Paradise Island, a long, narrow barrier island connected to Nassau by a toll bridge, is as different from Nassau as Key West is from Miami. While Paradise Island is a world of hotels, restaurants and exciting nightlife, it's also a world still quite unspoiled where you can enjoy the sea and beaches that lie close to the bustling streets of the city.

About the Bahamas

■ Freeport

Freeport, on **Grand Bahama Island**, is the second largest city in the islands. With a steadily growing population, now more than 50,000, Freeport, which adjoins the Lucaya Beach area, is a more modern city than Nassau. The carefully planned, landscaped streets are a product of the sixties, and of the dreams of American entrepreneur and financier, Wallace Groves.

■ Grand Bahama

Grand Bahama, through the efforts of dedicated individuals and institutions such as the Rand Memorial Nature Center and the Lucayan National Park, has become something of an environmental headquarters for the islands. With its miles of sandy beaches, excellent shopping, two casinos, a dozen or so large hotels, a waterfront district and many restaurants, Grand Bahama is quickly becoming a major vacation destination.

■ The Out Islands

There's another world beyond those two major tourist destinations: the Out Islands of Abaco, Andros, the Berry Islands, Bimini, Cat Island, Crooked Island, Eleuthera, the Exumas, Harbour Island, Long Island, and so on. The Out Islands have long been a popular destination for sailors, sport fishermen and divers. Today, due to some aggressive marketing and increased accessibility, they are fast becoming popular with other active travelers.

Far away from the bustling streets and tourist attractions of Nassau and Freeport, the rest of the Bahamian population, some 40,000 people, pursue their everyday lives. They live in sparsely settled little towns and villages from one end of the island chain to the other. Most Out Island residents have never left their island.

The little towns and villages are an odd mixture of the old and the new. Here and there across the Out Islands you'll find impressive colonial manor houses right alongside half-finished concrete structures that will one day, as money permits, become the homes of fishermen and farmers.

In the many villages of the outer islands to the southeast, the traditional pattern of farming and fishing prevails. Fruits and vegetables are grown throughout the Out Islands, along with pigs, sheep, goats and turkeys, while crayfish (Bahamian lobster), lumber, and pulp-wood are exported, chiefly to the United States.

Thick vegetation, mostly shrubs and bushes, covers most of the Out Islands. Each is a tiny land of dunes and rocks, sea grass, spider lilies, seagrape, mangrove, casuarina and palm. Each is a land of endless shores, tiny bays and rocky inlets, where the colorful families of the ocean live, play and die in the crystal-clear waters of the reefs.

Marsh Harbour, on Abaco Island, is the third largest city in the islands. This dusty little town is somewhat reminiscent of an American frontier cattle town of the 1880s. In contrast, the neat little painted villages of **Hope Town**, on Elbow Cay, and **New Plymouth**, on Green Turtle Cay, might well have been lifted up and flown in straight from New England.

If it's seclusion you're after, you'll find it in the Out Islands. The flat terrain and the long dusty roads, often devoid of travelers and always in various stages of disrepair, lend themselves well to walking or bicycling. Anglers no longer will need to tell tales of the one that got away. The bonefish here fight each other to take the hook and big game fish aren't as wary as they are off the coast of Florida. Shipwrecks, coral reefs, and mysterious blue holes dot the vast stretches of empty flats and shallow reefs. There are beaches where the sand is the color of pink champagne and there's not an empty soda can to be seen any-

School children in the Out Islands.

where; where you can wade in the shallow waters, lie in the sun, or cast a line into the gently rolling surf. You might hook a chunky snapper and bake it over a small fire as the sun goes down. Get lucky and you could be eating fresh lobster instead of snapper.

The people of the Out Islands are friendly. They are real people, people without pretensions, their roots anchored firmly in the past. They say "God bless you" rather than good-bye, and think nothing of letting a stranger into their home to use the bathroom, or for a drink of water. They are a jolly people who look forward only to the next day, and are grateful for it.

Perhaps you'll meet the tourist guide who lives alone with her small son and drives an aging Chevrolet that rarely starts. It doesn't phase her a bit. She carries on with life, never complaining, knowing that, one way or another, she'll get there in the end; and she always does.

Maybe you'll meet the taxi driver whose small, three-bedroom home shelters not only him and his wife, but five grown-up children and six of his grandchildren as well. Far from being harassed by the situation, he'll tell you how happy he is that they are all around for him to enjoy.

These aren't isolated cases. Of course, you'll find the occasional bum lounging on the beach, and there are certainly some strange characters wandering the streets of Nassau. There's a certain amount of petty crime on the islands and everyone wants more money. But on the whole, there's an overwhelming air of tranquility, a "don't worry; be happy" attitude that pervades the islands, and it's infectious. Visitors returning home often find the easygoing Bahamian ways, the shrug of the shoulders, and an almost overpowering desire to put everything off until tomorrow, has returned with them.

Only a few of the Out Islands offer any sort of tourist accommodations. Some are small hotels where the air-conditioning is nothing more than the soft trade winds blowing in through the window, and the only telephone is a lonely pay phone somewhere in the vicinity of the hotel office. There are also rental cottages, villas, luxurious hotels, private islands, and even resorts.

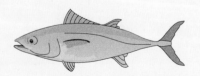

History

■ Early Settlement

 Before the Europeans arrived, the Bahamas were inhabited mostly by **Lucayan Indians**. **Christopher Columbus**, on his way to the New World, made landfall on San Salvador – so it's generally accepted – in 1492.

 DID YOU KNOW?

The islands became known as Bahama, from the Spanish "baja mar," or shallow sea.

Almost immediately, Europeans began enslaving the Lucayans. By the turn of the 16th century, they had almost been wiped out and a new source of cheap labor was needed. As early as 1503, the **Portuguese** were enslaving Africans and for several years they controlled the burgeoning industry. By 1520, however, white slave traders of assorted nationalities were going directly to the source.

In 1649, **Captain William Sayle** and a band of Englishmen arrived in the islands from Bermuda. They came with slaves of their own, seeking religious freedom. They called themselves the **Eleutherian Adventurers**, hence the island of Eleuthera. The name is based upon the Greek word for freedom.

Edward Teach, known as "Blackbeard."

■ Pirates & Privateers

In 1666, New Providence was settled by a second group of Englishmen. They, too, arrived from Bermuda seeking a better life. By then, however, other adventurers had already realized that the Bahamas, close to the already busy shipping routes from the New World to Spain and Portugal, offered quick and easy pickings. By 1660, privateering (officially sanctioned and often royally commissioned piracy) was already an established industry.

A Voyage to Remember

Sir John Hawkins had already made several journeys to the Caribbean selling slaves when he was joined in 1567 by **Francis Drake**, still a teenager, who made the journey as captain of his own ship, *Judith*. Their voyage ended in disaster when Hawkins and Drake, with a fleet of five ships, took refuge from a storm in the Spanish port of San Juan de Ulua, now called Vera Cruz. There, they were treachorously attacked by a superior Spanish fleet under the command of the new viceroy and Captain General of New Spain, Don Martin Enriquez. Hawkins' flagship, *Jesus of Lubeck*, and two other English ships were destroyed. Only the *Minion* and Drake's little bark returned to England. Thus began Drake's life-long personal war with Spain.

Drake and Hawkins were followed by an endless stream of privateers and pirates that, by the turn of the 18th century, included such notables as **Sir Henry Morgan**, **Blackbeard** and **Captain Kidd**. **Captain Henry Jennings** established a base in the Bahamas from which to raid the Spanish treasure ships sometime around 1714. **Major Stede Bonnet**, a wealthy French landowner of Barbados, turned to piracy simply for the adventure. He equipped a 10-gun sloop, *Revenge*, and in 1717 began to raid ships off the Virginia coast. He was hanged for piracy in November 1718.

Calico Jack

Captain John Rackham, called "Calico Jack" for the striped trousers he wore, was a pirate captain for the two years 1718 to 1720. During this short time he plundered many ships. He and his men were captured by the crew of a government ship and brought to trial at St. Jago de la Vega, Jamaica. Among Rackham's crew were his mistress, Mary Read, and Anne Bonney. They are the only female pirates on record. Rackham and Read were hanged in Port Royal on November 17, 1720.

The pirates were finally driven out of the Bahamas after **Captain Woodes Rogers** was appointed Royal Governor in 1718. When he arrived at New Providence, about 1,000 pirates were living on the island. Rogers blocked the harbor with two ships so that the outlaws couldn't escape. A fierce fight followed, during which the pirates set fire to one of their own ships and sailed it toward the English ships, forcing Rogers' ships back out to sea. Nevertheless, Rogers finally

Anne Bonney and Mary Read, Calico Jack's female pirate crew.

took possession of the island and the pirates were driven away. A statue of Rogers stands in front of the British Colonial Hotel in Nassau.

Captain Jean Lafitte, who died in about 1826, was the last colorful figure in the history of piracy. Lafitte, a patriot as well as a pirate, privateer, and smuggler, was enormously successful, but eventually he too lost his land base and his power dwindled.

■ The 19th Century

Just prior to the turn of the 19th century, after the American Revolution had drawn to a close, a new breed of immigrant arrived in the islands. These were one-time English colonists in America who were still loyal to England and its government. They left Virginia with their slaves and settled in the Bahamas.

By 1800, the black population of the islands had tripled. Emancipation came to the Bahamas in August 1834, and the newly liberated slaves left Nassau and moved "over the hill" to establish settlements of their own. The descendants of those slaves still live in Grant's Town, Carmichael, Gambier and Adelaide, as well as on the Out Islands of The Exumas, Rum Cay, San Salvador, Long Island and others. Unfortunately, the one-time slaves were unequipped for life on their own; the new settlements endured but didn't prosper. The black Bahamians became the poor people of the islands.

■ The Modern Era

By the early 1900s, people of African descent had become the majority of the Bahamian population, but power remained in the hands of the white minority. By the 1930s, the islands had been discovered by the millionaire developers from America and Europe, and the gap between the races grew even wider.

Things continued in much the same vein for more than 40 years until 1951, when women and people who didn't own property were given the right to vote. Eight years later, the black majority took the Bahamas into independence as a commonwealth nation, despite fierce opposition from the British government and white property owners.

Today, with the boom in tourism, the black population is doing better. Many of the new businesses on the islands are owned by Bahamians of African descent and there's a real sense of pride in this ownership.

Getting There

■ By Air

Both Nassau and Freeport are major US and international gateways. Dozens of airlines regularly fly between the islands and Europe, Canada and various US terminals, including most major cities such as New York, Chicago, Boston and Atlanta; and locations in Florida. Visitors can fly freely between the islands by **Bahamasair**, the national carrier. Charter flights between the islands are also available. See the *At a Glance* section at the end of this guide for full details.

■ By Cruise Ship

Four major cruise lines offer three- and four-night, regularly scheduled cruises to the Bahamas. **Royal Caribbean International** operates the *Sovereign of the Seas*

out of Miami. The ship does its three-night itinerary leaving port on Fridays for Nassau and their private island of Coco Cay. The four-night cruise leaves port on Mondays, and it too visits Nassau and Coco Cay. Rates start at around $350 per person, depending upon the season. ☎ 800-453-4022. www.royalcaribbean.com.

Premier Cruise Lines is the only line that includes visits to both Freeport, on Grand Bahama, and Nassau. They too offer three- and four-night itineraries on the *Oceanic*. The *Oceanic* is a themed ship – Looney Toons – and, with extensive children's programs, it's ideal for families. Ships leave Port Canaveral on Friday and Monday. Rates start at around $275 per person for the three-night cruise, and $330 for the four-night option – children cruise for substantially less. ☎ 800-990-7770. www.premierecruises.com.

Carnival Cruise Lines operates ships out of Miami and Port Canaveral on three- and four-night itineraries. The *Ecstasy* leaves Miami on Fridays for the three-night cruise. The *Fantasy* leaves Port Canaveral for three nights on Thursdays, and on Sundays for four nights. Rates start at around $350 per person, depending on the season. ☎ 800-CARNIVAL. www.carnival.com.

The latest addition to the ships cruising the Bahamas is **Disney's** *Magic*. It sails out of Port Canaveral on three- and four-night itineraries, and is the most expensive option. The three- and four-night cruise itineraries, usually combined with a three- or four-day visit to Walt Disney World, include a stop in Nassau and a visit to Disney's private island, Castaway Cay. Rates start at $450 per person for the three-night cruise and $530 for the four-night option; these rates are for the cruise only and do not include the Disney World option. ☎ 800-511-1333. www.disneycruise.com.

▪ By Mail Boat

 Traveling between the Out Islands by mail boat is an adventure. You won't find many reference to these little ships, and you can't make reservations. Operating out of Potter's Cay dock at the Paradise Island bridge, some 20 mail boats leave daily, usually in the afternoons, and return two or three days later. The schedules, though posted as regular, often can be haphazard. But, if you have the time and patience, this can add to your experience. Just sit back, relax, and enjoy yourself. To sail the mail boats, simply pick a time and destination – you'll find details in each chapter and in the *At a Glance* section at the end. You should get to the dock a few hours before sailing to book your passage. Sailing time to the Abacos is five hours; to the Inaguas, 18 hours.

Don't even consider taking the mail boats if you suffer from sea sickness.

■ By Private Boat

The Islands of the Bahamas have, since the dawn of recorded history, held a special interest for sailors. Spanish explorers, pirates and privateers and blockade runners have plied these waters. Today, private watercraft make up the bulk of traffic. Yachts and cruisers in all sizes range from little Hobie Cats to multi-million-dollar mega-yachts. The close proximity to the Florida mainland makes the crossing possible for sailors of even limited experience. Boating facilities are plentiful, diverse, and spread throughout the islands. You'll find marinas and anchorages listed throughout this book.

■ Package Vacations

A number of tour operators provide air/hotel packages. **Delta Dream Vacations**, **American FlyAAWay Vacations**, **Vacation Express**, **Travel Impressions**, and **Apple Vacations** all offer packages to Nassau. American FlyAAWay Vacations, **Princess Vacations**, Travel Impressions, Vacation Express and Apple also offer packages to Grand Bahama.

A WORD TO
THE WISE

If you want to visit the Out Islands, namely the Abacos, Eleuthera, Long Island and the Exumas, your best option is American FlyAAWay Vacations.

A couple of Out Island hotels also offer vacation and dive packages – check in the appropriate chapter for details. One other option worth considering is **Club Med**. They have resorts on Paradise Island (Nassau), Eleuthera and San Salvador.

If you want to visit one of the more remote islands, you'll need to enlist the services of a creative travel agent. It might take a little arranging, but it is possible, and the experience will be well worth the extra effort. You'll find options listed throughout this book.

If you're traveling to Nassau you should choose packages by American or Delta, and to Freeport, Princess Vacations. Especially where large airlines are concerned, all portions of the package are controlled by the package operator. This can make a difference, especially if something should go wrong – delayed or cancelled flights, for instance. Major air carriers are more inclined to look after their own customers before those of other suppliers.

Package vacations are usually arranged by a travel agent and will typically include airfare from a major US or European gateway, round-trip airport/hotel transfers, accommodations at a hotel chosen from the package operator's inventory, and hotel taxes. Another option is an "all-inclusive" package. This will include, not only your round-trip airfare, airport/hotel transfers, and accommodations, but all of your meals and drinks (alcoholic and soft), gratuities, golf and watersports.

Is an all-inclusive package worth the extra cost?

In general, yes; especially when you consider the cost of beverages: even the non-alcoholic versions of the exotic drinks will cost $5 to $6, and soft drinks are $2 to $3.

Hotels in most packages range from Tourist Class to Superior Deluxe, and are supposed to be inspected by the tour operator on a regular basis; some do, indeed, carry out such inspections. Remember, however, that you are not dealing with the same standards as in the United States, Canada or England (see the definitions under Accommodations on pages 20-21). I recommend that you NOT book a package with a hotel rated less than "Deluxe."

Before You Go

■ Travel Documents

To enter the Bahamas you'll need two things: **proof of citizenship** and a return or **onward-bound ticket**. A valid passport is the preferred proof of citizenship. For US citizens, a birth certificate and a photo ID are also acceptable. A voter's registration card is no longer acceptable. A visa is not required. US immigration officials will want to see proof of US citizenship on your return. See the State Department website for details at http://travel.state.gov/bahamas.html.

Canadian and British citizens visiting for three weeks or less may enter by showing the same documents as required for US citizens. Citizens of British Commonwealth countries do not need visas.

■ Customs

Dutiable items, such as furniture, china and linens, must be declared. Each adult may bring in duty-free 200 cigarettes, or 50 cigars or one pound of tobacco and one quart of alcohol.

US residents, including children, may take home duty-free purchases valued up to $600, and up to 32 ounces of alcohol per person over the age of 21. Canadian citizens may take home up to $300 in purchases. Residents of Great Britain may take home up to £32 in duty-free purchases and each adult visitor is allowed 200 cigarettes or 50 cigars or one pound of tobacco and a liter of alcohol without paying duty.

■ Departure Taxes

At the time of writing, air travelers must pay a departure tax of $15 at Nassau and $18 at Freeport.

■ Disabled Travelers

 If you're disabled, or traveling with someone who is disabled, make all your arrangements well in advance. Be sure that you let everyone involved know the nature of the disability so that accommodations and facilities can be arranged to meet your needs. On the whole, you'll find most hotels, tour operators, and other facilities are well equipped to handle the needs of disabled visitors.

The People

 The Bahamas, still very much steeped in their traditional British heritage, are inhabited by a hodgepodge of black and white races of African-American, Continental European, and African origin, among others. Less than 40 years ago, blacks on the islands were not allowed in any of the nation's restaurants, theaters, and hotels, although they represented more than 80% of the population. That is all changed now and, although several islands remain predominantly white, Bahamians of all colors integrate freely with one another.

With independence from Britain in 1973, and with tourism becoming the mainstay of the Bahamian economy, black people, once the poorest members of the population, have increasingly improved their lot.

The bulk of the wealth is still in white hands, but more and more black-owned business are making a contribution. Where once they were not allowed, black Bahamians have found their way into administration and management. And while many young Bahamians still leave the islands in search of something better, it seems most of them return sooner or later.

Bahamians, black or white, are very friendly and outgoing. The always cheerful "good morning," the happy smile, and the eagerness to help, whether it's with directions or service, often borders on the cloying. But rest assured, it's done with an almost naïve genuineness and a desire to please.

■ Language

The language spoken on the islands is English – at least it's called English. The old language has been shaped and reshaped over more than 300 years by a potpourri of cultures, of which the British and Caribbean have had no small influence. Some say the Bahamian accent is decidedly West Indian, others say it has a sound all its own. If it's spoken quickly, it's almost impossible for an outsider to understand. The secret is to listen carefully, and don't be afraid to ask the speaker to repeat – that will often bring a delighted grin to his or her face.

People to People

If you want to get to know the real Bahamians, go out and meet the people. This is easily achieved through the government-sponsored "People to People" program offered by the Ministry of Tourism. It gives visitors the opportunity to meet and socialize with Bahamians, meeting them in their homes and participating in their social and cultural events. Get involved and you'll be invited to a variety of activities and social events. These might include performances by a local theater group, sporting events, or afternoon tea with a Bahamian family. For more information, contact the People-to-People Unit at the Tourist Information Center at Rawson Square in Nassau, at one of the information booths at the Nassau International Airport, or on Bay Street next to the Straw Market, at Prince George Dock, where the Ministry of Tourism's main office is located. In Freeport, there's a tourist office at the International Bazaar. In the Out Islands there are offices on Abaco, Eleuthera and the Exumas. To find out more on the Internet, go to www.bahamas.com, click on People at the left of the screen, then click on People-to-People Programme.

Eating & Drinking

Bahamian food is an adventure in itself. The larder of the Bahamas is the sea that surrounds it; seafood is the staple.

▪ Feast from the Sea

The **conch** – pronounced "konk" – is chief among the many varieties of goodies gathered from the ocean. Claimed by the locals to be an aphrodisiac, conch can be prepared in numerous ways: for conch salad the flesh is chopped, spiced, and eaten raw with vegetables and lime juice; cracked conch is beaten and fried; and, finally, there are conch fritters. Be sure to try conch salad before you leave; it's delicious.

Fish, especially grouper, is the principal fare of the Bahamian people. It's served many ways, for breakfast, lunch and dinner. The **Bahamian lobster** (Americans call it crayfish) is plentiful, often large, and not as expensive as it is in the States. Try minced lobster, a mixture of shredded lobster meat cooked with tomatoes, green peppers and onions, and served in the shell.

Fishy Delights

Fish is prepared in a number of ways, the names of which are often confusing. **Boil fish** is served for breakfast. It's cooked with salt pork, green peppers and onions, and served with a generous portion of grits. **Stew fish** is prepared with celery, tomatoes, onions, and spices, all combined in a thick brown gravy; it is also served for breakfast. **Steamed fish** is cooked in a tomato base and is as tasty as it is novel.

▪ Traditional Foods

Bahamians also eat a lot of crab, chicken, pork, and mutton. Almost everything is served with huge portions of **peas and rice** – a concoction of pigeon peas, peppers, celery, tomatoes, and rice, seasoned and cooked until golden brown.

For dessert, try **guava duff**, a Bahamian delicacy made by spreading guava fruit pulp on a sheet of dough. It's then rolled and boiled, cut into slices and served with a thick white sauce.

Other than fish, most of the food eaten on the islands is imported, which makes it somewhat expensive. While restaurants on the Out Islands tend to serve mostly Bahamian foods, more and more American fare is making its way onto Bahamian tables. You can find a good steak or prime rib and the inevitable French fries at most of the popular restaurants in Nassau and Freeport. And almost all of the American fast-food chains are represented: McDonalds, Burger King, KFC.

There's even a Pizza Hut on Abaco. But to avoid the local food is to miss a great eating experience.

■ Drinks

AUTHOR PICK

Popular drinks are the **Bahama Mama**, the **Goombay Smash**, and the **Yellow Bird**. Bahamians also drink lots and lots of beer, mostly the local brew: a fine golden beer called **Kalik**. Be sure to try it. Imported beers from America and Europe are also available but, like everything else that has to be imported, they're expensive. For something really different, try one of the locally brewed sodas with exotic names.

All drinks on the islands are expensive. Be prepared to pay up to $5.50 for a bottle of beer in a restaurant, $5.50 for cocktails. Even non-alcoholic cocktails kids can consume in large quantities are pricey. A Coke or locally made soda can cost up to $3.

During the day, **hot tea** is the drink of preference. If you want iced tea, be sure to specify that when ordering. On most of the islands, the water is pure and safe to drink straight from the tap.

WORD TO THE WISE

Nassau's water is imported from Andros by ship and, by the time it reaches the consumer, the taste is not what you might like. It's best to drink only bottled water in Nassau because of that.

■ Tipping

It's standard to add a 15% service charge to restaurant checks and the same with room service in the large hotels. If you don't see a gratuity on the bill, ask. Hotels add an 8%-10% service charge to their rates, so there's no need to leave a room tip. Tour guides expect to receive $2 to $5 per person, and cab drivers usually receive 10%-15% of the fare.

Accommodations

Hotels on the two main islands, New Providence and Grand Bahama, range in quality from Tourist Class through Superior Deluxe. Remember, however, that you are not dealing with the same standards you have grown used to in the United States, Canada or England. Even the top-rated hotels are almost always busy, and geared to accommodate the vacationing public, rather than business people. In general, this means that, unless you book the best room your particular hotel has to offer, your accommodations will probably be no better than average. Clean and comfortable, yes; luxurious, number

Hotel Classification Guide

SUPERIOR DELUXE: Exclusive, elegant, luxury hotels offering the highest standards of accommodations, service and facilities.

DELUXE: Outstanding hotels with many of the features and amenities offered by those classed as Superior Deluxe, but less expensive.

SUPERIOR FIRST CLASS: Above-average hotels, often older, but well-maintained. Accommodations are comfortable and tastefully furnished.

FIRST CLASS: Facilities are not as extensive as those at hotels in the more expensive categories, but these hotels are dependable and comfortable.

SUPERIOR TOURIST CLASS: Budget properties, mostly well-kept and maintained. Facilities are few, but the rooms are generally clean and comfortable, if sometimes spartan.

TOURIST CLASS: Low budget, with few or no facilities. Not for the discriminating traveler.

■ Out Islands

On the Out Islands – the Abacos, Eleuthera, the Exumas, Andros, Long Island, Cat Island, etc. – accommodations can be basic; many are not air-conditioned. There are very few hotels rated better than First Class. Also, most Out Island hotels do not have TVs or telephones in the rooms, although they all have them in the main buildings. If you want to get away from the stresses of everyday living, it can be nice to leave the television and telephone back on the mainland.

About the Bahamas

■ Package Deals

If your vacation is a package provided by a major operator, you can generally expect your hotel to be clean and comfortable. Package operators inspect their client hotels regularly and require certain minimum standards. This doesn't mean you get better service or accommodations, just that you can be assured of certain standards.

Restaurant & Hotel Prices

Restaurant Price Scale
$ . . . . less than $20 per person
$$ . . . . $20-$50 per person
$$$ . . . . $50+ per person

Hotels are listed in order by rate, the least expensive first. Actual rates, when not quoted within the text, are shown at the back of the book in the *At a Glance* section.

Meal Plans

- **CP** (Continental Plan) includes a continental breakfast.
- **EP** (European Plan) denotes no meals, although restaurant facilities are available either on the property or nearby.
- **MAP** (Modified American Plan) denotes breakfast and dinner.
- **FAP** (Full American Plan) includes all meals.
- **All-Inc.** (All-Inclusive Plan) includes all meals, beverages (alcoholic and soft), watersports, tennis and golf, if available.

All hotel rates quoted are subject to a 4% room tax and a 4% resort levy; gratuities are extra.

Practical Information

■ Banking

Banking is big business in the Bahamas. Long recognized as a tax haven, both Nassau and Freeport are home to more than their fair share of counting houses. And for visitors to the islands that's good. There's always a bank around the next corner.

In Nassau and Freeport/Lucaya, banks are open from 9:30 am until 3 pm, Monday through Thursday, and from 9:30 am until 5 pm on Friday. If you rely on credit cards for your cash, there are international ATMs located at strategic spots on both of the major islands, including the casinos. As one might expect, banking hours vary in the Out Islands. In fact, banks on some islands open only on certain days of the week, and then only for a few hours.

■ Bicycles & Mopeds

Bicycles are popular on the islands. Visitors love them. They are inexpensive to rent, convenient, easy to park, and nowhere is really too far away. The only concern is that you'll be riding on the "wrong" side of the road. You can rent mopeds and bicycles at most hotels and resorts, or at nearby cycle shops. The going rates for mopeds range from about $20 to $30 a day – a half-day might cost anywhere from $10 to $20 – and you'll be asked to leave a small deposit, usually about $30. Bicycles run about $18 a day.

■ Buses

Bus travel can be an adventure. And if you want to meet the people, there's no better way to do it than finding your way around Nassau by bus. For 75¢, it's a great way to travel. Bahamians are very friendly and will come to your aid quickly with directions. (The only problem is understanding the waving hands and the fast talk.) On Grand Bahama, the buses connect Freeport with Lucaya, the hotels, the beaches, Port Lucaya and, of course, the International Bazaar.

■ Casinos

 Visitors over the age of 18 may gamble at all four casinos in Nassau and Freeport. Children are allowed to enter the casinos only to attend shows in the casino theaters. In Nassau, there is a casino on Paradise Island at the **Atlantis Resort** and one at **Nassau Marriott Resort** on Cable Beach. In Freeport, one casino is at **Our Lucaya**. The other is at the **Royal Oasis Resort & Casino**. There is more information on gaming and casinos in the regional chapters.

■ Climate

 The trade winds blow almost continuously here, creating a warm, agreeable climate that varies little throughout the year. September through May, when the temperature averages 70-75°F, is the most refreshing time to visit. The rest of the year is somewhat warmer, with temperatures between 80° and 85°.

May is the rainy season.

■ Currency

 Legal tender is the **Bahamian dollar**, which is always equivalent in value to the US dollar. Both US and Bahamian dollars are accepted interchangeably throughout the islands, and visitors are likely to receive change in mixed American and Bahamian currency.

Traveler's checks are accepted throughout the islands and may be cashed at banks and hotels. They will, however, add a service charge. **Credit cards** are widely accepted in Nassau and Freeport/Lucaya, and to a lesser extent on the Out Islands, where cash is still king. Be prepared to pay a service charge if you use American Express.

WORD TO THE WISE

British visitors should buy Bahamian dollars before traveling. The exchange rate often will be more favorable at home than in the Bahamas.

■ Dress

The dress code is casual and comfortable. Days are spent in shorts, swimsuits, slacks or jeans. Although the islands have been independent for more than 25 years, the influence of more than 250 years of British rule is still evident. You shouldn't wear swimsuits except at the pool or on the beach. Do not wear them in shops, restaurants, and on the streets of Nassau and Freeport/Lucaya.

In the evening, most people prefer to dress casual but smart – sport shirts and slacks. For more formal dining at some of the first-class restaurants and larger hotels, gentlemen should wear a tie and jacket; long skirts or cocktail dresses are preferred for ladies. On the Out Islands, except at some of the large resorts, dress is much more casual.

■ Electricity

All US and Canadian appliances can be used without adapters. Visitors from the United Kingdom will need adapters to 120 volts.

■ Ferries

Ah, this is the way to travel. Ferries in Nassau run between Prince George Dock and Paradise Island. On the Out Islands the ferry is often the only way of getting around. On Abaco, ferries run every hour or so between Treasure Cay, New Plymouth on Green Turtle Cay, and the Green Turtle Club (also on Green Turtle Cay), with various stops along the way. This round-trip takes about an hour to complete. From Marsh Harbour the ferry runs to Man-O-War Cay and back, and from Marsh Harbour to Hope Town on Elbow Cay and back. Once again, a round-trip takes about an hour. It's a lazy way to travel, but most enjoyable. There's nothing quite like a boat ride on a warm sunny day, especially when the scenery is spectacular and the sea the color of the palest jade.

■ Mail Boats

 Even though the Out Islands are now almost all accessible by airplane, mail boats still ply the waters back and forth between the islands. The boats leave Nassau from Potter's Cay – located off East Bay Street under the east Paradise Island bridge – about once a week, stopping at one or two of the Out Islands along the way. The journey takes about 12 hours, usually overnight. Schedules are somewhat random, subject to change and postponement. The mail boat is, however, an economical way to travel the islands, a lot of fun, and perhaps the most understated and unusual adventure available. The decks are crowded with Bahamians, freight, livestock and a variety of weird cargoes.

This is also a great way to make short trips to the Out Islands. For instance, the *Bahamas Daybreak III* leaves Nassau on Mondays at 7 pm, arrives at Governor's Harbour on Eleuthera at midnight, and returns to Nassau at 8 pm on Tuesday. You could spend the night at the Duck Inn or the Rainbow Inn, spend the next day sightseeing, swimming, snorkeling or whatever, then catch the boat and be back in your hotel by 1:30 am, just in time to get some sleep. Unfortunately, passage cannot be arranged in advance, but only after arrival in the Bahamas. For more information, call the dock master at Potter's Cay, ☎ 242-393-1064. You'll find detailed schedule and fare information within each regional chapter, and in the *At a Glance* section at the end of the book.

■ Photography

 The ocean wears a coat of many colors, ranging from the palest emerald green to the deepest indigo. The colors of the flowers – hibiscus, bougainvillea, goat's foot, and spider lily – seem a little brighter than anywhere else. The sand varies just a little from the palest pink to the tint of fine champagne. And then there's the clothing. Bahamians love bright colors. Light colored dresses, shirts, and hats set against rich brown skin offer rare opportunities for great photography. Gaily painted cottages, bustling streets alive with color, roadside fish markets, vast mangrove swamps, tiny harbors crowded with sailboats, lighthouses, and thousands of scenic bays, inlets, and beaches offer even more vistas for shutterbugs. If that's not enough, you can always dive into the underwater world.

Here are some simple techniques to help you shoot better photos:

- Take more film than you think you'll need, along with spare batteries, especially if you are shooting slides. Film is expensive locally and the type you prefer might not be available, especially in the Out Islands.

- Use low-speed film. The fine grain of a 50 or 100 ASA film will produce the best results. A rule of thumb is: the lower the film speed, the sharper the image will be. In the interest of great pictures, use a low-speed film whenever you can, especially on bright, sunny days. Use a high-speed film only with low light or when using a telephoto lens.

■ Shoot at the highest possible shutter speed. This will reduce camera shake. The longer the lens, the faster the shutter speed." You should never hand-hold a camera at a shutter speed slower than the focal length of the lens. For example, you would only hand-hold a camera fitted with 180mm lens when the shutter speed is set to 1/250 of a second or more; never slower. Likewise, a 50mm lens could be hand-held with the shutter set to 1/60th of a second, but no slower.

■ The best light for photography is in the early morning and late afternoon. The colors are warmer and the shadows deeper. At noon, when the sun is overhead, the lighting is flat and uninteresting.

■ Good composition means good photographs. Dull days and skies without detail mean dull photographs. Such situations call for a little thought before you shoot. A technique called *framing* will eliminate large, detail-less areas from your pictures. Shoot from beneath tree branches, through doorways and windows, and include odd sections of wall and pieces of furniture in the picture. Walk around the subject until you find something – anything – you can place in the picture that will break up those large, uninteresting areas of sky. Never place a dominant point of interest in the center of your picture; move it up or down just a little, or place it a little to one side. Finally, look around. Make sure there is no trash – soda cans, scraps of paper – lying around.

■ Never shoot into the sun. For the best effect, the sunlight should be coming from behind you, never from in front, unless you're looking for silhouettes.

■ If you can, take notes. There's nothing worse than getting a half-dozen rolls of film back from the lab and not knowing what it is you're seeing.

■ Don't miss the opportunity to shoot under water. Even if you don't intend to go diving, you should take a camera to the beach; the fish in the shallow waters are colorful and abundant. You can purchase one of those neat little ready-made under-water cameras that come ready to shoot. You simply take it into the water, shoot until it stops, and then take the whole thing in for processing. The second option is to rent a more sophisticated under-water camera from one of the many dive shops.

■ Medical

 The Bahamas are blessed with an excellent health service. Hospital facilities, public and private, are available in Nassau and Freeport. The Out Islands are served by health centers, clinics and general practitioner doctors. In an emergency, patients are flown to Nassau and treated at Princess Margaret Hospital.

You should be aware that most US medical insurance plans will not cover you while traveling abroad.

WORD TO THE WISE

Most package operators offer what's called travel protection insurance. This may or may not cover some limited medical emergencies. Several insurance companies also offer travel protection insurance as well as cancellation insurance. They can be well worth the extra cost. Perhaps the best of these is **CSA Travel Protection Insurance** *offered through travel agents and underwritten by Commercial Union Insurance Company. For more information, call your local travel agent or* ☎ *800-348-9505.*

Insects are not much of problem, but take along some insect repellent just in case. And don't leave home without a good sunblock.

■ Rental Cars

 If you have a valid US, Canadian or British driver's license, you can rent a car – even on the Out Islands, although what you get there might bring on a mild heart attack.

Be sure to check the car's condition before you drive away.

Rates vary from around $60 to $90 per day, but are much cheaper if rented by the week. Special rates can be arranged through most agencies in advance of travel. In Nassau, the world-wide agencies – **Avis** (www.avis.com), **Budget** (www.budget.com), **Dollar** (www.dollar.com) and **Hertz** (www.hertz.com) – as well as several local companies, are found at the airport, hotels and several downtown locations. In Freeport, there's also an Avis office in the International Bazaar.

Remember, Bahamians drive on the left side of the road. It can at first be a little disconcerting, but you'll soon get used to it.

■ Shopping Hours

Although shops throughout the Bahamas are now permitted to open on Sundays and some national holidays, you'll find many remain closed. In Nassau, shops open daily from 9 am until 5 pm. In Freeport/Lucaya they open from 9 am until 8 pm, although many of the stores in the International Bazaar and at Port Lucaya stay open until 9 on Saturday evenings.

■ Taxis & Tours

In Nassau and Freeport/Lucaya, as well as most of the Out Islands, taxis are readily available. On the Out Islands, however, some taxis are showing their age. Almost always reliable, these taxis often offer a ride that can be an adventure all its own.

The Ministry of Tourism and the Bahamas Training College have established a number of specialty tour guide qualifications: ecotour guides, bird-watching guides, etc. On the Out Islands there are no tour buses and, as yet, few tour guides. This is where the taxi comes into its own. For as little as $16 an hour, your friendly driver will show you his island and tell you all about it. These drivers are experts on the history of their particular island, and are often able to tell the story in a form that's as entertaining as it is interesting.

Rates are often negotiable, especially if you are prepared to hire by the day. Meters are present in most cabs on the main islands, but they may not be activated. It's always best to negotiate a particular fare before embarking.

Taxis in Nassau and Freeport are always metered – make sure your driver turns his meter on – and can be found waiting for fares on busy downtown streets, and at the airports and hotels. Rates are generally reasonable. A ride from Nassau's airport to Paradise Island is about $20, and to Cable Beach about $15. In Freeport, the trip from the airport to the hotel district can cost anywhere from $8 to $12; the fare is the same from the hotel district to Pier One restaurant.

Tips are expected and a couple of dollars for a short trip will be enough. Taxis usually meet arriving flights and ferry boats, but it's advisable to make sure in advance. Speak with your hotel and have them arrange something for you if needed.

■ Telephones

 When calling from the US, dial 242 and the local number. To call the US or Canada from the Bahamas, dial 1 + the area code and the local number.

■ Time

 Time in the Bahamas coincides with that of the Eastern United States. If it's noon in Atlanta, it's noon throughout the Bahamas.

How to Use This Book

In the section on each individual island, you'll find everything you need to know to plan an enjoyable vacation. Travel planning tips, plus sections on sightseeing, shopping and the best beaches are offered. Then I focus on activities – from diving and hiking to bird-watching. The Out Islands are listed in alphabetical order after Grand Bahama and New Providence.

At the end of the book you'll find a section called *At a Glance* – a quick reference to all you need to know; no descriptions, just names and addresses listed by category.

Tourist Information

Information is readily available throughout the Bahamas. There are, for instance, two district offices of the Bahamas Ministry of Tourism on Eleuthera: one in Governor's Harbour, the other on Harbour Island. Ministry personnel are cheerful, ready and willing to help. Maps and brochures are free and yours for the asking.

Bahamas Ministry of Tourism, PO Box N-3701, Market Plaza, Bay Street, Nassau, Bahamas. ☎ 242-322-7501; fax 242-328-0945.

The Grand Bahama Island Tourism Board, PO Box F-40251, Freeport, Grand Bahama Island. ☎ 242-352-8365; fax 242-352-7849.

For information about the Out Islands, contact:

The Out Islands Promotion Board, 1100 Lee Wagener Boulevard, Suite 206, Ft. Lauderdale, Florida, 33315-3564. ☎ 800-688-4752 (USA and Canada). In Ft. Lauderdale ☎ 305-359-8099; fax 305-359-8098.

For brochures on the Bahamas, ☎ 800-8BAHAMAS.

Bahamas Tourist Offices

150 East 52nd Street, New York, NY 10022. ☎ 212-758-2777; fax 212-753-6531.

One Turnberry Place, 19495 Biscayne Blvd., Suite 809, Aventura, FL 33180. ☎ 305-932-0051; fax 305-682-8758.

3450 Wilshire Blvd., Suite 1204, Los Angeles, CA 90010. ☎ 213-385-0033; fax 213-383-3966.

8600 W. Bryn Mawr Avenue, Suite 820, Chicago, IL 60631. ☎ 312-693-1500; fax 312-693-1114.

121 Bloor Street East, Suite 1101, Toronto, ON M4W 3M5, Canada. ☎ 416-968-2999; fax 416-968-6711.

3 The Billings, Walnut Tree Close, Guilford, Surrey, England, QV1 4VL. ☎ 01483-448990.

About the Bahamas

A Land of Adventure

In a nation completely surrounded by the clearest waters in the world, there are plenty of watersports. And while the great outdoors is where most people want to be, there's a lot to do here beyond the beach and the ocean. The shops and the nightlife of New Providence Island and Grand Bahama Island provide diversions that allow you to have a great vacation.

General information about what's available throughout the islands is listed in this section. More specific information about the attractions and activities on individual islands is given in each chapter, and the *At a Glance* section at the end of the book.

■ Bird Watching

Guides & Self-Guided Tours

WATCHABLE
WILDLIFE

With more than 25 inhabited islands and thousands of smaller rocks and cays, there is plenty of opportunity to explore different habitats and spot some rare birds. The three endemic species are the **Bahama woodstar hummingbird**, the **Bahama swallow** and **Bahama yellowthroat warbler**. Other prized birds include the **white-tailed tropicbird**, **Bahama pintail**, **Bahama parrot**, **great lizard-cuckoo**, **loggerhead kingbird**, **Bahama mockingbird** and the **stripe-headed tanager**, to name but a few. These birds cannot be found on all of the Bahamian Islands, so a birding guide can ensure you make the best use of your time.

■ Boating

Rentals

There are endless possibilities for getting out and about on the water – from the self-drive rental boat available by the hour, to the full-blown chartered day-sailor yacht that comes complete with captain and crew, not to mention champagne and lobster lunches. Most of the hotels have Hobie Cats, Sunfish or Sailfish for rent. Some even have Boston Whalers and other outboard-driven craft available. All come at a great variety of hourly or daily rates. Sometimes they are free. It's worth checking before you make your hotel reservations.

The islands have vast expanses of calm, clear open water, safe bays and inlets, and numerous convenient anchorages and marinas that offer everything from a quick lunch and a glass of cold beer to chilled champagne and a gourmet lobster dinner. All sizes of sailboats are available, with or without crew.

Arrangements can be made through any number of outlets, including your travel agent, hotel or one of the many special outfits you will find listed throughout the pages of this book.

Sea Kayaking & Sailing in the Exumas

If it's real adventure that you're looking for, consider a sea kayaking expedition in the Exumas. You can look forward to long hot days paddling the open waters between the islands of the chain, balmy nights under canvas, good food, and good company. You have to be fairly fit to handle the often-strenuous exercise of paddling for hours at a time. But the sheer vastness of the seascapes, the pristine beaches, and the crystal waters make this a one-of-a-kind experience. See pages 247-49 for details on the various outfitters.

Powerboat Adventures

Not for the faint-hearted, this is your chance to experience the thrills of off-shore powerboat racing in a certain degree of comfort, at least as much as one might be able to expect at speeds in excess of 50 miles per hour. Several companies offer this type of adventure, most of them operating out of Nassau. One offers day-trips to the Exumas – a truly excellent experi-

Golfing in the Bahamas.

ence – and another has rides around Paradise Island. They'll take you anywhere in the Bahamas, provided you can afford the cost of a private charter. You'll find more detailed information in the chapters on Nassau and Paradise Island (page 83) and the Exumas (page 251).

■ Golf

Across the islands are a number of fine courses, some laid out by famous names in golf architecture: Robert Trent Jones Jr. and Sr., Pete Dye, Dick Wilson and Joe Lee, to name but a few.

The Best Courses

The best courses are on the two most populated islands: New Providence and Grand Bahama. But the Out Islands, too, have some good courses. Most notable are those at the now defunct Cotton Bay Club on Eleuthera (page 226), The Treasure Cay Golf Club (page 185), and the small but challenging nine-hole course on Great Harbour Cay in the Berry Islands (page 266). All 18-hole courses on New Providence, Grand Bahama and the Out Islands have a complete range of facilities, including a resident pro, rental carts and clubs. Most facilities also offer clinics and private lessons.

The Land of Adventure

Long Island, like the other Out Islands, offers plenty of places for walking.

■ Hiking & Bicycling

 Opportunities to enjoy an afternoon, or even a week, hiking the quiet country lanes and beaches are just about endless. There's not a single island in the entire archipelago that doesn't offer some sort of hiking route.

 Most hiking routes are lonely, often dusty, and without facilities. Be sure to carry everything you need, especially an adequate quantity of water and sun block.

Bicycling offers the opportunitys to see the land at a more leisurely pace than by car or taxi. While bicycles are available for rent on the two main islands, they are not quite so easily come by in the Out Islands. Some of the hotels in the Out Islands offer them free of charge to their guests, and some do rent them to guests staying at other hotels. Check with your travel agent.

There are virtually no designated walking, hiking or bicycling trails on any of the islands. These activities are very much go-as-you-please affairs, especially on the Out Islands. The main roads are the first and most obvious choice, but there are also the beaches, of course, and hundreds of unmarked side roads that often end up at a secluded beach where you can enjoy a picnic lunch and a swim. At least in the Out Islands, there's no reason why you shouldn't wander at will. The locals are friendly and willing to give ideas, directions and the benefit of their knowledge about the best places to go and sites to see. Don't be afraid to ask.

Guided bike rides are offered by some of the larger hotels on New Providence Island, **Pedal & Paddle Ecoventures** in Nassau, ☎ 242-362-2772, and **Kayak Nature Tours** on Grand Bahama Island, ☎ 242-373-2485. Both offer guided rides and day-trips. Both use modern, off-road bikes.

WORD TO THE WISE

If you are going to one of the more remote islands, consider taking your own bike. Check with the airline as to procedure and costs.

■ Honeymooning

The Bahamas epitomize romance. From the soft sounds of the steel drum and calypso wafting gently over the beaches on a warm evening under a spectacular sunset, to deserted beaches where the palms wave gently over an emerald sea, the islands have much to offer.

There are extensive opportunities for honeymooning, or even getting married, in the Bahamas. All major hotels and resorts on Grand Bahama and New Providence offer a full range of facilities, including

Bahamas parasailing.

The Land of Adventure

everything from priest to cake. To get away from it all, consider honeymooning on one of the Out Islands – the Abacos, Eleuthera, or the Exumas. And for a really remote, even primitive, location, try Andros.

Here are some websites specializing in Bahamas weddings and honeymoons:

- www.islanddreaming.com
- www.weddinginthebahamas
- www.coordinators.thebahamian.com
- www.out-island-wedding.com
- www.honeymoontravel.com
- www.honemooncruiseshopper.com
- www.wedding-world.com

WORD TO THE WISE

Check first with your travel agent when making your booking and be sure to do so well in advance. The Bahamas are a very popular honeymoon destination and many suites are booked up a year or more in advance.

■ Horseback Riding

There's not much horseback riding on the islands and outfitters are often booked weeks in advance. There are stables on both Grand Bahama and New Providence. On New Providence, you can contact **Happy Trails Stables**, ☎ 242-362-1820; on Grand Bahama, **Pinetree Stables** is at ☎ 242-373-3600. The going rate is $25 per hour, and you have a choice of English or Western saddles. Long rides along quiet country lanes lined with seagrapes, cocoa plums, casuarinas and white sandy beaches provide hours of quiet relaxation and often new friends and good company.

■ Parasailing

Parasailing is available from private operators at most of the major resorts both on New Providence Island and Grand Bahama Island.

■ Jet-Skiing

Jet-skiing is offered at most of the beachfront hotels on Grand Bahama and New Providence Islands, but not on the Out Islands because the skis damage the fragile coral heads. Rates vary from hotel to hotel, but start at around $40 for 30 minutes.

■ Shelling

Shelling is a hobby that can bring back memories of your vacation for years to come. Put on your swimsuit, leave the big cities behind, and go to the east end of Grand Bahama or New Providence at low tide. Wade out to the dark spots in the water where the seaweed grows. There, conch feed in the thousands. There's always someone around willing to clean the shells for you. Sand dollars are common, and literally hundreds of exquisite shells lie on the high water line of Out Island beaches.

■ Sport Fishing

For many Bahamians, fishing is not just a sport, it's the way they make their living. But sport fishing here is spectacular, and you don't have to be a world-class angler to take advantage of what the islands have to offer. In fact, it's okay if you've never fished before in your life. There are plenty of

Fishing off Bimini.

The Land of Adventure

skilled guides willing to take you in hand and show you exactly how it's done. A couple of hours of instruction, a fast boat or a calm, shallow-water flat, and you're in business.

The Lure of Fishing

Nothing compares with the feeling you'll get aboard a slowly trolling boat on a calm sea under a hot summer sun, a heavy rod between your knees, and a can of something cold in your hand. And then it happens. There's a jerk on your line; something's taken the bait, and in seconds you're involved in the fight of your life. But wait, the line goes slack, it's gone. No, it's still there, and suddenly the water a hundred yards from the boat explodes and the great fish is in the air. Your first sailfish hurls itself out of the water in a breathtaking arc. The sight leaves you speechless, awed and, for a moment, not knowing what to do next. And then it hits again and the fight is on. Slowly you reel in, the clutch slipping under the strain, three winds on the crank for every inch of line you gain. As suddenly as it began, it's over. Your opponent, exhausted at the side of the boat, is gaffed and hauled aboard. It's more than five feet long and weighs perhaps as much as 90 pounds – you won't know until you get it back to the scale on the dock, but it's a good one; you know it is. You go home at day's end satisfied and tired, but still excited, ready to do it all again tomorrow, the next day, next year.

There are many ways to fish in the Bahamas. Off-shore fishing is the premier choice, but there really is something for everyone and you don't need to charter an expensive deep-sea boat. You can do it from a small rental boat all by yourself, or even wade to your waist in the crystal waters of one of a hundred or more bonefish flats for a day of sport.

Blue-Water Fishing

Other than the **sailfish**, the king of them all is perhaps the **blue marlin**. Catches of the big blue typically range from 100 to 300 pounds or more. Four and five hundred pounders are not uncommon and stories of the one that got away tell of fish in excess of 1,000 pounds. Fantasy? Perhaps; perhaps not.

Tuna is another fine blue-water catch. Every spring the bluefin make their annual run through the Bahamas, and anglers leave the docks in droves to participate in any one of a dozen or more tournaments from Bimini to Walker's Cay. Catches weigh from 100 to 800, even 900 pounds. There's also blackfin and yellowfin tuna – smaller, but no less fun to catch.

Other excellent deep-water species include the **kingfish** or **king mackerel**. They can be caught through the year, although peak time is during the spring and summer. **Dolphin** (the fish; not Flipper) are usually found fairly close in along the shoreline, weigh anywhere from five to 20 pounds, and are excellent to eat. **Wahoo** weigh 15 to 30 pounds; even 60 pounds is not unusual. They, too, make for good eating and are highly prized by sport fishermen. Wahoo are most often found lurking in the deep water off the edge of a reef. The **amberjack** is another prized sporting fish found most often during the summer months in the cooler, deep waters just off the edge of the reef and closer in-shore the rest of the year. Amberjack can run 20 to 40 pounds.

Sharks are common throughout the Bahamas, especially the Out Islands, and can be found in both shallow waters and deep. Bull sharks, blues, hammerheads, and tiger sharks abound. The truth is, however, that when one is caught, the fight usually lasts only as long as it takes for the shark's razor-like teeth to bite through the wire traces that hold him. Even so, you'll remember the battle for a long time to come.

The wily **barracuda** is found in large numbers, in shallow or deep waters. They can often be seen swimming close to the surface in the clear waters over reefs and sandy banks. Barracuda range in size from a few pounds to about 15 or 20 pounds and, small though they might be, you're sure of a good fight if you can get one on your hook.

Unfortunately, barracuda are often the victims of ciguatera poisoning and are, therefore, risky to eat.

For good eating, you can't beat **grouper**. Grouper – black, Nassau and yellowfin – can be found swimming lazily around, close to the bottom on the reefs throughout the Bahamas. Catches ranging from 15 to 25 pounds are the norm, and fish of 30 to 45 pounds are not uncommon. Often, your hotel will be willing to clean and cook grouper for you. There's nothing quite like a grouper steak, caught in the afternoon and eaten the same evening. The **snapper** too, may be caught on reefs throughout the islands. Most common are the red and gray variety and, though a fish may weigh only a pound or two, fresh-caught snapper is delicious.

Bonefishing

Inside the reef, before you reach the deep waters of the ocean where glamorous, deep-water sportfish hog the limelight, there's a second, very exciting sporting opportunity – bonefishing. The elusive bonefish, often called the ghost fish, is rapidly becoming one of the most popular sportfish on the islands. Until quite recently, bonefishing was almost unheard of among mainland anglers. Today, people from around the world flock here in search of this hard-fighting denizen of the flats.

Bonefish, so named for the huge numbers of bones in their bodies, live in deep water and come up onto the flats to feed. That's where you'll have to go to find them. Unlike most deep-water sportfish, they offer not only a good fight, but the thrill of a hunt as well.

Bonefish, like deer, must be stalked, and they are just as skittish. Make a wrong move at the wrong time and your quarry will be gone in a flash, leaving you standing alone in the water, totally frustrated, and wondering what went wrong.

Bonefish are not very big. They weigh in around six to 15 pounds, with some growing as large as 20 pounds.

WORD TO THE WISE

You'll need a guide who knows the area and where the best flats are found. Many hotels offer bonefishing packages that include the services of a reliable and experienced guide. If not, don't be afraid to ask. The hotel desk is the best place to start, but many taxi drivers know just who to put you in touch with. Most boat rental companies and dive companies will also know of someone.

Bonefishing is good almost everywhere in the islands, from Abaco to the Acklins, and from Bimini to Eleuthera. Unlike most other sportfishing, it is good throughout the year. There are a number of ways to go about it. It's claimed that in some areas bonefish can be caught from the dock, or by casting into the surf, or from a skiff. But the best way is to hunt them down on foot on the lonely flats of the Out Islands. This is where your guide will earn his fee. He will know where to go, what bait to use – fly or jig – and he'll guide you through the basics of how to fish for the ghost.

Bonefish come up onto the flats in schools and can be seen first in the near distance as a dark stain in the crystal-clear water above the white sandy bottom, then as a vast, surging ripple on the surface of the water as maybe a hundred fish move like a flock of birds, this way and that, across the flats, tails cleaving the water. Then you see them, shadowy gray streaks flashing over the white sand, ghostly, moving fast.

To hunt bonefish, move slowly, disturbing the water as little as possible. Keep your eyes on the school, not on the sandy bottom beneath your feet. Take one step at a time, until you're close enough to try a cast. Aim tour fly or jig close to the center of the school. If you're lucky, there's a slight tug, then a stronger one, and the surface of the water explodes in a frenzy of white water and struggling fish; and he's off like a runaway horse leaving you hanging on to your rod, reel screaming, spinning, as 150 yards of line disappears seaward in what seems less than a second. Then he turns, heads in another direction as you wind in frantically to take up the slack, beginning to reel him in, fighting every inch of the way.

Dolphin caught off Bimini.

The Land of Adventure

Bonefishing guides cost about $250 for a full day, or $150 for a half-day. Bring food and beverage. If you don't have your own gear, your guide can supply everything you need.

WORD TO THE WISE

If you've never bonefished before, the best way is to purchase one of the packages offered by many of the islands' hotels. These require only that you bring yourself and a willingness to do as you're told. You can expect to spend anywhere from $350 for a three-night stay, to more than $2,000 for seven nights in a luxury accommodation (see individual chapters for specific details).

Tournaments

There's a year-round series of competitive fishing events designed to make things as interesting as possible for all participants, novice and veteran alike. The best-known and most popular is the **Bahamas Billfish Championship Tournament**, held during the spring and early summer each year at five different locations. Anglers are welcome to take part in all or as many legs as they wish. The first two legs are held in April at Bimini and Walker's Cay. In May, the tournament moves to Treasure Cay and Boat Harbour, and then ends at Chub Cay in June. For details and registration, ☎ 305-923-8022.

The Bimini Big Game Club sponsors a number of tournaments. These include the mid-winter **Wahoo Tournament** in February, the **Annual Bacardi Rum Billfish Tournament** in March, the **Bimini Festival** in May, the **Family Tournament** in August, the **Small B.O.A.T. Tournament** for boats under 27 feet in September, and another **Wahoo Tournament** in November. The **Bimini International Light Tackle Bonefish Tournament** consists of two legs – one in January, the other in February. ☎ 800-327-4149 for more information and reservations.

The **Penny Turtle Billfish Tournament** is held at the Great Abaco Beach Resort each May; ☎ 800-468-4799. The **Billfish Foundation's Tag Tournament** is held in May at the Walker's Cay Hotel and Marina on Abaco; ☎ 800-WALKERS. The Green Turtle Cay Yacht Club hosts a fishing tournament in May; ☎ 242-365-4271. The *What's Out There* **Tournament** is held at Great Harbour Cay in April; ☎ 800-343-7256. The **Boat Harbour Billfish Championship** is held at the Marsh Harbour Resort in Abaco in June; ☎ 305-920-7877.

The **Bahamas Bonefish Annual Bash** is held in February at the Club Peace and Plenty on Exuma; ☎ 800-525-2210. The **Andros Big Yard Bonefishing and Bottom Fishing Tournament** is held in June; call the Bahamas Tourism Office at ☎ 800-32-SPORT. There's also a bonefishing tournament held in mid-July at the Staniel Cay and Yacht Club on Exuma; ☎ 242-355-2011. Bonefishing, as well as big game fishing, is a part of the **Bahamian Outer Islands International Gamefish Tournament** held in March; ☎ 800-426-0466 for location, details and registration.

For a full listing and schedules, contact the **Bahamas Tourism Office**, ☎ 800-32-SPORT, or the **Bahama Out Islands Promotion Board** at ☎ 800-688-4725.

Licenses & Permits

There are no restricted fishing seasons; it's open season throughout the year on whatever you want to catch. Licenses are not required if you're fishing from a Bahamian-registered boat. You will, however, need to obtain a sport-fishing permit if using your own craft. A single-visit permit costs $20 and is available at your legal port of entry into the Bahamas. An annual permit will cost you $250. You can also obtain your permit in advance by contacting the **Department of Fisheries**, PO Box N-3028, Nassau, Bahamas, ☎ 242-393-1777.

- Only hook and line fishing is allowed in the Bahamas; use of a **speargun is illegal**. In fact, spearguns themselves are illegal in the Bahamas.

- The **number of lines** per boat is limited to six in the water at any one time.

- The **bag limit** per person per boat for dolphin, kingfish and wahoo, or any combination of the three species, is six. Above that limit, fish should be released unharmed, as should all fish unless they are to be used for food.

Planning your fishing trip is easy. Many hotels offer packages of between three and eight days, with everything you need included in the rate: boat, bait, box lunches and gear. In some cases, even the use of a small sailboat is included (see specific chapters for package details).

The Land of Adventure

■ Marine National Parks

 More and more, the government of the Bahamas is concerned with protecting the fragile ecosystem and expanding the national park system, especially marine parks. At the time of writing, these included:

- **Peterson Cay National Park** of Grand Bahama, a 1½-acre cay and its surrounding reef system.

- **Black Sound Cay National Reserve** on Green Turtle Cay, Abaco, a two-acre mangrove reserve.

- **Tilloo Cay National Reserve**, Abaco, 11 acres of exposed shoreline.

- **Pelican Cays Land Sea Park**, Cherokee Sound, Great Abaco, a 2,100-acre undersea park with an extensive system of caves and reefs.

- **Exuma Cays Land & Sea Park**, more than 112,640 acres of land and sea marine reserve of outstanding natural beauty.

- **Conception Island National Park**, a 2,100-acre island bird and turtle sanctuary.

- **Union Creek Reserve**, Great Inagua, a 4,940-acre enclosed reserve incorporating a tidal creek.

 While you are welcome to visit these parks and reserves, preferably with a guide, it is an offence to remove anything from the parks, alive or dead. This includes seashells.

■ Sea Kayaking

 This is one of the most exciting ways to reach out-of-the-way areas. Kayaks are faster than regular canoes, easier to maneuver, and some can be equipped with sails. Best of all, anyone can do it; no experience is necessary. See page 246 for detailed information.

▪ Sightseeing

Local operators on Grand Bahama and New Providence offer a wide variety of sightseeing tours. Many taxi drivers also psrovide specialized sightseeing tours and will often know more about the sights and sounds of the islands than the scheduled tour operators. In Nassau, one such driver who comes readily to mind is **Mr. Pemmi Sutherland**. The man is an absolute mine of information and trivia, and a great source of fun in the bargain. Pemmi can be reached through **Li'l Murph Taxis**, ☎ 242-325-3725.

On the Out Islands, sightseeing tours are provided by local taxi drivers, who can be hired by the hour, but come much cheaper if contracted for the full day.

▪ Snorkeling & Diving

Scuba Diving

Diving off the Bahamas is excellent. Dive operators on most of the islands can take you on scheduled dives, or to locations of your own choosing.

For the most part, the waters off the Bahamas are very clear, shallow and offer an abundance of coral reefs and gardens for you to explore, as well as shipwrecks, modern and ancient.

WORD TO THE WISE

Unless you are an experienced diver, it's probably best to work with an operator, especially if you want to go wreck or shark diving.

Dive Sites

The dive sites listed throughout this book are, for the most part, remote and difficult to get to without a qualified guide. The locations of most listed sites in the Out Islands are not marked in any way – on maps or in the ocean – and are the closely guarded secrets of the local dive operators who make their living taking divers out on guided tours. If you want to see a particular site, ask your operator. If there are enough people interested in the site to make a full boat, it will cost no more than the regular half-day or full-day tour. If not, you'll have to rent the boat and guide on your own, which can be expensive.

The Land of Adventure

It is not recommended that you go off on your own. Local knowledge of the waters and currents is essential, and it's dangerous to dive without such knowledge, especially where shipwrecks are concerned.

Snorkeling

Snorkeling can be enjoyed almost anywhere with clear waters. The only place you need permission to swim is off private beaches.

WORD TO THE WISE

You should seek professional advice before taking off into the deep. It matters little where you might be staying; even on the most remote of the Out Islands there will always be someone available to warn you about the currents or other dangers at any given spot.

Jean Michel Cousteau Adventures

If you're really interested in a snorkeling vacation, arrange a stay at one of the hotels participating in the Jean Michel Cousteau "Snorkeling Adventures" program. It's a great value. For $98-$99 you can "immerse yourself into an exciting new world of wondrous corals and colorful fish...." Unlock the secrets of thousands of miles of coral reefs, more than 700 islands, and over 100,000 square miles of ocean.... Receive snorkeling instruction by trained professionals on guided excursions, a snorkeling instruction book, reference books and a custom T-shirt. And, within 10 days of your return home you'll receive your very own set of US Divers Limited Edition Jean-Michel Cousteau diving mask, fins, snorkel and gear bag. You'll also receive a personalized certificate from Jean-Michel Cousteau welcoming you to the exciting new world as well as the *Snorkeling Guide To Marine Life* and the accompanying *Underwater Identification Cards*." Participating Out Island hotels are listed throughout the book and in the *At a Glance* section. Your travel agent can book the program for you or you can book it yourself through the **Bahama Out Island Promotion Board**, ☎ 800-688-4752, fax 954-688-4752, sboipb@ix.netcom.com.

Dangers

Sharks, predators of the deep, have gained an undeserved reputation. But sharks kill only when hungry. Shark attacks are extremely rare, especially in the Bahamas. They say you have more of a chance of being twice-struck by lightning than of being attacked by a shark.

Moray eels, on the whole, are nocturnal creatures and like to be left alone inside their chosen lair. There are a few that might have become accustomed to humans – and the handouts they have come to expect from them – but those that haven't can, if disturbed or threatened, give you a very nasty bite. Stay at a respectful distance.

Barracuda are not really dangerous, just scary-looking, especially with their rather frightening and ever-present grin. The sleek, silver tiger of the ocean is a curious creature, however, and will often follow you around, which can be a little unnerving. If you happen to be feeding the local reef fish, **which you shouldn't do**, you should always be on the lookout for something bigger. A barracuda after his share of the pie will attack like lightning and, although he's only after your hand-out, it might be your hand he takes.

Reef fish tend to be curious. They're not dangerous, but you might find them nipping at your fingers, toes and hair.

Rays, on the whole, are not dangerous. Tread on a stingray buried in the sand, however, and you're probably in for a trip to the local hospital. The ray's first reaction is self-preservation, and its natural instinct is to lash out with its murderous tail. Unless threatened or trodden on, however, it's pretty much harmless and fascinating to watch as it flaps over the sandy bottom. Just be careful where you're putting your feet.

Bahamas diving is some of the best in the Western Hemisphere.

Scorpionfish lie in wait for the unwary on coral heads or close to the ocean floor. They

The Land of Adventure

Opportunities for snorkeling are abundant in the Bahamas.

have a set of thick spines on their backs that can inflict a nasty sting. Keep your hands clear.

The stonefish, often hard to see due to its camouflage, can also give you a nasty sting. Look carefully before you touch anything.

Jellyfish, transparent and often difficult to see, are almost all harmless. There are, however, some that are not. It's best to avoid them all.

Coral is often sharp, and tiny pieces can become dislodged in cuts and abrasions. If this should happen, you'll be in for a painful couple of days. Fire coral should not be handled at all. Your best bet is not to touch any coral – not only because it can hurt you, but also because it's a delicate, living organism.

Sea urchins are spiky little black balls that lie on the sandy ocean floor or in nooks and crannies among coral heads in the shallow waters of the reef. Step on a sea urchin with bare feet at your peril. The spines are brittle, often barbed, and will give you a very nasty experience. Fortunately, urchins are easily seen and thus easily avoided. Keep a sharp lookout and don't touch.

DID YOU KNOW? *If you do happen to get stung by coral, jellyfish, or an urchin, you can treat the sting first with vinegar. This will neutralize the poison. Then you should get some help from the local drugstore to ease the pain.*

Wreck Diving

It is said that there are more than 500 shipwrecks in the Bahamas, and it's probably true. Some of these wrecks, especially those that allow access to their interiors, can be dangerous and even experienced divers should not go into them alone. There are plenty of guides and dive operators who do know their way around. Many wrecks are infested with fire coral. Many more are home to moray eels that are not dangerous if you give them space.

Safety

Take reasonable precautions and stay alert. You'll get into trouble only if you do something you shouldn't, are neglectful, or fail to take note of expert advice. Never dive alone.

■ Sun Seeking

There are literally thousands of beaches here – some crowded, some so deserted you won't see another human being for weeks at a time. Great expanses of sugar-white sand and the palest of green waters stretch for mile after sun-soaked mile. On New Providence and Grand Bahama, almost every hotel is either on or close to a beach. Those that aren't provide free shuttle services back and forth to a carefully selected and monitored beach.

The Out Islands boast of some of the finest beaches in the world, including **Fernandez Bay** on Cat Island, **Harbour Island** off Eleuthera, **Rolleville** on Great Exuma, **Great Harbour Cay** on the Berry Islands, **Staniard Creek** on Andros, **Stocking Island** off George Town on Great Exuma, and the entire shoreline of **Mayaguana Cay** just east of Acklins Island.

The Land of Adventure

■ Tennis

Many of the larger and resort hotels have excellent tennis facilities. The largest is the 20-court tennis complex at **Club Med** on Paradise Island (see page 102). There are also fine facilities at other hotels on Paradise Island, Cable Beach, on Grand Bahama at Freeport/Lucaya, and on Eleuthera.

■ Water Skiing

The best sites for water skiing are off **Paradise Island** and **Cable Beach** in Nassau, and off the beaches at **Freeport/Lucaya**. Many of the big hotels on the two main islands of New Providence (Nassau) and Grand Bahama offer water skiing, as do some of the larger hotels and resorts on the Out Islands.

■ Windsurfing

Warm trade winds blow almost constantly, providing never-ending opportunities. Equipment can be rented quite easily on New Providence and Grand Bahama, and some of the largest hotels and resorts offer windsurfing free of charge. On the Out Islands, however, windsurfing gear is harder to find.

■ Nightlife

Nassau and **Freeport/Lucaya**, with four casinos and a number of nightclubs and theaters between them, are the hot-spots for nightlife and entertainment. To experience the warm summer evenings, the colorful dress of the Bahamians, and the lilting sounds of West Indian steel drums and calypso music, is to capture some of the real feeling of the islands.

■ Shopping

The Bahamas have shopping with a difference. The prices are not always what you might hope for, but searching for a bargain is half the fun. From the tiny street market in George Town on Great Exuma to the International Marketplace in Freeport to the world-famous Straw Market on Bay Street in Nassau, there are thousands of opportunities to browse, argue and bargain. Haggling over price can be a fun experience.

■ Holidays

Bahamas Calendar

January: **New Years' Day** (Jan 1) is a public holiday.

April: **Good Friday** (1st Friday in April) and **Easter Monday** (Monday following Easter) are public holidays.

May: **Whitmonday**. This public holiday follows **Whitsunday** (also known as Pentecost), the seventh Sunday after Easter.

June: **Labor Day** (June 1) is a public holiday.

July: **Independence Day** (July 10) is a public holiday that celebrates the Bahamas' independence from Britain. Parades and fireworks.

August: **Emancipation Day**, the first Monday in August, commemorates the end of slavery in the Bahamas in 1834.

September: **Annual Bahamas Jazz Festival** – an international event held the first week in September.

October: **Discovery Day** (Oct 12) is a public holiday celebrating Christopher Columbus' first landing in the Bahamas.

November: **Guy Fawkes Festival** (Nov 10) is celebrated on Eleuthera in honor of the capture of Guy Fawkes, who attempted to blow up the Houses of Parliament in England in 1605.

Central Banks Art Exhibition and Competition (Nov 16) is a national competition for artists under 26 years old, who showcase their works in a variety of media.

December: **Christmas Day** is a public holiday.

Boxing Day/Junkanoo Parade (Dec 26): The biggest public celebration on the islands, especially in Nassau. This is a traditional British holiday, when the wealthy boxed their Christmas dinner leftovers and presented them to their servants.

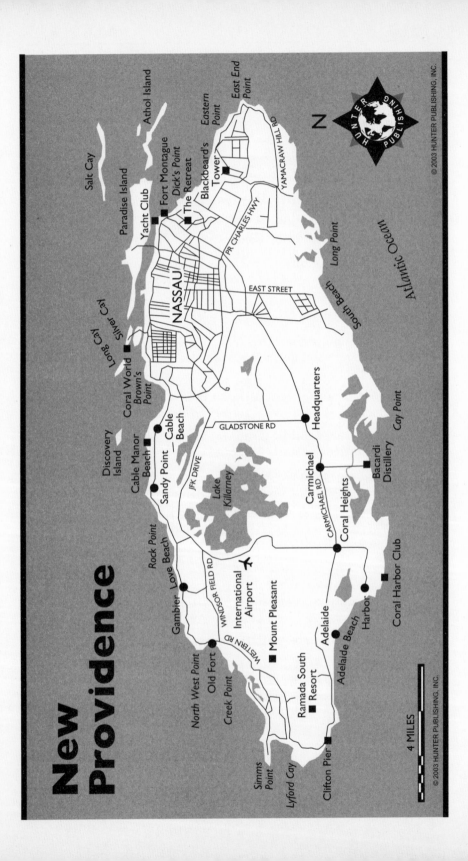

Nassau & New Providence Island

Nassau, the capital city of the islands and a bustling sea port, is a microcosm of Bahamian cultures. It's the largest city on the islands, with a population of more than 150,000, and has long been a center, not only for tourism, but for much of the world's banking. There are more than 400 banks in the city, offering tax shelters to one and all. But Nassau is more than the Bahamas' commercial center. Each year, some two million tourists enter the country through its international airport and a million more arrive by cruise ship and private boat. Most of them stay for at least a day or two.

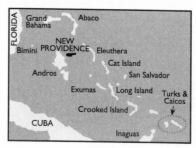

New Providence island, which measures 21 miles long by seven miles wide, offers a diversity of accommodations, from ultra-modern luxury resorts to intimate hotels.

There's a wide variety of attractions, from the all-in-one world of the Atlantis International Resort & Casino on Paradise Island, to Crystal Cay Marine Park, deep-sea fishing, diving, walking, swimming, bicycling, driving, windsurfing, parasailing, waverunning, shelling, and snorkeling, to diving beneath the waves in a full-blown submarine.

History

New Providence was first settled by the **English** in 1656. The colony was administered, somewhat loosely, by the colonial government on the North American mainland. During the early years, the people of the little settlement of

Charles Town lived their lives without much interference from the outside world. Then the island became a haven and base of operations for pirates, who raided the Spanish fleets plying the seas homeward to Cadiz laden with the king's treasures from the New World. It wasn't long before the Spanish Governor General decided that enough was enough, and Spain invaded the island. Spanish occupation of the island was, however, short-lived; there was a new king on the English throne, who was ready to exert his power.

Charles Town was renamed **Nassau** in honor of **King William of Orange-Nassau**, and the pirates returned to the island. Men like Blackbeard, Major Bonnet and Calico Jack Rackham set up shop and soon became more active than ever. Privateers sailing under royal sanction from the Netherlands, France and England soon joined them, making the voyage from the New World to Spain extremely hazardous.

Finally, however, the pirates were driven off the island by Woodes Rogers, a ruthless and dedicated man who became governor in 1718. Things then settled down for awhile.

Slavery had long been established on New Providence. After the native Lucayan Indians died out, sometime shortly after Europeans arrived on the islands, men like Sir John Hawkins and Sir Francis Drake made their early fortunes slave trading in the West Indies and other islands of the Caribbean. By the turn of the 18th century, the black population on the island had more than tripled. Emancipation came to the Bahamas in August 1834 and the newly liberated slaves left Nassau and moved "over the hill" to establish settlements of their own.

The outbreak of the American Civil War brought new activity to New Providence, Nassau in particular, and with it a new era of prosperity. Nassau became second only to Bermuda as a center for blockade-running activities. Both English and Confederate companies established agencies on New Providence, and the large numbers of blockade runners operating out of Nassau harbor became a matter of grave concern for US authorities.

Nassau & New Providence

DID YOU KNOW?

During four years of the American Civil War, 397 vessels entered Nassau from Southern ports, and more than 580 ships – most of them flying the English ensign – sailed from Nassau to the Southern ports of Charleston and Wilmington, and to hidden inlets and havens along the Florida coastline.

The blockade runners brought much-needed supplies to the Confederacy, arms and medical supplies especially, but their motives were not all patriotic. Profit was the driving force, and from Nassau just as many luxury items were carried into Southern ports as were essential supplies. It was a two-way street. Ships returning from Confederate ports carried cargoes of cotton, turpentine, and tobacco for sale in European markets. The profits were enormous – often exceeding 800%.

With the end of the Civil War in 1865, Nassau and New Providence returned to their quiet ways. But by the turn of the 19th century the island was discovered again, this time as a playground for the rich and famous. This new period of prosperity began after the laying of the international telephone cable from what is now Cable Beach to Jupiter, Florida. Cable Beach, with its magnificent stretch of unspoiled sand, drew the wealthy from around the world like a magnet. This period saw its peak during the Duke of Windsor's tenure as Governor of the island.

Today, New Providence, and Nassau in particular, is the center of the thriving Bahamian **tourist industry**. There is more to do, more to see, and more to enjoy on New Providence, tiny though it is, than on all the other islands of the Bahamas combined.

Getting There

Nassau is one of the easiest Bahamian destinations to reach. Most major US airlines and several European carriers offer scheduled service. Air/hotel-inclusive package vacations are available from a number of major tour operators, and several cruise lines include Nassau in their three-, four- and seven-day itineraries.

■ By Air

Options are extensive. Direct flights on major US carriers are available from New York, Boston, Atlanta and Miami, with connecting flights to and from most major mainland gateways. From Europe, flights are available from London and Paris, and from other gateways in Germany, Spain and Italy. (Some, however, may require US connections in Miami, New York or Atlanta.) Fares fluctuate depending on the time of year. From Atlanta, it's possible to buy a round-trip ticket for as little $200, the same from Miami and New York. From London and Europe, the fares vary according to the carrier and, in many cases, a diverse assortment of package operators.

WORD TO THE WISE

With so many options, it's best to enlist the services of a reputable travel agent.

■ By Cruise Ship

See page 12.

■ Package Vacations

Most package operators prefer that you book vacations through a travel agent. The theory is that they have less trouble dealing with an agent, with whom they will build a long-term relationship. Many, though, will deal with you directly, though only on-line. This being so, most operators prefer not to publish their phone numbers. In the *At a Glance* section at the back of the book you'll find listings for package operators, along with websites. Those that do offer on-line booking will often have discounted rates and seasonal specials.

Package options to Nassau and New Providence Island are varied. Most major airline vacation departments, and literally dozens of independent tour operators, can provide packages to over a dozen major hotels on Cable Beach and Paradise Island, from two days to as long as you like.

Delta Vacations: Air/hotel-inclusive packages from Atlanta with connections from most major US cities. Hotels include Sandals Royal Bahamian, Radisson Cable Beach, Marriott Cable Beach Resort &

Crystal Palace Casino, Nassau Beach Resort, Breezes Bahamas, British Colonial Beach Resort. On Paradise Island: Bay View Village, Comfort Suites Paradise Island, Atlantis - Paradise Island, Paradise Beach Resort, Radisson Grand Resort - Paradise Island, and the Ocean Club. At the low end, the British Colonial Beach Resort is a good choice; for those with a bigger budget, the Ocean Club is the ultimate choice, closely followed by Atlantis. Rates, depending on the season, start at $550 for three nights from Atlanta. www.deltavacations.com/ourpicks/all_inclusive.asp

American FlyAAWay Vacations: Air/hotel-inclusive packages from Miami with connections from most other major US cities. Their packages include all the hotel options as listed for Delta. Rates start around $450 for three nights from Miami. www.aavacations.com.

USAir Vacations: The same options as Delta and American, but the gateway is Charlotte, North Carolina. Rates are about the same. www.usairwaysvacations.com.

Vacation Express: An independent tour operator offering the same options as the major airlines. However, customers can choose their air carrier and, thus, are able to shop for the best rates. Packages often can run a little less than those of the major carriers. However, gateway options and availablity may be limited. www.vacation-express.com.

Travel Impressions: A subsidiary of American Express offering the same options, restrictions and advantages as Vacation Express. Travel Impressions is the only operator other than American Airlines FlyAAway Vacations that offers an extensive array of vacations to the Out Islands. These include trips to Abaco, Eleuthera, Harbour Island, the Exumas, and Long Island. www.travelimpressions.com.

Club Med - Paradise Island: Club Med rates this village as one of their best. The minimum stay is seven nights, and children are welcome, although there are no special facilities for them. Accommodations are gaily painted beachfront or garden-front lodges. Each is decorated in rich earth tones and comfortably furnished. All rooms are air-conditioned. Guests have access to all of the island excursions, along with the variety of on-site activities and facilities Club Med is famous for: aerobics, golf, kayaking, scuba diving, windsurfing, sailing, deep-sea fishing, tennis, etc. Club Med's gateways are Boston, Chicago, Los Angeles, New York, San Francisco, and Washington, DC. Rates start at $1,299 from Boston (air-inclusive for seven nights), rising to $1,499 from California. You can leave from other US cities, but you'll be required to pay add-on airfares. If you've not been to a

Club Med village before, you'll be required to pay a one-time initiation fee of $30 per person, and membership of $50 per person. ☎ 800-CLUB MED or call your travel agent. www.clubmed.com.

■ Vacation Planning Online

 There are online bargains to be found; it's just a matter of knowing where to look. But keep in mind that a good travel agent will often have first-hand knowledge of the popular resorts and will be able to recommend good hotels, restaurants, etc. Better yet, the same travel agent may be able to steer you away from the traps. He/she will be able to provide trip insurance, day-trips, itineraries, etc. In short, a good agent can ensure you get value for money and real back-up when you need it. I've been a traveler almost all my life and even I hesitate to entrust my hard-earned cash to my own expertise, and I was once a travel agent.

I recommend you use only well established companies, such as **Expedia.com** and **Travelocity.com**. Here you can book airline tickets – often at a discount – hotels and rental cars. Make sure you understand exactly what you're buying. Are there restrictions on your airline tickets? Can you cancel or are they non-refundable? What are the penalties that would apply if you needed to cancel close to the departure date? Understand that a cheap airline ticket almost always means there are restrictions. Be sure to shop around; there's always a better deal a few mouse clicks away.

Most major airlines and some large package operators have websites with online booking facilities. Delta Airlines, American Airlines, USAir, and many more, all offer a range of package options that include airfare, car, hotel, insurance, and airport/hotels transfers, often at big discounts (depending upon when you want to go). These companies are good at what they do. They have inspectors visiting resorts on a regular basis to make sure that standards are maintained. They own the airline, which means if a flight is cancelled you are their first priority for the next available flight. And it's true one-stop-shopping – a few clicks and you're done. More convenient and still reliable is the new website, **Orbitz** (www.orbitz.com), which was started by five leading airlines, American, Continental, Delta, Northwest and United. You can book online with 450 different airlines on Orbitz. They also offer rental cars, hotels, vacation packages and other travel services.

For hotels, **www.wheretostay.com** has huge listings of hotels in the Caribbean and the Bahamas, each with a link that will take you directly to the individual hotel's website. They also include guest reviews of many of the hotels.

Websites	
Air Jamaica Vacations (yes, they do packages to the Bahamas)	www.airjamaicavacations.com
American Airlines Vacations	www.aavacations.com
Apple Vacations	www.applevacations.com
Bahamas Tourism	www.bahamas.com
British Airways Vacations	www.britishairways.com
Classic Custom Vacations (packages sold through travel agents, but you can visit their website to see what they offer)	www.classicvacations.com
Club Med	www.clubmed.com
Delta Vacations	www.deltavacations.com
Horizon Tours	www.horizontours.com
Hotel Information	www.wheretostay.com
Orbitz	www.orbitz.com
Providenciales Information	www.provo.net
Travel Impressions	www.travelimpressions.com
Turks and Caicos Tourism	www.turksandcaicostourism.com
US Airways Vacations	www.usairwaysvacations.com
Vacation Express	www.vacationexpress.com

Getting Around

New Providence is small and fairly easy to navigate. Roads are all well paved and maintained, though somewhat narrow in Nassau, and they will take you quickly to most of the island's many attractions. **Bay Street**, the main highway, flows east-west along the shoreline, and makes traveling from one end of the island to the other relatively simple.

> *The speed limit on New Providence is 40 miles an hour and, while it's not often enforced, you should remain within the limit. Unfortunately, most of the islanders do not. You'll find them honking behind you and whizzing past at high speeds.*

Transportation comes in all the usual forms: rental cars, motorcycles, bicycles, taxis, and jitneys. New Providence's answer to public transportation, the jitney is a 32-seat Bahamian public bus, and riding it can be something of an adventure in itself. Often, it's difficult to know exactly where you are or where you're going when riding a jitney. But your fellow passengers will be happy to offer directions and instructions – if you can understand them, that is. The 75¢ fare makes the jitney a bargain.

■ Taxis

Taxis on New Providence are metered, so make sure your driver turns the meter on. This is an expensive way to travel. You can, however, make arrangements to rent a taxi by the hour, half-day, day, or longer. Be sure to negotiate the rate; drivers will work with you. Hire a taxi for island sightseeing and you'll get the best of both worlds. First, you can custom-build your tour. Second, Nassau taxi drivers are the most knowledgeable and helpful guides on the island.

■ Horse & Carriage

In Nassau, you can tour the city by horse and carriage. Unfortunately, though, some of the poor animals are not treated as well as they should be. If you have a soft spot for animals, skip this option.

■ Car Rental

People in the Bahamas drive on the left, which can be unnerving if you aren't accustomed to it. But with an hour or so at the wheel, and some serious concentration, you'll soon be whizzing along the highways and byways like a native.

Car Rental Companies in Nassau

Avis: Nassau, downtown, west of the British Colonial Hotel, ☎ 326-6380; Paradise Island at the Holiday Inn, ☎ 363-2061; Cable Beach at 1 West Bay Street, ☎ 322-2889; Nassau International Airport, ☎ 377-7121.

Budget: Nassau International Airport, ☎ 377-9000; Paradise Island Airport, ☎ 363-3095.

Hertz: Nassau International Airport, ☎ 377-6321; Paradise Island, ☎ 242-377-6866.

Dollar: Nassau International Airport, ☎ 377-7231; British Colonial Hotel, ☎ 242-325-3716; Sheraton Hotel, Paradise Island, ☎ 242-363-2500.

■ Tours

If you like to be escorted around to the hot spots and attractions, take a taxi or join an organized tour. You'll find details in the following pages or at the travel desk of your hotel.

Shopping

Nassau, New Providence's most populous city, provides more shopping opportunities than any other city on the islands. **Bay Street** and the adjoining side streets are jam-packed with everything from local arts and crafts to the very best fashions and perfumes from London, Paris, New York, and Milan. You can spend hours wandering the tiny side streets, browsing the shops, and enjoying snacks and cups of coffee. You'll find hundreds of unusual bargains and gifts, all at duty-free prices far below those you'll pay at home. The sample listed below is simply to whet your appetite.

■ The Best Spots

The International Bazaar, 95 Bay Street, offers a large selection of swimwear and beach clothing. The Bazaar carries lines by Jag, Just Take Cover, Tonga, Ipanema, and Mashua.

The Big Kahuna, on Bay Street, carries a wide range of brand name tee shirts, sandals, sun-tan products, and Caribbean steel drums.

The Brass & Leather Shops – one is on Charlotte Street and another is in the Mall at Marathon – are specialty shops. They carry lines by such designer companies as Bottega Veneta, Furla, and Pierre Balmain.

Cole's of Nassau, on Parliament Street, is the place to go for fine fashions and accessories. They carry a wide range of designer dresses for day and evening wear, as well as coordinated sportswear and separates.

Cartier, on Bay Street, is Nassau's latest attraction for shoppers. There, you can choose from a wide range of items, all carrying the Cartier name: watches, jewelry, fragrances, china, pens, and sunglasses.

Cameo Parfums, on Bay Street opposite the Straw Market, carries a variety of fragrances and skin care products by most of the world's famous manufacturers.

Bye-Bye Bahamas, on East Street North, is Nassau's hottest store for casual and sports clothing. High-quality silk screened shirts, pullovers, shorts, bags, kid's wear and a variety of accessories, are a sample of what's on sale.

The Burns House, on Bay Street, is the best place for your duty-free liquor at prices as much as 45% off what you pay at home. See page 16 for customs restrictions.

■ The Straw Market

Unfortunately, the Straw Market as I knew it, just off Bay Street, is no more. Only a week before terrorists hit the World Trade Center in New York the old Straw Market burned to the ground taking with it the Ministry of Tourism and more than a block of the surrounding buildings and businesses.

It was a microcosm of Bahamian culture, where tiny stalls and cafés crowded together almost on top of another. But no one was hurt in the fire, and the good people who made the old market what it was rallied round and put the whole thing under canvas, while a new Straw Market rises out of the ashes to be better than it was before. So, while the old, bustling little corner of Nassau is now gone, along with its atmosphere, you can still brave the same singsong voices of the vendors and haggle for bargains.

In the Straw Market, even now, the fun of striking a deal is as important to the traders as it is to you. Crafts, clothing, gifts, antiques, collectibles and bric-a-brac of every description are piled high with little or no thought for security or shoplifters. Pick the stuff up, turn it over, and rummage until you find what you want. And then it begins: a laughing, fun-filled session of bantering back and forth over just how much you'll pay for your prize. You'll walk away happy, and sure that you've struck the bargain of a lifetime, only to turn and see your adversary waving with a smile, and you wonder....

Aerial view of Nassau.

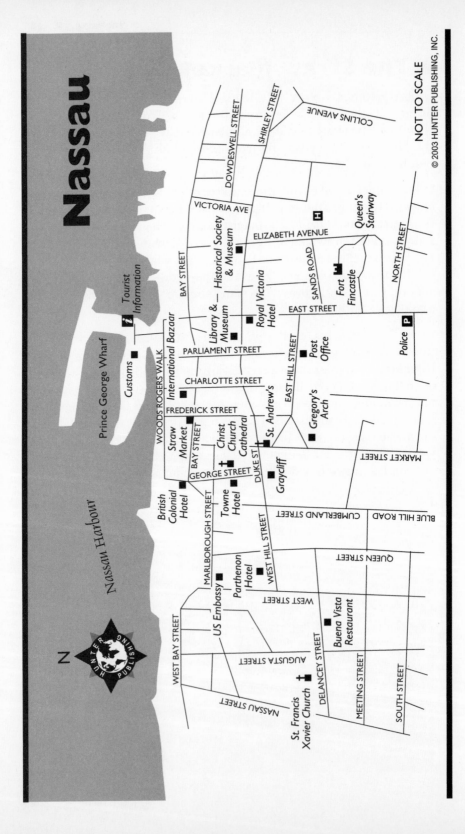

Nassau

Nassau Harbour

Prince George Wharf

Customs

Tourist Information

International Bazaar

WOODS ROGERS WALK

BAY STREET

Straw Market

BAY STREET

British Colonial Hotel

MARLBOROUGH STREET

Towne Hotel

GEORGE STREET

Christ Church Cathedral

FREDERICK STREET

CHARLOTTE STREET

PARLIAMENT STREET

Library & Museum

Royal Victoria Hotel

Historical Society & Museum

VICTORIA AVE

DOWDESWELL STREET

SHIRLEY STREET

COLLINS AVENUE

ELIZABETH AVENUE

Queen's Stairway

SANDS ROAD

Fort Fincastle

NORTH STREET

EAST STREET

Post Office

EAST HILL STREET

Gregory's Arch

St. Andrew's

DUKE ST.

Graycliff

MARKET STREET

Police

P

CUMBERLAND STREET

BLUE HILL ROAD

WEST HILL STREET

Parthenon Hotel

WEST STREET

QUEEN STREET

US Embassy

WEST BAY STREET

AUGUSTA STREET

NASSAU STREET

St. Francis Xavier Church

DELANCEY STREET

Buena Vista Restaurant

MEETING STREET

SOUTH STREET

N

HUNTER PUBLISHING

NOT TO SCALE

© 2003 HUNTER PUBLISHING, INC.

Sightseeing

■ The Atlantis Resort & Casino

One of Paradise Island's major resort hotels, is also one of New Providence's top tourist attractions. The centerpiece of Atlantis is its magnificent 14-acre Waterscape – a complex of six lagoons, three underwater grottos, and a transparent pedestrian tube that takes you beneath one of the lagoons, to cross a rope suspension bridge onto an artificial coral reef for an underwater habitat of more than 3.2 million gallons of saltwater.

DID YOU KNOW?

At a cost of more than $65 million, Atlantis is the largest outdoor, open-water aquarium in the world.

The six lagoons provide a home for more than 35,000 pounds of live tropical fish, coral and other marine life. The **Predator Lagoon** provides a unique look at some of the most feared denizens of the deep. Via a 100-foot, transparent underwater tunnel, visitors can view, up close, a variety of deep-sea predators, including three tiger sharks and a number of barracuda, plus stingrays, moray eels, turtles and crabs, all in their natural environment. There's something a little unnerving about watching a seven-foot shark swim slowly and silently by, just a couple of feet above your head. The other lagoons include **The Seagrapes Ocean Tower Lagoon**, which displays a tide pool and mangrove habitats, along with myriad forms of small marine life; **The Water's Edge Lagoon**, home for a variety of small sharks, rays, turtles, tarpon, jacks, and snappers; and **The Cascade Lagoon**, a series of cascading waterfalls. Finally, **The Paradise Lagoon** – claimed to be the perfect alternative to the ocean – is open to guests for swimming, diving and snorkeling. The eight-acre lagoon is, in places, more than 17 feet deep, and guests can dive beneath its surface to enjoy all the wonders of the ocean.

The Atlantis is a place of luxury where you can enjoy outdoor watersports such as windsurfing and waverunning, gamble away the evening in the casino, or watch a Las Vegas-type show.

■ Beaches

New Providence has some spectacular beaches. If you're visiting the island by cruise ship, you owe it to yourself to get out of town for a couple of hours and visit at least one of them. So many people take a two- or three-night cruise to Nassau, but never explore beyond the dock area and couple of blocks of the city. Get out of town. Visit the beaches.

Cable Beach

Cable Beach is New Providence's premier resort area. It is to Nassau what South Beach is to Miami. The only problem is that the hotels and resorts have gobbled up all the best sections. Of what's left you can pick your spot. Take the time to drive West Bay Street from Nassau to and beyond the resorts and you're sure to find something to suit you. Be careful, though. In some places the water can be rough, and the underlying rocks sharp. Some of the public areas are very popular with the locals, especially on weekends, and can become crowded. All along the beach are snacks, ice cream, activities, and vendors hawking trinkets and souvenirs; ladies can even get their hair braided. Here and there you'll find little fruit stands where the goodies are almost always fresh and cool. For lunch, a variety of cafés and restaurants offer local cuisine, fresh seafood and, of course, as much local libation as you can handle. All in all, Cable Beach comes highly recommended.

DID YOU KNOW? *Cable Beach takes its name from the undersea telephone cable that was laid between the beach and Jupiter, Florida in 1892.*

Buses and tours leave Nassau and Paradise Island for Cable Beach from the shopping center at the foot of Paradise Island Bridge.

Western Esplanade (Junkanoo Beach)

The Western Esplanade is the city beach for Nassau itself. It stretches westward from the British Colonial Hotel and has fine, soft sand, but it often is littered. It does have public restrooms, changing facilities, and one or two snack bars close at hand, and there are a number of fast food restaurants within walking distance. Its popularity lies in its closeness to the city and to the relatively inexpensive small hotels on West Bay Street. During Spring Break this beach becomes a seething mass of hot, excited, sweating bodies writhing to the rhythms of a hundred blaring radios. Still, if you're staying close at hand, and don't want to make the trip to either Cable Beach or Paradise Island, this might be the place for you.

Saunders Beach

Take West Bay Street to Fort Charlotte; the beach is just across the way. You might want to make a day of it: grab a box lunch from the hotel, visit the fort (see page 75), then spend the afternoon on the sand. If you go on a weekend, don't be surprised find it busy; this is a favorite spot for the locals. Weekdays, though, you can be sure of a quiet afternoon. During the summer you might even get to see a cricket match being played on the field just below the fort.

The Beach at Atlantis

This private stretch of sand at the grand resort on Paradise Island is rated – by experts such as the gurus of the Travel Channel – as one the top 10 beaches in the world. Certainly it's one of the best stretches of beach on New Providence and Grand Bahama Islands. But there are some spots in the Out Islands that are better. Unfortunately, unless you're staying at Atlantis, the beautiful beach is off-limits. If you *are* staying there, you'll find the section of beach close to the hotel complex is crowded most of the time. Walk the half-mile or so to the far end of the horseshoe-shaped bay where the sand is pure and white and often there's lots of room to spread out. If you're not staying at Atlantis, there are a number of smaller beaches dotted around Paradise Island; Cabbage Beach is one of the nicest, but also try Smugglers Beach, Shell Beach, and Honeymoon Cove. Ask any of the local taxi drivers to take you.

■ Ardastra Gardens

This is New Providence Island's zoological garden. Privately owned, the zoo and tropical gardens are home to a variety of birds and animals, many of them endangered species. You can wander the tiny pathways through the lush tropical undergrowth, where you'll see the endangered Bahamian parrot, jaguar, assorted monkeys and sloths, raccoons and other nocturnal animals.

Ardastra Flamingos

Ardastra is home to a flock of pink flamingos. And these are flamingos with a difference. Ardastra's are the only *trained* flock of flamingos in the world, and they perform daily for the public. Their trainer barks orders at a covey of flapping soldiers who line up as if on parade. Then they march back and forth upon command. The birds are happy and having fun. And when the show is over, you'll be given the opportunity to get out among them. They'll even pose with you for a photograph or two.

I've visited this unique animal park on a number of occasions, and it never fails to delight and entertain. The last time I was there several of the flamingos were egg-sitting and one couple already had tiny, fluffy offspring that could easily be seen on the far side of the flamingo pool. Needless to say, the kids were all intrigued.

Ardastra has instituted a breeding program for the endangered Bahamian parrot. The birds were once so plentiful that Columbus wrote in his log that flocks of this colorful bird darkened the sky. It is now found on only two of the 700 Bahamian islands. With its numbers down below 3,000, it is a rare and endangered species. At the time of writing, three chicks had been born in the park: all three survived and can be seen roosting in the trees along with their mother.

Because of the natural setting, many of the mammals, birds and reptiles are allowed to wander the park at liberty, and it's not unusual to find a peacock at your feet, proudly strutting its stuff and flouting its feathers.

This 5½-acre escape is only a few minutes drive from downtown Nassau. Alternatively, the #10a bus will take you from downtown Nassau to Arawak Cay, or a taxi will will take you to the zoo for a few dollars. If you are making your own way, the zoo is about four minutes walk from Arawak Cay. Open 9-5, seven days a week. ☎ 242-323-5806, www.ardastra.com, info@ardastra.com.

■ Pirates of Nassau

This is a brand new attraction that appeals to the kid in all of us. It's a step back in time to a world we've only been able to experience in the movies.

The golden age of piracy lasted for about 30 years, from 1690 to 1720; Nassau was at its heart. It was well suited as a pirate center of operations: its waters were too shallow to allow passage for the men-o-war, but deep enough for the shallow-draft vessels favored by the buccaneers. Consequently, Nassau attracted the largest concentration of pirates ever seen in the New World. From here they infested the trade routes, devastating merchant shipping, and causing havoc across the shallow seas. Pirate gold and stolen goods formed the basis for a thriving economy in and around Nassau and attracted rogues and merchants from far and wide. It was said that when a pirate slept he did not dream of going to heaven, but instead of returning to Nassau.

This attraction is unique. As you enter the dark building, it takes a moment or two for your eyes to adjust. Then you find yourself standing on the dock under the bow of the pirate ship *Revenge*. It's not full-size, but it's big enough to create the illusion. Across the street, just a few yards from the side of the ship, are reproductions of the dockside inns, shops, and tenements that might have been found in any port of the times. As you pass along the dock your guide provides a running commentary explaining exactly what it is you're seeing. The tour takes you onboard the ship for a look at the living quarters, gun decks, surgeon's quarters, and so on. From there you move on through the exhibit to experience a shocking true-to-life depiction of pirate lives and times. It's all rollicking good fun and an educational experience as well. Give it a try; you won't be disappointed. Pirates of Nassau is at the junction of Marlborough and George Streets. Admission: $12 adults, $6 children age three-18, free for kids under three. Open Monday through Saturday from 9 to 5. ☎ 242-356-3759; www.pirates-of-nassau.com.

■ The Cloisters

On Paradise Island, the Cloisters offer a unique photographic opportunity. These columns and structures, standing above a beautiful formal garden, are the remains of a 14th-century French monastery brought to the island by grocery chain magnate, Huntington Hartford. The stones were disassembled in France, brought over by ship, and then reassembled in their current location. They present an attractive, though somewhat incongruous, spectacle.

■ The Water Tower

The Water Tower, off Prison Lane just across the way from Fort Fincastle, is the highest point on the island. You'll take either a small rickety elevator or a long and winding staircase to the top of the tower, a spot that offers one of the finest views on the island. To the north are the cruise ship docks. To the west, Cable Beach and fancy-colored resort hotels; to the east lies Paradise Island; and to the south, Nassau. If you're lucky, there may be an unofficial guide at the top of the tower. He'll point out and comment about the attractions you see. For his service, he'll expect a tip. You can give a dollar, if you like; it's well worth it.

■ The Queen's Staircase

Just across the way and a short walk from the Water Tower, this is a stone stairway of 65 steps – one for each year of Queen Victoria's rule. The staircase climbs 102 feet to Fort Fincastle and the Water Tower. Alongside the steps, water cascades to a pool below, causing a mist full of rainbows in the sunshine. At the bottom of the steps, a walkway goes between high stone walls. Tropical plants and trees line the way. There, you'll find a dozen concession stands selling local crafts and tee-shirts. And then you're back on the main highway once more, only a short walk from the Water Tower and the parking lot.

■ Pompey Museum

This museum on Bay Street in Nassau, close to the Straw Market, contains such exhibits as *The Road To Freedom*, which interprets the course of slavery, abolition and emancipation in the islands through a variety of artifacts and historical documents. Open 10 until 4:30, Monday through Friday, and 10 until 1 on Saturday; closed Sunday and national holidays. Admission is $1 for adults; 50¢ for children under 12. ☎ 242-326-2566.

■ Historical Society Museum

Home to the permanent exhibition, *A Reservoir of History*, this museum houses one of the largest collections of Bahamian historic, anthropological and archaeological artifacts on the islands. It is located on Elizabeth Avenue and Shirley Street in Nassau; you can visit weekdays from 10 until 4, and on Saturdays from 10 until noon. Admission is $1 for adults; 50¢ for children under 12. For information, ☎ 242-326-2566.

■ Junkanoo Expo Museum

Junkanoo is a uniquely Bahamian celebration of the Islands' traditions and culture, culminating in a grand, lively and colorful parade through the streets of Nassau on New Year's Day. The parade is a kaleidoscope of sound and spectacle – Mardi Gras, Mummer's Parade and ancient African tribal ritual, all rolled into one. Revelers, dressed in colorful costumes of crêpe paper, parade through the streets to the sounds of cowbells, goatskin drums, whistles, horns and other homemade instruments. Parades are also held on other islands in the Bahamas. For more information, ☎ 242-394-0445.

The museum, on Prince George Wharf, houses a fascinating collection of Junkanoo memorabilia, including many large and colorful, intricately designed artistic creations from recent Junkanoo parades. There's a souvenir boutique selling unique paintings and crafts. Open daily from 9 to 5; closed on national holidays. Admission is $1 for adults; 50¢ for children under 12. ☎ 242-356-2731.

■ Changing of the Guard Ceremony

This is a little bit of pomp, pageantry and tradition left over from the days when the islands were part of the British Empire. Just as Buckingham Palace in England has its guards, so does Government House, the residence of the Governor General, personal representative of Her Majesty Queen Elizabeth II. And just as they do in London, they change the guard at pre-set times. You can watch the ceremony at 10 am every other week in the Government House Grounds, Blue Hill Road, just five minutes from downtown Nassau. For specific dates, ☎ 242-322-2020.

■ The Retreat

This is the home of the Bahamas National Trust on Paradise Island, where environmentalists and nature lovers can enjoy a natural haven of native flora. Thirty-minute tours are conducted Tuesday, Wednesday and Thursday from 11:45; the cost is $2. ☎ 242-393-1317.

■ Guided Walking Tours

Guided walks are the best way to visit Nassau's historic sites and points of interest. Tours depart daily from the Tourist Information Centre at Rawson Square, downtown Nassau, at 10 am and 4 pm, and take in all the interesting stops in and around the city. Tours are conducted by independent Bahamahost-trained guides, and group tours can be pre-arranged. The fee is a donation – $2 is the suggested rate. For more information and group tours, call the Ministry of Tourism and Transportation at ☎ 242-302-2055, or visit the Tourist Information Booth at Rawson Square, ☎ 242-326-9772/328-7810.

■ The Botanical Gardens

The Botanical Gardens, near Fort Charlotte, off Columbus Avenue in Nassau, is an 18-acre tropical garden with more than 600 species of tropical plants, trees, and flowers. There's also a lily pond, a children's playground and a cactus garden. Admission is $1 for adults; 50¢ for children under 12. Open Monday-Friday, 8-4; Saturday-Sunday, 9-4. ☎ 242-323-5975.

■ Fort Fincastle

Fort Fincastle, under the Water Tower at the head of the Queen's Staircase on Bennett's Hill, is a strange-looking structure shaped somewhat like an old-fashioned flat-iron. The tiny fort was built in 1793 by the Royal Governor of the islands, Lord Dunsmore, the Viscount Fincastle, to protect the island from invaders. Its garrison never fired a shot in anger. Today, you can climb to the top of the fort where guns, though not the original ones, still stand guard over the surrounding landscape. No admission charge. Open Monday-Saturday, 9-4. No phone.

■ Fort Montague

Off East Bay Street in Nassau, this is the oldest of the island's three forts. It was built in 1741 to defend the island from attack by Spanish invaders and faces the eastern end of the harbor. It, too, never saw a shot fired in anger. The little fort, barely large enough to justify the title, is always open to the public, day or night. You simply walk in, climb the stone stairs to the upper floor and look out over the harbor, much as its garrison must have done 250 years ago. While you're

Capturing the denizens of the deep on film.

the **Rand Nature Centre** in Freeport, ☎ 242-351-4187. Both agencies offer monthly field trips through the Ornithology Group; all are welcome.

■ Golf

There are three major resorts and country clubs on New Providence.

The Cable Beach Golf Club, managed by the Radisson Cable Beach, is the Bahamas' oldest golf course. It was built in 1974 as the Nassau Country Club and offers a number of unique challenges. Water comes into play at 11 of the 18 holes, and the 12th is a unique double dog-leg. ☎ 242-327-6000.

The South Ocean Golf and Beach Resort has a championship-length course of more than 6,700 yards. Designed by the legendary Joe Lee, the course incorporates four par-fives, each more than 550 yards long, including the 16th, a tough, tight, tree-lined monster that will challenge even the best. ☎ 242-362-4391.

Ocean Club Golf Club (formerly the Paradise Island Golf and Country Club) was originally designed by Dick Wilson to take advantage of the natural but challenging contours of the Paradise Island coastline, but it has recently been redesigned by Tom Weiskopf. The beautiful course is a delight to play, and offers a number of challenges along the way, including the 431-yard par-four ninth, with its long narrow green, and the 471-yard par-four 17th, which has water all along the right side of the fairway. ☎ 242-363-3000.

Golf Packages are offered by many of the island's hotels, including the South Beach Resort, ☎ *877-766-2326.*

■ Gambling

On Paradise Island, the action takes place at the **Atlantis Resort & Casino**. If you've never been to a casino before, you have to make the trip across the bridge to Paradise Island, even if it's only to take in the spectacle. After a general $650 million renovation, the new casino covers several acres, all within the greater confines of the resort. It's all glitz and glass, and rivals anything in Las Vegas. Built over water and invoking the spirit of lost Atlantis, its rooms are themed around the ancient temples of the lost civilization: the Temple of the Sun, the Temple of the Moon, etc. Five huge glass sculptures designed and built by Dale Chihuly draw the eye from wherever you might be in the building. Surrounding the casino is a massive shopping mall, with 35,000 square feet of retail outlets that cater mainly to the rich and famous, with Lalique, Versace, Cartier, Armani, Gucci, Ferragamo, Bulgari, and so on.

In the casino itself, are slots, hundreds of them, and all the other games of a world-class casino. They have blackjack, craps, poker, Caribbean poker, and more.

At **Dragons**, the casino's disco, you can dance away the hours to some of the best music in the islands. It's *the* place to see and be seen and a great place for singles. The party goes on all night long. Live music starts at 9 pm. If you're not a guest at Atlantis, you can still join the party but, on Friday and Saturday, you'll pay a $25 cover.

Jokers Wild is the casino's comedy club. The comics, at least three each evening, many of them locals, do a great job. They're not quite as sophisticated as those you'll find on the mainland, but extremely entertaining nonetheless. ☎ 242-363-3000.

With its comedy club and Las Vegas-style shows, the Atlantis is the more traditional of the two casinos on New Providence.

The Crystal Palace Casino, at the Nassau Marriott Resort on West Bay Street, gives its patrons something a little different. There is fast action at the slots and all the regular games of chance, but the Crystal Palace is a glitzy, upbeat establishment; very modern and very bright.

International currencies can be exchanged at the going rate inside both casinos. You will pay the standard commissions charged by local banks for exchanging all foreign currencies, except for the American dollar. Traveler's checks and most major credit cards are also accepted.

The slots accept coins and bills in denominations from a quarter through $100. You choose the stakes. Some tables limit stakes to between $5 and $15, another might have a minimum stake of $10 with a high limit of $25, while at yet another the minimum stake will be $25, with a high limit of $50. Some games, blackjack and Caribbean stud, take side bets and insurance bets.

The roulette wheels have numbers from 1 to 36, plus a "0" and "00." You set the value of your chips when you buy a stack.

WORD TO THE WISE

There is no specific dress code in the casinos, but you will be expected to dress reasonably – casual, but no swimsuits or bare feet are allowed.

Adventures on Water

■ Dolphin Encounters - Blue Lagoon Island, Nassau

I've seen the dolphins on Grand Bahama and in Nassau a couple of times, but I never get tired of seeing these intelligent animals perform. At the encounters on Blue Lagoon Island, just to the northeast of Paradise Island, you really get close to these finny creatures. Whereas you only get to touch, or simply swim with, the dolphins at the encounter in Freeport, there's a lot more interaction here in Nassau.

Dolphin Encounters Nassau is home to 16 Atlantic bottlenose dolphins, including the internationally famous "Flipper." Blue Lagoon Island is just three miles offshore, northeast of Paradise Island. The idea is for you to really get to know these beautiful and intelligent animals, one-on-one. This is done through a couple of programs: "Close Encounters" and "Swim With The Dolphins."

Close Encounters delivers exactly what it promises. Once in the water, usually to waist level or a little bit more, your trainer brings the chosen dolphin to you. After a moment or two, the dolphin is encouraged to move in close, real close. It will put its head over your shoulder and you can give it an intimate cuddle while the dolphin squeaks sweet nothings in your ear. Dolphins weigh between 600 and 800 pounds, so the experience can be intimidating, but don't let their size put you off; your time with one of these lovely creatures will become a memory to last forever.

AUTHOR PICK

Swim With The Dolphins brings you even closer to these fantastic creatures. The staff puts you into a life vest and you get into one of the pens. Swim around for a moment or two and you'll be joined by steel-gray dolphins that swirl the water around you, zipping off to far reaches of the pen, leaping out of the water and high into the air as they go. Then, the activity subsides. You're asked to lie in the water, on your stomach, stiff-legged, with your feet together; not the easiest thing to do, especially when you don't know what's about to happen. A few seconds go by and you feel something gently touch the soles of your feet. Then it happens: sudden pressure from behind. Faster and faster you move through the water as the dolphin pushes against the soles of your feet until you're planing across the surface of the water like a powerboat. The whole experience – the push – lasts for just a few seconds, but it's a great experience. You'll need to take along towels, swimsuit, sunscreen.

This is one of Nassau's premier attractions. It's almost always sold out, so be sure to call and make a reservation at least 24 hours in advance. They operate in rain or shine, daily from 8 am until 5 pm. Fees: Close Encounters, $75; Swim With The Dolphins, $145; observers, $15. ☎ 242-363-1003; www.dolphinswims.com.

■ Hartley's Undersea Walk

At the Yacht Basin on East Bay Street is one of Nassau's unique attractions. Reminiscent of the undersea walk depicted in the movie *20,000 Leagues Under The Sea*, the 3½-hour cruise is sure to be a highlight of your vacation. You'll leave the Yacht Basin aboard *Pied Piper*, a 57-foot diesel-powered catamaran, along with a captain and crew of two, and head out to the reef. There, you'll don your helmet –

you can keep your glasses on and you won't even get your head wet – then descend the ladder to the ocean floor. The price is $150 per person (adults and children). Generally, they go out Tuesday through Saturday, two trips a day, depending on demand.

Check-in times are 9 am and 1 pm. Reservations are required. You need to bring bathing suit and towel. There are changing facilities on board. You do not need to bring any sea walking shoes/sandals, because the walk takes place on a sandy ocean bottom. A credit card number is necessary for direct bookings. They are sometimes booked a week in advance, but generally you can get reserved seats about three days in advance. Another reason to contact them well in advance is to give them your hotel room number. Transportation service to and from your hotel is included in the $150 price and is arranged through our office. A local charter bus, Johnson's Charter Bus, provides the transportation for Hartley's. ☎ 242 393-8234, www.underseawalk.com, hartley@batelnet.bs.

■ Seaworld Explorer Semi-submarine

The *Seaworld Explorer* is a cruising, underwater observatory offering a guided marine tour. The term semi-submarine is a bit misleading. It is, in fact, a large surface vessel complete with observation deck, air-conditioning and shade canopy. What makes it unique is its undersea observatory just below the main deck. A cruise aboard the *Explorer* takes you out from the dock on Bay Street, through Nassau's docks, and on to the Sea Gardens Marine Park, where you'll get a close-up look at the undersea preserve. In the underwater observation lounge, just five feet below the surface, you'll have your own window on the world beneath the waves. The cruise comes with a running commentary and a fish identification chart. Along the way you're likely to see all sorts of marine life: sharks, rays, turtles and barracuda, along with a variety of brightly colored reef fish. The tour lasts about 1½ hours and costs $37 for adults and $19 for children. It's well

worth it. The *Seaworld Explorer* departs several times daily. Call for times. ☎ 242-356-2548.

■ Sport Fishing

Sport fishing opportunities on New Providence abound. Advertisements for boat charters and sport fishing trips are everywhere. And, no matter who you choose for your adventure, you're not likely to be disappointed. While it's never possible to guarantee a significant catch, it's also true that your chances off New Providence are greatly enhanced by the huge population of game fish: wahoo, marlin, sailfish, kingfish, barracuda, dolphin, tuna and shark. To get you started, all of the following charter companies provide good service. For a more complete list, contact the Bahamas Ministry of Tourism at ☎ 242-322-7501, fax 242-328-0945, or visit the Nassau office on Bay Street next to the Straw Market. A great resource is www.worldwidefishing.com/bahamas/salt.htm.

Fishing Charters

Brown's Charters, ☎ 242-324-1215, offer a variety of services aboard three boats. Captain Michael Brown will organize a deep-sea fishing cruise to any of a number of locations, or take you cruising the islands in one of his luxury air-conditioned boats. The 51-foot *White Cloud* is fully equipped for off-shore fishing, and can carry up to 40 persons for half-day or full-day-trips. The boat is air-conditioned and has two private bathrooms and two staterooms. They also have *Top Gun II* at 52 feet. And at 38 feet, *Fantasea* is Brown's smallest boat. Half-day charters are $400-$700; full-day, $800-$1,400. Online booking available. Shuttle from Paradise Island hotels. www.brownscharter.com.

Captain Arthur Moxey operates a 41-foot Hatteras off-shore fishing boat and is available for fishing charters and cruising. The boat has a capacity of four guests and a crew of two. ☎ 242-361-3527 for reservations and information.

Captain Mike Russell operates **Chubasco Charters** out of Nassau. The company has four boats: a 32-foot Trojan, 35-foot Chris Craft, 45-foot Hatteras, and a 42-foot Post. Russell is one of the most successful charter captains on the island. In 1991, Eddy Pack, along with Captain Russell, caught a record-breaking 10-foot, 7-inch blue marlin, the largest for that year. An added bonus, and a perfect end to a day's fishing, is an island picnic where you can make a meal of your fish, expertly grilled by a member of your crew. ☎ 242-322-8148, day or evening.

Born Free, operated by Captain Philip Pinder out of Nassau, has three boats: two 48-foot, air-conditioned Chris Crafts, and a 35-foot Alman. The company offers a variety of trips, including off-shore fishing, shark fishing, sightseeing, cruising, and snorkeling. ☎ 242-363-2003. www.born-free.com.

■ Powerboat Adventures

Here's your chance to experience the fast-paced world of powerboat racing. Two companies operate out of Nassau.

AUTHOR PICK

Island World Adventures, ☎ 242-363-3333, offers day-trips to the Exumas – definitely not your ordinary excursion. If you have a need for speed and a taste for adventure, this is a not-to-be-missed experience. Some of the islands are uninhabited. Authentic Bahamian cuisine is served, and you will experience the thrills of a high-speed chase across the crystal waters between the islands. If you have a day to spare, take my advice and book this day-trip; you won't regret it. The adventure begins in Nassau in the early morning – you need to be at the dock by 8:30 am. See page 251 for more information. www.islandworldadventures.com.

Thriller Powerboat Tours, ☎ 242-363-4685, will take you anywhere in the Bahamas, but their main clam to fame is the local rides they offer around Paradise Island and along Cable Beach. The boats, reminiscent of the cigarette boats made famous by such television shows as *Miami Vice*, cut through the waters off Nassau at speeds in excess of 45 miles per hour. It's all a great thrill, but not suitable for small children, people with heart conditions, or pregnant women. www.thrillerboat.com.

■ Diving & Snorkeling

With all that's happened over the region's long and sometimes violent history, it's no wonder this is now one of the richest dive sites in the Bahamas, if not the Western world. From the days of the great Spanish treasure ships, through the age of the pirates, privateers, and the Confederate blockade runners – right up to the present – literally hundreds of ships have gone down off New Providence. Add to all that an underwater world of coral reefs and deep clear waters, all teeming with the life of the ocean, and you have a great variety of diving experiences.

Huge expanses of coral reef lie in waters shallow enough for even the most inexperienced snorkeler or scuba diver to enjoy. You can explore dozens of shipwrecks, some barely covered by the rise and fall of the tide, some in water 90 to 100 feet deep. You'll enter great caverns, coral clusters, and shallow flats where bonefish run, barracuda hunt, sharks lurk, and spotted eagle rays lie hidden beneath the sand.

A dozen or so dive operators stand ready to take you out – they also offer instruction. If you want to do it all on your own, there are as many boat rental companies as there are dive operators. If you want to snorkel, the chances are you can do it right from the beach.

Best Dive Sites - North Side

There are more exciting dive sites off New Providence than anywhere else in the Bahamas. The most popular and well-known of those sites are visited regularly by most of the dive operators on the island.

Barracuda Shoals

This a vibrant and colorful underwater community lies in only 25 feet of water and is one of New Providence's most popular dive sites. Formed by several separate and distinct reefs, this triangular formation of shoals provides homes to a variety of marine life, including the barracuda that give the site its name. Underwater photographers love the colorful sponge colonies on the shoals. Barracuda Shoals is also the site of at least six shipwrecks lying in varying depths, from an easy 30 feet to a much more difficult 100 feet.

The Lost Blue Hole

About 10 miles east of Nassau, this is one of the most exciting blue holes in the islands. Seen from the air, the Lost Blue appears as a deep blue disc against the white sandy bottom. In reality, it's a vast opening in the ocean floor, some 100 feet in diameter, with isolated coral heads clinging precariously to its rim. Below, the sea rapidly darkens as you swim toward the depths.

DID YOU KNOW?

> *Each of the coral heads, much larger than they first appear, supports a marine colony all its own: sergeant majors, moray eels, Nassau groupers, and snappers. An assortment of colorful fish and animals play out their lives within the confines of their own particular coral head.*

The Fish Hotel

Though somewhat disappointing as far as reef formations go, this is home to perhaps the greatest concentration of fish on a single reef anywhere around New Providence. The holes and cavities in the hard rock shelves team with colorful fish of all shapes and sizes: sergeant majors, snappers, trumpetfish, parrotfish, grunts and even the occasional moray eel.

The Graveyard

This is the location of four shipwrecks. They lie at depths from 30 to 100 feet. The wrecks, and the marine life that lives within and around them, provide for great photographic opportunities.

Thunderball Reef

This is where the spear-gun scene was filmed for the James Bond movie, *Thunderball*. The site, located to the northeast of Athol Island, is comprised of a long, narrow reef, where the maximum depth is only 25 feet. The coral rises to within 10 feet of the surface, making it easily accessible to both snorkelers and scuba divers. The 100-yard-long reef is home to all sorts of marine life, including sponges, shrimp, and lobsters.

Best Dive Sites - South & West

Experts will tell you that the best diving is on the south and west sides of New Providence. There, also, is where you will find most of the dive operators.

The Shark Wall

This is the place to go if you want to observe these somewhat maligned denizens of the deep. At any one time, a half-dozen to a dozen sharks patrol the waters off the edge of the coral-encrusted drop-off known as the Tongue of the Ocean. The sharks – looking for free hand-outs of food – vary in size from four feet to more than eight feet, and include reef, bull, and lemon sharks. Divers interested in this unique, though contrived, situation position themselves on the sand between the coral heads in about 50 feet of water, while the organizers feed the great fish tidbits from the ends of spiked poles.

The Runway

The Runway is a neat, yet underrated, dive site on the south side of the island, and almost anyone with a little diving experience can visit it. Though there's not much to see, the site is a popular gathering place for Southern stingrays. It's not uncommon for divers to see rays as big as six to eight feet across. And even if the rays are not present, the resident barracuda, a silvery four-footer named Barry, will be pleased to entertain you.

The Southwest Reef

This is one of New Providence's most spectacular and most popular dive sites. Magnificent, multi-structured coral heads – elkhorn, fan, brain, tube, and more – host a multitude of colorful fish and crustaceans, such as flags, squirrelfish, parrotfish, sergeant majors, grunts and barracuda. It is all in only 15-30 feet of water, making the site easily accessible to scuba divers and snorkelers alike.

The Tunnel Wall

A part of the Clifton Wall on the southwest coast, this is an interesting and colorful system of caves, crevices and tunnels. It's a drop-off dive beginning in about 30 feet of water, descending to exit the tunnel system some 70-100 feet down along the near-vertical wall.

Shipwrecks

There are a number of shipwrecks on the reefs off New Providence. Some of them are readily accessible in only 10 or so feet of water to both snorkelers and scuba divers. Others, at depths of up to 120 feet, are not so accessible. Those listed here are the best-known and can be visited with any of the dive operators listed in this chapter.

The Alcora

The *Alcora* sits upright in 80 feet of water just northeast of Athol Island. The ship, a 130-foot freighter, had been involved in drug smuggling until confiscated by the Bahamian government, which then turned it over to Sun Divers for disposal. The only proviso was that it not cause a hazard to shipping. The ship was stripped of any object that might be dangerous to divers, the ports and hatches were opened to allow easy access, and then she was towed out to her present location, where she sits on the sandy bottom surrounded by corals. The wreck presents a major photographic opportunity and is well worth the long boat ride. The cost of the ride, however, unless enough people sign up for the dive, could make the trip prohibitive. You'll need to be a diver of at least intermediate experience to visit the *Alcora*. You'll also need to let the operators know you're interested well in advance.

The Antinque

Another confiscated drug smuggler ship, this is much smaller than the *Alcora* and therefore less interesting. It lies some 200 yards west of the *Tears of Allah* (see page 88), the James Bond wreck off the southwest coast.

The B-25

The B-25 is the wreck of a World War II bomber that crashed into the sea off the north side of Golden Cay more than 50 years ago. As you might imagine, there's not much left of her today. Still, if sunken aircraft excite you, it's worth a visit. The wreckage lies on the sand in less than 30 feet of water.

The Cessna

This is yet another scripted wreck, a part of the Bond film, *Never Say Never Again*. Bond crash-landed a twin-engine aircraft in the ocean, and then climbed out and swam to safety. This is that plane, and it lies in 40 feet of water, close to the Clifton Wall off the southwest side of the island. Novice divers, with supervision, can make it to this one.

WORD TO THE WISE

The site is sandy, so, if you're visiting as part of a large group of divers, make sure you get down there first, before the sand gets stirred up and obscures the view.

The LTC Wreck

The LTC Wreck is the remains of a WW II landing craft that saw extensive service ferrying freight between New Providence and Exuma. During one run, the vessel began taking on water and, in a desperate effort to save her, the crew ran her aground just southwest of Athol Island. Over the years, she's shifted and settled until finally she ended up at her present location in 10 to 20 feet of water. With the top of her wheelhouse almost on the surface, she's the ideal wreck for novice divers. Living beneath her hull you'll find all sorts of marine animals and crustaceans, including the tiny arrow crab. Still fairly intact, and liberally covered in seafans and sponges, she presents a nice photographic opportunity.

Be careful; LTCs' decks and door openings are covered in fire coral. It's best to wear a wet-suit.

The Mahoney

The *Mahoney* is not the real name of the wreck that lies in 45 feet of water off the north coast of Paradise Island. The 212-foot steel-hulled ship apparently sailed the oceans under a number of names, none of them *Mahoney*. She went down in a hurricane in 1929, breaking in two. What's left of the bow and stern portions are lying more than 100 yards apart. Unfortunately, because of the hazard she would have presented to other shipping, she was blown up with dynamite and laid out pretty flat on the ocean floor. Today, there's not much of a profile for divers to explore, but her boiler, and other machinery, make for wonderful photographic backdrops. Because of the fast currents caused by the ever-turning tides, you'll need to be fairly experienced to dive here.

Once again, watch out for fire coral, which is everywhere.

The Royal James

The *Royal James* was once an old Mississippi ferry boat that once worked the channel between Nassau and Paradise Island. Her useful life as a ferry ended with the building of the Paradise Island Bridge. For a while she continued to provide service as a dive boat. In 1988, however, the ravages of old age and her constantly failing machinery brought about her demise. Local dive operators stripped her, towed her out to sea and sank her in 45 feet of water close to the Golden Cay drop-off. And so her useful life began again as a regular stop on the operators' list of dive sites.

The Tears of Allah

The *Tears of Allah* is a 100-foot, steel-hulled wreck, perhaps the finest photographic opportunity of them all. The site was designed and dressed by experts. This was the freighter used to transport nuclear weapons in *Never Say Never Again,* the James Bond film. She, too, fell afoul of the Bahamian government when she was caught running drugs. The confiscated ship was taken under tow and, with help from Stuart Cove, the owner of Nassau Undersea Adventures, she was sunk in about 50 feet of water off the southwest coast. The ship's profile is gorgeous: a rounded wheelhouse, short bow, broad fantail, and a long cabin with plenty of doors and hatches to allow easy access. Looking down from the surface she's a little disappointing, but close-up she's a delight. There are no significant currents here, the water is clear, and even novice divers, under supervision, can have a great time exploring.

The Vulcan Bomber

A set from the early Bond film, *Thunderball*, this is not really a bomber at all – just a movie prop, a framework of steel pipes and tubes that looks for all the world like part of some giant construction kit. The site, located only yards away from *The Tears of Allah*, is a jungle of seafans, anemones, and corals. Who could forget the great Vulcan bomber – they called it a Vindicator in the movie – as it lay intact on its wheels in less than 30 feet of crystal water? The site is now alive with fish, all waiting for you to feed them. Be sure to take along a camera.

The Willaurie

The *Willaurie* lies in about 70 feet of water off Clifton Point on the southwest end of the island. This 150-foot wreck, a steel-hulled freighter and sometime mail boat, now sits upright on the sandy bottom, hatches wide open, looking as if it had been sunk only yesterday. The ship's demise is still something of a mystery. For a time it lay by Clifton Pier, seemingly abandoned. Then, one dark night, it disappeared, possibly towed away by one of the local dive operators, for it ended up on the bottom in its present location. The wreck has not yet had time to become inundated by the marine growth that will surely take over. Even so, the site offers a great many interesting photographic opportunities.

The Spiyva

The *Spiyva*, often called the Wreck on the Wall, is a 40-foot wooden fishing boat that was sunk just to the south of the *Tears of Allah*. It sits teetering on the edge of the abyss, offering an interesting dive. The coral of the Clifton Wall, upon which the boat lies, begins some 40 feet below the surface and drops off very quickly to a depth of more than 1,000 feet. The site is a wonderland of coral heads, marine life of all shapes, colors and sizes, and is very photogenic. You'll find large groupers, yellowtails and parrotfish, snappers, surgeon fish and, now and again, a shark lurking in the darker waters beyond the edge of the wall.

Dive Operators

Bahama Divers

On East Bay Street in Nassau, they have been in business for 30 years. They operate mostly on the north side of New Providence, and conduct regularly scheduled dives in the morning, afternoon and at night. They have a staff of 17, nine of whom are fully qualified instructors. Bahama Divers, affiliated with PADI, operates three dive boats with carrying capacities for 10 to 30 divers. The large company store sells a wide range of gear and equipment, and carries 100 sets of rental gear. Dive packages can be arranged through any of the hotels on the island. Rates: one day, one tank, $45; two days, two tanks, $130; night dive, $50. ☎ 242-393-8234, 800-398-DIVE, or write to PO Box 21584, Fort Lauderdale, FL 33335. www.bahamadivers.com.

Custom Aquatics

One of Nassau's newer companies, in business for only four years. The great advantage of working with this company is that they don't have regularly scheduled dives. This means that if a boat is available, you can charter it and go out diving at any time of day; you'll have the boat and instructor all to yourself. They will also take you to any site, wreck or reef that you might specify. The small staff of two operates two boats, each with a carrying capacity of eight divers. ☎ 242-362-1492, or write Box CB12730, Nassau, Bahamas. E-mail youngegrouper@batelnet.bs.

Dive Dive Dive

This is a very professional outfit, located in the Coral Harbour Hotel. In business for some 17 years, it works primarily on the south side with three boats that can carry from eight to 20 people. The company has a retail store where you can purchase and rent gear. The staff of 12 includes five fully qualified instructors. Agency affiliations include PADI, SSI, NAUI, NASDS, and ANDI. Dive Dive Dive specializes in shark dives and night videos. Packages can be arranged through the six villas on the property. Rates: two dives, $70; night dives, $70; starter courses, $99. ☎ 800-368-3483, or write to 1323 SE 17th Street, Fort Lauderdale, FL 33316. www.divedivedive.com.

Diver's Haven

This is one of Nassau's long-established operators, in business for more than 27 years. The staff of 17 includes five fully qualified guides and instructors. The four company boats have carrying capacities from 15 to 40 people. There's an on-site training pool, where first-timers can learn to dive in safety. By arrangement, this company will take you to any and all of the remote wreck and reef sites. Packages can be arranged through a number of island hotels, including the Comfort Suites, Red Carpet Inn, and the Radisson Cable Beach Resort. ☎ 242-393-0869, or write to PO Box N1658, Nassau, Bahamas.

The Nassau Scuba Centre

This is another of Nassau's newer companies, in business less than five years. The company schedules dives throughout the day and evening. The staff of 12 includes four instructors. Their three boats can carry from 12 to 22 passengers. Agency affiliations include PADI, SSI, NAUI, NASDS and BSAC. Specialties include shark dives, and packages can be arranged through Le Meridian Cable Beach, Orange Hill, and the Radisson Cable Beach Resort. Rates: two dives, $75; night dives, $55. ☎ 800-327-8150, or write to PO Box 21766, Fort Lauderdale, FL 33335. www.nassau-scuba-centre.com.

Stuart Cove's Dive South Ocean

One of Nassau's premier dive operators specializing, as the name implies, in dive sites off the south side of the island. Stuart has first-hand knowledge of the Bond sites, having helped with their construction during the filming. The company, in business for more than 17 years, has a staff of 20 – 10 of whom are fully qualified instructors. They operate six boats with capacities ranging from six to 24 passengers. You can arrange custom dives, or join one of the scheduled dives in the morning, afternoon, and evening. There are daily shark dives. Packages can be arranged on the property through the South Ocean Golf and Beach Resort. Pick-up service is available at all Nassau hotels. ☎ 800-879-9832, or write to PO Box CB11697, Nassau, Bahamas.

Sunskiff Divers

In business for about nine years, they have a staff of two (both instructors) and operate one boat with capacity for six people. This company doesn't have a regular schedule of dives and so can be very flexible. For years, they've specialized in blue hole, shark and night diving, and they will take you to any site, even the remote ones. They offer custom dive packages including accommodation in a three-bedroom house on the canal. ☎ 800-331-5884, local 242-362-1979, or write PO Box N142, Nassau, Bahamas.

Where to Stay & Eat

Restaurant Price Scale	
$	less than $20 per person
$$	$20-$50 per person
$$$	$50+ per person

■ Dining

 $ The Blue Marlin, at Hurricane Hole Plaza on Paradise Island, overlooks the Paradise Island Bridge and the busy docks below and across the water. It serves lunch and dinner and also has a Happy Hour from 4 to 6 pm. The large picture windows offer splendid views of the boats and yachts tied up at the nearby dock. The menu, filled with a variety of Bahamian specialties, includes conch served in all the traditional ways, and an assortment of fresh seafood dishes, such as grouper and snapper, all served with peas and rice. ☎ 242-363-2660. www.bahamasnet.com/bluemarlin/.

$$$ Buena Vista Restaurant, Buena Vista Hotel, Delancy Street, Nassau. This is one of Nassau's top dining spots, and it's been open for business for more than 50 years. It's expensive, but the experience is well worth the cost. The cuisine is French, the atmosphere cozy and intimate, the décor elegant, and the desserts are decadent (try the cherries jubilee). Specialties include veal dishes, rack of lamb and beef. It's best to make a reservation and men should wear a jacket. Open Monday through Saturday for dinner from 7 to 9:30 pm. ☎ 242-322-2811. www.buenavista-restaurant.com.

$$$ The Courtyard Terrace, at the Ocean Club Golf & Tennis Resort on Paradise Island, is the epitome of elegance and quiet luxury. Tables line the edge of a pool where the fountain plays against a backdrop of tropical palms and plants. Meals are served on fine china at tables dressed with Irish linen, flowers and candles. Gentle strains of classical and island music complete the experience. It's an expensive evening, but one you're likely never to forget. ☎ 242-363-2222.

$$$ The Graycliff, on West Hill Street, Nassau, has been rated as one of the world's 10 best restaurants by *Lifestyles of the Rich and Famous,* and has received *The Wine Spectator's* Grand Award for its wine cellar, which contains more than 175,000 bottles. The restaurant also claims to have the best collection of Cuban cigars in the world. The Graycliff is the only five-star restaurant in the Caribbean. You'll need a jacket, a tie, and a reservation. ☎ 242-322-2796.

$$$ The Humidor Bistro and Smokehouse, Graycliff Cigar Company, West Hill Street, Nassau. A part of the Graycliff complex, this fine restaurant caters to the ever-expanding company of cigar aficionados. Do you have to smoke cigars here? Of course not. If you don't smoke, though, or if you can't handle a smokey atmosphere, this is not the place for you. If you are one of tobacco's elite, then you really are in for an experience: the stogie is king here. The food is French, but more down to earth than you might expect at a high-end international restaurant, with lamb, beef, fish, veal, and lots more. No jacket is required, but reservations are a must. Open Tuesday through Sunday for dinner until 9:30 pm. Credit cards are accepted. ☎ 242-322-2796/7.

$$ Passin' Jacks, on East Bay just east of the Paradise Island Bridge, is located on the top floor of the Nassau Harbour Club. The restaurant offers not only great food, but good views of the harbor and boats as well. Passin' Jacks is a local favorite, and one of those places where you can enjoy the atmosphere just as much as the meal. Bahamian favorites include cracked conch, fresh boiled grouper, smothered chicken and peas and rice. ☎ 242-393-8175.

$$ The Prince George Roof Top Café, Restaurant & Lounge, on Bay Street in Nassau is another of the island's most popular haunts. You can dine inside or out on the rooftop, and enjoy a traditional Bahamian meal. All the standard dishes are on the menu, including the best conch salad anywhere, and excellent fried grouper. ☎ 242-322-5854.

$$ The Reef, on Thompson Boulevard at Moss Street, also offers home-cooked Bahamian fare. A best seller here is grouper; they can cook it any way you like. Other island specialties include fish stew, conch, mutton and curried goat, along with an extensive and interesting dessert menu. ☎ 242-323-5506.

$$$ The Sun And... , on Lakeview Drive off East Shirley Street, is one of those places that always seems to be waiting to be discovered; it's an atmosphere that the management works hard to maintain. To enter the restaurant, you walk across a drawbridge, through an archway, and into an enclosed garden, where you'll find an elegant, intimate setting for fine dining in traditional French style. Rack of lamb, stone crabs, duckling with raspberry sauce, and marnier soufflé are just a few of the culinary delights. You'll need a reservation, plus a jacket and tie. ☎ 242-393-1205.

$$ The Tamarind Hill Restaurant & Music Bar, on Village Road, is an out-of-the-way dining event. The relaxed atmosphere, the primitive motifs and paintings, and the live shows make the short drive to the restaurant well worth the effort. The menu includes seafood crêpes, fried calimari, chicken in mango glacé, and their own gourmet vegetarian pizza. ☎ 242-393-1306.

■ Accommodations

 With rare exceptions, hotel standards in the Bahamas are not what you'd expect on the US mainland or in Europe. Due to the fact that almost everything has to be imported, and is therefore expensive, there is a definite trend to put off until tomorrow what should be done today. Hotels that might have been considered fairly upscale five years ago can quickly become slightly seedy as time and weather take their toll. Don't expect too much, but don't let a little inconvenience spoil an otherwise wonderful experience.

Hotel Meal Plans

- **CP** (Continental Plan) includes a continental breakfast.
- **EP** (European Plan) denotes no meals, although restaurant facilities are available either on the property or nearby.
- **MAP** (Modified American Plan) denotes breakfast and dinner.
- **FAP** (Full American Plan) includes all meals.
- **All-Inc.** (All-Inclusive Plan) includes all meals, beverages (alcoholic and soft), watersports, tennis and golf, if available.

Dillet's Guest House is an elegant, authentic Bahamian home just off West Bay Street, and a short walk from the Ardastra Gardens, Fort Charlotte, the Botanical Gardens and a half-dozen nice beaches. It is only minutes away by taxi from downtown Nassau and Cable Beach. All accommodations are air-conditioned suites, some with cooking facilities. Rental bicycles are available. Meals are served on request. Dillet's is the best buy on the island. On Dunmore Avenue and Strachen Street, Nassau, ☎ 242-325-1133, $50 EP.

The Parliament Inn is a small hotel dating back to the early 1930s. Close to the Victorian Gardens, the Cenotaph, and Government House. Pleasant, individually furnished guest rooms. Bay Street, with its shops and restaurants, is a short walk away, but the beach is quite a trip. Box N-4138, Parliament Street, Nassau, ☎ 800-327-0787, $70 EP.

The Buena Vista Hotel, Delancy Street, is an old mansion, much like a luxurious private home, situated near Government House in the downtown area of Nassau. It's close to the shops and restaurants, but quite a hike to the beach. Five beautifully furnished guest rooms, all with refrigerators. The restaurant, for dinner only, offers good food served on fine china. See page 92. Box N-564, Nassau, ☎ 242-322-2811, $95 EP. www.buenavista-hotel.com.

Casuarina's of Cable Beach has well-appointed guest rooms with refrigerators, nice views and a landscaped courtyard. There are two swimming pools and two great restaurants. It's quiet here. Located about a mile from the Crystal Palace Casino. Box N-4016, ☎ 800-325-2525, $105 EP.

Paradise Paradise. A pleasant, well-appointed hotel on the beach with extra services that make the already modest rates very attractive. There's a quiet beach, pool, changing rooms, plus volleyball and basketball facilities. Organized activities, including a daily bicycle tour, are all included in the rate. Box SS-6249, Nassau, ☎ 800-321-3000, $115 EP.

Nassau Beach Hotel, Cable Beach. Not quite as upscale as its sibling resort, Nassau Marriott, just a short distance away, Nassau Beach is still one of Cable Beach's best. Marriott took over the property in the early 1990s and promptly spent mega-bucks bringing it up to the chain's stringent standards. In 1999 they spent a further $12 million to renovate most of the guest rooms. Even so, it's still one of the beach's older hotels – built in the 1940s – and, as such, doesn't have the charisma of its more glitzy neighbors. But that's not a bad thing. If you like a quiet, comfortable atmosphere, this is just the place for you. It has most facilities, with more than 3,000 feet of beautiful, well-kept beach, nice restaurants, and bars and cafés. There are scenic gardens and stone paths, wrought iron outdoor furniture by the pool and on the lawns, plus comfortable guest rooms with balconies, ocean views, and dressing alcoves. The casino is right next door. Guests have tennis and golf privileges. There are seven restaurants, three bars, a health club, baby-sitting service, and a range of watersports. Rates are affordable and start around $140 per night for a double room. Reasonably priced packages are available from most of the major operators, and Marriott usually has a deal or two, to offer as well. Check their website at www.marriott.com. ☎ 888-627-7282.

The South Ocean Golf & Beach Resort is 15 minutes by taxi from Nassau's airport. This large resort has its own golf course, four tennis courts, two pools, and a private beach. There's always lots going on, from scuba diving to sightseeing tours. The rooms are comfortable, nicely decorated, and all have balconies or patios. 808 Adelaide Drive, ☎ 800-228-9898, $140 EP.

WORD TO THE WISE

Rooms on the ground floor can be very noisy at South Ocean, especially with late-night revelers and children coming and going from the pool or beach.

Superclubs Breezes. Look at the travel brochures and you'll find little difference, on the surface, between this resort group and its main competitor, Sandals. The ads look alike, but there the similarities end. Breezes is not quite as expensive as Sandals and it doesn't have the same stringent rules: singles are allowed and gays are welcome too. There are two restaurants – the quality of the food is okay but never outstanding – and there's a beachside café-grill. What's really remarkable about Breezes is its outdoor ice rink (open 24 hours), not exactly what you'd expect in the Bahamas. It's a lot of fun and the use of ice skates is complimentary. There are five pools, often overcrowded; a disco, always overcrowded; a nightclub, almost always overcrowded; and a piano bar, rarely overcrowded. If you like lots of people, lots of noise, and a busy get-down-and-have-a-real-good-time resort, this is the place for you. Very expensive. Rates start at $400 per night for a double, and quickly rise to more than $750. Having said that, the package operators seem to have an inside track, and it's almost always possible to find something at a more reasonable rate. Even Breezes, from time to time, comes up with something special. Check their website at www.breezes.com, and the package operators listed on page 58. ☎ 242-327-8231.

The British Colonial Beach Resort is a Best Western Hotel. Even though it's in the general downtown area, it has its own private beach. The hotel is one of Nassau's major landmarks. Large, well-appointed guest rooms offer views over the ocean, city, and harbor. Box N-7148, Nassau. ☎ 800-528-1234, $150 EP.

Comfort Suites, Paradise Island. A large, but quiet, hotel just across the way from the action at the Atlantis Resort and Casino, where Comfort Suites guests can charge meals to their hotel rooms and have access to all of the facilities. Each suite – really a divided room – has either a king-sized bed or two double beds, and a pull-out sofabed. The open-air restaurant, overlooking the pool and the water-side bar, serves breakfast and lunch. The traditional Comfort Suites continental breakfast is included in the rate. Box SS-6202, Nassau, ☎ 800-228-5150, www.vacationparadiseisland.com, $150 EP.

The Bay View Village. This quiet, getaway hotel set in four acres of lush, landscaped gardens offers one- , two- , or three-bedroom cottages, individually decorated and privately owned. All have private balconies, built-in safes, irons, TVs, and hair dryers. There are three swimming pools. Box SS-6308, Nassau, ☎ 800-327-0787, $165 EP.

The Graycliff Hotel is a historic mansion situated just behind Government House in downtown Nassau. It houses one of the top restaurants in the Caribbean (see page 92). The atmosphere at the hotel is one of private opulence and old-world charm. All guest rooms are comfortably furnished with dressing rooms and large bathrooms. There are lots of extras, including Jacuzzi, gymnasium, solarium, porches, and patios. Box N-10246, Nassau, ☎ 242-322-2796, $170 EP.

Atlantis Paradise Island Resort and Casino. I first stayed at Atlantis some six years ago. It was beyond description even then. Today, after the owners have spent more than $600 million, I find myself at a loss to do it justice. In truth, it probably deserves a chapter all to itself, far more space than I have available here. Its sheer size makes it unique. And size, while it does offer many advantages, can also create problems. Personally, I like Atlantis, because of its size. My wife and daughter, though, find it overpowering. Every attraction is just a little too far away. There are always lines at the waterslides and amusements, so the waits can be long. The service, because of the vast numbers of guests and visitors, is a little slow. But all that, in my opinion, is to be expected, and the pros far outweigh the cons. The guestrooms, new and old, are luxurious by any standards. The restaurants, all 20 of them, are, with the exception of slower service, excellent. The best of them is the **Bahamian Club**. Their cuisine is French, the food absolutely beyond reproach, and even the service is efficient. The prices, of course, reflect this. There are some 15 bars and clubs at Atlantis, all of them almost always crowded. The beach, while exclusive to guests of the resort, is also often packed, especially close to the towers. The amusements, like everything else at Atlantis, are larger than life.

Atlantis is a vast water world. Its theme is the Lost Continent. No expense has been spared to bring the illusion to life. Nothing does this better than **The Dig**, a believable representation of an undersea archeological site. It's like something straight out of a Jules Verne novel, complete with Atlantian diving suits, underground passages, artifacts and ruins, all done on a grand scale. The Dig is surrounded by huge plate glass windows that turn the ocean itself into a vast aquarium and provide fantastic underwater views of still more ruins and ocean life, including a giant manta ray and innumerable sharks. The Dig is open to guests at no charge, and to visitors – admission is included in the visitor fee of $25. The Dig is a must.

The amusements include a floating pool (no, it doesn't float; you do). You take to the gently moving waters in an inner-tube and for 20 minutes or so meander along a concrete-lined river that makes its way around a number of ornamental gardens, through palm-covered glades, past closely manicured lawns. It's great for kids, and for grown-ups who like to take things slowly; in fact, it's about the only amusement at Atlantis that does go slowly. Water slides come in various levels of scary: there's one for the smaller kids that's quite tame, one that even I could probably handle, but that still provides a thrill; and then there's one with an almost vertical drop that takes you down, by way of a clear acrylic tunnel, through the waters of a shark-infested lake to drop you with a huge splash in a shallow wading pool. You might have to wait in line for 20 minutes or more to enjoy a thrill that's over in a matter of seconds. Still, you've got to give it a go.

The gardens of Atlantis are worth a visit too. Acre upon acre of fantastic and exotic landscapes and plant life, dotted here and there with ornamental pools and vast lakes, some of which are stocked with predators of the ocean: sharks of every size and description, rays, even barracudas patrol the larger lakes. There are also hammerhead sharks, tiger sharks, swordfish, and more.

The Atlantis casino is done in a grand style (see *Gambling*, page 78). Again, the theme is that of the ocean and the ancient god of the ocean, Neptune. The décor is sumptuous, the furnishings luxurious, and the play international. The entertainment, nightclubs, shows, lounges and bars, are also international in scope; there's even a superb cigar shop (don't forget, you can't take Cuban cigars into the United States). Above all, though, is the opulence. You don't have to gamble to enjoy this casino. Just walk around; you'll see what I mean.

If you're in Nassau, don't miss Atlantis. If you can afford the rates, and they are expensive, try to spend at least a few days on the property. Rates start at $295 per night for a double room, and rise to $25,000 – that's right, thousand – per night for the Bridge Suite. If you can handle that, I'm told you'll be in good company: Michael Jordan and Michael Jackson, to mention just a couple of names, have stayed here. ☎ 800-ATLANTIS; wwwatlantisresort.com.

The Radisson Cable Beach Hotel. This is one of the most under-rated accommodations on the island. I've stayed a number of times on the property and I've watched it grow into a classy, family-oriented resort that can compete with any in the Bahamas or the Caribbean. The Radisson has undergone a major renovation and now shares the casino with the Nassau Marriott Resort. The hotel forms a great protective semi-circle along one of Cable Beach's finest stretches of sand. Plus, it's barely more than walking distance from Nassau proper. There's not nearly as much going on at the Radisson as there is at Atlantis, but it's not lacking in appeal, especially if you prefer things a little less crowded, less noisy, and less expensive. There's always plenty of space on the beach, the three pools are rarely crowded, and the bars offer drinks at reasonable prices, comparable to anywhere else in the Bahamas. On the downside, the staff is a little off-hand, and the service in the two most popular restaurants is slow. In general, you should always expect to get what you pay for; here at the Radisson I think you get a little more than that.

There are six specialty and gourmet restaurants. Comfortable guest rooms have fabulous views of ocean, beaches and grounds. One of the best private beaches on Cable Beach is here. Eighteen holes of golf, tennis, and racquetball are available. There are three pools, three squash courts, 15 tennis courts, Camp Junkanoo for the kids, baby sitting, a beauty salon, shops and a casino next door. Rates start at $225 for a double. EP or all-inclusive packages are available. See listings on pages 58 and 350. Highly recommended. ☎ 800-333-3333; www.radisson.com.

Sandals Royal Bahamian. This is an exclusive, luxurious hotel and the perfect spot to spend a few days alone with the one you love. It's also for your honeymoon, or even as a place to get married. If you decide to take the plunge right here on the island, Sandals will make everything easy for you. They can provide a wedding councilor, preacher, photographer, flowers, champagne and cake. Honeymoon accommodations include 27 luxury suites, each with its own plunge pool. The hotel's main pool borders on the decadent, flanked by towering marble columns with a wide, glittering mosaic floor, all reminiscent of ancient Rome. The guest rooms are a bit fancier than most, but seasoned travelers will feel right at home. The rooms that face the ocean all have small balconies. There are a half-dozen restaurants, cafés and bars, ranging from the intimate and comfortable to the best of fine dining. Take a short boat ride to the resort's private island, with its palm-covered restaurant, bar and secluded beaches – a veritable Gilligan's Island. Back ashore you can visit the spa, which is rivaled only by those high-end spas in Arizona, Las Vegas, and New York. Then there are the fountains, courtyards, English Pub, and tennis courts; golf is available on a championship course that's almost within walking distance of the resort. It's all-inclusive and for couples only. Sorry – no gay couples.

What does all this cost? This is one of the most expensive destinations in the Bahamas. Rates begin at a whopping $4,000 per couple for seven days, or $1,200 for two days; prices do include all meals and beverages. The smart shopper can always find a deal, so be sure to consult your travel agent early. You can also try going direct to ☎ 800-SANDALS, or visit their website at www.sandals.com. From time to time some of the major carriers, American Airlines Vacations, Delta Vacations, Vacation Express, and Travel Impressions all offer Sandals packages. See listings on pages 58 and 350.

West Wind II. Sounds like a sailboat, but it's not. At the western end of Cable Beach, it's a collection of two-story units comprising some 54 two-bedroom time-share apartments. From the road (West Bay Street), it looks exactly like what it is: an exclusive, upscale, private estate. But there's almost always one or more units available for rent. It's a great place for families. The two-bed apartments are completely self-sufficient; they all have full-service kitchens. There's a large (by Bahamian standards) supermarket within easy walking distance of the complex. There's also a Subway sandwich shop less than a block away, which I found extremely convenient (prices are about the same as in the US, so families can eat cheap). Downtown Nassau is a short bus ride away. There are two pools and a private beach, but little else on-site. The Marriott casino is also an easy walk. Rates in the off-season (May through October) begin at $1,250 per week; in the high season (November through April), they start at $1,400 per week. ☎ 242-327-7019.

Paradise Island Fun sits at the water's edge, on Harbour Drive, with stunning views over Paradise Island and the harbor beyond. It has an excellent restaurant and guest rooms. There are tennis clinics, use of snorkeling equipment and live entertainment. The beach is not too distant. An all-inclusive property. Rates are $129-$179 per night. ☎ 800-952-2426, $200 EP.

Pirate's Cove. This luxury hotel has quiet sandy beaches, a swimming pool, open-air bar, landscaped gardens, fitness room, and a romantic atmosphere that makes it an ideal honeymoon spot. The guest rooms are standard Holiday Inn. They are comfortable, roomy, and offer a variety of excellent views. Box 6214, Nassau, ☎ 800-HOLIDAY, 242-356-0000 (local), www.holiday-inn.com. $200 EP.

Sheraton Grand Resort Paradise Island. Formerly the Radisson Grand Resort, this property has undergone a $10 million renovation. It reopened in early 2000 and, to a great extent, it lives up to the hype. The 340 guest rooms are all spacious, decorated in cool relaxing colors, air-conditioned and they have cable TV and pay-per-view options. Some rooms have balconies and all have spectacular views overlooking the three-mile stretch of beach and the ocean. All guest rooms also have all the modern conveniences: coffee makers, hair dryers, irons and boards, modems for Internet access, and mini-bars. Other hotel facilities include lighted tennis courts and a huge pool and patio. Indoors, there's a fitness center, three bars and four restaurants. The resort is within walking distance of Atlantis and its casino so there's plenty to see and do for the entire family. It's expensive. Room rates start at $250, rising to $280 per night in the summertime (suites run from $290 to $650) and in the winter they range from $290 to $325 per night (suites go for $355 to $900). Casino Drive, Box SS-6307, Paradise Island, ☎ 242-363-3500 and 800-782-9488; www.sheratongrand.com.

Nassau Marriott Resort & Crystal Palace Casino. There was a time when Marriott had every reason to be ashamed to call this resort one of its own. Not any more. Today it's one of New Providence's finest, most lavish, glitzy, luxurious and, at times, jumpin' resorts. It offers a little bit of everything: watersports, fine dining, fast food, a fine beach, more than a dozen restaurants and bars, a huge pool, an upscale shopping mall and an 18-hole golf course. Add a little nightlife, a Las Vegas-style theater, the casino, and you have more than enough entertainment on-site to keep you busy for a week or more. Guest rooms have satellite TV, floor-to-ceiling windows and balconies with spectacular views of the beaches and ocean. It's fairly expensive. Rates start at $199 per night for a double and rise to more than $500 for a suite. Even so, you're sure to get your money's worth. Highly recommended. West Bay Street, PO Box N8306, Nassau, ☎ 800-222-7466. www.marriott.com/NASBS.

Club Land'Or. This is a time-share resort on Paradise Island, with some hotel rooms available. It's very expensive, considering the beach is a good 10-minute walk away. All units have kitchens, dining areas and living rooms. There's a nice pool with a patio and view of the lagoon. $230 EP. Box SS-6429, Nassau, ☎ 800-321-3000, www.clublandor.com, info@clublandor.com.

Ocean Club. This is one of Paradise Island's truly opulent hotels. And its Courtyard Terrace is one of the most romantic restaurants on New Providence. The rooms have patios, ocean or garden views, and spacious bathrooms. Lots of watersports are available and the hotel beach is a long, pristine expanse of sugar-white sand. The Ocean Club also has three restaurants, including the famous **Courtyard Terrace** and a new venture called **Dune**. The décor of the guest rooms reflects the overall opulence of the resort: gilded mirrors, dark woods and plush upholstery. The atmosphere is one of quiet, secluded luxury, almost museum-like. This is an excellent choice. Rates begin at $400 per night, rising to $725 for a double during the summer season ($725 to $850 for a suite) and range from $625 to $750 for a double during the winter season (suites from $1,125 to $1,350). There also are five private villas where the rates range from $650 to $1,350 per night, depending upon the season. Box N-4777, Nassau, ☎ 800-321-3000, 242-363-2501; www.oceanclub.com.

Club Med Paradise Island. This 21-acre village is a hive of activity targeted to the young at heart. Single rooms are available if needed, but might be subject to a surcharge. All recreational activities are included in the rates. Club Med is a worldwide chain of resorts, some dedicated only to adults, where the food is good, the accommodations sometimes primitive, but always clean and inviting, and the activities are organized to promote a friendly, lively atmosphere. The resorts are almost always situated on private beaches and the grounds heavily landscaped to make them tropical paradises, ultimate upscale getaways. Box N-7137, Nassau, ☎ 800-CLUBMED, 242-363-2640 (local). Call for rates. www.clubmed.com

Grand Bahama

Grand Bahama is located some 50 miles and less than 30 minutes by air from the east coast of Florida. It's an island of "cosmopolitan glitz and glamour coupled with miles of pristine beaches and endless turquoise seas." Sounds like a travel brochure, doesn't it? Well, that's because it's quoted from one of Grand Bahama's promotional releases. And, far from overstating the qualities of the island, in fact, it *understates* them.

The **Freeport/Lucaya** area, a modern, well-planned urban metropolis with a population of around 55,000, is the economic center for the island. It's also the hub of activity for visitors who arrive daily by airplane, cruise ship and private boat. Sightseeing, shopping, gambling, watersports, golf, tennis and, of course, sun and sand are just a few of the attractions.

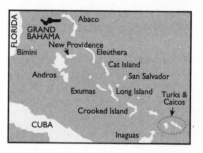

Grand Bahama is surrounded by crystal-clear emerald seas, sugar-white beaches, and spectacular coral reefs. You can dive with and feed sharks, or spend a quiet moment in the soothing company of an Atlantic bottlenose dolphin. You can, after a week of instruction, become a fully certified diver. If that sounds a little too much, after just three hours of instruction, you can take to the deep sea – complete with fins, tanks, and weights – for an underwater experience you'll never forget. Too old? Nonsense! It's never too late.

Golfers are in for a rare treat. There are three golf courses on the island – three of the best courses in the Caribbean: the PGA-rated Ruby and Emerald courses at the Royal Oasis Golf Resort & Casino, and the Quality Atlantic Beach Resort's Lucayan Country Club Course.

If shopping appeals to you, head for **Port Lucaya**, where more than six acres of shopping, dining, and entertainment await you at The Marketplace. In downtown **Freeport**, you'll find more than 90 shops

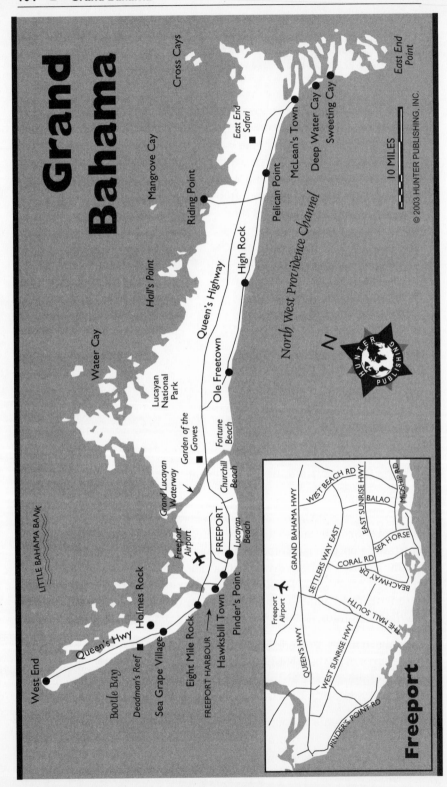

Grand Bahama

Freeport

© 2003 HUNTER PUBLISHING, INC.

and stores in the International Bazaar. And the Straw Market just next door is a treasure house of crafts and specialties.

Aside from the ocean and beaches that teem with life, there's also a unique national park, a magnificent botanical garden, and a nature center devoted to preservation of the island's wildlife. Throughout the center, dozens of nature trails and woodland paths meander back and forth among the mangrove swamps, flower gardens, and forests. For those who really like to get away into the outback, there are more than 90 miles of virtually untouched wilderness and deserted shores to explore – a world of casuarina, seagrape, mangrove, palmetto, seagrass, and scrub, where buzzards, lizards, and crabs, along with a fisherman or two, live out the great cycle of life.

At the far ends of the island, the villagers in the tiny communities of **West End** and **McClean's Town** will extend a warm welcome and create some of the finest Bahamian cuisine you'll ever taste.

Grand Bahama also offers two world-class casinos – at the **Royal Oasis Golf Resort & Casino** and **Our Lucaya**.

Grand Bahama has a wide variety of accommodations, from the sprawling deluxe resorts to the beachfront hotels, self-catering apartments, secluded getaways inns and small economy hotels.

History

 Grand Bahama is the fourth largest of the Bahamian islands, and Freeport is the second largest city. The island's modern history began in the 1950s with the development of Freeport and Lucaya.

The first inhabitants of the islands were **Stone-Age Indians** from Cuba. They were replaced almost 1,000 years ago by the **Lucayans**. They, in turn, were displaced and pretty well exterminated with the arrival of the Europeans shortly after Columbus discovered the islands in 1492. From then on, Grand Bahama was the forgotten island of the Bahamas. Except for the occasional band of pirates or loyalists, it remained virtually uninhabited for almost 300 years.

DID YOU KNOW?

Grand Bahama was given its name by the Spanish – "gran bajamar" means "great shallows" – for the vast reaches of flats and shoals in the waters off the island.

The first permanent settlers arrived during the late 19th century. Most of them scratched out a living from the sea as fishermen, or by harvesting the abundant timber from the land. During the American Civil War, the small population declined even further when people began abandoning their farms and flocked to Nassau to join the economic boom brought by the blockade runners. Prohibition in America during the 1920s created something of a mini-boom in the island's economy when the rumrunners moved in. But the new prosperity was short-lived.

In 1955, American financier **Wallace Groves**, who had extensive lumber interests on the island, made a proposal to the Bahamian government to build a tax-free city on Grand Bahama. In return, Groves would be granted tax exemptions and exclusive development rights. His proposal was accepted, and modern Freeport is the result. Groves also built the resort city of Lucaya, just five miles south of Freeport. His innovations attracted more investors to the island and, between 1963 and 1967, investment, along with the population of Grand Bahama, more than tripled.

Today on Grand Bahama, as everywhere else in the islands, tourism is king. Every year thousands upon thousands of tourists visit to take advantage of its many attractions and its tax-free status.

Getting There

■ By Air

Several major airlines provide scheduled service into Freeport. Of these, **American Airlines** (☎ 800-433-7300, www.aa.com) offers the most options, although everything must connect through Miami.

■ By Cruise Ship

 Premier Cruise Lines is the only line that visits both Freeport, on Grand Bahama, and Nassau. They offer three- and four-night itineraries on the Big Red Boat, *Oceanic*. The *Oceanic* is a themed ship – Looney Toons – and with extensive children's programs it's ideal for families. Ships leave Port Canaveral on Friday and Monday: rates start at around $275 per person for the three-night cruise, and $330 for the four-night option – children cruise for substantially less. ☎ 800-990-7770. www. premiercruises.com.

■ Package Vacations

Package options to Freeport and Grand Bahama are not as readily available as those to Nassau and New Providence. Several independent operators offer packages to one or two designated hotels. Other than that you'll need a creative travel agent's help to build your own package.

Perhaps the strongest provider is **Princess Vacations**, based in Fort Lauderdale, Florida. They own Resort & Casino, and have arranged exclusive charter services with Laker Airways Ltd. This means they can offer package rates other suppliers can't even meet, let alone beat. The Royal Oasis Golf Resort & Casino and its packages are described in detail on page 123. Contact your travel agent, or call Princess direct at ☎ 800-545-1300. www.princess-vacations.com.

American FlyAAWay Vacations has air/hotel-inclusive packages from Miami with connections from most other major US cities. Their package includes only one hotel option: the Royal Oasis Golf Resort & Casino. Rates start around $600 for three nights from Miami. ☎ 800-321-2121, www.aavacations.com.

Getting Around

In a city the size of Freeport, getting around is not difficult. Everywhere, taxi drivers await. They know the best places to go for entertainment, where the best beaches are, and more about the local history and traditions than most of the accredited guides. Rental cars, mopeds and bicycles are always available from a number of international and local agencies. You can also choose from a number of guided trips and tours to the many attractions around the harbor, under the sea, and into the outback.

The main roads are mostly good, especially around Freeport/Lucaya.

Remember to drive on the left side of the road and, when crossing the road, look to the right.

■ By Bicycle

Bicyclists will be pleased to learn that the terrain is mostly flat. Many attractive locations are within easy pedaling distance of Freeport and Lucaya. You might want to give **Taino Beach** a try. It's less than three miles from the hotel district of Lucayan Beach and well worth the effort. Take Seahorse Road from Lucaya to Midshipman Road and turn right. Cycle about a mile and turn right again onto West Beach Road. Turn right at the Stoned Crab sign and follow the road down to Taino Beach, where you'll find a long stretch of sugar-white sand dotted with umbrellas.

■ By Car

Suggested Trips

The settlement of **West End** is a leisurely 45 minutes away from Freeport. Take the West Sunrise Highway and the Queen's Highway along the well-paved road to the oldest settlement on Grand Bahama. You'll find a number of other small towns and villages along the way, each with unique attractions.

If you decide to go east, you'll need to set aside the entire day. The two- to three-hour drive will take you through a number of odd little settlements. Take the East Sunrise Highway from Lucaya, past Fortune Beach and on to **Gold Rock Beach**, a part of the Lucayan National Park, where you can enjoy caves and mangrove swamps and feed fish and ducks. From Gold Rock Beach, continue on through Bevan's Town to **High Rock**, where you can enjoy the scenery. Then it's on to **Pelican's Point, McClean's Town**, and perhaps a boat ride out to **Sweeting's Cay**, a tiny settlement right at the end of Grand Bahama. Electricity did not come to this quaint little community until 1994 and, from all accounts, it generated quite a celebration. The locals turned out in force to see the first light turned on. It's a long way to McClean's Town, but the trip is well worth the effort.

Car Rental Companies

Avis: ☎ 242-352-8144, 800-230-4898, www.avis.com. $65 and up per day, plus $12 per day insurance.

Courtesy: ☎ 242-352-5212. $69 and up per day; insurance is included.

Econo Car & Motor Bike Rental: ☎ 242-351-6700. $55 and up per day, including insurance.

Hertz: ☎ 242-352-9277, 800-634-3131, www.hertz.com. $60 and up per day, plus $12 per day insurance.

Dollar: ☎ 242-352-9308, 800-800-3665, www.dollar.com. $50 and up per day, plus $10 per day insurance.

Sears Rent-A-Car: ☎ 242-352-5953. $55 and up per day, plus $10.50 per day insurance.

Shopping

You'll find a world of goodies, trinkets, jewelry, perfume, and gifts, and almost everything at bargain prices – taxable goods, that is. Grand Bahama's duty-free status makes it a mecca for those with money to spend and the time to shop around.

Grand Bahama has taken advantage of its unique status and, far from being a center for cheap and shoddy goods, you'll find it *the* place for brand names at good prices.

Of course, alcohol and perfumes have always been at the top of most lists to take home. Top-of-the-line imported brands available duty-free save around 40% off list prices in the United States, and even more if you are from the UK.

Beyond bargain drinks and fragrances, there are many other dutiable products you might want to buy: luxurious crystal and china, fine jewelry, leather goods, silver, gold, emeralds, all sorts of electrical goods and electronic gadgets; even cashmere and pure woolen goods.

WORD TO THE WISE

The rainbow ends when you reach Customs on your return home. Make sure you know exactly what your duty-free allowance is; if you exceed it, you'll have to pay.

Of all that's available to shoppers on Grand Bahama, and there is an awful lot, most of it is sold at the International Bazaar and the Port Lucaya Marketplace.

Sweeting's Cay.

■ The International Bazaar

Next to the Royal Oasis Golf Resort & Casino, this is a vast complex of shops, stores, boutiques, restaurants, cafés and interesting little diversions. You can spend hours perusing the diversity of goods and sampling the food. www.grand-bahama.com/bazaar.htm.

Be sure to check out the **Bahamian Souvenir Outlet** in the Indian section of the Bazaar. This is a one-stop shop for gifts and souvenirs. Some are made locally. The list includes Bahamian perfumes, music, books, shell jewelry, Anna Karina Bahamian coin jewelry, sealife jewelry, coconut shell figurines, clocks, and straw products.

For liquor, head to the **Burns House**. They carry just about every international brand you can think of, plus the local stuff. **Butler & Sands** is the place to go for fine wines.

For resort wear, cruise wear, and other casual clothing, **Bye-Bye Bahamas** is the hottest new outlet on the island.

To find something very special, visit to **Colombian Emeralds International.**

Fragrance of the Bahamas offers a complimentary tour of the working perfume factory. **Parfum de Paris** is in the heart of the French section of the Bazaar, but there are many more options.

■ The Port Lucaya Marketplace

Just across the way from the Atlantik Beach Hotel, this is a vast complex of shopping and dining opportunities, with all sorts of duty-free outlets. One that's not to missed is the **Golden Nuggets** store, which offers terrific buys on close-out jewelry, a vast selection of gold chains, bracelets, bangles and precious and semi-precious gemstone jewelry at prices that are hard to believe.

Linens of Lucaya has a selection of quality linens and exotic gifts – all at savings of up to 50% from prices of similar goods in the United States.

Pusser's is the place to go for lunch or dinner. This very British pub, restaurant and boutique offers great food and drink, as well as upscale clothing, including slacks and shirts.

Grand Bahama

Sightseeing

 Grand Bahama is crammed with attractions and light adventures. Those described here are some of the most worthwhile.

■ Garden of the Groves

At the intersection of Midshipmen Road and Magellan Drive, this 12-acre botanical garden (☎ 242-373-5668) is dedicated to the memory of Freeport's founders, Wallace and Georgette Groves. It's acknowledged as one of the finest botanical centers in the Caribbean, a floral and water paradise of hibiscus, bougainvillea, powderpuff, chenille, screw pines and Washington palms. A walk through the garden will take you through tiny floral communities, including the Citrus Grove, Fern Gully and Bougainvillea Walk. Along the way, keep an eye out for curly tailed lizards and wander beneath ornamental waterfalls. Take a rest in the tiny Chapel on the Hill, visit the Cactus Garden and the Hanging Gardens, and pause to look at a replica of Freeport's first airport terminal building, a tiny wooden hut with barely enough room for two people. The walk through Fern Gully will take you 20 feet below the surrounding gardens to a 400-foot pathway lined with exotic plants and flowers, heady with the sweet smells of the island's year-long summer. Guided tours available. Petting zoo. Wedding ceremonies offered. $9.95 for adults; $6.95 for kids. www.gardenofthegroves.com.

■ Hydroflora Gardens

Hydroponics is the art of growing plants and food in water rather than soil and that's what Hydroflora is all about. Visitors learn all about the conch, which has a museum all its own, and are given a flower as a memento of their visit. Guided tours of the facility are conducted by experienced and knowledgeable members of the staff. There's a 3,000-foot floral trail and a number of rooms and gardens where you can learn about the various programs conducted at the center. Open Monday-Friday, 9-5:30; Saturday, 9-4. On East Beach Drive, ☎ 242-352-6052. E-mail: hfloral@batelnet.bs.

■ Lucayan National Park

AUTHOR PICK

This park is 20 miles east of Lucaya on the East Sunrise Highway and is easily accessible by taxi, tour bus, moped, auto, or public bus (take the bus to High Rock and make arrangements with the driver to drop you off and pick you up). The park can be reached at ☎ 242-352-5438. www.grand-bahama.com/lucayan.htm.

The park is the result of efforts by the Bahamas National Trust, with some help from Operation Raleigh.

Operation Raleigh

This is an international group of young people who travel by boat – in the tradition of their namesake, Sir Walter Raleigh – and lend a hand with various scientific projects. They laid most of the trails and boardwalks throughout the Lucayan National Park.

In addition to its wealth of flora and fauna, the 40-acre park has a number of special and interesting features. Extending on both sides of the highway, it features a long, looping walk and a series of caves to the north, with a large mangrove swamp and deserted beach area to the south.

Lucayan National Park.

Grand Bahama

The parking lot is on the north side of the road. From there, follow the path to **Ben's Cave**, the first of two caves, named for Ben Rose, the diver and biologist who discovered it. Ben's Cave is part of an underground, underwater system of caverns said to be among the largest of its kind in the world. The cave is also home to the tiny remipedia (oar foot), a crustacean found nowhere else in the world. A little further on along the trail you'll see another opening. This is the **Burial Mound Cave**, where, in 1986, archaeologists found four skeletons on the floor, along with evidence of pre-Columbian settlement. The skeletons were the remains of a group of local Lucayan Indians.

On the south side of the road a narrow trail takes you across a large expanse of mangrove swamp and a section of **Gold Rock Creek** to the ocean and Gold Rock Beach. Be sure to take your swimming gear along. For most of the walk you'll hike across a vast watery area via a series of narrow boardwalks. Along the way, you'll see a wide assortment of plants and wildlife. The trail will take you past strange-looking, bonsai-like ming trees and, if the season is right, a variety of colorful orchids.

In the saltwater creek you may see a lurking barracuda and other saltwater fish, including gray snapper. There's also a covey of small wild ducks, all quacking and flapping, busily pursuing their daily lives in the swamp.

Beyond the mangrove swamp lies one of the highest coastal dunes on the island, a richly vegetated area of cocoplum, casuarina, seagrape, cinnecord, and other species of tropical trees.

At the far end of the trail, **Gold Rock Beach** lies on the windswept south side of the island. It's often deserted, but always appealing, with magnificent views of the wide sandy shore, emerald waters, and Gold Rock itself jutting up out of the ocean a half-mile offshore. Gold Rock Beach is one of those places you see in commercials. It's a strip of tropical paradise where, in all likelihood, you'll find yourself alone to swim and snorkel in the clear shallow waters.

Return to your vehicle by continuing on along the trail, which loops around the park, over the mangroves, to end at the park entrance where it began.

■ Rand Memorial Nature Center

On Settler's Way, just two miles from Freeport and three miles from Lucaya, this is a 100-acre nature reserve where you can spend an interesting hour or two learning about Grand Bahama's flora and fauna. If you enjoy bird watching, this is the place for you. More than 40 species of birds, including turkey vultures, hairy woodpeckers, Bahama yellowthroats, indigo buntings, American redstarts, Greater Antillean pewees, and American red-tailed hawks, inhabit the park.

Take a **guided tour** of the facility, the only way to see and really understand its scope, and you'll be introduced to many of the smaller birds as they fly in for a tidbit casually tossed into the air by your guide; it's very entertaining. The tour will take you on a pleasant walk along the 2,000-foot nature trail that meanders back and forth among the flowering plants, orchids, poinsettias, periwinkles, hibiscus, impatiens, morning glories and more, to a freshwater pond at the end. There, a flock of West Indian flamingos will rush to meet you, ready for their treat – a morsel of dog food, which they'll devour with great relish. You may also see butterflies, blue-tailed lizards, tree frogs and curly tailed lizards.

Traditional Lucayan Village

A replica of a Lucayan village includes small *canayes*, round family dwellings, thatched with palm leaves. The chieftain's house is square, reflecting his all-powerful image, while the *cacique bohio*, a place of worship, is hexagonal.

The nature center is open Monday through Friday from 9 am until 4 pm, and on Saturdays from 9 am until 1 pm. Guided tours of the sanctuary are conducted daily at 10 am and 2 pm. If you want to do the tour alone, you can.

Ask for a bird checklist to help you recognize those you see.

Grand Bahama

■ Seaworld Explorer

Seaworld Explorer (☎ 242-373-7863), owned by Superior Watersports of Freeport, is one of the best ways to explore the undersea world and certainly the most reasonably priced. The *Explorer* is half-sightseeing cruiser and half-submarine. The neat thing about it is that you'll have the excitement of the submarine experience without ever being submerged.

The cruise costs just $29 per person. It begins with a ride, topside, of about a mile out to the reef, where you'll descend the stairs to the observation deck. This is where things get really interesting. The lower deck is a narrow chamber with seats for up to 30 people. The large undersea windows are angled so that you can look downward as well as outward, a definite advantage over the *Atlantis*-type submarine in Nassau. For the next hour you'll move slowly over the coral reef, observing all sorts of coral formations and a multitude of gaily colored marine life. Be sure to take along your camera and some high-speed film. You may see sharks, spotted eagle rays, stingrays or barracuda, and you'll certainly see parrotfish, sergeant majors, triggers, queen angels, puffers, and a lot more. The *Seaworld Explorer* excursion is one of the best values on the island.

■ The Dolphin Experience

The Dolphin Experience (☎ 800-992-3483, 954-351-9889, info@unexso.com, www.unexso.com), on the dock in Freeport in the same building as, and owned by, UNEXSO, also offers a unique encounter. It's a fascinating and often soul-stirring experience where you'll meet, close-up, one of nature's most lovable and intelligent creatures: the Atlantic bottlenose dolphin. Be sure to wear clothes that you don't mind getting wet.

Your experience – actually, there are a couple of different programs – starts at UNEXSO's headquarters on the dock across from Our Lucaya. You'll board a boat for a 20-minute ride out to Sanctuary Bay where the dolphins live.

DID YOU KNOW?

UNEXSO is an acronym for the organization's full title: The UNderwater EXplorer's SOciety.

The first things you'll see when you arrive at the facility are the tops of the huge pens that keep the dolphins separated from each other and safe from marauding sharks. Then, you'll take the boardwalk over the water and the dolphin pens to the observation platform, where you'll actually meet the animals.

Close Encounter

The Dolphin Close Encounter program allows you meet the dolphins face-to-face; well, bottlenose-to-face. Before you do, however, you'll listen to a 15-minute talk that dispels the myths and legends that have built up around this finny creature. While the talk is being given, a couple of your soon-to-be playmates are carousing about the pool near where you're sitting.

Dolphins are not quite the close cousins you've been led to believe, and they don't have supernatural healing powers either. It's true that they are extremely intelligent and love to play, as you'll soon find out.

When the talk is ended, your instructor will call you into the water – it's not deep – where you'll stand in pairs facing each other. The two dolphins then swim into the gap between you and your partner, and you'll be allowed to stroke, pet and rub them down; they love it. You'll be surprised, too, at the size of these creatures. They are some eight to 12 feet long and can weigh in at 500-700 pounds, but they are as gentle as kittens and, big as they are, you'll never get bumped or pushed. The cost for the two-hour experience is $59 per person; age four-seven, $29.50; children under three, free.

Assistant Trainer Program

The second dolphin experience is the Dolphin Assistant Trainer program. This allows participants to sign on for one, two or more days in order to spend the time from early morning till late in the afternoon working with the animal care staff and the dolphins in a wide variety of activities. The program costs $219 per person.

There's also a Snorkel with Dolphins program at $169.

Guided Tours

■ East End Adventures

East End Adventures (☎ 242-373-6662, eastendsafari@ yahoo.com, www.bahamasecotours.com) offers one of the most enjoyable all-day, outdoor experiences available.

This trip to the outback and the east end of the island – 50 miles by road and seven more in a small boat – begins at your hotel when an open 4X4, trailing the boat, picks you up at 8 am. Don't eat breakfast before you leave; you'll get plenty to eat along the way.

The first stop, at about 8:30 am, is **Casuarina Bridge** on the Grand Lucayan Waterway, a man-made canal that cuts the island into two parts between north and south. It was built primarily to enhance the value of the surrounding property. Here, you'll eat a light breakfast of biscuits, muffins and coffee.

From Casuarina Bridge, you'll turn off the main highway and head into a dense jungle of native pine and palm trees to Owl Hole. Along the way, the guides will identify trees and plants used for bush medicines.

Owl Hole, an inland blue hole and home for the past several years to a family of owls, is a short hike from the main trail through dense undergrowth. This is really a large sink hole, and the entrance into an underground, underwater system of caves and caverns connected to the ocean.

After Owl Hole, you'll be treated to a selection of fresh Bahamian fruit: pineapple, mango, melon, grapefruit, and sugar cane. And you'll be introduced to a wonderful local concoction called "gullywash," a strange-looking mixture of gin, coconut water, and condensed milk, seasoned with cinnamon. Whew!

From Owl Hole, if the tide permits, your 4X4 will head for the beach and a ride along the oceanfront to the **Lucayan National Park** (see page 101). There, you'll explore the park, the mangrove swamp, Gold Rock Beach, and you'll feed the barracuda, snappers, needlenose, and a busy little family of ducks. Then its on the road again to your next stop, McClean's Town, the furthest settlement you will reach by road.

From McClean's Town you head out to sea at great speed in a small boat. Some 20 minutes and seven miles later, you'll land at the dock of the **Fig Tree Restaurant** on Sweeting's Cay, where you'll be met by Ola and Pinna. To describe the Fig Tree as a restaurant is, perhaps, a little misleading. The one-room establishment combines bar, café, and social club all rolled into one. Pinna, the owner, is also the cook, waitress, bartender and general bottle washer. Ola, something of a local celebrity, demonstrates how to extract the conch – part of your lunch – from its shell while your guide picks up the catch of the day. Take a lei-

Traditional house on Grand Bahama.

surely walk along the seafront, past huge piles of empty conch shells, and watch the crabs fighting among themselves on the sandy bottom of the tiny harbor. Back on the boat and you're off again at high speed to a deserted island for a picnic lunch of conch salad, fresh fish, and a bottle of wine, prepared on the spot by one of your guides. You can stroll the deserted beaches, wade, swim or snorkel in the clear green waters, or just relax under the palms.

After lunch, you'll take to the boat again and, if time allows, skim across the flats, looking for blue holes. When you reach one, you can wade and look into the depths at the hundreds of fish swimming around in the sanctuary of the rocky hole.

Be sure to keep your eyes on the bottom as you go wading; you'll find all sorts of sand dollars, seabiscuits and shells to take home with you.

After the boat ride back to McClean's Town, you'll board the 4X4 once again for the ride back to Freeport and your hotel. By now it's close to 4 in the afternoon, and you're just about ready for another round of gullywash. An hour or so later, you'll arrive back at your hotel, happy, tired and with a whole lot of memories. The cost for all this? Just $110 per person for adults, $55 for kids under 12. $10 discount for cash.

The company also offers the the Blue Hole Snorkeling Safari ($85, $35), the Gone Fishin' Safari ($85, $55) and Bonefishing Trips ($250 half-day, $350 full day).

■ Shorex International

Shorex International in Port Lucaya, ☎ 242-373-7863, offers a number of tours in and around Freeport/Lucaya, all well organized, and all at reasonable prices.

- The **Highlights Tour** goes to all the popular attractions, both in Freeport and Lucaya, with plenty of stops along the way for snacks and shopping. Traveling aboard an air-conditioned coach, you'll visit Taino Beach, the Garden of the Groves, Millionaire's Row, where all the rich folks live, the open-air fruit market, and the International Bazaar. Pick-up from your hotel is at 9 am and the cost of the tour, which lasts about three hours, is $21 per adult and $17 for children under 12.

- The **Robinson Crusoe Beach Party** provides lots of fun on the ocean. You'll depart Port Lucaya at either 11 am or noon, depending on the season, on *Bahama Mama*, a 72-foot catamaran, and return either at 4:30 or 5:30 in the afternoon. The first stop is Treasure Reef, where you can snorkel among the coral heads and observe the colorful fish and other marine life. Then it's on to Barbary Beach for a buffet lunch, followed by an afternoon of sunbathing, swimming, and volleyball. There's dancing all the way back to Port Lucaya. The cost for the trip, which lasts about 5½ hours, is $40 per adult, $27 for children under 12, and includes pick-up at your hotel.

- The **Bahama Mama Sunset Booze Cruise** takes you day-sailing on the 72-foot catamaran, *Bahama Mama*, along the coastline of Freeport to watch, if you're lucky, a magnificent ocean sunset. While cruising, you can dance, enjoy the romantic music, eat a variety of hot and cold hors d'oeuvres, and drink all the wine and Bahama Mamas you like. You'll depart Port Lucaya at 5:30 and return at 7:30. The two-hour cruise costs $25 per person and includes pick-up from your hotel.

■ The **See & Sea Tour**, a narrated excursion around the best of Freeport and Lucaya, includes stops at Taino Beach, Millionaire's Row, the open-air fruit market, and the International Bazaar. Having done all that, you'll board the *Seaworld Explorer* (see pages 81 and 116), a semi-submarine, for an exciting 90-minute voyage out to Treasure Reef. There, you'll view the magnificent coral structures, colorful reef fish, sharks, rays and barracuda – all from the comfort of the lower deck observation chamber. The cost of this tour, including pick-up at your hotel, is $39 for adults and $29 for children under 12.

■ Bus Tours

Although there are several bus companies, they all offer much the same in the way of tours and services. You'll also find that most of the major hotels, and some of the smaller ones, have travel desks where you can book your tour. If you wish, you can call the company direct.

WORD TO THE WISE

Be sure to ask the travel staff at your hotel to show you all that's available; some of them tend to have favorites and will steer you to them if they can.

A **Grand Bahama Day-Trip**, offered by most bus companies, is a great value, and will take you out to the village of West End, the Garden of the Groves, and then back again to Freeport for a look at Millionaire's Row and the city. The cost is $25, which is not bad for the five-hour round-trip.

A bus tour of **Freeport/Lucaya** costs about $17 per person. It takes in all the interesting attractions along the way, including the residential and commercial areas.

A number of operators offer round-trips to the **Garden of the Groves** for about $10. You can find a variety of combinations that include Freeport/Lucaya, the Garden of the Groves, the Rand Nature Center, the Hydroflora Gardens, Lucayan National Park, and more. All you need do is ask any driver.

■ Boat Tours

 The number of tours available on the sea outnumber those on *terra firma*. Once again, your hotel travel desk will be able to point you in a number of directions. All tours include pick-up in the hotel lobby. And you'll need to make sure the hotel staff shows you all that's offered. If your hotel doesn't have a travel desk, drop in at one that does. The staff there will be pleased to help you out, whether you are a guest or not.

You can take a cruise or go on a beach party with **Reef Tours** (☎ 242-375-5880); go sailing on *Tri-wind*, a 55-foot trimaran; take a glass-bottom boat trip on *Mermaid Kitty*; go sailing and snorkeling on the 50-foot *Bright Star*, another trimaran; sail on a 35-foot racing catamaran, the *Lucky Lady*; or board a 50-foot motor yacht and take a snorkeling, lunch and party cruise with **Pat & Diana Tours** (☎ 242-373-8681). They have a "reef and wreck" party cruise for $40 per person and a "sunset sailing cruise" aboard a 52-foot trimaran for $30 per person. *Island Time*, a 40-foot catamaran docked at the Britannia Pub, leaves twice daily for lunch and booze cruises.

Adventures on Land

■ Golf

 Golf on Grand Bahama comes in some impressive packages: the Lucayan Golf & Country Club, the Royal Oasis Golf Resort & Casino Emerald Course, and the Royal Oasis Golf Resort Ruby Course. All three courses are PGA-rated.

Each of Grand Bahama's four top courses offers a driving range, putting green, plus club and shoe rentals.

The oldest course is at the **Our Lucaya** (Royal Palm Way, Lucaya, ☎ 800-LUCAYAN). It was designed by Dick Wilson and built in 1963. For many years it was the home course of Masters Champion Craig Woods.

The design of the 6,800-yard course places a premium on accuracy. The greens are all well bunkered, with generous fairways that meander through stands of pine trees and areas of dense tropical brush and undergrowth. Wilson designed the course with privacy in mind, and it's rare that foursomes see each other during a round. The Lucayan Country Club has a fully stocked pro shop, a snack bar, and a fine restaurant. The fee is $67 per 18 holes, which includes mandatory use of a golf cart. Reservations are required.

The Emerald Course at the **Royal Oasis Golf Resort & Casino**, on West Sunrise Highway, across from the resort, was also designed by Dick Wilson. If you've never played a Dick Wilson course you're in for a rare treat. The fairways and greens are lush and green, but one has to wonder if Dick had a bit of mean streak. The par-72 course, almost 6,700 yards in length, is a wonderful combination of deceptively wide fairways, doglegs, water and the smoothest greens, but all are guarded by more than 80 bunkers, most placed with a hint of malice to snare even the gentlest of fade. Add to this the small, odd-shaped, elevated greens, and this course becomes a monster to challenge even the best of golfers. Green fees are reasonable for the class of course – $75, which includes half-share of a cart. Packages are available. For more information and reservations, ☎ 800-545-1300; the local number in Freeport is ☎ 242-352-6721; fax 242-352-8487.

The other Royal Oasis course, **the Ruby**, was designed by Joe Lee, who learned his craft from the venerable Dick Wilson, and it shows. The course winds through a lush forest of native pines, rubber trees and flowers, and was the site of the Michelin National Long Driving Championship. The Ruby Course has more water holes than the Emerald, and features 78 bunkers. The signature hole, the fifth, is a beguiling 384-yard par-four, left-hand dogleg with a lake wrapped around the fairway and green. The Ruby offers a challenge, even for the best golfers.

Beyond its two fine courses, the Royal Oasis Golf Center offers a variety of services from lessons to club storage and cleaning. The clothing on sale in the shop is attractive and reasonably priced, and the staff is friendly and ever-ready to lend a helping hand.

The Reef, on Royal Palm Way (☎ 242-373-2002), is an 18-hole course designed by Robert Trent Jones II and opened in 2001. It's a tight par-72 course of more than 6,900 yards, with lots of water (13 of the holes feature water hazards). You'll need all your skills to score well at the The Reef. Fees are $100 for 18 holes; $66 for nine holes. Both include a cart. Reservations are required.

Golf Packages

Special golf packages are available at the resorts listed below.

The Royal Oasis Golf Resort & Casino offers several basic packages, and can accommodate groups. It will build custom packages on request.

- The basic three-day, three-night package includes round-trip airfare from any one of 12 gateway airports in the United States, hotel accommodations with private terrace, round-trip transfers between hotel and airport, all taxes and gratuities, and a welcome cocktail. The golf package includes unlimited golf on your choice of the two courses, shared golf cart for unlimited golf in the low season and for 18 holes in the high season, club storage and cleaning, and golf center staff gratuities. All-inclusive packages, which include all meals and beverages, are available at a reasonable extra cost. The rate, depending upon the US gateway, in the high season – November 1st through April 30th – is $370 per person, double occupancy. The low-season rate can be as low as $285.

- The basic four-day, four-night package includes all the above but the rate in the high season is $470 per person, double occupancy. In the low season the rate can be as low as $345.

- The rate for the basic seven-day, seven-night package starts around $699 per person, double occupancy. In the low season the rate is significantly lower.

■ Gambling

Grand Bahama has two world-class casinos.

The **Royal Oasis Golf Resort & Casino** offers its guests plenty of action with more than 600 slots, a roulette wheel, several craps tables, a big six wheel, a couple of dozen blackjack tables, almost as many Bahamian stud poker tables, baccarat, horseracing, and an international sports book, The Casino Royal theater features Las Vegas-style shows with new artists and performers every two weeks. ☎ 800-545-1300; the local number in Freeport is ☎ 242-352-6721.

Our Lucaya's Casino is smaller than the one at the Royal Oasis, but offers basically the same amenities. It, too, has a casino theater. ☎ 800-LUCAYAN.

International currencies can be exchanged at the going rate inside both casinos. Traveler's checks and most major credit cards are also accepted at both. You will, however, pay the standard commissions charged by local banks for exchanging all foreign currencies.

The slots will accept coins and bills in denominations from a quarter through $5. The card tables offer high or low stakes: some tables will limit stakes to between $5 and $1,000.

The roulette wheels have numbers from 1 to 36, plus a "0" and "00."

There is no specific dress code in the casinos, but you will be expected to dress reasonably – casual, but no swimsuits or bare feet are allowed.

Adventures on Water

■ Sea Kayaking

Kayak Nature Tours, 140 Seagate Lane, Freeport, Grand Bahama, ☎ 242-373-2485; kayaknaturetours@ aol.com, www.bahamasvg.com/kayak.html. This outfit offers a comprehensive choice of nature and kayaking tours. Erica Gates and her staff of 10 have many years of experience in the eco-adventure business. They offer short or extended trips, birding opportunities, and much more.

- *Lucayan National Park Kayak Nature & Cave Tour.* $69
  Six hours.
  Safe in any weather – no dangerous creatures.
  Suitable for all ages; beginners welcomed.
  Kayaking portion of trip is approximately 90 minutes of light to moderate paddling in inland creek through a mangrove forest.
  Lunch on private, shady beach.
  Time for swimming or beachcombing.
  Guided nature walk and visit to caves.
  Park entrance fee included.

- *All Day Water Cay Kayak Excursion.* $110

  Eight hours – moderately strenuous.

  Kayak through the coastal mangroves to this small inhabited island off the North Shore.

  Walk through the quaint native settlement.

  Visit the church and school and meet the friendly local people.

  Have a guided nature walk through the hardwood forest, with bird watching.

  Taste a native lunch of home-baked bread and local specialities.

- *Peterson Cay Kayak / Snorkel Tour.* $69

  Five hours.

  Paddle time to Peterson Cay is about 30 minutes.

  Peterson Cay is the smallest national park on Grand Bahama and protected from fishing.

  Beginners are welcome and both kayak and snorkeling instructions are provided.

  All equipment is provided.

  Guides are certified divers and lifeguards and accompany guests throughout the snorkel experience. Snorkel time is about 90 minutes.

  Snorkeling commences from beach on Peterson Cay, giving guests time to become acclimatized and adjust gear.

  After snorkeling a light lunch and beverages are provided on Peterson Cay.

  Peterson Cay is home to a variety of sea birds some of which are returning to this area for the first time in many years.

- *Biking Nature Tour.* $69

  This tour can also be conducted as a day-hike on foot.

  Tour is five hours – total distance 12 miles.

  The bike trail goes along the uninhabited south shore and the trail heads through pine forest, wetlands, sandy and rocky shoreline.

  Stops are made for flora and fauna highlights and picturesque vistas.

  All equipment is provided.

  Also included: lunch, snacks, beverages, backpacks and binoculars for bird watching.

- *Water Cay All-Day Kayak Tour. $150*

  Water Cay is a remote, tiny island off the north shore of Grand Bahama that can be visited only by shallow-draft boats. Once populated by over 400 people; barely 10 families live on island today.

  This tour is for experienced paddlers and requires two hours of paddling to the island and two hours return. Part of trip is through challenging mangrove creeks and partly through open water that can be choppy.

  All equipment, transportation, food, beverages and logistics provided.

■ Sport Fishing

Grand Bahama is great for sport fishing. The waters are home to many fighting fish, including blue and white marlin, sailfish, bluefin and yellowfin tuna, wahoo, bonito, barracuda, kingfish and dolphin.

Of the many deep-sea operators on the island, you should probably choose from one of the five members of the Charter Fishing Operators Association. They're all pretty well known, both by name and reputation and, while a catch is never guaranteed, you'll get expert advice and guidance. They all charge about the same for their services, and will supply tackle, bait, rods, reels and ice, but not refreshments. The minimum charge per person, for a party of six, is $300 for the half-day (four hours), or $600 for the full day.

- **Captain Ted Been**, ☎ 242-352-2797, has a 34-foot Luhrs.

- **Captain Tony Cooper**, ☎ 242-352-6782, runs a 38-foot Bertram.

- **Captain Steve Hollingsworth**, ☎ 242-352-2050, fishes from a 36-foot Chris Craft.

- **Captain John Roberts**, ☎ 242-352-7915, at the Running Mon Marina, has a 36-foot Chris Craft.

- **Captain Doug Silvera**, ☎ 242-373-8446 (ask to leave a message), in Port Lucaya, runs a 34-foot Hatteras.

Grand Bahama

■ Snorkeling & Diving

 There are hundreds of opportunities for snorkeling on Grand Bahama and several companies offer snorkeling tours, day-trips, etc.; you'll find them listed on page 130. There are also many exciting dive sites that can be visited with professional operators, who offer a range of services from basic diving instruction for beginners to courses that end in full certification.

UNEXSO

Of all the operators on the island – for facilities, support, and all-around professionalism – UNEXSO, The Underwater Explorer's Society, is the premier outfit. UNEXSO is open to one and all, beginner and experienced diver alike. Even as a beginner, with some basic instruction, you can dive with a pair of Atlantic bottlenose dolphins, visit Shark Junction – where you'll watch and photograph a steel-suited diver feeding the sharks – or you can go wreck and cavern diving. All it takes is a little effort and, in the case of the shark dives, nerves of steel.

For $99, you can learn to dive in a three-hour course and go diving the same day with UNEXSO. They also offer a full range of guided dive options for certified divers, including a three-dive package for $105; a four-dive package for $140, six dives for $210; and nine dives for $315. They also run a two-hour snorkeling trip for $39, departing at 9 am.

In the recent past, they offered a variety of certification courses as well. These have been suspended temporarily, but may be reinstated by the time of your visit. Check with them if you are interested.

Contact: ☎ 800-992-DIVE, 954-351-9889, www.UNEXSO.com.

Xanadu Undersea Adventures

Xanadu will teach you how to scuba dive in only three hours, and then take you out to dive over the coral reef. The cost for your first diving adventure with Xanadu is $79. Once you've learned to dive, you can join in single-tank packages from one to nine dives, special night dives, shark dives, and your open water certification.

Contact: ☎ 800-327-8150, 242-352-3811, www.xanadudive.com.

Best Dive Sites

The Tunnel

Off Grand Bahama, The Tunnel is named for its swim-through channels. These are populated by large schools of snappers, yellowtails, and jacks.

The Pygmy Caves

The Pygmy Caves are a 65-foot section of the outer reef with a system of caves and caverns running through an extensive formation of coral heads and walls.

Ben's Caverns

A part of the Lucayan Cavern Complex, this is reputed to be the most extensive system of underwater river, cavern and cave systems in the world. The caverns were named for the man who discovered them, Ben Rose, UNEXSO's resident naturalist.

Shipwrecks

There are three shipwrecks off Grand Bahama Island worthy of note. All are accessible with any one of the dive operators on the island.

The José

The *José* is a steel-hulled workboat, 45 feet long and 20 feet wide. It had been abandoned and left to rot at the rear of a closed hotel. When the hotel eventually reopened, the new owners asked that the hulk be removed. UNEXO's dive master, Ollie Ferguson, obliged and in 1986 it was towed to its present location. The hulk now sits upright in about 65 feet of water and is an excellent dive for beginners.

The Sugar Wreck

Thought to be the remains of a barge, this is a steel-hulled wreck lying in about 18 feet of water. Lately, it's become home for several large barracuda. The wreckage is pretty well scattered but consists of three fairly large heaps of debris.

Theo's Wreck

Named for the engineer whose idea it was to sink the ship, this is the remains of the cargo vessel, *Logna*. Built in Norway in 1954, it lies on its port side in 100 feet of water. The ship, 228 feet long with a 35-foot beam, is still intact and is a great underwater spectacle. After a long and useful life, the *Logna* was sunk as a joint venture between UNEXSO and her owners, the Bahama Cement Company. The idea was to provide an unusual and exciting diving adventure. Holes were cut in the deck to allow access by divers. The hatches were removed, along with anything else that might pose a danger to an unwary diver, and then the ship was towed out to its present location. It lies off the Silver Beach Inlet on the edge of the Grand Bahama Ledge, where the continental shelf drops off more than 5,000 feet. Theo's Wreck is one of the most photogenic underwater sites in the Bahamas.

Dive Operators

Under Water Explorers Society (UNEXSO)

In business for 33 years, UNEXSO has a staff of 80, with 16 instructors. The company operates seven modern boats with a carrying capacity of 10 to 30 divers. The company's professional affiliations include PADI, SSI and NAUI. The retail store sells a large line of diving equipment, accessories and clothing, and has on hand 60 sets of rental gear. UNEXSO offers diving packages of its own (see page 114), and participates in packages offered by many of the hotels, including the Royal Oasis Golf Resort & Casino, Our Lucaya, the Clarion Atlantik Hotel, the Radisson Resort on Lucaya Beach, and the Port Lucaya Resort & Marina. UNEXSO has the only recompression chamber on the island. ☎ 800-992-DIVE, 954-351-9889, www.UNEXSO.com.

Xanadu Undersea Adventures

In operation for nine years, Xanadu has a staff of 10, with five instructors, and runs three dive boats with carrying capacity for six to 20 passengers. The company's professional affiliations include PADI, SSI and NAUI. Xanadu, in addition to their regularly scheduled dives (see page 128), offers shark dives three days a week and participates with the Xanadu Beach Resort and Marina, and with other hotels on Grand Bahama, in providing a selection of dive packages. ☎ 800-327-8150, 242-352-3811, www.xanadudive.com.

East End

At the Deep Water Cay Club, ☎ 242-359-4831, there is a smaller operator specializing in guided dives and snorkeling trips. There are no instructors on the staff so you'll need to take instruction elsewhere before you go. The company has two boats and, at the time of writing, has no professional affiliations.

Sunn Odyssey Divers

This company operates out of Freeport/Lucaya. It has two dive boats, three guides, and its professional affiliations include PADI and NAUI. Qualified guides will take you on a variety of diving and snorkeling expeditions to the reefs, caves, and wrecks around the island. ☎ 242-373-4014, www.sunodysseydivers.com.

Where to Stay & Eat

Restaurant Price Scale	
$	less than $20 per person
$$	$20-$50 per person
$$$	$50+ per person

■ Dining

$$ The Brass Helmet is at the waterfront on Bell Channel Bay Road, above UNEXSO's store. You are in for quite a surprise when you reach the top of the stairs, for the head of a huge great white shark is bursting through the wall and into the room. The restaurant, filled with all sorts of underwater memorabilia, has an old-world atmosphere reminiscent of the deep-sea diving movies of the 1950s and early 1960s. The food is always good, and the menu includes such Bahamian specialties as chicken patties, Jamaican beef, and that good old Bahamian standby, peas 'n rice. Be sure to try the conch salad. ☎ 242-373-2032.

$$ The Buccaneer is on the beach at Deadman's Reef, almost at the west end of the island. The drive itself is an experience well worth the trip, as is the great European and Bahamian food. The menu includes conch fritters, crabmeat salad, broiled lobster tail, beef tenderloin, wienerschnitzel and rack of lamb, all served in an atmosphere of island greenery. Call ☎ 242-349-3794 for reservations and free transportation.

$$ The Captain's Charthouse, on East Sunrise Highway in Port Lucaya, is Bahamian-owned and -managed and, while the menu is definitely aimed at the American visitor, traditional Bahamian specials are available. Conch, lobster, grouper and crab are all served with lavish portions of good old peas and rice. ☎ 242-373-3900.

$ Georgie's Restaurant, in Port Lucaya on East Sunrise Highway, is a rare authentic Bahamian restaurants with a traditional island atmosphere. You'll sit beneath ceiling fans, among the memorabilia, and listen to the soft lilt of island music as you sip your Bahama Mama. The menu includes conch salad, minced lobster, steamed grouper, and cracked conch, all served with the best peas and rice you'll ever eat. ☎ 242-373-8513.

$ Geneva's Place, on West Mall Street, is another of Freeport's authentic island restaurants. The menu is a small one, but includes all the traditional Bahamian dishes, as well as New York strip steak and barbecued chicken. The food is prepared by Bahamian chefs. Their local dishes are spicy and well seasoned for a flavor that's unique. ☎ 242-352-5085.

$ Guanahani's, at the Royal Oasis Golf Resort & Casino in Freeport, is known for its home-smoked dishes. These include smoked chicken, beef and baby back ribs, but that's not all. The restaurant also offers fresh seafood dishes, all with a pronounced island flavor, including conch stir-fry, Bahamian-style pan-fried red snapper with peas and rice, and island lobster tail, split and char-broiled – all at reasonable prices. There's nothing on the menu priced above $19. ☎ 242-352-6721.

$$ The Lobster Reef, at the Port Lucaya Marketplace, serves really fresh fish. The restaurant operates its own boat, so the catch is always fresh. The restaurant is steeped in a nautical atmosphere; the walls and ceilings are hung with fishing nets, pictures, and marine memorabilia. The food reflects the restaurant's name and atmosphere, with such delicacies as lobster Bimini, Lobster Reef special, cracked conch and grouper Kahlua. The wine list is one of the most extensive on the island and includes a selection of fine champagnes. ☎ 242-352-8044.

$$-$$$ Luciano's, located upstairs at the Port Lucaya Marketplace, may be Grand Bahama's most elegant and romantic restaurant. The décor is subtle, the lighting intimate, and the cuisine decidedly French, with just a dash of the islands thrown in. You can dine indoors or outside overlooking the marina. ☎ 242-373-9100.

$$ Morgan's Bluff is in the Royal Oasis Hotel on West Sunrise Highway, next to the International Bazaar in Freeport. There's a definite island atmosphere about the place. The menu consists primarily of seafood dishes tied to the prevailing season. The food is excellent and cooked to perfection – try the strip steak; it's to die for. Morgan's Bluff is open for dinner only, from 6 until 11. ☎ 242-352-9661.

$ The Outriggers, at Smith's Point, just beyond Taino Beach, is a small, very Bahamian restaurant. A fine conch salad and minced lobster are served, along with an appealing assortment of other authentic local specialties. ☎ 242-373-4811.

$$$ Pier One at Freeport Harbour, is actually located on and beneath the pilings. The restaurant has many qualities that might persuade you to stop by for a romantic dinner. The food, mostly from the sea, is excellent, though a little pricey. You could watch the sun set in the west, and see the ships as they come and go. However, you're more likely to ignore such mundane, everyday happenings and watch the sharks instead. That's right, sharks. Every evening, just as the sun goes down, the restaurant staff feeds the sharks, and you can watch them do it right from your outdoor table. You'll see sharks lurking in the waters below the restaurant. The menu features a vast collection of seafood dishes, including everything from lobster to lemon shark, and from mahi-mahi to fresh Bahamian stone crab claws. Shark feeding is at 7, 8 and 9 pm. ☎ 242-352-6674.

$ The Pub on the Mall, at Ranfurley Circus on Sunrise Highway, is Freeport's oldest and most authentic English pub. The menu includes such British staples as fish and chips, English bangers (sausages), shepherd's pie and steak and kidney pie. The ale, too, is English; John Courage's ale is served either in bottles or on draught. The atmosphere is very casual. It's a great place to mingle. ☎ 242-352-5110.

$ Pusser's, in the Port Lucaya Marketplace off Sea Horse Road, claims to be "the place to see, and the place to be seen" on Grand Bahama. Pusser's is another English-style pub. There are large numbers of antiques, model ships, and other nautical memorabilia and artifacts reflecting an establishment you'd more likely expect to find in England, close to the docks in Bristol or Portsmouth, than on a tropical island. The food includes such traditional English dishes as shepherd's pie and fish and chips, along with a pleasing variety of local seafood dishes. ☎ 242-352-5110.

$$ Taino's by the Sea, at the Taino Beach Resort & Club, 5 Jolly Roger Drive in Port Lucaya, is one of Grand Bahama's newest restaurants. The atmosphere is French, the waiters are dressed in tuxedos, the décor elegant and intimate, and the food is cooked to order, often at table-side. Specialties include *canard à la bigarade* (roast duckling in a zesty orange sauce), *escalopes de veau "Sirena"* (veal scalopine

Grand Bahama

sautéed in Marsala wine with creamed mushrooms and green noodles), and *filet mignon au poivre noir* (fillet of beef in crushed black peppercorns, pan-fried at the table). ☎ 242-373-4677.

$$$ The Rib Room, in the Royal Oasis Golf Resort & Casino on West Sunrise Highway in Freeport, is a quality restaurant, in English pub style. The atmosphere is close and the lights are low. The food is top quality and therefore on the pricey side, but if you like prime rib, the best cuts of steak, and fresh lobster, this is the place for you. Dress is casual, but it would be wise to make a reservation. ☎ 242-352-6721.

$$ Ruby Swiss, next to the Royal Oasis Tower on West Sunrise Highway in Freeport, is another elegant restaurant specializing in French cuisine and table-side cooking – a restaurant for gourmets. If you like French food, you'll love their *entrecôte "Café de Paris"* (a strip steak served in garlic butter with a baked potato), *poulet au vin blanc* (sliced chicken in white wine, brandy and fresh cream served with onions and mushrooms), and their famous *fondu "Bourguignon"* (cubes of prime rib dipped in boiling oil right at your table) and served with a sauce of your choice. ☎ 242-352-8507.

$$ Scorpio's, at the corner of Explorer's Way and West Atlantic in Port Lucaya, is the oldest restaurant in downtown Freeport. If you like the food of the islands, you're in for a treat at Scorpio's. The Bahamian chefs specialize in cracked conch, steamed grouper, steamed chicken, and minced or broiled lobster. The restaurant is open from 7 am and serves breakfast, lunch and dinner. ☎ 242-352-6969.

AUTHOR PICK

$$ The Stoned Crab, on Taino Beach, is famed for its fine dining. It's the only restaurant on the island where you can eat right next to the ocean. For more than 20 years the restaurant's exceptional setting and nautical décor have made it an island institution, and a watering hole for locals and visitors alike. Long considered the "in place," The Stoned Crab, with its good food, casual atmosphere, and spectacular views over a moonlit ocean, turns an ordinary night out into something really special. The house specialties include wahoo, yellowfin tuna, swordfish, red snapper, grouper, lobster, stone crab claws, crab cakes and escargots. ☎ 242-373-1442.

$ The Tradewinds Café, in the Port Lucaya Resort and Yacht Club next to the Port Lucaya Marketplace, is a neat little place where you can enjoy a cup of coffee and a slice of Bahamian cheesecake at lunch time, or a full-blown lobster dinner in the evening. The café's peach melba is a delight, and the Lucayan chicken (marinated in rum, seasoned with sage, roasted with peppers, onions, olives, tomatoes, and served with peas and rice) is out of this world. ☎ 242-373-6618.

$$ Zorba's, in the Port Lucaya Marketplace, off Sea Horse Road, claims to be the only truly authentic Greek restaurant on the island. Freshly made Greek salads, *tyropitas, spanakopitas, kebabs, moussaka, baklava* and *galatobouriko* are just a few of the treats to enjoy. ☎ 242-373-6137.

■ Accommodations

Old Bahama Bay, some 25 miles west of Freeport, was formerly the Jack Tar Village resort. It has undergone extensive remodeling and renovation over the past several years. Today, it holds its own with any of its more glitzy competitors in Lucaya and Freeport. Set on the oceanfront at the West End of Grand Bahama Island, the complex includes a marina, 47 guest units – cottages and suites – a restaurant, bar, tennis courts, pool, dive shop, and a variety of on-site watersports. The guest units are comfortably furnished, the bathrooms are large and modern, and each unit has its own refrigerator, coffee maker, TV, fax, and Internet connection. The resort boasts more than 25 acres, most of it waterfront, and white sandy beaches. The restaurant – **The Conch Shack** – is open for breakfast, lunch and dinner; the cuisine is Bahamian and American. Old Bahama Bay, West End, Box F-42546, ☎ 800-572-5711 or 242-346-6500. Rates from $250 per night for a double.

Our Lucaya, centered upon the two finest beaches on Grand Bahama, is arguably the largest resort in the entire Bahama chain. Lucayan Beach and Taino Beach provide almost eight acres of pristine white sand and some of the most beautiful waters anywhere. The seas banded by the two vast beaches are the perfect setting for a great resort that just about lives up to all the hype that has preceded it. It replaces two old resorts, the Alantik Beach and the Lucayan Beach Resort and Casino. These two grand old ladies became the media event of century, at least as far as the Bahamas are concerned, when they were spectacularly demolished several years ago to make way for Our Lucaya. The guest rooms at Our Lucaya are all comfortable, beautifully furnished and come with all modern conveniences. The list of amenities is long and all-encompassing. They provide just about everything you desire to make a vacation a memorable event: two championship golf courses, three pools, watersports of every description, 14 restaurants, bars and lounges. Rivaled only by Atlantis on Paradise Island, Our Lucaya is highly recommended. Rates are from $155 to $490. PO Box F-42500, Royal Palm Way, Lucaya, ☎ 800-LUCAYAN.

The Royal Oasis, on Sunrise Highway in Freeport, is the Phoenix that rose from the ashes of another grand old lady, the Bahamas Princess Resort and Casino, which was always my favorite place to stay in the Bahamas. Since it was first built in the early 1960s, it has undergone several remodelings, renovations – call them what you will – but nothing ever quite seemed to work. Still, I loved it just as it was. Today, after some $50 million has been pumped into remodeling, it's not quite the hotel I fell in love with, but it does work. They still don't have a beach – the shuttle wends its way back and forth throughout most of the day – but the rooms have all been modernized, the restaurants upgraded, and the general appearance has been vastly enhanced, no longer a dowdy old lady. There are two championship golf courses, 12 tennis courts, pools, and whole range of organized trips available on-site. Rates range from $118 to $350. The Mall at Sunrise Highway, Freeport, ☎ 800-545-1300.

The Castaways Resort, in Freeport at the International Bazaar, offers a choice of king or double rooms close to the casino action at the Royal Oasis Golf Resort & Casino. The pool is surrounded by a magnificent tropical garden, and shops, beaches, and watersports centers are only a short stroll away. Rates begin at around $75 per night, per person in the off-season (May to mid-December). ☎ 242-352-6682, PO Box F-2629, Freeport.

The Coral Beach Hotel in Lucaya is actually a condominium complex. Consequently, there are never many guest rooms available. The facilities are, however, fairly extensive, and include a swimming pool, one of the best beaches on the island, and **The Sandpiper**, a popular island night spot. Off-season rates start at $75 per person. Box F-2468, Freeport, ☎ 242-373-2468.

The Running Mon Marina & Resort, at 208 Kelly Court in Freeport, is located on the water's edge and offers an outstanding array of facilities and organized activities. Guests can choose from a variety of accommodations that include double and king-sized beds. There's also the Admiral's Suite, which has a furnished living room, kitchen, dining area and a Jacuzzi. The hotel's **Mainsail Restaurant** serves both Bahamian and American dishes. They own and operate a glass-bottom dive boat. Guests can enjoy an exclusive evening cruise complete with tropical drinks and the music of the islands.

Rates in the off-season begin at $90 per person, per night. Box F-2663, Freeport, ☎ 242-352-6834.

The Port Lucaya Resort & Yacht Club, which adjoins the Port Lucaya Marketplace on Bell Channel Bay Road, is only minutes away from the beach. The hotel has its own pool complex and an outdoor Jacuzzi. Guests have a choice of first- or second-floor accommodations, with stunning views of the Marketplace and the marina. You can enjoy a variety of American and Bahamian dishes in the hotel's restaurant. Off-season rates start at around $95 per night, per person. Box F-2452, Freeport, ☎ 800-582-2921.

Xanadu Beach Resort & Marina, set on a small peninsula in Freeport, has its own beach and a 72-slip marina. The resort, once the hideaway of legendary recluse, Howard Hughes, offers a variety of first class accommodations and facilities designed to provide an all-in-one vacation. The resort has its own pool complex complete with a bar and poolside service. Watersports of all types are within easy reach, and golfers can play the two PGA-rated courses at the Royal Oasis Golf Resort & Casino. The rooms are comfortable, have been refurnished and redecorated, and all have balconies and tables. Rates begin at $140 per person, per night. Box F-42438, Freeport, ☎ 242-352-6783.

Club Fortuna Beach Resort at 1 Dubloon Road in Freeport is another of the island's popular luxury resorts. The typical guest at Club Fortuna is young, outgoing, and uninhibited – topless bathing is commonplace. The atmosphere is definitely European – all of the staff members seem to speak Spanish or Italian – and the food includes a selection of Italian dishes. Designed to get you away from the hustle of everyday living, the guest rooms do not have televisions or telephones, but they are sumptuously furnished and decorated. The rates include three meals per day, and all the windsurfing, kayaking, archery, tennis, and snorkeling you might wish. Rates start at $240 per person, per night. ☎ 800-898-9968.

The Deep Water Cay Club is Grand Bahama's most expensive and exclusive sanctuary for members, mostly male, of the corporate world. The club offers its guests (non-members can stay here) an opportunity to relax or fish in an atmosphere of quiet luxury. Each morning, you'll head out for a day's bonefishing or deep-sea fishing. In the evenings you'll relax in the club lounge for a quiet drink, after which you'll enjoy a meal for gourmets in the Club's luxurious dining room. The rustic guest rooms all have ceiling fans and air-conditioning, thick, heavy towels, and embroidered bed linens.

Grand Bahama

Each room faces the sea, and all have porches, umbrellas, and easy chairs; some even have hammocks. Deep Water Cay is located at the east end of the island, almost an hour from the airport, so you'll need to make arrangements with the hotel for a pick up before you arrive. Box 40039, Freeport, ☎ 242-353-3073, $350 per night for a minimum of three nights.

The Out Islands

Beyond Nassau and Freeport lie the 13 inhabited islands or island groups that make up the Out Islands of The Bahamas. These are the Abacos, Andros, Eleuthera, Cat Island, Long Island, Bimini, the Berry Islands, Crooked Island, San Salvador, the Inaguas, the Exumas, Ragged Island and Rum Cay. They are magical places, each with a character all its own. It's here in these tiny backwater paradises that adventures really begin. This is the land of the treasure hunter, scuba diver, beachcomber, explorer and hiker. It's where the old world ends and the new one begins, a land of emerald seas, snow-white sands and mysterious blue holes, where you can wander deserted beaches for hours on end and never set eyes on another living soul. Although there are no shopping malls, night clubs, casinos or any of the other major attractions that lure visitors to the two main islands of the Bahamas, life goes on here much as it has for more than 300 years, quietly, unchanged.

These are the islands of romance where couples can leave the bustling mainland and all its distractions behind. Sunshine, warm breezes, tropical drinks, soft music and solitude make for an unforgettable experience. If, after a week together here in the Out Islands, you don't get to know one another intimately, you never will.

Dotted around the Out Islands are a dozen or so resorts (some more deserving of the title than others) and perhaps five times as many small hotels and B&Bs. Accommodations run the gamut from spartan to delightful and almost luxurious. Don't expect all the modern conveniences here: telephones and televisions are rarities. Air-conditioning is available almost everywhere, but be sure you confirm before you book. The absence of climate control in your room, if you're not prepared for it, can be a vacation breaker.

Upscale restaurants and fine dining, as we know them, are the exception rather than the rule, but these islands do boast of some of the best little holes in the wall I've ever come across. The atmosphere in these sometimes raunchy little cafés and restaurants, and the often outrageous local cuisine, makes eating out an experience to remember. But even those who like fine dining and a good bottle of wine, will find opportunities to indulge. The Romora Bay Club on Harbour Island is one (see page 233), the Green Turtle Club on Green Turtle Cay in the Abacos is another (see page182).

Adventures on land and sea abound in the Out Islands. Most of them, though, require a modicum of self-organization. Throughout the following pages you'll find references to beaches, dive sites, snorkeling, bicycling and walking opportunities. Very few of these activities, with the exception of scuba diving, can be formally structured. A good map and the ability to make friends with the locals – local knowledge can produce golden opportunities – is all you need. Hotel employees are also a good source for local secrets. Other than that, you'll need to head out on your own and see what you can find.

Beyond the Out Islands, far to the south, lie the Turks and Caicos Islands. These are not a part of the Bahamas per se, but they are a part of the Bahamian archipelago and an increasingly popular destination for Americans, Canadians and Europeans. So, it seems only right that we give them coverage in these pages. The section begins on page 311.

Most people have heard of Nassau, some have heard of Freeport and Grand Bahama, but very few have heard of the Out Islands. If you really want to get away from life in the fast lane, enjoy a few quiet days in the sun on some of the most beautiful and unspoiled beaches in the world, the opportunities offered by the Out Islands are almost limitless. Start your quest by visiting the Bahamas website: www.bahamas.com.

WORD TO THE WISE

With rare exceptions, hotel standards in the Bahamas are not what you get on the US mainland, or in Europe. Due to the fact that almost everything has to be imported, and is therefore expensive, there is a definite trend to put off until tomorrow what should be done today. Hotels that might have been considered fairly upscale five years ago can quickly become slightly seedy as time and weather take their toll. Don't expect too much, especially in the Out Islands and Turks and Caicos. But don't let a little inconvenience spoil your vacation.

The Abacos

Often referred to as Abaco, this cluster of islands, islets, and rocky outcrops forms an archipelago that stretches for more than 100 miles, from Walker's Cay in the northeast Bahamas, all the way down to Hole in the Wall in the southwest. It is the second largest grouping of islands in the Bahamas. Abaco, aside from being the most affluent and most-visited of the Out Islands, is also the most developed. **Marsh Harbour**, its capital city, is the third largest city in the Bahamas.

But, with more than 650 square miles of almost deserted land and a total population of around 11,000, Abaco is hardly a bustling metropolis. Still, there's plenty to see and do and the available amenities are, for the most part, modern.

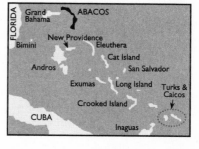

The Abacos are a mixture of isolated, dusty settlements and neat towns and villages that might have been lifted straight out of New England. Pastel-colored clapboard houses and white picket fences contrast sharply with dusty, bumpy, deserted roads. The Abacos offer sun-drenched beaches, warm ocean breezes, tropical trees and flowers, and quiet country lanes. More than 50 species of wild and tropical birds inhabit the islands, along with wild boar, several species of lizards and, in the surrounding waters, bonefish. Most of the men earn their living from the ocean.

The Abacos offer all sorts of spectacular outdoor activities, including sailing, sport fishing, sea kayaking, snorkeling, wreck diving, boating, guided island hopping, beach picnics, all-day island safaris, bird-watching and nature tours, hiking, fishing, biking, shelling, and on and on.

The Abacos

Most of the settlements on the Abacos sprang up along the east side of the main island. On the other islands, including Great Guana, Man-O-War Cay, Green Turtle Cay, Elbow Cay, and Little Abaco, a number of quaint little towns have grown up, named New Plymouth, Hope Town, Cooper's Town and Treasure Cay.

The principle city, Marsh Harbour, is a dusty little town somewhat reminiscent of a frontier town in the American west. Stand here for a moment or two and you might expect to see a tumbleweed roll across the road beneath the town's single, lonely stop-light.

Founded by American loyalists in 1784, Marsh Harbour is located close to the center of the Abaco island chain and is the gateway to the nearby island settlements of Great Guana Cay, Man-O-War Cay and Hope Town. Almost everything begins and ends in Marsh Harbour.

History

 The first foreigners to visit the Abacos were **Spanish** explorers. They called the islands Habacoa, from the Spanish phrase, "haba de cacau," a rough description of the islands' limestone substructure.

Juan Ponce de Leon is supposed to have stopped by the islands in 1513, during his search for the fabled Fountain of Youth, but he found nothing of value except the local inhabitants, a small number of Lucayan Indians. These he quickly enslaved and, by 1550, the poor Lucayans had died out completely.

Then the pirates arrived. They, too, found little of value. They realized, however, that the remote location and the hundreds of tiny cays, bays and inlets made fine hideouts, and the rocky coastline was a great asset in increasing their second source of income, wrecking.

 DID YOU KNOW? *It's said that more than 500 galleons, some still laden with treasure, lie at the bottom of the ocean around the Abacos; many of them are the victims of wreckers.*

Following the pirates, and after the end of the American War of Independence, a new breed of adventurer arrived on the Abacos. **Loyalists** from Virginia, the Carolinas and New England put down roots at **Charleton**, near Treasure Cay in the center of the Abacos. But their crops failed and, finally, the town was destroyed in a hurricane. By the late 1700s, Charleton had been abandoned and, in 1784, a new settlement, **Elizabeth Harbour**, some 18 miles to the south, had been established with help from friends on nearby Eleuthera. There, the colonists took to fishing and, once again, to farming. The little settlement of Elizabeth Harbour eventually became **Marsh Harbour**.

New settlers came and stayed on the Abacos, bringing with them an assortment of skills. The islands became an important center for small shipbuilding. Soon, due to the high quality of the islanders' craftsmanship, sloops, fishing boats, and dinghies built on the Abacos became prized throughout the Bahamas.

In the early 1970s came the movement toward Bahamian **independence**. The white population of the Abacos remained fiercely loyal to Britain; they even tried to secede from the Bahamas. In the end, however, independence came to the islands.

Today, although the little settlements on Man-O-War Cay – Hope Town and Green Turtle Cay – are still predominantly white, the residents of the Abacos have somewhat reluctantly come to terms with their new situation. The Abacos are prosperous – a popular tourist destination – and they are playing an increasingly important part in the Bahamian tourist industry.

The Abacos

On the beach in the Abacos.

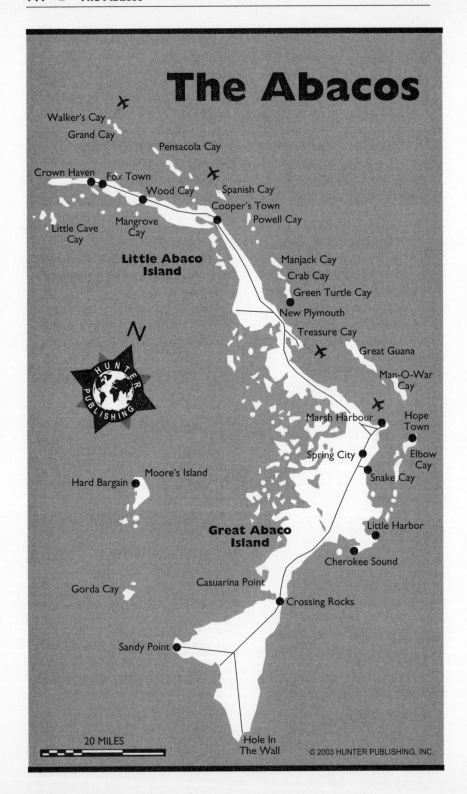

The Abacos

Walker's Cay
Grand Cay
Pensacola Cay
Crown Haven
Fox Town
Wood Cay
Spanish Cay
Cooper's Town
Little Cave Cay
Mangrove Cay
Powell Cay

Little Abaco Island

Manjack Cay
Crab Cay
Green Turtle Cay
New Plymouth
Treasure Cay
Great Guana
Man-O-War Cay
Marsh Harbour
Hope Town
Spring City
Elbow Cay
Moore's Island
Snake Cay
Hard Bargain

Great Abaco Island

Little Harbor
Cherokee Sound
Gorda Cay
Casuarina Point
Crossing Rocks
Sandy Point
Hole In The Wall

20 MILES

© 2003 HUNTER PUBLISHING, INC.

Getting There

■ By Air

The Abacos are well served, both locally and from the mainland. **American**, **Continental**, and **USAir** offer service from most US gateway cities.

Visitors from Europe can travel from London and other major continental cities on the same three airlines, or on other code-sharing partner airlines, making connections in the US through Miami, Atlanta, Orlando, and elsewhere. Also, your travel agent can hook you up with package operators – British Airways Holidays, Thomas Cook, or American Express Holiday, to mention just a few. See *Package Vacations*, pages 14 and 350.

Flying in to the Abacos, you arrive at one of two international airports, both tiny. **Treasure Cay Airport** is in the middle of that island and serves Green Turtle Cay, Manjack Cay, Cooper's Town, and the rest of Little Abaco, while **Marsh Harbour Airport**, farther south, serves Hope Town, Man-O-War Cay, and Great Guana Cay.

The Abacos

Marsh Harbour Airport	
Access to Elbow Cay, Guana Cay & Man-O-War Cay	
FROM	**AIRLINE**
Nassau	**Bahamasair** operates regular daily schedules, ☎ 800-222-4262. Round-trip fare, $96.
Freeport	**Major Air**, ☎ 242-352-5778.

Fort Lauderdale	**Gulfstream** (Continental Airlines Connection), ☎ 800-231-0856; **Island Express**, ☎ 954-359-0380; **Air Sunshine**, ☎ 800-327-8900; **Bel Air Transport**, ☎ 954-524-9814. Round-trip fare, $99.
Miami	**American Eagle**, ☎ 800-433-7300; **Gulfstream** (Continental Airlines Connection), ☎ 800-231-0856. Round-trip fare, $158.
Orlando	**USAirways Express**, ☎ 800-622-1015. Round-trip fare, $158.
West Palm Beach	**Bahamasair** operates regular daily schedules, ☎ 800-222-4262, **USAirways Express**, ☎ 800-622-1015. Round-trip fare, $160.

Treasure Cay Airport
Access to Green Turtle Cay & Spanish Cay

FROM	AIRLINE
Nassau	**Bahamasair** operates regular daily schedules, ☎ 800-222-4262. Round-trip fare, $96.
Freeport	**Major Air**, ☎ 242-352-5778. Round-trip fare, $99.
Fort Lauderdale	**Gulfstream** (Continental Airlines Connection), ☎ 800-231-0856; **Island Express**, ☎ 954-359-0380; **Air Sunshine**, ☎ 800-327-8900; **Twin Air**, ☎ 954-359-8266. Round-trip fare, $160.

Miami	**Gulfstream** (Continental Airlines Connection), ☎ 800-231-0856. Round-trip fare, $158.
Orlando	**USAirways Express**, ☎ 800-622-1015. Round-trip fare, $160.
West Palm Beach	**Bahamasair** operates regular daily schedules, ☎ 800-222-4262; **USAirways Express**, ☎ 800-622-1015. Round-trip fare, $160.

■ By Mail Boat

Mail boat schedules depend on the weather, and therefore can be a little erratic. They do stick to the schedule most of the time but it's best to call ahead and make sure. ☎ 423-339-1064.

Mia Desa leaves Potter's Cay, Nassau, for Marsh Harbour, Treasure Cay, Green Turtle Cay and Hope Town on Tuesday at 8 pm, returning on Thursday at 7 pm. Sailing time is 12 hours. The fare, one-way, is $45.

Champion II sails for Sandy Point, Moore's Island and Bullock Harbour on Tuesday at 8 pm, returning on Thursday at 10 am. Sailing time is 11 hours. The one-way fare is $30.

■ By Private Boat

During recent years, the Abacos have become a popular sailing destinations. For more than 130 miles, stretching north and south, the two major islands, along with dozens of tiny islets and cays, present a wealth of opportunities. While you can visit a limitless number of secluded, often deserted, inlets, bays and anchorages, you're always secure in the knowledge that civilization is never very far away. Official ports of entry are Walker's Cay, Green Turtle Cay, Marsh Harbour, Sandy Point, and Spanish Cay.

The Abacos

There's a marina at the south end of **Spanish Cay**. Facilities include 75 slips with a maximum depth of nine feet, showers, fuel, a laundromat, shops and a restaurant. ☎ 888-722-6474, fax 561-655-0172, VHF 16.

Green Turtle Cay has two facilities, the **Green Turtle Club** and the **Green Turtle Shipyard**. They have a combined total of 44 slips and a maximum depth of eight feet. Other facilities include showers, fuel, shops, restaurant, laundromat and satellite TV. ☎ 242-365-4271, fax 242-365-4272, VHF 16.

The **Bluff House Beach Hotel** on Green Turtle Cay at White Sound offers 20 slips with a maximum depth of 10 feet. There's also a restaurant, laundromat, showers, fuel service, and a shop. ☎ 242-365-4247, fax 242-365-4248, VHF 16.

At **Treasure Cay**, the **Treasure Cay Hotel Resort & Marina** is a full-service operation with 150 slips with a maximum depth of 12 feet. It also has on-shore accommodations, a repair shop, fuel service, a laundromat, showers, a restaurant, and several shops. There's a 50-ton travel lift nearby. ☎ 800-327-1584, fax 242-365-8847, VHF 16.

The marina at the **Guana Beach Resort** on Abaco offers 22 slips with a maximum depth of 10 feet, along with on-shore accommodations, a popular bar and restaurant, an excellent beach with pink sand and several shops close by. If, however, you're looking for fuel or showers, you'll need to go elsewhere. ☎ 242-365-5133, fax 242-365-5134, VHF 16.

The **Abaco Beach Resort and Boat Harbour Marina** is very popular. Facilities include 180 full-service slips with a maximum depth of 10 feet, repair service, fuel, a modern bathhouse with hot showers and dressing rooms, shops, a great restaurant, and a sailor's bar. ☎ 800-468-4799, fax 242-367-2819, VHF 16.

There are more marinas scattered across the Abacos: **Admiral's Yacht Haven, Harbour View Marina, Hope Town Harbour Marina** on Elbow Cay, **Marsh Harbour Marina, Mango's Marina,** and the **Conch Inn Marina,** which has a great outdoor/indoor bar and restaurant, as well as more than 30 full-service slips, postal service, and mini-market; there's even a dive shop on the property. Call the Conch Inn Hotel and Marina at ☎ 800-688-4752 or 242-367-4000.

■ Package Vacations

Unless you're a completely independent traveler, a package vacation is the best way to visit the Abacos, especially if you've not been before. Several companies offer air/hotel-inclusive packages with a variety of hotels to choose from; contact a reliable travel agent for a presentation of all the options. I recommend a package by **American Airlines FlyAAWay Vacations** (☎ 800-321-2121, www.aavacations.com) because they supply their own air portion of the vacation. This is an advantage if something goes wrong, especially when flights are delayed or cancelled. An airline will always see that their own customers are looked after before those of package operators.

American Airlines does not offer packages into Treasure Cay International Airport because they do not serve that airport. **Destination Bahamas** is a wholesaler that packages a more diverse number of properties with air on Abaco. Their number for reservations is ☎ 1-800-224-2627. More information on this wholesaler or alternatives can be found at www.bahamas.com.

Both of the airports and the docks are well served by independently owned taxis, and you'll find them waiting to meet all of the inter-island ferries. Fares are reasonable, starting at around $12 for two people to ride from Treasure Cay or Marsh Harbour to any of the local hotels or ferry docks.

If you're traveling to Green Turtle Cay or Hope Town, take a taxi from the airport to the dock. The inter-island ferries are scheduled to coincide with incoming air services.

Getting Around

On Great Abaco a taxi is the most convenient mode of transportation. If you're headed on to the islands, it's the ferry.

■ By Ferry

To get to **Green Turtle Cay**, catch the ferry near Treasure Cay Airport. Taxi fare from the airport to the dock is $5. The ferry ride over to Green Turtle Cay will take about 50 minutes and cost $8; a same-day, round-trip ticket costs $12.

The taxi fare from Marsh Harbour Airport into town, or to Albury's Ferry Station, is about $12. Boats depart for **Man-O-War Cay** and **Elbow Cay** from Crossing Beach twice each day at 10:30 am and 4:30 pm. The one-way fare is $8; a same-day round-trip ticket costs $12. The ferry to **Great Guana Cay** leaves twice a day from the dock at the Conch Inn Marina at 9:30 am and 4:30 pm. The fare is $8 one-way and $12 for a same-day round-trip ticket. Children ride for half-fare.

WORD TO THE WISE

If you miss the ferry, either at Marsh Harbour or Treasure Cay, don't worry, you're not stranded. You can arrange a special charter by calling **Albury's Ferry Service** *at* ☎ *809-367-2306. A one-way ride will cost around $40. At Treasure Cay you can call the* **Green Turtle Ferry** *at* ☎ *809-365-4166 or 4151.*

■ By Bicycle, Moped or Car

Bicycles are available to rent at many of the hotels and resorts throughout the Abacos and at **Brendal's Dive Shop** (☎ 800-780-9941) on Green Turtle Cay. Rental cars, bicycles and mopeds are also available in Marsh Harbour. At the time of this writing, the going rate for a rental car was negotiable, starting at about $60 per day. It's cheaper by the week. For a bicycle, you'll pay at least $10 per day or $50 per week. A moped will cost $40 for 24 hours, or $200 by the week – maybe less if you're prepared to haggle.

Marsh Harbour

With a permanent population of just over 3,000 and a single traffic light (the only one on the Out Islands), the Bahamas' third largest city could be regarded as a major commercial center for the islands. It is, in addition, a major boating center, with craft of all shapes and sizes coming through for fuel, rest, food and water.

The little town has a shopping center of sorts, several small hotels, a couple of gift shops, and a number of restaurants.

Vacationers using Marsh Harbour as a center of operations will find the tiny community refreshingly quiet and well-equipped for most of your needs. From Marsh Harbour you can drive Great Abaco, or cruise the cays in a rental boat.

■ Walking

There are a number of good hikes. A leisurely half-hour stroll will take you to most of the sights and sounds of Marsh Harbour, while longer walks of up to three miles can provide a pleasant afternoon in the sunshine and some excellent views of the small off-shore cays and tiny outlying settlements.

A good place to begin is the **Conch Inn** (☎ 242-367-4000; see page 184). This is where the yachting fraternity congregates in ever-increasing numbers. The water here is crystal clear, and you can watch the fish, crabs, and the boats as they come and go. You can even rent a boat yourself and take a leisurely cruise. Visit the Conch Inn for breakfast, lunch or dinner. The dockside bar and restaurant with its open-air dining is famous across the islands as a gathering spot and watering hole. There are several other restaurants close to the waterfront, including **Wally's** and **Mangoes**. The waterfront is also home to **Dive Abaco** (see page 172), one of the largest scuba and snorkeling centers in the Abacos. Along the way, bicycles can be rented at **Abaco Towns by the Sea**, a time-share apartment complex in downtown Marsh Harbour off Bay Street on the South Shore.

South from Town

A short walk from the old harbour to the south you will find Marsh Town and the **Abaco Beach Resort & Boat Harbour**

The Abacos

(☎ 800-468-4799; www.abacoresort.com; see page 184), with its full-service marina and 160 slips. The hotel, set back a little from the water, is also the location of one of the most popular watering holes: the **Angler's Restaurant**. The Great Abaco Beach Resort is also home to **The Dive Shop**. On the waterfront in Marsh Harbour, **Seahorse Boat Rentals**, ☎ 242-367-2513, at Boat Harbour Marina on Bay Street, has boats, bicycles, windsurfers and snorkel equipment for rent. Follow Bay Street a little way to the east from Marsh Town and you'll pass through the tiny settlements of Pond Bay, Pelican Shores, Fanny Bay, and Upper Cut. The walk is a pleasant and leisurely way of spending an hour or two, and there are shady rest stops conveniently placed along the way.

North from Town

Go north from the waterfront in Marsh Harbour for an agreeable three-mile walk along Harbour Road to the quaint little fishing villages of **Dundas Town** and **Murphy Town**, two little communities with little churches and tiny clapboard houses. Be sure to drop in at **Mother Merle's Fishnet** in Dundas Town for conch salad, fresh fish, or a lobster plate that's excellent (take-out service only).

Marsh Harbour.

■ Driving

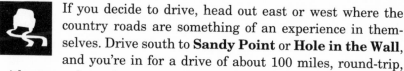

If you decide to drive, head out east or west where the country roads are something of an experience in themselves. Drive south to **Sandy Point** or **Hole in the Wall**, and you're in for a drive of about 100 miles, round-trip, with stops along the way at **Cherokee Sound** and **Casuarina Point**, where you'll find one of the island's most fascinating and not-to-be-missed characters, Nettie Symonette (see page 160). Go north and a scenic drive of similar length will take you through Treasure Cay and on to the tiny villages of **Cooper's Town, Cedar Harbour, Mount Hope, Fox Town** and **Crown Haven**.

Man-O-War Cay

Man-O-War Cay is a small island community some three miles by boat from Marsh Harbour. It's the boat-building capital of the Abacos, and home to the Albury family, whose roots on the Abacos go back for many generations. They have something to do with almost everything that happens on the island – they operate the Albury ferry, the grocery store, the famous Albury's Sail Shop, the Harbour Store, Aunt Mady's Boutique, the Man-O-War Marina, Joe's Studio and many more of the island's prosperous businesses. Man-O-War Cay is a delightful place. There are no cars; the main mode of transport is either the golf cart or walking. There is just one hotel, **Schooner's Landing Resort** (see page 183 for details), and a few rental cottages and apartments.

■ Exploring

Along the **Queen's Highway**, a big name for such a narrow thoroughfare, is an assortment of quaint gift shops, stores, churches and the island's tiny post office. A few yards down one of the miniscule side roads is Man-O-War's magnificent beach, often deserted, but always inviting. If you enjoy walking, there's probably no nicer hike than the couple of hours it will take you to walk from one end of the island to the other. To visit Man-O-War, take the ferry from the Marsh Harbour dock. A same-day round-trip will cost you $12, and it's well worth the money.

The Abacos

Elbow Cay & Hope Town

Hope Town is a quaint little place reminiscent of old New England. The town is a labyrinth of tiny streets, of gaily painted blue, yellow, pink and white clapboard cottages, small-town stores, and old-fashioned churches. And the town is ablaze with flowers growing in tiny gardens and along the sidewalks: pink oleander, purple bougainvillea, and yellow and red hibiscus. Boats bob at anchor in the harbour, above which the famous candy-striped lighthouse dominates the land and seascape for miles around.

Hope Town's harbor is almost completely enclosed. Only when you've navigated its narrow entrance does the town heave into view. As with Man-O-War, you won't find any cars in the city.

Located on the narrow northern end of Elbow Cay, Hope Town faces the harbor to the west. To the east is the ocean and, only yards from the main highway at the end of a narrow street, a magnificent stretch of white sandy beach. Almost always, there's the irresistible smell of fresh-baked bread, cakes and pies that permeates the air.

■ Exploring

The town's two museums – the **Wyannie Malone Museum**, off Bark Street at Hope Town Beach (open 10 am to 12:30, Monday-Saturday; entrance fee $1) and the **Hope Town Lighthouse**, across the harbour, close to Club Soleil – offer a peek into the town's and Elbow Cay's past.

You can stop for a cold drink at the **Hope Town Harbour Lodge Hotel** on Bay Street and enjoy lunch at **Captain Jack's**. From there, you might like to take a stroll up the hill to the **Bryle Patterson Memorial Garden**; a more peaceful or picturesque view would be hard to find. Hope Town is one of those story-book settings you may read about, but rarely find.

Green Turtle Cay & New Plymouth

Green Turtle Cay is perhaps the Abacos' most popular vacation destination. **New Plymouth**, the island's only town, is another quaint little colonial community. It was founded by English loyalists in 1783 after the close of the American War of Independence, making it one of the oldest settlements in the Abacos. Once the second largest city in the Bahamas after Nassau, the old town is a photo album of neat clapboard cottages, picket fences, and a profusion of flowers. Unlike Hope Town and Man-O-War Cay, however, New Plymouth is open to vehicular traffic.

■ Exploring

With the **Albert Lowe Museum** as the focal point of your tour, New Plymouth's narrow streets, galleries, quaint shops and restaurants are wonderful to explore. The museum, on Parliament Street among the bougainvillea, is in an old colonial building. It contains a fine collection of maritime memorabilia and will provide you with a unique peek into the life and times of the loyalist settlers. They are located at

The Albert Lowe Museum, Green Turtle Cay.

The Abacos

Parliament and King Streets. Open from 9 to 11:45 am and 1 to 4:30 pm, Monday through Saturday. Entrance fee is $1. Other places of interest include the **Loyalist Memorial Sculpture Garden**, the **New Plymouth Cemetery** with gravestones dating back to the 18th century, and the old **New Plymouth Jail**, unused now for more than two centuries.

But there's more to Green Turtle Cay than New Plymouth. The island boasts a number of **fine beaches**, some of the **best diving** locations in the Bahamas, and a network of roads that will take you on long hikes to **romantic bays and inlets**, quiet little harbors where boats sit at anchor, and a number of out-of-the-way restaurants and cafés where you can enjoy fish and lobster straight from the ocean.

Green Turtle Cay has three hotels, one in New Plymouth, the others on the harbor at White Sound (see page 182 for details). The island can be reached only by private boat or by the ferry. The ferry service is good. You can leave for New Plymouth early in the morning from either Treasure Cay or the Green Turtle Club, returning to either dock in the mid-afternoon. There are also a couple of local tour operators who run trips to the island on a weekly basis.

Treasure Cay

Treasure Cay – the name is misleading, for it's not a cay at all – is on Great Abaco Island some 25 miles north of Marsh Harbour, and was the scene of the first major tourist development in the Abacos. During the 1950s, work began on the resort community. It has continued ever since. Today, the small town offers a variety of accommodations and facilities. There are luxury villas, condos, and time-share units. There's also a hotel, a 150-slip marina, several shops, a post office, grocery store, health clinic, dive shop and more. Best of all, Treasure Cay boasts one of the best beaches in the Bahamas. The four-mile crescent of sugar-white sand and waving palms, offset against a background of shallow, pale green sea, is the sort of stuff you see on the quintessential vacation poster. A major attraction is the golf course at Treasure Cay Hotel Resort & Marina, the only one in the Out Islands. There is also a dive shop at the resort, Treasure Divers.

Treasure Cay Beach Resort & Villas.

DID YOU KNOW? *Treasure Cay is close to the site where the first settlers of the Abacos built their homes in Charleton, near the northern end of Treasure Cay. It lasted only a year or two before its population moved on to what would eventually become modern-day Marsh Harbour.*

Great Guana Cay

Great Guana is one of the largest of the outer Abaco cays. It's also the location of one of the smallest settlements on the Abacos, **Guana Harbour**. The community is set at about the midway point on the seven-mile-long island, and you won't find it until you've navigated the tiny harbour entrance. Guana Harbour has a permanent population of only 80. Most of the men make their living either by farming or fishing. Those that don't are employed at the Guana Beach Resort and Marina.

Like most of the cays in the Abacos, Great Guana is accessible only by private boat or ferry. The ferry runs a scheduled service from Marsh Harbour. The tiny village with its clapboard cottages, café, gift shop, liquor store, and grocery store, is a quiet retreat with narrow streets

The Abacos

and waving palms. So, for the most part, Great Guana remains an unspoiled tropical paradise with more than seven miles of pristine white
beaches, grassy dunes, and emerald waters, all set against a deep
blue sky.

The Guana Resort & Marina and Seaside Villas, the only hotel
on the island, sits amid the palms, seagrapes and casuarina trees on a
tiny peninsula. The resort is a sportsman's dream. Here you can
windsurf, snorkel, water-ski, sail, and go deep-sea fishing. See page
182 for details.

Walker's Cay

Far away at the northern tip of the archipelago, two tiny islands,
Walker's Cay and Grand Cay, represent the end of the world, at least
as far as the Abacos are concerned. Walker's Cay, reached only by private plane or boat, is the last stop in the Bahamas – a mecca for sport
fishermen from around the world. It's a lonely place, with only one hotel, a marina, and a population of marine life that will delight angler
and diver alike. Walker's Cay, protected and unspoiled, was once a
refuge for pirates and ne'er-do-wells. Today it's a haven for anglers,
divers, and sailors. It's also a sanctuary for those who want to spend a
few days in total seclusion – where the air is sweet, the beaches deserted, the sea clear, and the sunsets spectacular.

Guided Tours & Sightseeing

■ Sand Dollar Tours

Sand Dollar Tours, Marsh Harbour, ☎ 809-367-2189, offers a variety
of scheduled sightseeing tours throughout the week. These include a
Monday or Saturday sightseeing and swimming tour to Treasure
Cay, with a quick look at **Marsh Harbour**, **Dundas Town** and
Murphy Town along the way. You'll be able to go swimming off
Treasure Cay's beach, do some beachcombing or shelling, and visit
Treasure Cay's blue hole, where you can snorkel.

On Tuesdays and Thursdays, Sand Dollar Tours heads south for sightseeing at **Spring City** and **Snake Cay**, with visits to Pete's Pub and the Gold Shop in Little Harbour. They also conduct trips to Snake Cay for swimming and to **Wyndham Bay** for beachcombing.

On Wednesdays and Sundays the tour heads south again. This time you'll visit the site of the old **Bail Sugar Mill**. Here, there's sightseeing at Crossing Rocks, beachcombing at Long Bay, then on to **Bahama Palm Shores** for swimming, shelling or beachcombing. Finally, you'll stop at **Casuarina Point** and a visit to "The Different of Abaco" (see below).

Friday's tour goes north through **Blackwood**, **Cooper's Town**, **Cedar Harbour**, **Wood Cay**, **Mount Hope**, **Fox Town**, and **Crown Haven** for a round-trip of more than 100 miles.

Tours leave Marsh Harbour at 9 am and return at 4 pm, and they include a complimentary soft drink or beer. Rates: $30 per tour for adults, children under 12, $15.

▪ Bird Watching & Nature Tours

These tours, operated by **Bahamas Naturalists Expeditions, Ltd.**, give you the opportunity to explore the nature trails in the Caribbean pine forests of the **Abaco National Park** with an experienced naturalist guide, who will explain everything of interest. You'll go in search of the endangered Bahama parrot, see a variety of orchids and bromeliads, and enjoy a catered picnic lunch on a deserted beach in southern Abaco. You'll also be able to snorkel in a freshwater, inland blue hole and see colossal stalagmites and stalactites that were formed more than 10,000 years ago.

Tours depart Marsh Harbour at 10 am and return at 4 pm. They cost $75 per person, including lunch and beverages. Snorkeling equipment is not included (you must bring your own). ☎ 809-359-6783 for reservations, or inquire at Sapodilly's Restaurant & Bar on Bay Street in Marsh Harbour, or at Sea Horse Boat Rentals, either in Hope Town or Marsh Harbour at Boat Harbour Marina.

■ The Different of Abaco

This is at **Casuarina Point**, Abaco. Also the home of the Great Abaco Bonefishing Club, the Different of Abaco is the dream of Nettie Symonette. The natural resort, a small, rustic hotel in the wilds of southern Abaco off Cherokee Sound, is an on-going development of naturally landscaped gardens, rock gardens, freshwater ponds, and saltwater inlets, where bougainvillea, hibiscus, croton, oleander, star of Bethlehem and native orchids provide a riot of color and greenery. The rock gardens are a natural home for a variety of land and marine life that includes crabs, curly tailed lizards and snakes, while Nettie's personal collection of wildlife includes the Exuma iguana, the Abaco wild boar, dozens of friendly ducks, local chickens, and a lovable old donkey – all living happily together in a habitat that closely emulates their own natural environments.

To visit The Different of Abaco you must take either a taxi or rent a moped or bicycle. Once there, you can enjoy a home-cooked meal, wander the grounds, spend hours watching the more than 50 species of wild birds that inhabit the area and, before you leave, enjoy a cup of Nettie's famous Bush Tea. Hike a mile or two south on Great Abaco Highway and you can see hundreds of Abaco parrots. A little farther on, about five miles from The Different, is the village of **Cherokee**, a picturesque colonial town at the edge of Cherokee Sound. If you're interested in staying for a few days, call Nettie at ☎ 242-366-2150 or 327-7921. If you want to try some bonefishing, there's no better place than here (see *Fishing Packages*, page 164).

■ Ibis Tours

Sea Kayaking is a neat way to see the islands of the Abacos. Ibis Tours of Boynton Beach, Florida, offers an eight-day package to the Abacos, during which you'll paddle the sheltered waters around the cays in a sturdy kayak that's almost impossible to overturn. For more information and rates, ☎ 800-525-9411, www.ibistours.com.

Adventures on Water

■ Sport Fishing

 The waters off the Abacos offer some great sport fishing. The flats around Cherokee Sound and Casuarina Point teem with bonefish. Boats are available for rent from a number of operators and the hotels on the islands offer a wide variety of sport and bonefishing packages. There are also several deep-sea charter fishing outfits that will take you right to the best waters to catch marlin, sailfish, wahoo, kingfish and barracuda.

Boat Rentals

- **Rich's Rentals**, Marsh Harbour. 17- and 21-foot Paramounts, daily, three-day, weekly and monthly rates. From $95 to $140 per day. ☎ 242-367-2742.

- **Conch Inn Resort & Marina**, operated by The Moorings. Charter sailboats, bareboat and crewed. Expensive – call for rates. ☎ 242-367-4000.

- **Island Marine**. Boston Whalers and Aquasports, Rates start at $40 per day for a 15-foot Boston Whaler. ☎ 242-366-0181.

- **Sea Horse Boat Rentals**, Great Abaco Beach Resort. 18- to 21-foot Boston Whalers, $85-$140 per day, depending on size. ☎ 242-367-2513.

- **B & E Boat Rentals**, Marsh Harbour. 21-foot Paramount, 21-foot Proline, 21.3-foot Chris Craft, 23-foot Mako. Daily, three-day, and weekly rates. ☎ 242-367-2182.

- **Robert's Boat Rentals**, Marsh Harbour. 20-foot native boats, daily, three-day, and weekly rates. ☎ 242-367-2758.

- **Rainbow Rentals**, 17-foot Paramounts and 21-foot Chris Craft. ☎ 242-367-2452.

- **Donny's Boat Rentals**, Green Turtle Cay. 14- to 17-foot Boston Whalers and 19- to 23-foot Makos. Daily, three-day and weekly rates. ☎ 242-365-4119.

- **Dames Rentals**, Green Turtle Cay. 14- to 23-foot boats available at daily and weekly rates. ☎ 242-365-4247.

- **Hope Town Dive Shop & Boat Rentals**, Hope Town. Boats from 13 to 23 feet available, with daily, three-day, and weekly rates. ☎ 242-366-0029.

Fishing Tournaments

One of the first two legs of the **Bahamas Billfish Championship Tournament**, which takes place during the spring and early summer each year at five different locations, is held in April at Walker's Cay. The third and fourth legs are at Treasure Cay and Boat Harbour. For details and registration, ☎ 305-923-8022 or 242-367-2158.

The **Penny Turtle Billfish Tournament** is held at the Great Abaco Beach Resort in May. ☎ 800-468-4799 or 242-367-2158.

The **Billfish Foundation's Tag Tournament** is held in May at the Walker's Cay Hotel and Marina. ☎ 800-WALKERS.

The **Annual Treasure Cay International Billfish Tournament** is held in June. ☎ 800-327-1584.

The **Green Turtle Cay Yacht Club** hosts its annual fishing tournament in May. ☎ 242-365-4271.

The **Boat Harbour Billfish Championship** is held in June at the Marsh Harbour Resort. ☎ 305-920-7877 or 242-367-2158.

Fishing/Accommodation Packages

Sport fishing packages are offered by several hotels on the Abacos, including those listed here. The rates quoted below are, unless otherwise stated, per person, double occupancy. For a full list of package operators, call either the **Bahamas Tourism Office** at ☎ 800-32-SPORT, or the **Bahama Out Islands Promotion Board** at ☎ 800-688-4725.

The Tangelo Hotel

Wood Cay, Abaco. ☎ 242-365-2222 for reservations. http://oii.net/tangelo. This hotel specializes in bonefishing. Their basic package is a four-day/three-night stay that includes breakfast, lunch, and dinner, round-trip ground transfers, and two full days of fishing. The basic four-day package costs $778 for two persons based on double occupancy – a significant saving over the single rate of $686 per person. The package rate does not include airfare, taxes, or gratuities. An additional day of fishing will cost $200. Fly to Treasure Cay and take a taxi to the hotel or call for a pick-up.

Sea Spray Resort & Villas

Elbow Cay, Abaco, ☎ 242-366-0065, www.seasprayresort.com. Fly into Marsh Harbour, then take the ferry to Elbow Cay. This operator offers two options:

- The basic four-day, three-night package is based on a group of four people and includes stay in an oceanfront villa with maid service and dinner each day. It also includes use of a 22-foot boat for three days, with bait and a boxed lunch each day, and 2½ days fishing with a local guide. $1,272.

- The seven-night package includes use of the boat for six days, 3½ days fishing with a local guide, bait, and boxed lunches on fishing days. Four people: $2,072.

Both packages also include use of a Sunfish sailboat, freezer space, ice, local charts, gratuities, and the 8% hotel tax. Airfare, breakfast, and fuel for the boat are not included.

Schooner's Landing Resort

Man-O-War Cay, Abaco, ☎ 242-365-6072, http://oii.net/schooners. Fly into Marsh Harbour then take the ferry over to Man-O-War Cay. A resort representative will meet you at the ferry dock. Schooner's Landing offers two packages:

- The basic four-day, three-night package includes a beachfront, two-bedroom townhouse, fully equipped; maid service; use of a 20-foot boat for three days, including ice and bait; a local fishing guide for 2½ days; a box lunch on fishing days and evening meals. $1,295.

- The extended eight-day, seven-night package includes all the above, with the boat for six days and the guide for 3½ days, boxed lunches for three days and evening meals for three nights. $2,252.

Both packages include freezer space, private dock, local charts, gratuities and the 8% hotel tax. Airfare, fuel for the boat, tackle, taxi and ferry transportation are not included in the rates.

The Abacos

WORD TO THE WISE

Note: Visa / Mastercard and American Express charges are subject to a 5% surcharge.

The Conch Inn

Marsh Harbour, Abaco, ☎ 242-367-4000. Fly into Marsh Harbour Airport and take a taxi to the hotel. The Conch Inn offers a basic four-day, as well as an extended eight-day, package. Included in the rate is transportation to and from the Marsh Harbour Airport; accommodations; use of the private pool and beach; daily maid service; a half-day of bonefishing, including bait, tackle and ice; and one full day of deep-sea fishing, including bait, tackle and ice. Meals, beverages, taxes and gratuities are extra. Four days/three nights: $862. Eight days/seven nights: $1,202.

Guana Beach Resort

Guana Cay, Abaco, ☎ 800-227-3366, wwwguanabeach.com. Fly into Marsh Harbour Airport, take a taxi to the ferry dock, and then take the ferry to Guana Cay. Guana Beach Resort's package includes five days (four nights) of deluxe accommodations; a welcome "Guana Grabber" cocktail; use of a Sunfish sailboat and beach boat; and three half-day fishing trips for $550. Airfare and meals are not included, but breakfast and dinner are available for an extra $32 per person, per day.

The Great Abaco Bonefishing Club

Located at The Different of Abaco, Casuarina Point, Abaco, ☎ 242-366-2150 or 327-7921. The Different of Abaco is a small, naturally developed retreat/resort with 10 guest rooms located just off Cherokee Sound. If you are looking for something different, want to get back to basics and away from it all for some fine bonefishing, this is the place. The Different offers four days of bonefishing and seclusion for $1,000 per person. The rate includes accommodations, meals, and three days of fishing with an expert local guide. More than that, though, you'll be taken to virgin flats where, rather than the elusive, skittish quarry you might expect, the bonefish have never seen a fly and will fight each other to take your bait. The bonefish here, from the tales of those who stalk them, fight harder and longer than anywhere else. The Different operates 10 boats, all with expert local guides, for fishing the flats of the Cherokee Sound or the flats at the Marls, some 18 miles down water.

Fishing Guides

Rates shown are per boat. Where no rates are given, they will be comparable to those that are shown.

Will Key is available all year. He can take up to four people fishing on his 21-foot offshore boat, *Day's Catch*. Will specializes in bonefishing, reef and deep-sea fishing, snorkeling, sightseeing and shelling. Rates: $150 for a half-day; $250 for a full day. ☎ 242-266-0059.

Robert Lowe runs charters April through August. His 30-foot Stapleton, *Sea Gull*, has a capacity of six persons for deep-sea fishing. Rates: $220 for a half-day; $440 for a full day. ☎ 242-366-0266.

Maitland Lowe, an expert bonefisherman as well as deep-sea fisherman, takes anglers out in his 19-foot boat and charges $200 for a day's bonefishing; $150 for a half-day deep-sea fishing; and $250 for a full day. ☎ 242-366-0004.

Truman Major is a guide for all types of fishing, except bonefishing, year-round. Truman takes anglers out in his 30-foot Sea Hawk, *Lucky Strike*, and supplies all tackle, bait and ice. Rates: $220 for a half-day; $320 for a full day. ☎ 242-366-0101.

Captain Creswell Archer is available for deep-sea fishing and sightseeing out of Marsh Harbour. ☎ 242-367-4000 for reservations.

Orthnell Russell, the "Bonefish King," is in Treasure Cay. Contact the Treasure Cay Marina, ☎ 242-367-2570, or in Copper's Town, ☎ 242-365-0125.

The King Fish II, Treasure Cay. Sportfishing daily. ☎ 242-367-2570.

Lincoln Jones, Green Turtle Cay, ☎ 242-365-4223.

Joe Sawyer, Green Turtle Cay, ☎ 242-365-4173.

Trevor Sawyer, Cherokee, ☎ 242-366-2065.

■ Diving & Snorkeling

 The Abacos have plenty of coral reefs and ancient shipwrecks to explore. Or just float around close to the surface and watch the thousands of brightly colored fish, crabs and other marine life.

From Walker's Cay to Sandy Point, the shoreline of the Abacos offers a huge and varied assortment of shallow flats, sand banks, patch reefs, and fringe and barrier reefs. Diving is mostly done in shallow waters, six to 15 feet deep, easily within the scope of inexperienced snorkelers. Visibility ranges, according to depth, up to a couple of hundred feet. The coral structures, which include everything from sea fans to brain coral, and from antlers to tubes, are often fissured, undercut and dotted with mysterious blue holes. Everywhere there is a never-ending parade of reef and pelagic (deep-sea) fish of every color imaginable. Add to that a dozen or so wreck sites and you have an underwater enthusiast's dream come true.

Best Dive Sites

It's generally acknowledged that the best diving in the Abacos is between its eastern shores and the long line of cays on the 150-mile eastern barrier reef. For snorkelers, almost every beach throughout the archipelago offers something special.

Marsh Harbour

- **The Towers.** Huge coral pinnacles extend upward some 60 feet from the ocean floor and are riddled with spectacular tunnels and caverns.

- **The Cathedral**, a huge cavern where shafts of sunlight filter through, splashing the seabed with color.

- **Grouper Alley**, where, in 40 feet of unclouded water, great coral heads are honeycombed with tunnels.

- **Wayne's World**, where the water approaches 70 feet in depth, and you can take a thrilling excursion along the outer wall of the barrier reef.

Pelican Cays National Land & Sea Park

Located just north of Cherokee Sound, this is a 2,100-acre undersea wildlife refuge where you'll swim among coral heads, dive into undersea caves, and visit with gaily colored fish and other reef dwellers. Pelican Cays incorporates the only inshore fringed reef in the Abacos and is home to some 170 different species of marine life, including green turtles and spotted eagle rays.

Green Turtle Cay

Green Turtle Cay is located some three miles off the northeast coast of Great Abaco, , a tiny island that measures no more than three and a half miles long by a half-mile wide. It has a coastline of small bays, inlets and sandy beaches, along with excellent diving.

- **Coral Canyons** is a series of great canyons with an overhang that goes back into the reef some 60 to 80 feet. Often filled with huge schools of silver fish, the site provides great opportunities for underwater photography.

- **The Catacombs**, another great site for underwater photography, is a shallow, sunlit cavern.

- **Coral Condos**, in 60 to 70 feet of clear water, are a series of huge coral heads that provide homes for dozens of brilliantly colored reef fish.

- **Tarpon Reef**, another magnificent series of coral formations, is home to a school of tarpon from which it gets its name, as well as a large green moray eel. The wrecks of the *Viceroy* and the *San Jacinto* (see *Shipwrecks*, pages 168-69) lie in some 30 to 50 feet of water and, although scattered over a wide area, present some unique photographic opportunities.

Walker's Cay

Accessible only by private plane or boat or through the services offered by the Walker's Cay Hotel and Marina, this is the northernmost of the chain of islands that makes up the Abacos. Because of its splendid isolation and inaccessibility, the island enjoys a reputation for fine diving and there's no shortage of facilities, guides, or support. Walker's Cay Undersea Adventures (see *Dive Operators*, page 172) will provide expert guides, rental gear, and instruction. The diving off Walker's Cay features bank, fringe and patch reefs, as well as drop-offs. It's dense with coral formations in shallow waters, crowded with marine life and, because of its isolation, is a world unspoiled and now well protected.

Spectacular dive sites can be found throughout the area. These include:

- **Spiral Caverns**, a dramatic series of caverns in less than 50 feet of water that meander through vast coral formations filled with clouds of silver minnows.

- **Pirates' Cathedral** is a magnificent reef cavern with a series of chambers and openings filled with fish and other marine life.

The Abacos

- **Barracuda Alley**, the home of Charlie, a scary-looking, six-foot barracuda, provides a dive through 45 feet of water into a canyon-like coral reef formation.

- **Shark Canyon**. A dive through almost 100 feet of crystalline water and coral formations into a canyon, where sleeping sharks can often be found on the sandy bottom.

Shipwrecks

Dozens of shipwrecks lie off the Abacos. Some of the wreck sites are spectacular; some are barely recognizable. Some are accessible only by private boat; others can be explored through the dive operators working out of Marsh Harbour, Hope Town, and Green Turtle Cay. Following is a list of some of the better known wrecks in the Abacos:

The USS Adirondack

The *USS Adirondack*, an Ossipee class, wooden, steam- and sail-driven sloop of 1,240 tons and 207 feet in length, was launched on February 22, 1862. Hers was a short life. She was a Federal gunboat, operating as a part of the South Atlantic Blockading Squadron, that went down on August 23, 1862 after running aground on the Little Bahama Bank during a voyage from Port Royal to Nassau. Every member of her crew was rescued, but attempts to salvage the ship failed. The wind and surf soon smashed her into pieces and she sank.

Today, there's not much left of her. What remains lies scattered in 10-30 feet of water over a wide area between No Name Cay and Man-O-War Cay. Two of her 11-inch guns, as well as several other smaller guns, can still be seen, but that's about all. The wreck can be reached via either Dive Abaco or Dave Malone at the Hope Town Dive Shop (see page 172). Dave will tell you that it's hardly worth the effort. Even so, if you're a Civil War buff, the *Adirondack* offers at least some historic significance.

The USS San Jacinto

The *USS San Jacinto* was also a Civil War gunboat. Launched on April 16, 1850, she was an experimental ship – one of the first to be powered by steam and sail. Unfortunately, her engines were not as reliable as those used in later ships and were a problem throughout her service. At the time of her demise she was employed as a part of the blockade against the Confederate ports on the east coast of the US. She ran aground off Chub Rocks on New Year's Day, 1865. In her time, although plagued by her unreliable machinery, she was credited with the capture of such Confederate blockade runners as the *Lizzie Davis*, the *Roebuck*, the *Fox* and others.

Today, what little remains of the *San Jacinto* lies scattered over a wide area in some 40 feet of water. Her superstructure is all gone, smashed to pieces by 145 years of pounding surf. She can be explored with Brendal's Dive International Shop of Green Turtle Cay (☎ 800-780-9941).

The Viceroy

The *Viceroy*, a turn-of-the-century steamship, lies in about 50 feet of water close to Chub Rocks, not far from the wreck of the *San Jacinto*. The ship's engines and props are still intact and make for some great close-up photography.

The Viceroy is also the home of "Pickles," a seven-foot green moray eel who likes to be fed tidbits.

The H.M.S. Mermaid

The *H.M.S. Mermaid* set sail from Charleston, South Carolina on December 1, 1759, bound for New Providence; she never made it. On the morning of December 4th, fighting gale force winds and heavy seas, she found herself driven relentlessly toward the breakers. In a futile attempt to save his ship, Captain James Hackman tried three times to anchor her, and each time the ropes snapped under the force of the storm. For hours, the captain and crew fought to save the ship. The heavy guns were thrown overboard in a last-ditch attempt to lighten the ship and float it over the reef; it was not enough. The *Mermaid* finally ran aground about a half-mile offshore. For almost a month, the ship lay on the rocks, the surf pounding at her hull. Finally, on January 6, 1760, she broke up and sank; her remains were to lie undiscovered for 227 years until 1987, when Carl Fismer of the Spanish Main Treasure Company found her resting in only 10 feet of water. Fismer, using a magnetometer, first found one of her anchors, then another. Then, one by one, he found her long-abandoned guns and, finally, what was left of her hull among the rocks and sand off Mermaid Beach.

The wreck is easily accessible to both divers and snorkelers, and can be reached via a guided tour by Gary Adkinson and Barry Albury at the Walker's Cay Hotel and Marina Dive Shop. ☎ 800-327-8150.

The Abacos

The Bonita

The *Bonita,* an English World War II transport vessel, was sunk in a location known only to Brendal Stevens of Brendal's Dive Shop, is now a grouper feeding station in 60 feet of water and is included in Brendal's schedule of dive sites.

The Barge

This wreck consists of the scattered remains of an old landing craft in 40 feet of water off Fiddle Cay.

The Demira

A 411-foot steel-hulled freighter that sank during a hurricane in 1928, she lies in 30 feet of water and is accessible to both scuba divers and snorkelers.

Best Snorkeling Sites

 Nine hotels in the Abacos participate in the Jean Michel Cousteau "Snorkeling Adventures" program (see page 48). All are featured at the http://oii.net website.

- **Abaco Inn**, Elbow Cay, ☎ 800-468-8799
- **Bluff House Club**, Green Turtle Cay, ☎ 800-688-4752
- **Great Abaco Beach Resort**, Marsh Harbour, ☎ 800-468-4799
- **Green Turtle Club**, Green Turtle Cay, ☎ 800-688-4752
- **Guana Beach Resort**, ☎ 800-227-3366
- **Hope Town Harbour Lodge**, Elbow Cay, ☎ 800-316-7844
- **Pelican Beach Villas**, Marsh Harbour, ☎ 800-642-7268
- **Spanish Cay Inn**, Cooperstown, ☎ 800-688-4752
- **Walker's Cay Hotel**, ☎ 800-WALKERS

The best sites are as follows:

Angelfish Reef

An area of the reef where angelfish school in large numbers. The water here is less than 20 feet deep; it's ideal for beginners.

Blue Strip Reef

Spawning grounds for a variety of reef fish. Lots of colorful underwater formations. Large schools of blue striped grunts.

Crawfish Shallows

A fun place to visit, great for lobsters and the occasional sleeping nurse shark.

Elkhorn Park

A vast area of reef with acres of elk and staghorn corals. Lots of colorful reef fish, and lots of octopus. Coral heads are close to the surface.

Fowl Cay Reef

A large expanse of coral reef just a few minutes swim from the beach. Many interesting formations, and a large friendly grouper named "Gillie."

Hope Town Reef

An area of reef with lots of soft and hard corals, multitudes of colorful reef fish. Great for beginners.

Jeanette's Reef

Lots of small invertebrates, schools of colorful fish, and the occasional marauding barracuda.

Meghan's Mesa

An area where you can see a variety of soft and hard corals, all sorts of little critters, and lots of plume worms.

Pirates Cathedral

A labyrinth of caverns and underwater arches, all safe to swim through. Great for experienced snorkelers.

Pelican Park

This is a great site to observe sea turtles and eagle rays, along with a wide variety of other marine life.

Smugglers Rest

Lots of fun to be had here. The remains of a plane wreck, now home to all sorts of marine life.

Spanish Cannon

Very little is left of the Spanish galleon that sank here on the reef. Look for the cannon scattered among the ballast stones.

Sandy Cay Reef

A great place to observe some of the larger inhabitants of the coral reef: southern stingrays, spotted eagle rays, etc.

Dive Operators

Dive Abaco

Marsh Harbour, Abaco, Bahamas. ☎ 800-247-5338, fax 242-367-2787, www.diveabaco.com. Dive Abaco, a small operation catering to divers and snorkelers, has been in business for more than 15 years and operates out of a wooden building on the waterfront at the Conch Inn, East Bay Street.. They have a staff of four, including two instructors, and their boat can carry up to 12 divers. Dive Abaco's retail store sells snorkel gear, accessories, and carries 35 sets of rental gear. The company is affiliated with NAUI, PADI, and CMAS.

Brendal's Dive Center International

Green Turtle Cay, Abaco, Bahamas. ☎ 800-780-9941, www.brendal.com. Brendal Stevens, in business now for more than 10 years, offers instruction and a variety of specialized and individual tours. There is an all-day dive, snorkel, and glass-bottom boat tour, plus a sailing trip to a secluded island with a seafood cookout. The shop offers two-tank morning dives, one-tank afternoon dives, and night dives (by special arrangement). The operation has two boats: a new custom dive boat with capacity of up to 24 passengers and a smaller boat with capacity of 12. There's a staff of three, including an instructor. The shop store sells a full range of gear and accessories, and it carries 30 sets of rental gear. Brendal's is affiliated with SSI, CMAS, and NAUI.

Walker's Cay Undersea Adventures

PO Box 21766, Ft. Lauderdale, FL 33335. ☎ 800-327-8150, www.nealwatson.com. With more than 21 years in business, they offer a wide range of diving options: two-tank dives in the morning and afternoon, two night dives each week, and shark dives three times a week. The outfit has a staff of six, including four instructors, and two boats with capacities of 16-25 passengers. The company store sells gear and accessories and keeps 15 sets of rental gear on hand. Walker's Cay Undersea is affiliated with PADI, SSI, NAUI, and YMCA.

The Dive Shop

Great Abaco Beach Resort, Marsh Harbour, Abaco, Bahamas. ☎ 800-468-4799, wwwabacoresort.com. This is operated by Doug Laurie, who offers diving and snorkeling excursions for novice and experienced divers.

The Hope Town Dive Shop

Hope Town, Abaco, Bahamas. ☎ 242-366-0029. A fully equipped shop: B/Cs, regulators, masks, fins, belts, and boat rentals.

Dive/Accommodation Packages

Dive packages are offered by several hotels on the Abacos, including those listed below. The rates quoted are, unless otherwise stated, per person, double occupancy, and were current at the time of writing. Credit cards are accepted unless otherwise stated.

The Conch Inn

Marsh Harbour, Abaco, Bahamas. ☎ 800-247-5338, fax 242-367-4004. This package includes professionally guided scuba diving trips from Dive Abaco's full-service dive shop, tank and weights, two dives per day, hotel accommodations, and use of the fresh-water pool. The package does not include airfare, meals, taxes, or gratuities.

- 5 days/4 nights (includes 3 days of diving): $396
- 8 days/7 nights (includes 4 days of diving): $572

Pelican Beach Villas

Marsh Harbour, Abaco, Bahamas. ☎ 800-642-7268, www.pelicanbeachvillas.com. The package includes a two-bedroom/two-bath air-conditioned beachfront villa with a living room, full kitchen, dishwasher and 8% tax. Also included are professionally guided two-tank dives, two days with Dive Abaco (extra two-tank dives are $60); a free Wednesday or Sunday night cookout at the Jib Room; free beach chairs; private beach; on-site caretaker and maid service; and a welcome bottle of champagne. Airfare, transfers, meals and beverages (other than those indicated), and staff gratuities are not included.

- 4 nights/2 persons: $899 (extra person $50)
- 7 nights/2 persons: $1,199 (extra person $50)

WORD TO THE WISE

A special airfare is available, either from Miami or Fort Lauderdale, for $150 per person, plus $15 tax. Airlines serving Marsh Harbour are US Air Express, American Eagle, Gulfstream, and Bahamasair (see page 351-52).

Schooner's Landing Resort

Man-O-War Cay, Abaco, Bahamas. ☎ 242-365-6072, fax 242-365-6285, e-mail info@schoonerslanding.com. Fly into Marsh Harbour, take a taxi to the ferry dock and ride the ferry to Man-O-War Cay, where you will be met by a Schooner's Landing Resort representative. They offer two packages based upon a four-person occupancy. The four-day package includes a fully equipped beachfront, two-bedroom townhouse with maid service; a 20-foot boat for two days to explore the surrounding islands or dive the national parks; a one-day professionally guided dive trip (two-tank dive); one full tank per person each day for two days; boxed lunches for three days; evening meals; use of a private dock; gratuities, and hotel taxes. The eight-day package includes all the above plus use of the 20-foot boat for five days and one full tank per person for five days. Packages do not include air fare, fuel for the boat, taxi and ferry transportation, snorkel gear, regulator, and B/C. Visa/Mastercard and American Express charges are subject to a 5% surcharge.

- 4 days/3 nights: $1,450
- 8 days/7 nights: $2,225

The Green Turtle Club

Green Turtle Cay, Abaco, Bahamas. ☎ 800-780-9941, www.greenturtleclub.com. Fly into Treasure Cay Airport, take the ferry to Green Turtle Cay and disembark at the Green Turtle Club. The lobby is just a few yards in front of you. Airlines serving Treasure Cay are USAir Express, American Eagle, Gulfstream, Island Express, and Bahamasair (see page 349 for contacts). The club offers a wide variety of dive package options for all seasons. Included in all rates are luxury accommodations at the Green Turtle Yacht Club, use of the freshwater swimming pool, windsurfing, beach chairs, tennis, two daily dive trips to the reefs or wrecks, tanks, back pack, weight belts, and a welcome drink. Not included are air fares, meals, transfers, the ferry from and to Treasure Cay, and airport departure taxes. Diving is with Brendal's Dive Shop on Green Turtle Cay, close to the Green Turtle Yacht Club. Call the toll-free number for rates.

Walker's Cay Hotel and Marina

Walker's Cay, Abaco, Bahamas. ☎ 800-327-8150. Walker's Cay Hotel and Marina operates its own plane service out of Fort Lauderdale. Dive packages include round-trip airfare from Fort Lauderdale; transfers to and from the hotel; deluxe air-conditioned accommodations; breakfast and dinner daily; three dives per day (two in the morning and one in the afternoon); tank, weights and belt; room taxes, maid, and MAP meal gratuities. Not included are bar charges, incidentals, US and Bahamian departure taxes. Non-divers may deduct $40 per night from the above. Private pilots may deduct $150 from the packages rate. Call the toll-free number for rates.

Dive packages are also offered by the following:

Marsh Harbour

- **Lofty Fig Villas** (☎ 242-367-2681)
- **Abaco Towns by the Sea** (☎ 242-367-2227)

Green Turtle Cay

- **Bluff House** (☎ 242-365-4246)
- **Coco Bay Cottages** (☎ 800-752-0166)

Hope Town

- **Hope Town Hideaways** (☎ 242-366-0030)

Where to Stay & Eat

Restaurant Price Scale	
$	less than $20 per person
$$	$20-$50 per person
$$$	$50+ per person

■ Dining

Elbow Cay

$$ The Abaco Inn Restaurant on White Sound is open to the public for breakfast, lunch and dinner. Free transportation is provided to and from Hope Town, so give them a call to get the ferry times – you'll need to make a reservation anyway. Conch fritters, conch salad, lobster, dolphin, grouper and rack of lamb are a few of the items you're likely to find on the evening menu.

\$\$ Club Soleil is at Hope Town Marina across the water from the Hope Town itself, so you'll need a boat to get there. If you don't have one, the restaurant will provide transportation. Located under the famous candy striped lighthouse, Club Soleil specializes in continental cuisine and fresh fish, with a champagne brunch on Sundays.

\$-\$\$ Captain Jack's is a great little waterfront café next to Hope Town Harbour. They serve breakfast, lunch, and dinner on the veranda in an easy-going atmosphere. Specialties include seafood of all sorts, home-made bread, and even turtle burgers.

\$-\$\$ The Harbour's Edge, as its name indicates, is right on the waterfront in Hope Town where you can enjoy a fine view. The restaurant, with its inside bar, is a popular watering hole for nautical types and locals alike. The food is always good, and the specialties include crawfish salad, conch chowder, and gullywings (chicken wings). Happy Hour is 5 pm until 6 pm. The restaurant is open for lunch and dinner only.

\$\$ Hope Town Harbour Lodge in Hope Town is a good spot for a quiet breakfast on the veranda, lunch by the pool, or candlelight dining in an intimate atmosphere. There is also a Sunday champagne brunch with fresh seafood, roast beef, and chicken.

\$\$ Reef Bar & Grill at the Hope Town Harbour Lodge is open for lunch, Monday through Saturday, and the bar is open from 4 pm. Ocean and poolside dining features Bahamian specialties, including conch burgers and complimentary conch fritters.

\$\$ Rudy's Place is about a mile from Hope Town and is open for dinner only. They do provide free transportation from the town and from many of the hotels, so you'll need to make a reservation. The atmosphere is simple but the food is always good and you can expect to find lamb, steak, turtle, and fresh fish on the menu, all complemented by excellent home-made bread.

Great Guana Cay

\$\$ The Guana Beach Resort Restaurant serves breakfast to hotel guests only, but opens up to everyone for lunch and dinner. Lunch can be eaten on the pool deck or inside. The dinner menu includes an assortment of Bahamian dishes, as well as fish, chicken, and steak.

Green Turtle Cay

$$ The Bluff House Restaurant sits on a hill overlooking White Sound and is a romantic spot for a candlelight dinner with breathtaking views of the ocean and the lights of New Plymouth in the distance. Your dinner includes complimentary wine and the menu offers a range of dishes such as fresh lobster, prime rib and roast duck. The restaurant provides free transportation to and from New Plymouth, and from hotels and boats.

$$ The Green Turtle Club is also on White Sound. Breakfast and lunch are served outdoors on the patio. Dinner is served at a single sitting at 7 pm in the opulent dining room. Reservations must be made before 5 pm. The menu offers a choice of three entrées each evening, which might include lobster, duck, chicken, veal, or prime rib.

$ Laura's Kitchen is on King Street in New Plymouth. You can eat inside or take out your order. The restaurant serves conch, fish, chicken, conch burgers, and ice cream.

$$ The New Plymouth Inn Restaurant is just across the way from the Sculpture Garden, right in the center of Hope Town. It is one of Hope Town's popular gathering places. You'll need to make a reservation, as the dining room is small and intimate. Dinner is served in a single sitting at 7:30 pm, and the menu will include a choice of three entrées.

$ Plymouth Rock Café is at the end of Parliament Street on the main government dock. The café is open only from 9 am until 3 pm, serving sandwiches and burgers at the counter.

$ The Rooster's Rest, over the hill near the school on Loyalist Road in New Plymouth, is open for lunch and dinner and serves local dishes, including conch cooked several ways and fresh fish.

$$ The Sea View Restaurant is on the south side of New Plymouth on Loyalist Road. Lunch is served from 10 am until 3 pm. Dinner is served from 5 pm until the last customer decides it's time to leave. You have a choice of both Bahamian and American cuisine.

$$ The Wrecking Tree, on New Plymouth Harbour, is open for breakfast, lunch and dinner. This is the place to enjoy a beer, or any one of a range of exotic tropical drinks. Specialties include Bahamian pastries, conch salad, and chicken.

Man-O-War Cay

Albury's Bakery is in a private home just across the way from the Man-O-War Grocery on Queen's Highway. They sell some of the best bread, home-made pies, and conch fritters on the islands. Call ahead to place your order.

$$ The Man-O-War Pavillion is an open-air reastaurant at the harbour. The menu is mostly Bahamian and includes a variety of seafood dishes – conch, grouper, dolphin, shrimp – along with chicken, burgers and an assortment of side orders. On a fine day, this can be a very relaxing dining experience.

■ Accommodations

Hotel Meal Plans

- **CP** (Continental Plan) includes a continental breakfast.
- **EP** (European Plan) denotes no meals, although restaurant facilities are available either on the property or nearby.
- **MAP** (Modified American Plan) denotes breakfast and dinner.
- **FAP** (Full American Plan) includes all meals.
- **All-Inc.** (All-Inclusive Plan) includes all meals, beverages (alcoholic and soft), watersports, tennis and golf, if available.

Elbow Cay

Hope Town Harbour Lodge sits on top of a bluff and, though still "in town," is just as close to the harbour as it is to the beach. The view from the Lodge is one of the best on the island. Some of the rooms are in the main building, some in quaint little cottages by the water, and some in the Butterfly House, one of the oldest buildings in Hope Town. Some rooms are air-conditioned. The others are cooled by soft breezes blowing in from the ocean and, except on the hottest days, remain comfortable throughout the year. The rate is $100 per night for one person, $115-135 for two, and $125-145 for three people. MAP is $33 extra per night. ☎ 800-316-7844, or write Hope Town Harbour Lodge, Hope Town, Abaco, Bahamas. www.hopetownlodge.com.

The Club Soleil at the Hope Town Marina is just across the harbour from Hope Town itself, so you'll need a boat or the ferry to get back and forth, but that's half the fun. From its romantic spot beneath Hope Town's famous candy-striped lighthouse, you have a fine view of the harbour and the town itself. Lunch is served on a deck that surrounds the pool. There's also a great place to eat, the Club Soleil Restaurant, close by, or you can take the ferry over to town for your evening meal. The rate per night for up to two persons is $115, and for three persons it's $125. MAP will cost $32 per night extra. ☎ 242-366-0003, or write Club Soleil Resort, Hope Town, Abaco, Bahamas.

The Abaco Inn is two miles south of Hope Town on Queen's Highway. It lies on a narrow ridge with the ocean at one side and White Sound at the other. This small hotel offers 12 guest units, six on the ocean side and six with harbour views. Some units are air-conditioned. There is a pool built right into the coral rock, hammocks for two, and a fleet of bicycles for guests to use free of charge. Complimentary transportation is provided into Hope Town. The rate is $120 per night for one person, $135 for two, and $155 for three. MAP is $33 extra per night. ☎ 800-468-8799 or write Abaco Inn, Hope Town, Abaco, Bahamas. http://oii.net/abacoinn.

Hope Town Hideaways is one of the newest and most luxurious accommodations on the island. Each of the four large, air-conditioned villas has a modern kitchen, breakfast bar, dining room, living room, and wrap-around deck so you can follow the sun – or stay in the shade – all day long if you wish. The villas are set on 11 landscaped acres across the water from Hope Town. The views of the town, harbour, and lighthouse are spectacular and, although Hope Town is a short boat ride away, you are within easy reach of shops, restaurants, and beaches. Rates start at around $140 per night, per person, and go up to $220 per night, EP only. ☎ 242-366-0224, or write Hope Town Hideaways, One Purple Porpoise Place, Hope Town, Abaco, Bahamas. www.hopetown.com.

The Sea Spray Resort & Villas is at the south end of the island about three miles from town on White Sound. The resort offers a selection of one- and two-bedroom ocean-view cottages and villas, all with air-conditioning and daily maid service. Each unit has a deck and a barbecue pit. The beach is a bit rocky, but has lots of character. You'll have the use of a Sunfish sailboat or windsurfer, free of charge, and you can rent a bike just down the road at the Abaco Inn. The resort is a great place for hiking, too. Hope Town is just an hour away on foot, and Tahiti Beach less than 30 minutes. Fly into Marsh Harbour

The Abacos

and take the ferry over to Elbow Cay; transfer from the dock to the resort is free. The daily rate per person is $150; EP only, but you can arrange to have your meals catered. ☎ 242-366-0065, or write the Sea Spray Resort, White Sound, Elbow Cay, Abaco, Bahamas. www.seasprayresort.com.

Great Abaco & Marsh Harbour

$-$$ The Conch Inn Restaurant at the marina is a popular gathering place for all sorts of interesting people, many of them sailors. Some are locals; others are visitors. The semi-outdoor, harbour-view dining room and bar, with its rustic décor and yachting memorabilia, has a beachcomber, waterfront atmosphere. It's relaxed and easy going – canvas shorts, colored shirts, and sandals are the standard dress. The restaurant is open for breakfast, lunch, and dinner. The menu offers a wide variety, mostly Bahamian, of ocean-fresh seafood, including conch salad, cracked conch, and lobster; or you can have steak or chops. ☎ 242-367-4000.

$$ Angler's Restaurant, at the Boat Harbour Marina, specializes both in Bahamian and American cuisine. If you want to enjoy a quiet drink at the poolside you can drop in at the Sand Bar, or go indoors for a little mother's ruin (gin) at Penny's Pub. Both are close by. ☎ 242-367-2158.

$$ Café La Florence. Located on Queen Elizabeth Drive, just across from Memorial Plaza, La Florence is open for breakfast, lunch and dinner, Monday through Saturday. Specialties include a variety of Bahamian dishes, lots of fresh seafood, including lobster and grouper, and a wide selection of fresh-baked goodies.

$$ The Castle Café is a charming little restaurant set high on a hill overlooking Marsh Harbour and the ocean. Unfortunately, they are open only for lunch, which is served daily from 11 am until 5 pm on the terrace. The house itself is a large, old-world mansion. It's a gathering spot for the locals and for the sailing fraternity. Home-made specialties, including wonderful soups, seafood salads, and sandwiches, are all prepared by the owner.

$ The Golden Grouper is in Dove Plaza. Open Monday through Saturday from 7 am until 3 pm daily for breakfast and lunch. It serves Cuban, Chinese, and Bahamian dishes.

$ The Main Street Grill at Royal Harbour specializes in fried chicken, home-made burgers, and gourmet potatoes. Open daily from 11 am until 10 pm.

This is a great place to take the kids for a quiet family meal.

$ Kool Scoops is *the* ice cream parlor in the Abacos. Located in downtown Marsh Harbour, next to the Canadian Imperial Bank, Kool Scoops offers a wide selection of flavors and an air-conditioned dining room. Open from 11 am until 10 pm, Monday through Saturday, and from 1 pm until 10 pm on Sunday.

$$ The Bayview Restaurant is on the water in Marsh Harbour, a mile west of the traffic light. Specialties include seafood and prime rib. Open daily for lunch and dinner from 11 am until 11 pm; champagne brunch is served on Sunday from 11:30 am until 3:30 pm. The restaurant has an all-tide dinghy dock.

$ The Sand Bar is a popular gathering spot at the Abaco Beach Resort. There's a pool with a swim-up bar. Snacks are available from 11 am until late, but you can also choose from a full bar menu. The specialty is frozen tropical drinks.

$$ The Jib Room is just across the water from the Conch Inn and is open for lunch daily and for dinner Wednesday through Sunday. You'll enjoy your meal on the waterfront at an umbrella-covered table in a Bahamian, rustic-garden atmosphere.

$$ Mangoes on the waterfront, just across the road from the Lofty Fig, is another of Marsh Harbour's institutions. The restaurant is open for lunch and dinner every day except Sunday, specializing in burgers and fresh seafood at lunchtime and candlelight dinners in the evening. The bar on the waterside veranda is the ideal spot for an evening drink while watching the sun go down.

$ The Tiki Hut on Bay Street near the Conch Inn is the place to go for American sandwiches, burgers and Bahamian dishes.

$$ Wally's, across the road from and facing the harbour, is the most famous restaurant in Marsh Harbour. The colonial-style, two-story building is reminiscent of a pink-and-white Southern mansion. Dine inside or outside on the veranda, but first sit at the bar and enjoy one of Marine's or Barbara's special island drinks. The Bahamian cooks specialize in local cuisine and, so they say, "you can't get fish any fresher anywhere in the Bahamas. It comes straight from the boat and into the kitchen." Try the fried grouper or, better yet, the coconut curried wahoo. If you don't like seafood, they also offer a number of beef and poultry dishes.

$ Mother Merle's, on Dundas Road about two miles north of the stoplight, is open for dinner only. Bahamian specialties include conch salad, cracked conch, chicken, home-made pies, and fresh fish. No credit cards.

Great Guana Cay

The Guana Beach Resort is the place where you can get away from life in the fast lane. There are no telephones or television sets in the guest rooms, but all are air-conditioned and some even have kitchens. There's also a bar and a restaurant that specializes in exceptional seafood. You can eat outside on the deck if you wish. Set back among the palms, the hotel is on a small peninsula with the marina on one side and the bay on the other. There are seven miles of deserted beaches, the crystal waters of the ocean, a fleet of Sunfish sailboats for guests to use free of charge, and an abundance of opportunities for snorkeling, fishing, shelling or exploring. The ferry makes pickups twice each day in Marsh Harbour, which is only a few minutes ride from the airport. The rate for up to two persons per night is $140 and $150 for three persons. MAP is $35 per night extra. ☎ 242-365-5133 or write to Guana Beach Resort, PO Box 474, Marsh Harbour, Abaco, Bahamas. www.guanabeach.com.

Green Turtle Cay

The New Plymouth Inn is in the heart of New Plymouth on Parliament Street among the shops and galleries and only a short walk away from the beach. Once the home of sea Captain Billy Roberts, the restored 150-year-old building has 10 comfortable guest rooms, each with private bath, some with canopied beds and some with twin beds. The hotel also has a bar and dining room, a saltwater pool, and a landscaped garden entrance with a wrought-iron table and chairs. The room rate is $85 per night for one person, $120 for two, and $180 for three persons MAP. ☎ 242-365-4161 for reservations, or write New Plymouth Inn, Green Turtle Cay, Abaco, Bahamas.

The Green Turtle Club & Marina is at the end of White Sound, north of New Plymouth. It's a place known around the world in yachting circles. The walls of the tiny bar and lounge are papered with autographed dollar bills – thousands of them – and the ceiling is hung with yacht club pennants of all shapes and sizes. Dinner at the Green Turtle Club is an experience in itself. Guests are escorted into an elegant, formal dining room for the single-sitting meal, and are served a series of delicious courses in candlelit splendor. Outside, the club's tiny strip of private beach faces the sun and the harbour where dozens of boats, large and small, bob at anchor. The guest rooms are devoid of phones and television sets, but all are air-conditioned and all have private decks with views of the harbour or sound. At night, you'll wend your way along a dimly lighted path from your room to the lounge or dining room. From Treasure Cay, take a taxi to the dock and then the ferry over to Green Turtle Cay. The rate for one or two persons per night is $145 and for three, $165. MAP is an extra $36 per night. ☎ 242-365-4271, or write The Green Turtle Club, PO Box 270, Green Turtle Cay, Abaco, Bahamas. www.greenturtleclub.com.

The Bluff House Hotel & Marina is up on a hill overlooking White Sound and offers fine views of the island and the town of New Plymouth in the distance. The hotel has 30 guest accommodations, including rooms, suites and villas. All are air-conditioned, have private porches, and views of the water. The clubhouse, overlooking the pool and the ocean, is decorated with original paintings and framed posters. Guests can use the tennis courts free of charge, and the staff will arrange diving and fishing trips. Daytime boat rides to New Plymouth are also free for guests. The daily room rate is $90 for up to two persons, and $125 for three people. MAP is $34 extra per day. ☎ 242-365-4247, or write Bluff House, Green Turtle Cay, Abaco, Bahamas. e-mail info@bluffhouse.com, www.bluffhouse.com.

Man-O-War Cay

Schooner's Landing sits on the water's edge a short walk from the marina. Each of the resort's two-story units has two bedrooms, two baths, and comes fully equipped with all the amenities you expect to find at a luxury resort, including a beach far away from the crowds and smell of the city. With no motor vehicles on the island except for those of the utilities, you must walk everywhere, but that's a large part of the resort's appeal. Nowhere is more than a mile away and the fresh air and splendid views, not to mention the exercise you'll get, are food for the soul. To get to Man-O-War, fly into Marsh Harbour, take a taxi to the ferry dock and then ride over to the island, where a representative from the resort will meet you. The rate per person per night is $150, EP only. ☎ 242-365-6072, or write Schooner's Landing, Man-O-War Cay, Abaco, Bahamas. http://oii.net/schooners.

Marsh Harbour

Island Breezes Motel is a small, but comfortable hotel with air-conditioned rooms that feature ceiling fans, televisions, refrigerators, and microwave ovens. There's no restaurant, but meals are available at a number of nearby eateries. The room rate is $75 per night, EP only. ☎ 242-367-3776.

The Conch Inn at Marsh Harbour is on the waterfront, East Bay Street, less than 10 minutes from the airport, and only five minutes from the ferry dock. There are 10 rooms, each with a view of the water, twin beds, private baths, televisions, and air-conditioning, but no telephones. The hotel restaurant, open for breakfast, lunch and dinner, is something of an institution and watering hole for locals and visitors. The room rate is $85 per night for one or two persons, and $95 for three persons, EP only. ☎ 242-367-4000 for reservations, or write to The Conch Inn, PO Box 434, Marsh Harbour, Abaco, Bahamas. www.go-abacos.com/conchinn.

Pelican Beach Villas, a small resort on Pelican Shores across from Marsh Harbour Marina, offers five comfortable, two-bedroom, two-bathroom villas, each with a full kitchen, living room, and private deck on the beachfront. With all the amenities of Marsh Harbour and its marina close by, you'll always have plenty to see and do, from deep-sea fishing to scuba diving, and from boating to hiking. The resort is only minutes away from the airport and ferry dock, where you can take a sightseeing trip around the islands. The rate is $145 per night for one person, $160 for two, and $175 for three; EP only. The weekly rate is $975, with an additional $75 per extra person. To make reservations, ☎ 800-642-7268, or write Pelican Beach Villas, PO Box AB20304, Marsh Harbour, Abaco, Bahamas. www.pelicanbeachvillas. com.

Abaco Beach Resort & Boat Harbour in Marsh Harbour adjoins Boat Harbour Marina. It's a modern hotel with an extensive range of facilities. The opulent rooms and two-bedroom villas, all facing the pool, beach and/or the marina, have air-conditioning, satellite television, telephones (a real luxury in the Abacos), balconies and well-lit dressing areas. You'll find there's lots to see and do. You can rent a boat at the marina and go exploring by yourself, take a guided boat trip around the nearby islands, or go deep-sea fishing or scuba diving. You can stroll the waterfront and pristine beaches, go shelling in front of the hotel, or grab a bike and head off into town or down the road for a day of sightseeing. There is also a fine restaurant with a five-star chef in charge of the cuisine. The daily rate, depending upon the season, varies from a low of $95 per person for an ocean-view room to a high of $350 for what they call a "Grand Villa." Fly into Marsh Harbour and take a taxi to the resort. ☎ 800-468-4799, or write the

Great Abaco Beach Hotel, PO Box 511, Marsh Harbour, Abaco, Bahamas. www.abacoresort.com.

Spanish Cay

Spanish Cay Resort & Marina. If you're looking for something really different, this is it. Spanish Cay is a private island, a world away from civilization. Privacy is the essence of a vacation here. With more than 180 acres of tropical forests and mangroves, miles and miles of secluded beaches where the water is the palest jade, and the reef at the ocean's edge only a mile away, you'll find seclusion easily. That's not to say that you'll have to give up all those little luxuries that make for an enjoyable vacation. With its five luxury suites and seven apartments, the Inn is a small, self-contained resort with two restaurants, four tennis courts, and the outgoing atmosphere of a local yacht club. While on the island, you'll have the use of a golf cart and a set of snorkeling gear. You can hike around the island, go fishing, or rent a boat and spend your days on the water. To get there, fly into Treasure Cay and take a taxi to the ferry dock, where you'll find a boat waiting to take you over to Spanish Cay. The rate per night per person is $180; EP only. ☎ 800-688-4725, or write the Inn at Spanish Cay, PO Box 882, Cooper's Town, Abaco, Bahamas.

Treasure Cay (not an island; a peninsula)

Treasure Cay Hotel Resort & Marina. Located some 17 miles north of Marsh Harbour, Treasure Cay is home to one of the largest resorts in the Out Islands. It caters to a wide cross-section of adventurers: golfers, boaters, divers, bone fishermen and -women, and blue water anglers. The resort is a a diverse complex of hotel rooms, cottages and condos – some 95 units in all. All guest units are air-conditioned and come with mini-fridges, hair dryers, coffeemakers, and ironing gear; the larger, deluxe units have microwave ovens too. The villas, recently renovated, have full kitchens and washers and dryers. Some of the suites have loft bedrooms, some have marina views, all are nicely furnished and tastefully decorated. Perhaps the most unusual facility on the property is its 18-hole golf course, the only one in the Abacos. Golfers take note: if you're looking for something really different, give this one a try. Also of note to blue water anglers is the resort's Annual Treasure Cay International Billfish Tournament held in June each year (call ☎ 800-224-2627 or visit www.treasurecayfishing.com for details). As to the rest of the property: the gardens are a riot of tropical color, the beach is spectacular, the restaurant menu includes cuisine from Europe and America, the bars serve just about any concoction you might be able to imagine. There's also a full service dive shop, six tennis courts, a 150-slip marina, and you can hire fishing guides and dive guides on the property. Treasure Cay, Abaco. ☎ 800-327-1584; fax 242-365-8847; www.treasurecay.com. Rates from $180 through $395. MAP available.

Walker's Cay

Walker's Cay Hotel & Marina provides the only accommodation on Walker's Cay. The 62 rooms and four villas make for a comfortable stay, although there are no telephones or televisions. The main house has a dining room, a shop, an indoor game room, and an indoor-outdoor bar. The island itself is a sportsman's paradise, and the hotel staff will be pleased to make arrangements for custom excursions to scuba dive, deep-sea fish, or shark dive. The nightly rate for two persons is $100, for three persons it's $120. MAP costs $32-50 extra per night. ☎ 800-925-5377; e-mail info@walkerscay@com, www.walkerscay.com.

Wood Cay

The Tangelo Hotel, on the main highway in Wood Cay, has 12 rooms with private baths, air-conditioning, ceiling fans, satellite TV, and complimentary pick-up for boaters in Fox Town, or from the airport. The restaurant, with its bar, is open for breakfast, lunch and dinner, specializing in Bahamian food such as stewed fish, conch salad, fresh grouper, and peas and rice. Fishing trips and guides can be arranged. The room rate is $66 per night, EP only. ☎ 242-359-6536 for reservations, or write to The Tangelo Hotel, PO Box 830, Cooper's Town, Abaco, Bahamas. http://oii.net/tangelo.

Andros

Andros, the largest island in the Bahamas, is even more laid-back than its neighbor to the north, Abaco. The island is some 104 miles long by 40 miles wide, with a population of about 8,000.

There are three main towns on Andros – **Nicholl's Town** to the north, **Fresh Creek** in the center of the island, and **Kemp's Bay** to the south. All three are accessible by boat, or by plane from Miami and Nassau. Lodging on the island runs the gamut from tidy little guest houses to grand resorts.

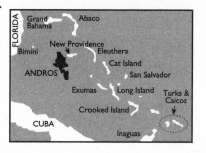

A diver's dream, Andros boasts the third largest barrier reef in the world, more than 120 miles long. From the reef, the ocean drops off to a depth of more than 6,000 feet. The reef, and its many mysterious blue holes, make Andros a popular destination for divers throughout the world.

DID YOU KNOW? *Blue holes are formed when subterranean limestone caverns collapsed to leave great, clear, deep-water basins in the shallow flats. They are magnets for all sorts of fish and marine life, as well as divers at every level of experience.*

Lost Treasures

An old legend says that pirate Captain Henry Morgan's treasure lies buried in one of the caves off Morgan's Bluff at the north end of the island. That, and a number of shipwrecks, provide possibilities for several interesting excursions.

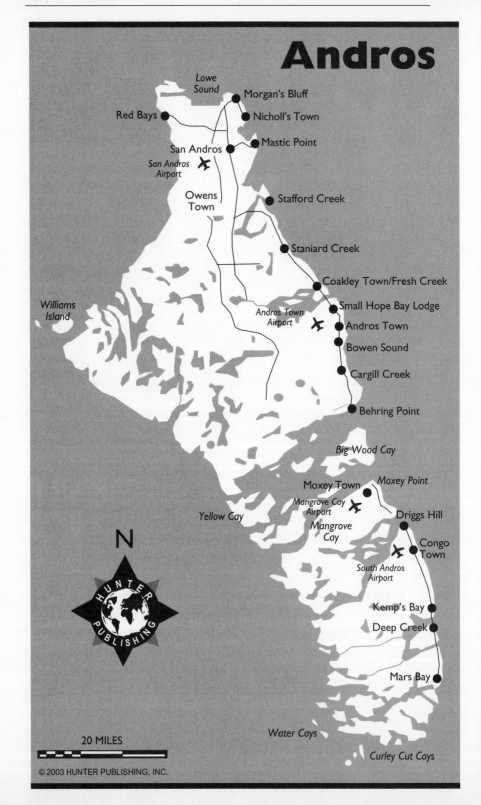

Andros

Lowe Sound

Morgan's Bluff

Red Bays

Nicholl's Town

Mastic Point

San Andros

San Andros Airport

Owens Town

Stafford Creek

Staniard Creek

Coakley Town/Fresh Creek

Small Hope Bay Lodge

Andros Town Airport

Andros Town

Williams Island

Bowen Sound

Cargill Creek

Behring Point

Big Wood Cay

Moxey Town

Moxey Point

Mangrove Cay Airport

Driggs Hill

Yellow Cay

Mangrove Cay

Congo Town

South Andros Airport

N

HUNTER PUBLISHING

Kemp's Bay

Deep Creek

Mars Bay

20 MILES

Water Cays

Curley Cut Cays

Andros is known as one of the world's finest deep-water fishing grounds. You can hunt great blue marlin, sailfish, bluefin tuna and the new hero of the shallow water flats, bonefish.

Geography & Wildlife

 The geography of Andros is both varied and interesting. The central portion of the island, known locally as the "The Big Yard," is densely forested with mahogany and pine. More than 50 varieties of orchids bloom in the undergrowth of The Big Yard. The west coast of the island, "The Mud," – actually part of the Great Bahama bank – is mostly marsh and scrub. The east coast flanks the great barrier reef. Southern Andros is where you'll find one of nature's last great mangrove forests in the Bahamas. The 40-square-mile tract is home to a variety of wild birds and animals, including the endangered Bahamian parrot, herons, egrets, lizards of every shape and size, iguanas that grow to more than six feet in length, and the Bahamian boa-constrictor – non-poisonous, but scary nonetheless. In the late spring each year, visitors are treated to a rare performance when the Andros land crabs migrate by the thousands from the forest to the sea.

In April of 2002 the Andros Conservancy and Trust (ANCAT) was successful in getting the Bahamas National Trust and the Bahamian government to declare a national park on the island of Andros – **The Central Andros National Park**. It encompasses the highest concentration of blue holes in the Bahamas, two portions of Andros Barrier Reef, a land crab management area, and North Bight mangrove/ wetland nursery. Approximate size: 288,000 acres.

Andros is guarded by one of the world's longest and best-preserved barrier reefs and houses the highest known density of blue holes in the world. Its extensive wetlands are of national, regional, and international importance and it boasts the "best bonefishing in the world." It provides critical habitat for endangered birds, crabs, and iguanas. It is also the country's largest reservoir of freshwater.

This first phase of park designation focuses on Central Andros – North Bight, Fresh Creek, Blanket Sound, Young Sound, and Staniard Creek – protecting forests, blue holes, coral reefs, wetlands, and mangroves, and paves the way for additional protection in the north and south. This park system will be co-managed by the Bahamas National Trust and the Andros Conservancy and Trust (ANCAT – www.ancat.org).

Chickcharnies

Andros is the place where, so they say, you'll find those funny little Bahamian gremlins known affectionately as Chickcharnies. These strange little creatures, with three toes and red eyes, are said to hang upside-down in the trees casting down good- or bad-luck spells upon passers-by, depending upon their mood.

History

 As with most of the islands in the Bahamas, Andros once was populated by the native **Lucayan Indians** and here, as elsewhere, the Indians became extinct not long after the **Europeans** landed.

For most of its history, little of note happened on Andros. It became a center for wrecking and a one-time base of operations for Captain Morgan, but it wasn't until 1845 that industry of any sort came to the island. That year, the **Andros Fibre Company** was established to manufacture sisal for use in the making of rope. The industry was short-lived, however. The poor quality of the soil contributed to the company's demise and, by the late 1920s, it had departed.

Next came timber production, but that too eventually died out, leaving the island with a serious unemployment problem and a system of roads almost beyond repair.

Then tourism arrived on the islands and things began to look up. Today, the tourist industry on Andros, while still in its infancy, is flourishing as more and more people discover the quiet beauty of this almost-deserted tropical paradise.

Getting There

■ By Air

Andros has four airports: to the north, **San Andros**; in the middle, **Andros Town**; and to the south, **Mangrove Cay** and **Congo Town**. All but Mangrove Cay are international ports of entry served by Bahamasair from Nassau, and several carriers from the mainland. The one-way fare from Nassau on Bahamasair to all airports on Andros is $45.

Visitors from Europe can travel from London and other major continental cities to make connections in the US through Miami, Atlanta, Orlando, and other cities. Also, your travel agent can hook you up with one of several package operators serving the United States and the Bahamas, such as British Airways Holidays, Thomas Cook, American Express Holidays (see page 350 for contacts).

Andros Town Airport	
Access to Cargill Creek, Behring Point & Fresh Creek	
FROM	**AIRLINE**
Nassau	**Bahamasair** operates regular daily schedules, ☎ 800-222-4262. Round-trip fare, $65.
Freeport	**Major Air**, ☎ 242-352-5778. Round-trip fare, $85.
Fort Lauderdale	**Island Express**, ☎ 954-359-0380. Round-trip fare, $230.
Miami	**Bahamasair** operates a daily schedule from Miami to Andros Town. Round-trip fare, $165.

Congo Town/South Andros Airport

Access to Driggs Hill

FROM	AIRLINE
Nassau	**Bahamasair** operates regular daily schedules, ☎ 800-222-4262. Round-trip fare, $96.
Freeport	**Major Air**, ☎ 242-352-5778. Round-trip fare, $99.
Fort Lauderdale	**Island Express**, ☎ 954-359-0380. **Lynx Air**, ☎ 954-491-7576.
Miami	**Bahamasair** operates a daily schedule from Miami to Andros Town. Round-trip fare, $165.

San Andros Airport

Access to Nicholl's Town

FROM	AIRLINE
Nassau	**Bahamasair** operates regular daily schedules, ☎ 800-222-4262. Round-trip fare, $65.
Freeport	**Major Air**, ☎ 242-352-5778. .
Fort Lauderdale	**Island Express**, ☎ 954-359-0380. Round-trip fare, $230.

■ By Mail Boat

Mail boats sailing from Potter's Cay make regularly scheduled stops at North, Central and South Andros. Schedules are listed below, and in the *At a Glance* section at the back of the book. Mail boat schedules depend on the weather so they don't always leave on time. It's best to call ahead and make sure. ☎ 423-339-1064.

Lisa J. II leaves Potter's Cay, Nassau, for North Andros – Nicholl's Town, Mastic Point, and Morgan's Bluff – on Wednesday at 3:30 pm, returning on Tuesday at 12 noon. Sailing time is five hours. The fare, one way, is $30.

Mangrove Cay Express sails for Mangrove Cay and Lisbon Creek on Wednesday at 6 pm, returning on Monday at 4 pm. Sailing time is 5½ hours. The one-way fare is $30.

The Captain Moxey sails for South Andros – Kemp's Bay, Bluff, Long Bay Cay, Driggs Hill, and Congo Town – on Mondays at 11 pm, and returns on Wednesday at 11 pm. Sailing time is 7½ hours. The one-way fare is $30.

Lady Gloria sails for Mangrove Cay, Sandy Point, Moore's Landing, and Bullock Harbour on Tuesday at 8 pm, and returns on Sunday (time varies). Sailing time is five hours. The one-way fare is $30.

There are several other sailings weekly with varying schedules on Wednesdays, Tuesdays and Thursdays. Call the dock master, ☎ 242-393-1064, for details.

■ By Private Boat

Andros is the largest of the Out Islands. It's a strange, sparsely populated, remote land of endless shoreline, and inland lakes intertwined with canals. Ports of entry are Nicholl's Town, San Andros, Congo Cay, Mangrove Cay and Fresh Creek, all on the east coast. The east coast is also the location of the world's third largest barrier reef, making it something of a mecca for scuba divers, as well as yachtsmen. Unfortunately, docking facilities around the island are still somewhat limited, although several new marinas are in the planning stage.

Andros Lighthouse Yacht Club & Marina at Andros Town offers 20 slips and most basic services and facilities: showers, fuel, water, ice, and electricity. Accommodations are available nearby, and there are a couple of nice restaurants. Maximum depth at high water is 12 feet. VHF 16. ☎ 242-368-2305, fax 242-368-2300.

Andros

Getting Around

On Andros most of the main roads are paved and in varying stages of repair from fair to quite good. Get off the beaten path, however, and it's a different story.

*All four airports and the docks are served by independently owned **taxis**. Fares are reasonable, starting around $8 for two people.*

▪ By Bicycle

If you have the time to ride, you can see an awful lot of the island. There's very little local traffic here, so you can peddle off down the highways and byways without a care in the world; just be sure to ride on the left side of the road. Bikes can be rented at **Small Hope Bay Lodge** in Andros Town (☎ 242-368-2013; $15 per day), and at many of the hotels on the island. From Andros Town you can head out to visit such places as Small Hope Bay, Calabash Bay, Coakley Town, and Fresh Creek. All are only a short distance from each other and easily reached by bicycle.

▪ By Car

This way you can see it all. The main roads are often deserted and, whichever direction you take, you can drive for miles without passing a single person along the way.

You can make arrangements to rent a car – often somebody's private one – through your hotel when you arrive, but there are also two rental agencies: one at Fresh Creek, called **Amklco**, ☎ 368-2056; the other at Calabash Bay, called **Berth Rent-A-Car,** ☎ 368-2102. The rates are $65 per day, with a $100 deposit.

When you head out northward for the deserted beaches and shallow water flats off the east side of the island, be prepared for a sometimes bumpy ride. The drive from Andros Town to **Nicholl's Town** in the north will take you along more than 40 miles of a dusty, deserted road; yes, it's paved and in relatively good condition.

Fresh Creek is the home of the **Androsia Batik Factory**. Since 1973 Androsia has been coloring the Bahamas with unique hand-waxed and hand-dyed fabrics and garments that are inspired by the beauty of the islands. Androsia is located on Androsia Street, a right turn after you make the turn onto Light House Club Drive from Queens Highway. Self-guided tours of the factory are available Monday-Friday from 8 am to 4 pm. Their outlet store is open Monday-Wednesday, 8 am-4 pm, Thursday and Friday, 8 am-5:30 pm, and Saturday, 8 am-1 pm. Worth a visit. ☎ 368-2020 or 2080; www.androsia.com; info@androsia.com.

A little further on you'll find the lovely beaches at **Small Hope Bay** and, eight miles further on, is **Staniard Creek**. It's a tiny settlement with neat little churches and a beach where, at **Jolly Boy's Enterprises**, you can hire a boat and go out cruising the bonefish flats.

From Staniard Creek, the road takes you past the **Forfar Field Station Marine Science Center** to **Stafford Creek**, and then on to **Owen's Town** and **San Andros Airport**. Continue northward to

On the beach at Small Hope Bay Lodge.

Nicholl's Town, Morgan's Bluff or **Red Bays**, whichever takes your fancy.

Go south from Andros Town along the coast road and you'll find a road leading off left to the **Atlantic Undersea Test and Evaluation Center**, one of several top secret British and American bases on the island. Take the road to the right, however, and you'll find yourself in **Bowen Sound**, and then **Man-O-War Sound**, **Cargill Creek**, and **Behring Point**, tiny settlements almost forgotten by the faraway world, where the beaches are great and the fishing is even better.

Fishing Camps

Cargill Creek is home to two of Andros' finest fishing camps: **Cargill Creek Lodge** (☎ 241-368-5129)and **Andros Island Bone Fishing Club** (☎ 242-368-5167). At Behring Point you'll find another popular fishing lodge: **Nottages Cottages** (☎ 242-368-4293).

The villages to the south of Behring Point, where the Northern Bight separates North and South Andros, are not accessible by private car. **Mangrove Cay** and **South Andros** can be reached by water taxi; the service runs twice each day in the morning and afternoon. Drive to Behring Point Dock and leave your car in the parking lot. You'll also need to take the water taxi to **Lisbon Creek**, and the ferry to **Drigg's Hill**. From there you can take a regular taxi to **Congo Town** and the other small settlements further south where you'll find some remote, unspoiled beaches.

Adventures on Water

■ Sport Fishing

The fishing off Andros is as good as anywhere else in the Bahamas – if not better. Andros is rapidly becoming known as the bonefishing capital of the world. The waters south of Behring Point consistently yield bonefish weighing in at more than 10 pounds. Offshore, marlin, tarpon, and sailfish can reach majestic proportions. On the barrier reef, huge groupers of 40 and 50 pounds are not unusual and are regularly taken, along with amberjack, snapper, and yellowtail.

There are three major fishing camps on Andros, any of which will be pleased to arrange whatever you might fancy: **Cargill Creek Lodge**, ☎ 368-5129; **Andros Island Bone Fishing Club**, ☎ 368-5167; and, at Behring Point, **Nottages Cottages**, ☎ 368-4293.

Boat Rentals

Andros Island Bone Fishing Club. Bone fishing charters from $250 per half-day, $480 per full day. ☎ 242-368-5167.

■ Diving

Andros' barrier reef – third largest in the world after Australia's Great Barrier Reef and the reef off the coast of Belize – is one of the planet's outstanding natural wonders. From the outer edge of the 120-mile reef that parallels the eastern shore, the ocean drops off more than 6,000 feet into a trench known as "The Tongue of the Ocean." To dive off the edge of the reef over the "Tongue" is to experience a feeling of insecurity like none you've ever known. Imagining the great depth below you will send you hurrying back to the security of the shallower waters.

Blue Holes

In addition to the wonders of the barrier reef, the flats around Andros are riddled with blue holes: mysterious circular depressions caused by the collapse of limestone caves far beneath the surface. These blue holes are home to thousands of species of fish and marine life. Blue holes come in all shapes and sizes, from small depressions inside the reef, to great tidal caverns in the bights and bays.

There are a number of shipwrecks for you to explore as well.

Perhaps you don't dive, but you do like to snorkel. Well, along the entire length of the eastern shore, bay after bay, beach after beach, and reef garden after reef garden await you. The shallow waters of the flats and inner reefs will provide myriad snorkeling opportunities.

Best Dive Sites

The Underwater Caverns at Lisbon Cay

The Underwater Caverns at Lisbon Cay provide an unusual diving adventure. The caverns, a network of limestone structures thought to have formed when the island was much larger and when more of its surface was above the ocean, make for a formidable and exciting dive. You'll need an experienced guide to take you. There are also underwater caverns to explore off Morgan's Bluff at the northern end of the island.

Blue Holes

There are at least 100 blue holes around Andros, of which the most famous may be **Uncle Charlie's Blue Hole**, which was featured in Jacques Cousteau's television series.

The Giant Staircase

The Giant Staircase is a spectacular series of coral steps descending steadily downward toward the drop-off, where you can swim among coral of every shape and size.

The Garden

The Garden is another wonderful coral formation. To name but a few, there are seafans, elkhorn, brain, and tube formations, and all the life-forms that inhabit the great reef are represented: snappers, sergeant majors, groupers, rays, eels, angels, and even the giant parrotfish.

Shipwrecks

Although there are many wrecks off Andros, most of them still await discovery. Only the two below are regularly visited.

The Marion

The *Marion* was a fairly large barge that capsized in the late 1980s. There were attempts to raise her, but all failed and she still lies in some 70 feet of water. The hulk, 100 feet long and 40 feet wide, has been gutted and permits easy access for divers.

The Potomac

This British tanker built in 1893, 345 feet long and 44 feet wide, ran aground in a hurricane off the north end of the island on September 26, 1929. She broke in half and went down in shallow water, 18 to 20 feet, where she lies today. The action of the ocean has smashed her to pieces and there's not much left for you to explore except the remains of the bow section and her boilers.

Best Snorkeling Sites

Cousteau Snorkeling Adventure

Only one hotel on Andros, **Small Hope Bay Lodge** at Fresh Creek, participates in the Jean Michel Cousteau "Snorkeling Adventures" program (see page 48). The experience is an exciting one, and that fact alone may have a direct bearing on your choice of accommodations. Those that are listed rank among the most popular sites, and are visited regularly under the Cousteau program. Remembering that Andros is home to the world's third largest barrier reef, it's no wonder that the island has more than its fair share of suitable snorkeling sites. As you can imagine, it would be impossible to list all of them here.

Central Park

Central Park is an area of the reef where you can see a great many unique coral formations, among them three major stands of elkhorn coral, all in less than 15 feet of water. It's an excellent site for beginners.

China Point

This is a great place to observe a grand variety of colorful reef fish: sergeant majors, blue tangs and trigger fish.

The Compressor

The Compressor is just that, an old compressor that has turned into a tiny reef. Lots of fun, and a highly unusual snorkeling experience.

Davis Creek

Not a creek at all, but a large tidal flat fringed by mangroves. A unique snorkeling adventure.

Goat Cay

Goat Cay is a great place to hunt sea biscuits and sand dollars.

Lisben's Point

Lisben's Point is a large area of reef with many unusual coral formations, including elk and staghorn, brain, seafan and star coral.

North Beach

Lots of small shoals and patchy areas that are home to all sorts of colorful fish and other species of marine life. Lots of fun, and easy, too.

Andros

Red Shoal

A patch of reef encrusted with elk and staghorn corals. Large schools of fish moving this way and that make this an unusual spot.

Trumpet Reef

A great place to watch the small invertebrates scurry about the ocean floor tending to their daily business.

Dive Operators

Small Hope Bay Lodge

They have been in the diving business for more than 42 years and they know the island waters well. The staff includes three instructors and four dive masters. They conduct two-tank morning dives, one-tank afternoon dives, and night dives, provided they have a minimum of six participants. Their professional affiliations include PADI, NAUI, SDI/TDI, and Universal Referrals. They offer comprehensive instruction for beginners and specialize in blue hole and wall diving. They offer several specialty dives with either one or two participants and the dive master. These are usually to inland blue holes, deeper exploration of the Ocean Blue Hole, and deeper wall dives, or you can plan your own dive with your dive master. They also offer a relaxed shark observation dive. Costs average $85 per dive. ☎ 800-223-6961. www.smallhope.com.

Dive/Accommodation Packages

Small Hope Bay Lodge

At Fresh Creek, they offer a flexible package based on double occupancy at a rate of $235-$245 per night, per person, depending on the season. Singles pay a $45 surcharge for a private room, or they can have a private room with a shared bath in a family cabin and then they pay no surcharge. Dive package discounts are offered for stays of seven days or more. Included in the rate is the round-trip transfer to and from the hotel; beachfront accommodations; three dives per day; breakfast, lunch and dinner daily; conch fritters and hors d'oeuvres every evening, all bar drinks and beverages (!); all hotel and food taxes; service charges; intro scuba diving lessons; hot tub, bicycles, sailboat and windsurfer. Complimentary baby-sitting services are provided during the cocktail hour. ☎ 800-223-6961. www.smallhope.com.

Where to Stay & Eat

Restaurant Price Scale	
$	less than $20 per person
$$	$20-$50 per person
$$$	$50+ per person

■ Dining

$$ The Beacon, ☎ 242-368-2305, at the Andros Lighthouse Yacht Club, is open for breakfast, lunch and dinner. Fresh seafood and local cuisine. Reservations suggested.

$$ Small Hope Bay Lodge, ☎ 242-368-2014. Open for breakfast, lunch and dinner, the restaurant serves a full American-style breakfast, a hot buffet at midday and dinner in the evening, with a variety of fresh seafood, including lobster, as well as beef, pork and chicken. Reservations required.

■ Accommodations

Hotel Meal Plans

- **CP** (Continental Plan) includes a continental breakfast.
- **EP** (European Plan) denotes no meals, although restaurant facilities are available either on the property or nearby.
- **MAP** (Modified American Plan) denotes breakfast and dinner.
- **FAP** (Full American Plan) includes all meals.
- **All-Inc.** (All-Inclusive Plan) includes all meals, beverages (alcoholic and soft), watersports, tennis and golf, if available.

Andros Lighthouse Yacht Club and Marina, in Andros Town, ☎ 242-368-2300, www.androslighthouse.com. The hotel is a five-minute walk from the beach, near the lighthouse from which it takes its name. The 20 guest

Andros

At Small Hope Bay Lodge, Andros.

rooms are all nicely furnished, with marbled tile, reproduction furniture, and all are cooled by ceiling fans. There's a swimming pool and a fine dining room where you can enjoy traditional Bahamian fare and great views of the marina. Fresh Creek is a short walk across the bridge. Rates start at around $130 per person, per night; MAP is $40 extra.

Small Hope Bay Lodge, at Fresh Creek in North Andros, ☎ 800-223-6961. The Lodge is pretty much dedicated to divers, but offers those who are looking for a real getaway something special. This resort has just 20 guest rooms in small cabins along the beach under the shade of the palm trees. All have ceiling fans, are tastefully decorated, and furnished with bed linens made from batik cloth manufactured at the nearby Androsia plant. Most rooms have private baths; others share one between two rooms. The atmosphere is definitely casual, as you'll find if you decide to wear a tie to dinner – you'll lose it quite quickly to one of the staff brandishing a pair of scissors. The resort is closed for four weeks during September and October (exact time varies). Rates are $175-$185 per night per person, meals, drinks, taxes and activities included. www.smallhope.com.

Coakley House, ☎ 800-223-6961, 242-368-2013, is also at Fresh Creek and is a good choice for independent travelers looking for a villa rental. It offers three air-conditioned bedrooms, 3½ baths, large living room, dining room, fully equipped kitchen and laundry room. The house takes full advantage of magnificent water views and breezes from any direction. Outside it has a lovely patio overlooking the sea and its own private dock. Boat or car rentals, fishing, diving, and maid/cook service can all be arranged through Small Hope Bay Lodge. Rates are as follows: November through April, $300 per night or $1,750 per week; May through October, $250 per night or $1,500 per week. www.coakleyhouse.com; coakleyhouse@smallhope.com.

Andros Island Bone Fishing Camp, at Cargill Creek, ☎ 242-368-5176. As the name implies, bonefishing is the essence of this community. The atmosphere is very relaxed, the accommodation rustic, but comfortable, with all sorts of amenities, and the lounge has a large, open, ocean-front deck with lots of heavy wooden chairs for relaxing. On the beach among the palms you'll find hammocks and more beach chairs free of charge. Rates per boat are $150-$200 per half-day; $275-$325 per full day. EP only.

Cargill Creek Lodge, at Cargill Creek/Behring Point, ☎ 242-368-5129, www.dalodge.com. The Lodge is expensive, but when you consider that the rate includes everything but your beverages, and when compared to what a day's fishing can cost you at the hands of a local operator, it's a very good value. Most people who stay at the Lodge are avid anglers. There is no beach to speak of, but there is a small pool. The hotel's 15 guest cottages are all well furnished and have television sets. Each has a private bath – very nice too – and ceiling fans to complement the air-conditioning. The restaurant is right at the water, and the lounge is one of the island's popular gathering places. Behring Point is about 35 miles south of the airport and 12 miles from Andros Town. The rate is $275 per night, per person. It includes all meals and unlimited fishing.

Andros Lighthouse Yacht Club & Marina.

Andros

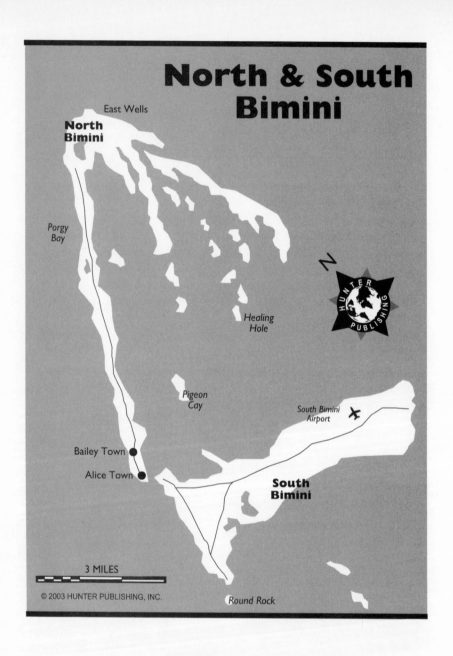

North & South Bimini

East Wells

North Bimini

Porgy Bay

Healing Hole

Pigeon Cay

South Bimini Airport

Bailey Town

Alice Town

South Bimini

3 MILES

© 2003 HUNTER PUBLISHING, INC.

Round Rock

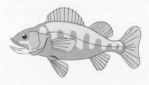

Bimini — No

Just 50 miles off the east coast of Florida, Bimini is one of the best known of the Bahamas. It's most popular with fishermen, and is within easy reach of amateur sailors from the American mainland. Bimini is actually two distinct islands separated by a narrow ocean passage and a number of minor cays. It has a total land mass of less than 10 square miles, a rich history and a wealth of natural resources.

Most of the community's population, about 1,600, lives on North Bimini in **Bailey Town**, while **Alice Town**, also on North Bimini, is the main tourist center where most of the hotels, restaurants, and fishing operations can be found. There's an airport on South Bimini, although most visitors arrive on the islands at North Bimini Harbour via sea plane from Miami.

The Biminis are perhaps the best-known of the Bahamian Out Islands thanks to the publicity provided by such famous fishermen as Ernest Hemingway, Adam Clayton Powell, Jr., and Zane Grey. Today, they are widely accepted as a sport fishing mecca. Beyond that, the Biminis are an excellent yachting and cruising center and an exciting destination for divers.

Most of Bimini's visitors come to fish. The seas off the tiny islands abound with white and blue marlin, tarpon, sailfish, swordfish, amberjack, wahoo, barracuda and shark. Bonefish, too, are plentiful on the flats off the coast of Alice Town. More than 20 fishing tournaments each year draw anglers from around the world in search of the great billfish and a place in angling history (see page 192).

Bimini

History

 Some say these islands were once part of the road system of the Lost Continent of Atlantis. Ponce de Leon visited Bimini in his search for the Fountain of Youth. Did he find it here? The locals will tell you that he did and, with tongue in cheek, will point out its precise location.

Bimini's modern history centers around the two people who made it famous. **The Compleat Angler**, a hotel and bar in Alice Town is where **Ernest Hemingway** spent most of his time when he wasn't writing or fishing. Its lobby is jam-packed with Hemingway memorabilia. His cottage, now a part of the **Bimini Blue Water Resort**, is thought to be the place where he wrote most of *To Have and Have Not*.

Adam Clayton Powell, a New York Congressman, spent a great deal of his time on the island fishing, as well as socializing in The End of the World Bar in Alice Town, a hole-in-the-wall with a sandy floor.

Alice Town, the home of the **Bimini Big Game Fishing Club**, is the fishing capital of the little island group. It's in Alice Town that you'll find the best restaurants and bars – such local institutions as **Captain Bob's**, where you can eat breakfast and buy a packed lunch for the day's fishing; **Fisherman's Paradise**, where you can eat excellent Bahamian fare for lunch and dinner; **The Bimini Breeze**, **The Wee Hours Club**, and **The End of the World Bar**.

Getting There

■ By Air

 The Biminis are not as well-served as other Out Islands. Several airlines offer scheduled service to South Bimini out of Fort Lauderdale, and there is regular sea plane service into Alice Town from Fort Lauderdale.

North Bimini	
FROM	**AIRLINE**
Fort Lauderdale	**Pan Am Air Bridge**, ☎ 800-424-2557.
Miami	**Pan Am Air Bridge**, ☎ 800-424-2557.
Paradise Island	**Pan Am Air Bridge**, ☎ 800-424-2557.

South Bimini	
FROM	**AIRLINE**
Fort Lauderdale	**Island Air Charters**, ☎ 800-444-9904, fax 954-760-9157; **Bel Air Transport**, ☎ 954-524-9814, fax 954-524-0115.
Freeport	**Major Air**, ☎ 242-352-5778, fax 242-352-5788.

■ By Mail Boat

Mail boats sail regular schedules from Potter's Cay, Nassau. Call ahead to make sure of departure times and arrivals. ☎ 242-393-1064.

Bimini Mack makes a weekly stop at Cat Cay and North Bimini. Call the dock master for schedules, ☎ 242-393-1064. Sailing time is 12 hours. The one-way fare is $45.

■ By Sailboat

The Biminis are the most popular sailing destination from mainland Florida. Less than 50 miles from the coast, they are well within reach of most sea-going sailers. While I was visiting the east end of Grand Bahama a couple of years ago, I ran into two adventurous types who had made the crossing from Florida on Hobie Cats. It took them almost 10 hours. Not something I would recommend, but it shows what can be done.

Flings

If you'll be crossing to the Biminis for the first time, the **Bahamas Boating Flings** might be the way to go. Sponsored jointly by the Bahamas Ministry of Tourism and the South Florida Marine Industries Association, the flings are organized fleets of not more than 30 vessels brought together to make the crossing from either Miami or Fort Lauderdale for boats of at least 22 feet, and from Palm Beach in boats at least 24 feet. Each boat pays a fee of $65 to participate. Flings are organized throughout the summer, when sailing conditions are best. For more information, call the Bahamas Tourist office in Miami at ☎ 800-327-7678 or 305-932-0051.

For seasoned sailors, the official port of entry is Alice Town on North Bimini. The **Bimini Big Game Fishing Club**, with 100 slips, is the premier marina on the islands. It can accommodate boats up to 100 feet, and offers services that include showers, fuel, groceries, engine repair, water, ice, and electricity. There's also a restaurant, accommodations and a swimming pool. You can radio ahead on VHF 9/16. ☎ 800-737-1007, fax 242-347-3392.

Bimini Blue Water Marina is a smaller, but no less popular, base of operations. It offers 32 slips, along with showers, fuel, groceries, engine repair, water, ice, electricity and much more. Restaurants and accommodations are available nearby. Call ahead on VHF 16/68. ☎ 242-347-3166, fax 242-347-3293.

The airport and the docks are served by independently owned taxis. Fares are reasonable, starting around $10.

Adventures on Water

■ Fishing

If you don't have your own boat, you'll need to charter one. Costs average $200-$300 per person for a half-day; $350-$400 per person for a full day. For more information, call the Bahamas Tourism Office at ☎ 800-32-SPORT.

- **The Bimini Big Game Fishing Club**, Alice Town, ☎ 242-347-2391 or 800-327-4149.

- **The Bimini Blue Water Resort & Marina**, Alice Town, ☎ 242-347-3166.

- **The Bimini Reef Club & Marina**, South Bimini, ☎ 305-359-9449.

- **The Sea Crest Hotel & Marina**, Alice Town, ☎ 242-347-3071, www.seacrestbimini.com.

- **Weech's Dock**, ☎ 242-347-2028.

Fishing/Accommodation Packages

The Bimini Big Game Fishing Club

On North Bimini, they offer two three-day, two-night packages. The deep-sea fishing package includes deluxe accommodations and a full day fishing from a 28-foot Bertram with a captain and mate for $372 per person (double occupancy). The Backwater Fishing package includes deluxe accommodations and a full day of bonefishing with a guide for $219 per person (double occupancy). ☎ 800-327-4149.

Bimini Blue Water Marina.

The Bimini Blue Water Hotel

They also offer two packages; you decide the length of each. The daily rate for a bonefishing package, including hotel accommodations and a half-day of fishing with a guide, is $215 for two persons. The daily rate for the deep-sea fishing package, including hotel accommodations and a half-day aboard the 46-foot *Sir Tones*, is $465 for two persons. ☎ 242-347-2166.

Fishing Tournaments

Below are the major tournaments conducted off Bimini throughout the year. There are also a number of smaller tournaments in the area. For more information call the Bahamas Tourism Office at ☎ 800-32-SPORT.

- **JANUARY**: The **Bimini Light Tackle Bonefish Tournament**, 1st leg, Bimini Big Game Fishing Club, ☎ 242-347-3391.

- **FEBRUARY**: The **Bimini Light Tackle Bonefish Tournament**, 2nd leg, Bimini Big Game Fishing Club, ☎ 242-347-3391.

- **MARCH**: The **Annual Bacardi Rum Billfish Tournament**, Bimini Big Game Fishing Club, ☎ 242-347-3391.

- **MAY**: The **Bimini Festival Tournament**, Bimini Big Game Fishing Club, ☎ 242-347-3391.

- **JUNE**: The **Big 5 Tournament**, Bimini Big Game Fishing Club, ☎ 242-347-3391.

- **JUNE**: The **South Florida Fishing Club Tournament**, Bimini Big Game Fishing Club, ☎ 242-347-3391.

- **AUGUST**: The **Bimini Native Fishing Tournament**, Bimini Big Game Fishing Club, ☎ 242-347-3391.

- **SEPTEMBER**: The **Small B.O.A.T. Tournament**, 1st and 2nd legs, Bimini Big Game Fishing Club, ☎ 242-347-3391.

- **NOVEMBER**: The **Wahoo Tournament**, Bimini Big Game Fishing Club, ☎ 242-347-3391.

■ Diving

 Diving off the Biminis is excellent and most of the popular dive sites can be reached quite quickly by boat. The main attraction of underwater Bimini is the abundance of fish and marine life, although the reefs are not quite as extensive or as spectacular as they are off Andros or Abaco. Expect to see huge schools of grunts, snapper, and goatfish. Groups of spotted eagle rays congregate in the channel between the two main islands, and the ever-present groupers grow to record-breaking proportions.

Best Dive Sites

The reefs off Bimini vary in depths from a shallow 15 feet to more than 100 feet.

Tuna Alley & the Victories

To the south you'll visit Tuna Alley and the Victories, where miles of coral reef and drop-offs are populated by almost every type of tropical marine life you can imagine. The area is riddled with caverns, channels and tunnels at depths varying from 30 to 90 feet.

Rainbow Reef

Rainbow Reef lies in an easy 25 to 35 feet of water and offers divers spectacular coral formations and lots of schooling fish, along with nurse sharks of varying sizes, turtles, groupers, and even barracuda.

The Bimini Barge

This is the wreck of an ocean-going barge now sitting on the bottom in some 100 feet of water. Its superstructure, however, is only 60 feet from the surface.

The Sapona

The *Sapona* is the wreck of a 350-foot concrete transport that was originally named the *Lone Star*. She ran aground in 1926 during a hurricane and broke in half under the relentless action of the sea. During World War II, the hulk was used as an aerial target by the US Navy and Air Force. Today, the *Sapona* sits in a mere 20 feet of water with her superstructure showing above the water like the bones of some motionless leviathan. The wreck lies in shallow waters and is accessible to both divers and snorkelers. She's a wonderland of dead machinery, ship's propellers, and interior locations, all lit by the rays of sunlight filtering down from the deck areas above.

Bimini

Dive Operators

Bill and Nowdla Keefe's Bimini Undersea Adventures has been in business for more than 14 years and has a well-deserved reputation for good service and an in-depth knowledge of the undersea Biminis. The company has a staff of seven, including four instructors, and conducts a regular schedule of dives that includes two-tank morning dives, one-tank afternoon dives, and night dives on Wednesdays and Saturdays. The newest attraction is a program called "Swim With The Wild Wild Dolphin." A pod of wild spotted dolphins has taken up residence off Bimini. The Keefes offer Dolphin Excursions two-three times weekly aboard their dive boats *Destiny* and *Adventurer*. Trips are done both in the morning and afternoon and can be anywhere from three-four hours in length. In most cases, once the pod has come to the boat, the dolphins allow you to swim and interact with them. It takes approximately an hour to reach the "Dolphin Grounds." The company's professional affiliations include PADI and NAUI. Pre-booked rates: adults, $109; children (eight-12), $69; guests, $89; children (under eight), no charge. On-island rates: adults, $119; children (eight-12), $79; guests, $99. ☎ 800-348-4644. e-mail dolphins@biminiundersea.com. www.biminiundersea.com.

Spotted Dolphins

Spotted dolphins are different in many ways from the more well known grey bottle nosed dolphins that you see in captivity. In the wild, spotted dolphins actually seek out human interaction. In contrast, the bottle nosed dolphins tend to be curious but tentative, more often than not shying away from swimmers. In captivity, their roles are reversed. Spotted dolphins are virtually un-trainable and do not do well in a captive environment. Bottle nosed dolphins are very trainable and adapt well to captivity.

Dive/Accommodation Packages

Bimini Big Game Fishing Club offers a series of all-inclusive dive packages. Off-season rates (September 15th to May 14th) for two nights, $350; three nights, $490; four nights, $629; five nights, $769; six nights, $908; seven nights, $1,048. From May 15th through September 14th, the rates are increased by some $80 to $280, depending upon the length of stay.

All rates are per person, per night, and are based on double occupancy. Each package includes three dives per day (two on arrival and departure days), one night dive, transfers to and from the hotel, deluxe air-conditioned accommodations, breakfast and dinner each day, all service charges, use of tanks, weights and belts, and use of tennis courts. ☎ 242-347-3391.

Best Snorkeling Spots

 Only one hotel in the Biminis participates in the Jean Michel Cousteau "Snorkeling Adventures" program (see page 48): **Bimini Big Game Club**. There are lots of opportunities to enjoy the sport, either on your own, or through the program, and there are a number of popular sites.

Bimini Shoreline

Bimini Shoreline is an area of the reef with lots of coral formations, colorful reef fishes, and a bird's eye view of everyday life on the reef.

Bimini Road

This is the most interesting snorkeling site in the Out Islands. A number of stone structures are believed by some to be part of the lost continent of Atlantis.

Eagle Ray Run

You'll see dozens of eagle rays swimming in formation. It's a rare experience.

Healing Hole

Thought to be the site of the fabled Fountain of Youth.

LaChance Rocks

A group of huge rocks on the ocean floor, inhabited by dozens of species of small marine life, including invertebrates.

Rainbow Reef

One of the most densely populated sections of reef in the Bahamas. Here you'll have the chance to observe many species of reef-dweller.

Rock Sound

A shallow water snorkeling experience over a rock and coral field.

Sapona

An unusual snorkel over a sunken concrete ship.

Stingray Hole

The place to observe lots of stingrays. You can feed them, too.

Where to Stay & Eat

Restaurant Price Scale
$ . . . . less than $20 per person
$$ . . . . $20-$50 per person
$$$ . . . . $50+ per person

■ Dining

$$ Bimini Bay, ☎ 242-347-2174, located in a mansion on North Bimini overlooking Paradise Point, is open from 3 pm until 6 pm for an early afternoon tea.

$$ The Gulfstream Restaurant and Bar, ☎ 242-347-3393, at the Bimini Game Fishing Club in Alice Town, offers an extensive menu of fresh seafood dishes, beef, chicken and a selection of fine wines. Open daily for breakfast, lunch and dinner. Reservations a must.

$-$$ The Red Lion, ☎ 242-347-3259, in Alice Town, is open Tuesday through Sunday for bar meals and dinner from 6 pm to 11 pm. The bar is open until 2 am.

■ Accommodations

Hotel Meal Plans

- **CP** (Continental Plan) includes a continental breakfast.
- **EP** (European Plan) denotes no meals, although restaurant facilities are available either on the property or nearby.
- **MAP** (Modified American Plan) denotes breakfast and dinner.
- **FAP** (Full American Plan) includes all meals.
- **All-Inc.** (All-Inclusive Plan) includes all meals, beverages (alcoholic and soft), watersports, tennis and golf, if available.

Bimini Big Game Fishing Club, Alice Town, ☎ 800-737-1007, $150 EP. The hotel, with its 50 guest rooms, including cottages and suites, and 100 boat slips, is headquarters of the Bimini sport fishing industry. The guest rooms are all luxuriously appointed and have TVs, tiled floors, rattan furniture, and are decorated in pastel shades of green and white to make for a cool, tropical atmosphere. The hotel has three bars, two dining rooms, a swimming pool, and a tennis court. The beach is nearby.

Bimini Blue Water Resort, Alice Town, ☎ 242-347-3166, $100 EP. Most of the hotel's 12 guest rooms overlook the beach, all are comfortably appointed, and sit adjacent to the private beach. Of special interest is the cottage once owned by Ernest Hemingway, now part of the hotel complex. If you make arrangements far enough in advance, you can stay here, surrounded by an atmosphere unlike anywhere else. The cottage, next door to Hemingway's other watering hole, The Compleat Angler, has a blue marlin hanging over the living room fireplace, a kitchen, three bedrooms, and a large patio.

The Compleat Angler Hotel, Alice Town, ☎ 242-347-3122, $85 EP. A cozy hotel with 13 guest rooms, huge shade trees, balconies, and courtyards reminiscent of New Orleans' French Quarter than on the islands. This was once the haunt of Ernest Hemingway, and his presence can still be felt among the memorabilia. In the bar, the walls are hung with nautical flags, pennants and old photographs. One of the

The Compleat Angler, a favorite haunt of Ernest Hemingway.

Bimini

photographs shows Hemingway with the remains of a 500-pound blue marlin, the victim of a shark attack, that might have been the inspiration for his famous 1952 work, *The Old Man and the Sea*.

Sea Crest Hotel, Alice Town, ☎ 242-347-3071, www.seacrestbimini. com, $90 EP. The Sea Crest is a small, comfortable hotel, though it lacks both a pool and a restaurant. The 10 guest rooms are neatly furnished, have TVs and either double or single beds. The beach is just across the road and a number of good restaurants are within walking distance.

Eleuthera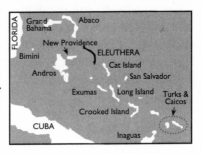

Eleuthera, playground to many of the rich and famous, is one of the longest islands in the Bahamian archipelago. More than 110 miles long, but less than two miles wide, the island is home to about 10,500 residents. It lies some 60 miles to the west of Nassau and, with three airports – Governor's Harbour, North Eleuthera and Rock Sound – and daily flights from Miami, Fort Lauderdale and Nassau, it's one of the most accessible of the Out Islands.

Map showing FLORIDA, Grand Bahama, Abaco, New Providence, Bimini, ELEUTHERA, Cat Island, Andros, San Salvador, Exumas, Long Island, Turks & Caicos, Crooked Island, CUBA, Inaguas.

CAUTION *Be sure to ask your carrier which airport is the correct one for your hotel. Get it wrong, and you could find yourself facing a taxi ride of 90 miles or more.*

History

 Founded by English settlers in the mid-1700s, and named for the Greek word meaning "Freedom," the island is a combination of white picket fences and pastel-painted cottages, with a wild and secluded landscape of stark cliffs, deserted beaches, rolling hills and bluffs, dusty roads, pine, casuarina, palms, seagrape and scrub undergrowth. It has miles and miles of scenic coastline and emerald waters of the northern Caribbean sea.

Getting There

Eleuthera and its nearby islands are served by three tiny international airports: **North Eleuthera**, **Governor's Harbour** at the center of the island, and **Rock Sound** to the south. All enjoy scheduled service from Nassau and, to a lesser extent, from the mainland. The main ports of entry for sailors are Cape Eleuthera, Governor's Harbour, Harbour Island, Hatchet Bay, North Eleuthera, and Rock Sound. And, the island is well served by mail boats out of Potter's Cay, Nassau.

■ By Air

Governor's Harbour Airport	
Access to Gregory Town, Hatchet Bay, Palmetto Point	
FROM	**AIRLINE**
Nassau	**Bahamasair**, daily. ☎ 800-222-4262. Round-trip fare, $74.
Freeport	**Major Air**, daily. ☎ 242-352-5778.
Fort Lauderdale	**USAirways Express**, ☎ 800-622-1015, **Twin Air**, ☎ 954-359-8266, **Bel Air Transport**, ☎ 954-524-9814. All operate a daily schedule. The round-trip fare starts at $264.

Eleuthera

Miami	**American Eagle**, daily. ☎ 800-433-7300. Round-trip fare, $175. **Bahamasair**, daily. ☎ 800-222-4262. Round-trip fare, $170.

North Eleuthera Airport

Access to Gregory Town, Harbour Island, Spanish Wells

Fares are comparable to those into Governor's Harbour.

FROM	AIRLINE
Nassau	**Bahamasair**, ☎ 800-222-4262, and **Sandpiper**, ☎ 242-328-7591, offer a daily schedule.
Fort Lauderdale	**Gulfstream** (Continental Airways Connection), **Twin Air**, ☎ 954-359-8266, and **USAirways Express,** ☎ 800-622-1015.
Freeport	**Major Air**, ☎ 242-352-5778.
Miami	**Gulfstream** (Continental Airways Connection), ☎ 800-231-0856, **Bahamasair**, ☎ 800-222-4262.

Rock Sound Airport

Access to Tarpum Bay

FROM	AIRLINE
Nassau	**Bahamasair**, daily. ☎ 800-222-4262.
Fort Lauderdale	**Island Express**, daily. ☎ 954-359-0380.
Freeport	**Major Air**, ☎ 242-352-5778.

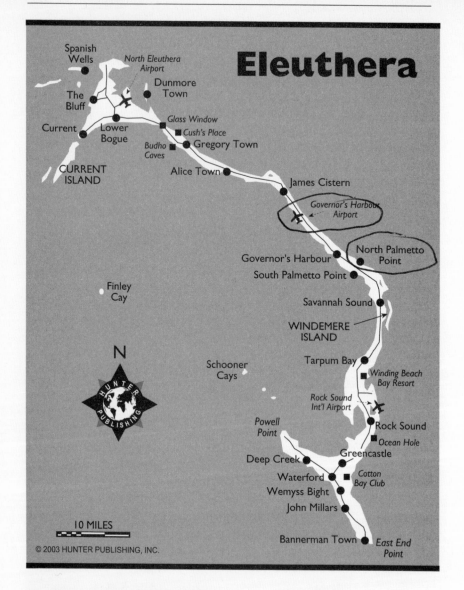

■ By Mail Boat

Bahama Daybreak III sails from Potter's Cay, Nassau, on Mondays at 5 pm, stopping at Rock Sound, Davis Harbour, and South Eleuthera. She returns on Tuesday at 10 pm. Sailing time is five hours. The one-way fare is $20.

Eleuthera Express sails from Potter's Cay, Nassau, on Mondays at 7 pm for Governor's Harbour and Spanish Wells. She returns on Tuesday at 8 pm. Sailing time is five hours. The one-way fare is $20.

Captain Fox sails from Potter's Cay, Nassau, on Fridays at noon for Hatchet Bay, and returns on Wednesday at 4 pm. Sailing time is six hours. The one-way fare is $25.

Spanish Rose sails from Potter's Cay on Thursdays at 7 am for Spanish Wells. Sailing time is five hours. The one-way fare is $20.

Eleuthera Express sails from Potter's Cay on Thursdays at 7 am for Rock Sound, Davis Harbour and South Eleuthera. Sailing time is five hours. The one-way fare is $25.

■ By Private Plane

All three airports are accessible to private pilots. Eleuthera's remote FSS frequency is 124.2.

■ By Private Boat

Eleuthera is one of the most popular cruising destinations in the Bahamian archipelago. Full-service marinas are available from one end of the 90-mile long island to the other. All marinas monitor VHF 16.

Spanish Wells

Spanish Wells Yacht Haven offers 30 full-service slips with access to fuel, water, ice, etc. There are several boat yards nearby where boats can be hauled out of the water for repairs.

Harbour Island

Valentine's Resort and Marina offers 39 full-service slips along with access to all of the restaurants in Dunsmore Town.

Harbour Island Club and Marina is a full-service operation with showers, a laundromat, fuel, water and ice. The 32 slips have 30- and 50-amp hookups.

Hatchet Bay Marine Services of Eleuthera offers 20 full-service slips and their own Harbour View Restaurant and Bar.

Palmetto Shores

The **Palmetto Shores Vacation Villa** offers eight slips.

Governor's Harbour

The harbor itself is a large, protected bay where you can drop anchor for just about as long as you like. A dock allows you to tie up and take a short walk into town for provisions.

Rock Sound

Rock Sound, at the southern end of the island, is Eleuthera's largest community. The town offers a large, well-protected bay where you can drop anchor and come ashore to replenish supplies.

■ Package Vacations

Several major operators offer air-inclusive vacations to Eleuthera. Unfortunately, the hotel options are limited to the Cove Eleuthera, which is a great place to stay, and a couple of other smaller hotels, but there's nothing available on Harbour Island. A creative travel agent could build a custom package for you, not a difficult proposition. Other than that I recommend the following:

American FlyAAWay Vacations

They offers air-inclusive vacation packages to the Cove Eleuthera from most major US cities, connecting to American Eagle in Miami. Typically, a five-night package for two – no meal plan – from Atlanta will cost about $1,200 for two persons, maybe a little less, depending on the time of year. Break that down and you see that you're paying around $600 per person, including airfare, which represents great value for money. Rates from other gateway cities are comparable. Facilities include tennis courts, a fresh-water swimming pool, and ocean fishing. Accommodations are in duplex-style cabins surrounded by tropical gardens. These are comfortably furnished, and enjoy either a garden or ocean view. There are no telephones or televisions in the rooms; these are available in the main building. If you're looking for a real getaway you'll enjoy the feeling of being beyond reach. You can book through your travel agent, or call American FlyAAWay, ☎ 800-321-2121, www.aavacations.com.

Apple Vacations

Apple Vacations offers packages to Eleuthera using scheduled air carriers which, in this case, means American Airlines. They offer several hotel options, including the Cove Eleuthera, Unique Village and, to the south, <u>Palmetto</u> Shores Vacation Villas. Rates run just a little higher than those offered by American FlyAAWay Vacations, but departure options are more extensive – they will provide connection flights from most cities with an airport. www.applevacations.com.

Club Med

Club Med has a village close to Governor's Harbour, with weekly rates starting at $1,300 per person, using the US gateway cities of Boston, New York, Chicago, Los Angeles, San Francisco and Washington, DC. Air add-ons from other cities are available but will cost upwards of $200 per person.

Club Med Eleuthera is a family-oriented village. Activities include circus training for the whole family – trapeze, trampoline, juggling, tightwire and other circus skills.

Accommodations are in two- and three-story affairs, air-conditioned, tastefully furnished and decorated in native Bahamian pastels. Each room has a private bathroom with shower – water is desalinated. Tennis is available on eight courts, two of them lighted, and there's an 18-hole golf course at the now defunct Cotton Bay Club, about 45 minutes from the village by taxi. Other activities include aerobics, bocce ball, ocean fishing, sailing, scuba diving, and snorkeling. For reservations, ☎ 800-CLUB-MED. www.clubmed.com.

Getting Around

Transfers from any of the three airports to your hotel must be by private **taxi**. Even package vacations do not include transfers. If you're visiting Harbour Island, you'll find taxis waiting for in-coming aircraft just outside the main building. They will transfer you to the ferry dock. It's not far – you could easily walk it in five minutes – and the fare should be just a couple of dollars. If you decide to walk, turn right out of the main building; it's all downhill from there. **Ferry boats** also meet in-coming aircraft. If you're visiting one of the hotels in the Governor's Harbour area – the Cove, Unique Village, etc. – your taxi fare will be about $40, one-way, for two persons. Once you've checked into your hotel, you can rent a car or bicycle to do your sightseeing.

The several towns on the island are separated by many miles of almost deserted beaches. Want to swim or snorkel? Simply leave the road, park your car – there are several rental agents on the island – and walk right into the water. You're in one of the finest reef locations in the world.

■ Island Driving Tour

There are two towns of interest on the north end of the island: **Spanish Wells** and **Harbour Island**.

Due to its thriving crawfish industry, Spanish Wells – named for the Spanish explorers who put ashore in search of fresh water and provisions – is one of the wealthiest communities in the Bahamas. Harbour Island, just off Eleuthera's northern coast, is a resort island where the beach is tinged with pink and the water is clear.

Harbour Island.

Above: Royal Towers, Atlantis, Paradise Island

Below: Beach at Atlantis (Blair Howard)

Above: Venetian Canal, Atlantis (Blair Howard)

Below: Predator Lagoon Viewing Tunnel, Atlantis

Above: Rawson Square, Nassau (Blair Howard)

Below: Prince George Dock, Nassau (Blair Howard)

Above: Boat docks, Nassau (Blair Howard)

Below: Ardastra Gardens, Nassau (Blair Howard)

Above: Flamingos, Ardastra Gardens

Below: Radisson, Cable Beach (Blair Howard)

COLUMBUS

1492

Bimini

Above: The Dolphin Experience, Sanctuary Bay, Grand Bahama

Below: Offshore racing

Hope Town Lighthouse, Elbow Cay, Abacos

Above: "The Bahamas Oldest Historical Museum," Abaco

Below: Store on Harbour Island, Eleuthera

East End, Grand Bahama

Above: Elizabeth Harbour, George Town, Exumas
Below: Peace & Plenty Pier, George Town, Exumas

Further south is **Gregory Town**, the pineapple capital of the island. This fruit is responsible for the tiny village's prosperity and is honored each June during the **Pineapple Festival**. The festival includes a Miss Teen Pineapple Pageant, a pineapple-eating contest, dancing in the streets, a basketball shootout, music and a street party on Saturday night. Along the way from Spanish Wells to Gregory Town, you'll pass through the Bluff, Upper and Lower Bogue, and then over a natural bridge called **Glass Window Bridge**. The narrowest point on the island, the bridge, with its spectacular views to the north and south, is the result of millions of years of erosion by wind and sea.

From Gregory Town, the road heads southward through Alice Town, past Hatchet Bay, James Cistern, on into Governor's Harbour at the center of Eleuthera.

Governor's Harbour is typical of the tropical towns you'll find dotted around the Out Islands. It's fairly remote, but has a charm all its own: a tiny church loaded with history, shops where you can buy local souvenirs and crafts, boats bobbing at anchor in the bay and, here and there, restaurants where you can sample real Bahamian food. It's not as upscale as other resort areas at Harbour Island and Spanish Wells, but it is interesting and enjoyable. Said to be the earliest settlement on the island, Governor's Harbour offers several places to stay, including a Club Med, and there's even a bank. If you really want a getaway vacation, Governor's Harbour might be just the place.

Continue south along the road from Governor's Harbour through Palmetto Point, Savannah Sound, past Windermere Island and on through Tarpum Bay. You'll then reach Rock Sound, the largest settlement on the island.

DID YOU KNOW?

Windermere Island was once the favorite getaway haunt of Prince Charles and Princess Diana.

Tarpum Bay is an artist's community. It was here that Mal Flanders, an American, came to paint the island life and scenery. His work is well known, and you might want to drop by the studio. Another good place to visit at Tarpum belongs to another artist. Scotsman MacMillan Hughes built the strange-looking structure he likes to call **The Castle** with his own hands. Take a moment to visit, view his work, and enjoy a tour of his home. Both are on Queen's Highway.

Eleuthera has plenty of good places for walking.

Rock Sound, along Queen's Highway, south of Tarpum Bay and north of Greencastle, boasts a number of attractions, including **Ocean Hole**, a large inland lake connected to the ocean by a labyrinth of subterranean tunnels. Some say the hole is bottomless. Its depth has been measured to more than 100 feet. Either way, it has become home to a variety of fish and marine animals, many of which are accustomed to being fed by hand. Steps cut into the coral make for easy access to the hole, the water, and the fish, providing a rare photographic opportunity.

If you're a golfer or tennis player, stop by **The Club**, on Queen's Highway at Rock Sound. The club's magnificent 18-hole golf course, designed by Robert Trent Jones, is considered one of the finest golfing challenges in the Bahamas. Greens fees are $70 for 18 holes; $45 for nine holes. Club rental, $15. No need to book tee times in advance.

Walking and bicycling are both popular pastimes on Eleuthera. The miles of deserted roads, vast stretches of pristine sand, tiny bays and coves, side tracks, pathways and trails all make for endless hours of peddling or hoofing. You can rent bicycles at almost all of the island's hotels for about $15 per day.

WORD TO THE WISE

Bicycling or walking, be sure to take something to drink. Once you leave your resort, rest stops and country stores are few and far between.

Adventures on Water

■ Fishing

 Deep-sea and bonefishing expeditions can be arranged through many of the hotels – just ask at the front desk. Rates average $150-$250 per person for a half-day; $325-$425 for a full day. The hotels listed below are particularly helpful at making advance arrangements for you. See www.eleu.net/marina-e.html for details on the marinas of Eleuthera.

- **Coral Sands Hotel**, Romora Bay on Harbour Island, ☎ 800-333-2368., www.coralsands.com.

- **Valentines Inn & Yacht Club**, Harbour Island, ☎ 242-333-2142.

- **Spanish Wells Yacht Haven**, Spanish Wells, ☎ 242-333-4255.

- **Spanish Wells Marina**, Spanish Wells, ☎ 242-333-4122.

- **Hatchet Bay Marina**, Hatchet Bay, ☎ 242-332-0186.

- **Harbour Island Club & Marina**, Harbour Island, ☎ 242-333-2427, www.harbourislandmarina.com.

Boat Rentals

Buccaneer Club. Guided boat rentals can be arranged from $200 per day and small boats from $65 per day. ☎ 242-332-2000.

■ Diving

 Most of the major dive sites are located around Harbour Island. Along the eastern coast of Harbour Island and Eleuthera, a long fringed reef guards the shoreline. It's a vast undersea continent of sand and coral, where ocean creatures congregate. Stop off at any of the tiny bays and inlets, put on your mask and snorkel, walk a few yards out from the beach, and you'll discover all the wonders of the inner reef at your feet. Take to a boat and venture a little further out toward the edge of the reef, strap on your scuba gear, and you'll enter a crystal world of color, marine life, coral cathedrals, and shipwrecks. See www.eleu.net/diving.html for details on diving on Eleuthera.

Harbour Island.

Best Dive Sites

Stingray Hole

Just to the north of Spanish Wells, this is a long stretch of fringed reef that has spelled disaster for dozens of ships over almost three centuries. In one spot, three wrecks lie one atop the other. The reef itself has a variety of reef and deep-sea fish, along with crustaceans, urchins, and anemones at depths varying from 10 to 80 feet.

The Plateau

Just off Harbour Island, this is a huge underwater plain of rolling coral, sandy crevices, ledges, cuts and channels at depths that vary from 45 to 100 feet, all densely populated with marine life.

The Arch

Also off Harbour Island, the Arch is a giant coral grotto with schools of gaily colored fish swimming back and forth, ever-changing their direction like some underwater flock of birds.

The Current Cut

AUTHOR PICK

An exciting adventure for experienced divers. Located between Eleuthera and Current Island, the 100-yard-wide channel is subject to the changing tides that send a mighty current eddying through the corridor. Divers enter the channel at one end and come tumbling out the other in a flurry of bubbles and churning water. You'll need to wear a wet suit to ride the Cut.

The Pinnacles

The Pinnacles represent part of a mountain of coral heads rising upward from the ocean floor and covered with giant sponges, elkhorn, seafans, plate, brain and tube corals. You'll need to go deep to explore this one.

Shipwrecks

The Arimoroa

The *Arimoroa*, often called the Freighter Wreck, is a 260-foot Lebanese freighter that ran aground in 1970. Apparently, the ship caught fire at sea and the captain decided to ground her on Egg Island to save the crew. The crew made it safely ashore and the fire continued to burn. Today, the hulk sits on the rocks in 20 feet of water. The burned-out shell is a haven for fish and other marine life. The wreck provides a wonderful photographic opportunity.

The Carnarvon

The *Carnarvon* is another old freighter that ran aground in 1919 and sank off North Eleuthera. She now sits on the sandy bottom in about 30 feet of water. The site is littered with wreckage, including the ship's anchors, boilers, engines, and propeller. It's an easy dive and, once again, a great photo opportunity.

The Cienfuagos

A 90-foot passenger liner launched in Pennsylvania in 1883, the *Cienfuegos* ran aground on February 5, 1895 in heavy seas north of Harbour Island. All the passengers and crew survived. Today, battered to pieces by the persistent action of the sea, what's left of the liner is scattered over a wide area in 30 to 40 feet of water. There's still plenty to see.

The Train Wreck

Not far from the *Carnarvon* wreck, this is what's left (wheels, etc.) of a steam locomotive from the Civil War submerged in 20 feet of water. It was lost when the barge carrying it went down in 1865 during a storm on the Devil's Backbone reef.

Best Snorkeling Sites

Bird Cay

Bird Cay has lots of fish, conch, and other small marine life.

Blue Hole

This area of reef around an old blue hole offers lots of corals and colorful marine fish.

Current Cut

Not for the fainthearted, this is a "roller-coaster ride through a tidal cut that attracts all sorts of marine critters."

Gaulding's Cay

One of the most beautiful reef gardens on the island. Lots of corals of every description, sea anemones and bonefish.

Glass Window Bridge

Once the bridge between north and south Eleuthera, the structure has now taken on new life as a sunken reef.

Muttonfish Point

This is home to large numbers of mutton snapper, from which the site gets its name, and many colorful reef fish.

Oleander Reef

Just a short swim from the beach, this is one of the island's most densely populated underwater areas, with plenty of reef fish.

Paradise Beach

Not far from the beach, the barrier reef here is home to a huge parrot fish, schools of jacks, and lots of other reef dwellers.

Pineapple Dock

This old wreck now hosts a multitude of colorful fish, invertebrates, and many other species of small marine life.

AUTHOR PICK

Sea Fan Gardens

If you're looking for a thrill, this is the site for you. The gardens are the home of "Baron," a large barracuda.

Cousteau Snorkeling Adventures

Five hotels on Eleuthera participate in the Jean Michel Cousteau "Snorkeling Adventures" program (see page 48): **Cambridge Villas**, in Governor's Harbour, ☎ 800-688-4752; **Palmetto Shores Villas**, Governor's Harbour, ☎ 800-688-4752; **Rainbow Inn**, Governor's Harbour, ☎ 800-688-4752; **The Cove Eleuthera**, Gregory Town, ☎ 800-552-5960; and **Unique Village**, Governor's Harbour, ☎ 800-688-4752. All of these hotels include most of the following popular snorkeling locations in their itineraries.

Dive Operators

Romora Bay Club Dive Shop

On Harbour Island, with a staff of four, including two instructors, they have been in business for more than 20 years. Regular daily dives are conducted in the mornings and afternoons. The staff will be pleased to organize custom trips to suit individual interests. The company's professional affiliations include PADI. Packages are available through most of the hotels on Harbour Island. One-tank dives cost $35; two-tank dives, $60. ☎ 242-333-2325. www.romorabay.com.

Valentine's Dive Center

In business for 17 years, the center has a staff of six, including three instructors. They conduct daily dives in the mornings and afternoons, and night dives once a week. The company operates two boats, with capacities of 10 to 28 persons. One-tank dives cost $35; two-tank dives, $60. A dive at the Current Cut is $125. Professional affiliations include PADI and SSI. Valentine's can cater to individual site requests and conducts excursions to many of the most popular dive sites. Packages are offered through Valentine's Yacht Club & Marina. ☎ 800-383-6480. www.valentinesdive.com.

South Eleuthera Dive

In Rock Sound, conveniently located for guests staying at the southern end of the island, this outfit can provide all the amenities and services you'll need, from customized trips to instruction. One-tank dives cost $35; two-tank dives, $60. ☎ 242-334-4083. www.bahamas-rental.com/southdive.html.

Where to Stay & Eat

Restaurant Price Scale	
$ . . . . less than $20 per person	
$$ . . . . $20-$50 per person	
$$$ . . . . $50+ per person	

■ Dining

Governor's Harbour

$$ Picchio, ☎ 242-332-2455. Open for dinner only, this 10-year-old Bahamian-style home-turned-restaurant offers a range of local and international specialties, such as French baby lamb chops and spaghetti with crayfish and conch. There is a fine selection of imported wines.

Gregory Town

$$ Cove Eleuthera, ☎ 242-335-5142. Open for breakfast, lunch and dinner, the restaurant has a view of the waterfront, poolside dining, and a menu that offers American and Bahamian cuisine.

Hatchet Bay

$$ Hatchet Bay Yacht Club, ☎ 242-335-0396. Open for breakfast, lunch and dinner, the Yacht Club has a nautical atmosphere, along with a casual Bahamian menu featuring burgers, conch, grouper and lobster.

$$ The Rainbow Inn, ☎ 242-335-0294, is open for dinner. It's a popular local watering hole and you'd be well advised to make reservations for dinner. The menu includes a large selection of Bahamian and continental dishes, including conch, lobster and escargots. Closed on Sunday and Monday during the summer, and on Sunday only in the winter.

Palmetto Point

$$ Unique Village Restaurant & Lounge, ☎ 242-332-1830, is open for lunch and dinner, specializing in local dishes, steak and seafood, peas and rice, and conch served several different ways.

Harbour Island

$ Coral Sands Beach Bar, Sundeck and Lounge, ☎ 242-333-2320, is open from 11 am until dark. No reservations are required. It overlooks the three-mile Pink Beach and serves lunch until 3 pm.

$$-$$$ Romora Bay Club, ☎ 242-333-2325. The restaurant features indoor or outdoor dining for breakfast, lunch and dinner. Fixed menu, with alternative choices. Dinner is served at one 7:30 sitting. An elegant dining experience. Reservation and proper dress required for dinner.

$$ Runaway Hill Club, ☎ 242-333-2150, is open to the public for dinner only. You need a reservation. A set menu is served at 8 pm in an elegant dining room. Cost is $40 per person.

$$ Angela's Starfish Restaurant, ☎ 242-333-2253, is open daily from 8:30 am until 8:30 pm for breakfast, lunch and dinner. The menu features authentic Bahamian cuisine.

Aerial view of The Cove.

$ The Bahama Bayside Café, ☎ 242-333-2174, is on the waterfront north of the Straw Market. Open from 7:30 am until 9 pm for breakfast, lunch, dinner and snacks.

$$ The Landing, ☎ 242-333-2707, a harbor-front restaurant, is open daily for breakfast, lunch and dinner. The menu is extensive and features Bahamian and Mediterranian dishes. Open until 10 pm.

$$ The Reach, ☎ 242-333-2142, is on the waterfront at Valentine's Resort and Marina. The atmosphere is casual, the service pleasant and fast, and the food is as good as it gets. Popular with yachting fraternity. Open from 7:30 am until 10 pm for breakfast, lunch, dinner and snacks.

■ Accommodations

See www.eleu.net/hotels.html for detailed information on hotels on Eleuthera.

Hotel Meal Plans

- **CP** (Continental Plan) includes a continental breakfast.
- **EP** (European Plan) denotes no meals, although restaurant facilities are available either on the property or nearby.
- **MAP** (Modified American Plan) denotes breakfast and dinner.
- **FAP** (Full American Plan) includes all meals.
- **All-Inc.** (All-Inclusive Plan) includes all meals, beverages (alcoholic and soft), watersports, tennis and golf, if available.

Hilton's Haven, on Queen's Highway at Tarpum Bay, ☎ 242-334-4231. This is a 10-room guest house without all the facilities of the larger hotels and resorts. Don't let that put you off, though. The lack of facilities is more than made up for by the close personal attention you'll receive at the hands of the owner. Rates start at around $55 per person, per night; MAP is $30 extra.

The Cove Eleuthera, Gregory Town, ☎ 800-552-5960, www.thecoveeleuthera.com. The Cove sits on 28 acres with its own secluded beach, swimming pool, and tennis courts. The 24 guest rooms are all nicely furnished, air-conditioned, and have covered porches. Bicycles are available for rent, and hikers can wander the grounds, the beaches, and the island roads. Rates start at $110 per person, per night; MAP is $38 extra.

The Romora Bay Club, Harbour Island, ☎ 800-327-8286, www.romorabay.com. The Club is a luxury resort surrounded by lush greenery and secluded trails. All guest rooms are tastefully decorated; each has several pieces of original art. Some have kitchens; most have rattan furniture, and all have air-conditioning, patios, and ceiling fans. The pool is new and there's plenty of room for relaxing. The bar overlooks the harbor and the beach is only a short walk away. The restaurant features an international menu prepared by a world-class chef. Rates are in the region of $190 per night; MAP is $50 extra per person, per day.

Coral Sands Hotel, Romora Bay, Harbour Island, ☎ 800-333-2368, www.coralsands.com. The guest rooms and suites, some in the main building and some in an annex, are all well appointed and have patios, large closets, and living areas. There's a lighted tennis court, indoor games, and bikes, motor scooters and boats available for rent. Meals are served on the patio overlooking the ocean. There's live music on weekends. Rooms start at $160 per person, per night; MAP plans are available.

Cambridge Villas, Gregory Town, ☎ 800-688-4752. This is a retreat for those who like to get away from it all to fish, snorkel, dive or simply sit back and do nothing at all. You can stroll the beach in search of shells by day and dance to the seductive sounds of the steel band by night. Accommodations include apartments with living room, bath, air-conditioning and fully equipped kitchenette; standard, superior double, triple, and quad rooms all feature private baths. The staff is happy to arrange fishing, diving, snorkeling, and sightseeing excursions. The resort even has its own five-passenger airplane on hand for island-hopping charters. There's a pleasant dining room, with great food, swimming pool, and complimentary transportation to the beach. Car rentals are available. Rates start at around $80 per person, per night. MAP plans are available.

For more hotel listings and rates, check the At a Glance *section at the back of the book.*

The Exumas ~~Maybe~~ ⊗

From a point just 35 miles south-east of New Providence, the Exumas – a chain of 365 islands and cays – lie strung out across some 95 miles of ocean almost to Long Island. The total population is about 3,550.

It's an area of great natural beauty with tiny cays, secluded inlets, isolated beaches, and great fishing, an ideal vacation spot for boaters, fishermen, and beachcombers.

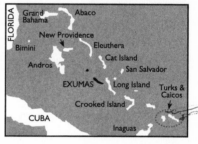

Most of the islands' inhabitants live on **Great Exuma** or **Little Exuma**, both of which are in the southern part of the island chain. **George Town** is the population center of Great Exuma, while **Williams Town** is the main town on Little Exuma. The Exumas are easily reached by air from Miami or Nassau on daily flights to Exuma's International Airport at **Moss Town**, just a few miles north of George Town.

Exuma Cays Land & Sea Park

To the north on Great Exuma and Staniel Cay lies the Exuma Cays Land & Sea Park. The park, administered by the Bahamas National Trust, is a 177-square-mile tract of islands, cays, and reefs where the underwater world can easily be seen through 10 feet or so of water. Accessible only by boat, this is a conservation area where you can observe the wildlife and marine life in its natural surroundings, unspoiled and beautiful. The park – specifically Allens Cays – is home to the **Bahamian Dragons**, rock iguanas that can grow to more than two feet long. Undersea are reefs, blue holes and shipwrecks. **Ocean Rock** features an underwater valley known locally as the **Iron Curtain**, with huge caves full of black coral.s

History

 The Lucayan Indians, the first inhabitants of the Exumas, were followed in the 1600s by the **Spanish** explorers, who virtually wiped out the Indians. About the same time, the discovery of salt sparked the Exumas' first prosperous industry. This prosperity, however, brought its own problems. The salt merchants' ships made easy pickings for pirates, and the islands were a natural haven for the corsairs.

In 1783, a group of loyalists fleeing from the aftermath of the American Revolution settled on the islands and, for a while at least, cotton brought new industry to the islands. Both the salt and the cotton plantations were manned by slaves, most of whom were imported from the former British colonies in America. This new prosperity didn't last, however. Insects destroyed the cotton, and it was found that salt could be produced more profitably on other islands in the Bahamas.

Rolle Town on Great Exuma is the direct result of the influx of the Loyalists in 1783. John Rolle settled in the area with his slaves, more than 300 of them, and soon acquired a great deal of land granted to

St. Andrews Church, George Town.

him by a grateful English king. Rolle was later knighted for his services.

Rolle's Heirs

After the slaves were freed by England's 1834 Act of Emancipation, most of those belonging to Lord Rolle took his name – and his land. Today, many of the inhabitants of the Exumas are named Rolle and it's not clear whether they were given the land by a philanthropic master or simply took it along with his name and their freedom. Today the land cannot be sold, but must be passed down from generation to generation.

Rolle Town sits on top of a hill. The houses are painted in bright colors of blue, pink and yellow. The view from the little town is spectacular.

The descendants of John Rolle's slaves are mostly **farmers** or **fishermen**, selling the day's catch, along with tomatoes, onions, mangoes, and avocados to hotels. Those who aren't farmers or fishermen earn their livelihood as a part of the burgeoning **tourist industry**, working at the hotels and marinas.

Parliament Buildings, George Town.

The Exumas

Getting There

■ By Air

Two international airports serve the Exumas, **George Town** and **Staniel Cay**, neither as grand as the designation "international" implies.

George Town Airport	
FROM	**AIRLINE**
Nassau	**Bahamasair** operates two daily schedules, morning and afternoon, ☎ 800-222-4262. Round-trip fare, $120
Fort Lauderdale	**Island Express**, ☎ 954-359-0380; **Air Sunshine**, ☎ 800-327-8900. Round-trip fare, $170.
Miami	**American Eagle**, ☎ 800-433-7300; **Bahamasair**, ☎ 800-222-4262. Both operate regular daily schedules. Round-trip fare, $175.

Staniel Cay Airport	
FROM	**AIRLINE**
Nassau	**Bahamasair** operates regular daily trips, ☎ 800-222-4262. Round-trip fare, $120.
Fort Lauderdale	**Island Express**, ☎ 954-359-0380. Round-trip fare, $170.

■ By Mail Boat

Mail boats operate weekly between Nassau (Potter's Cay Dock) and, as always, schedules depend on the weather so they can be erratic. The dock master can be reached at ☎ 423-339-1064.

Grand Master sails from Potter's Cay, Nassau, for George Town on Tuesdays at 2 pm, and returns on Fridays at 7 am. Sailing time is 12 hours. The fare, one way, is $55.

■ By Private Boat

The waters around these islands make sailing a great pleasure. To the north, **Allen's Cay** and **Leaf Cay** represent the northern extremity of the archipelago and, less than 40 miles from Nassau, they are easily accessible from the island's capital. There's a protected anchorage between the two.

*If you're interested in the local wildlife, you'll want to visit **Leaf Cay**; it's the home of the rare Bahamian iguana. The iguana is a protected species. So, if you have a dog on board, you are requested not to take it ashore because of the threat it will pose to the iguanas.*

From the south end of **Norman's Cay**, the **Exuma Cays Land & Sea Trust** extends some 22 miles to the north and seven miles to the east and west on either side of the islands. Since commercial fishing is banned within the boundaries of the Trust, the waters there are teeming with fish. And, as the average depth of the water is only eight feet, it represents one of the finest snorkeling grounds in the Bahamas.

Sampson Cay is just south of the Trust. Here, boaters have a choice of a 500-foot dock in the outer harbor, or the 30 full-service slips at the **Sampson Cay Club and Marina**. The VHF frequency is 16.

Staniel Cay Yacht Club is also just south of the Trust. They offer 15 full-service slips, along with showers, fuel service, water, ice, groceries and other sea-going necessities. The VHF frequency is 16. ☎ 242-355-2024, fax 242-355-2044.

Moving farther south, **Elizabeth Harbour**, at **George Town**, offers a sheltered anchorage within easy reach of the shops and stores.

Exuma Fantasea Marina is also at George Town. There you'll have access to 36 full-service slips, water, and fuel. There's a restaurant and shops nearby in George Town. The VHF frequency is 16. ☎ 242-336-3483, fax 242-336-3483.

George Town is the Exumas' official port of entry.

Getting Around

Most of the cays that make up the Exumas are accessible only by boat. **Staniel Cay**, north of George Town, is famous for its beaches, diving, and fishing, and for its great underwater grotto, where the James Bond movie, *Thunderball*, was filmed. Staniel Cay is the jumping-off point for the **Exuma Cays Land & Sea Park**; there are no organized trips. To reach Staniel Cay, charter a small plane at George Town and

Exuma Cays Land & Sea Park.

fly in, or rent a sailboat and crew and travel by sea. The sea voyage will take about a day and a half.

To see George Town and the surrounding area, you have two or three different options. You can take in the sights slowly on foot; you can rent a bicycle, motor scooter, or car and head out on your own; or you can hire a taxi and do it in relative style and comfort.

■ By Taxi

Your taxi driver will give you a running commentary and you'll soon know almost as much about the Exumas' principal town as he does. A taxi for a day will cost about $120, depending upon how good you are at bargaining. The easiest place to find a cab is at the airport.

■ George Town On Foot

To do the sights of George Town on foot – it won't take long – start in the center of town on the Queen's Highway. There you'll find the **Club Peace and Plenty**, named for the ship that brought John Rolle to the islands. The hotel was opened in 1955 and encompasses the remains of an old warehouse on Harbourfront. You can take a ferry from the Club to **Stocking Island**, where you might spend an afternoon on the beach or snorkeling in the clear green waters.

Walk a short distance north along Queen's Highway and you'll come to **St. Andrews**, a little church with a gabled roof and arched doorways. To the south is the **Government Administration Building**, which houses the local police station and post office. There's a small park opposite with a straw market offering locally made gifts and trinkets. A bit farther on to the northf is the **Town Café**, a good little restaurant for breakfast or lunch. Nearby **Exumas Transport**, ☎ 336-2101, has cars for rent. **Sam's Place**, a great seafood restaurant with the best conch salad on the island, is just a few steps farther. From there, it's back to Club Peace and Plenty.

■ Touring by Bus

Christine Rolle's Island Tours (no phone number) has a nice new air-conditioned bus, and the price of her three- to four-hour tours is $20 per person. There's an Eastern Tour

(Little Exuma, Shark Lady, Hermitage Plantation Ruins, and many secluded beaches), and Western Tour (Loyalist tombs, Emerald Bay, Barra Terre, and bush medicine. Contact Christine through your hotel.

■ Touring by Motor Scooter

You can see a lot of Great Exuma this way, and at a pace to suit yourself. You can rent a motor scooter at **Exuma Dive Center**, ☎ 242-336-2390. Rates are $35 per day; $240 per week. Once again, the place to start is right in the center of George Town at the Club Peace and Plenty on Harbourfront. Head out northward along the east coast via the Queen's Highway for about eight miles, past Hooper's Bay, Moss Town to the left, then Ramsey and Jimmy's Hill, until you come to **Ocean Bight**, a tiny, picturesque fishing village where you can spend a quiet afternoon swimming and walking before returning to George Town.

■ Touring by Bike

Starfish – The Exuma Activity Center, ☎ 242-336-3033, rents 21-speed specialized mountain and cruiser bikes for $15-$25 per day. Downtown George Town; e-mail starfishexuma@pocketmail.com.

■ Touring by Car

This is the way to do the island in style. It will take about four hours – longer if you stop for a snack or a swim – to see all the sights along the Queen's Highway from George Town to Barraterre at the northern tip of Great Exuma, a journey of only 30 miles or so. Follow the road along the coast to Hooper's Bay and then head into **Moss Town**, a tiny farming community with brightly painted houses and two little churches. From there, the road winds on and rejoins the coast road.

As you proceed from Moss Town to **Rolleville** – be sure to take in the tiny bays, inlets and beaches along the way – you'll pass through Farmer's Hill and Steventon, the remains of two of Lord Rolle's once-great plantations. The great houses are long gone, but the descendants of the slaves that once worked the cotton fields still live in and around the area.

Rolleville, one of the largest settlements here, is in fact a tiny community of a few small houses, a church, and **The Hilltop Tavern**, where you can enjoy a lunch of fresh grouper and an ice-cold drink.

From Rolleville, you must return the way you came for about a mile, where the road branches off to the west for **Alexander** – another old plantation settlement – and on to **Barraterre**, a quaint fishing village well worth the drive from George Town. Barraterre offers several stores where you can buy locally made handicrafts and gifts, an inn for something to eat and drink, and a beach where you can watch fishermen bringing in the day's catch.

If you drive south from George Town for about 15 miles on Queen's Highway, you'll cross a bridge to Little Exuma and the islands' southernmost community of Williams Town. Along the way you'll pass through **Rolle Town**. Turn left into the village, then head up the hill to the **old cemetery**, where you'll find several historic graves and tombs, including those of Captain Alexander McKay and his family.

DID YOU KNOW?

Alexander McKay arrived on the Exumas from Scotland in 1789 to farm 400 acres of land given to him by the English king, George III.

A little farther on you'll find the **Peace and Plenty Bonefish Lodge**, where you can arrange to go bonefishing with Captain Bob Hyde or one of his expert guides.

From Rolle Town, continue south and cross the bridge to **Little Exuma**. Just beyond the bridge you'll see a sign pointing the way to **Tara, Home of the Shark Lady**, and another sign proclaiming that the Tropic of Cancer runs right through the good lady's home. Be sure to visit Tara; it's an amazing experience.

The Shark Lady

The Shark Lady is Miss Gloria Patience. Now in her 70s, she gained her title and reputation from a lifetime of shark fishing. This grand old lady is a story-teller to rank among the very best. How true the stories are you'll have to judge for yourself. She claims to have caught more than 2,000 sharks, including an 18-foot tiger shark and a hammerhead that almost smashed her boat to pieces. And she's still at it. Every day she boards her boat and heads out to check her lines. When she's not fishing, she sells all sorts of little baubles and hand-made gifts.

From the Shark Lady's house head south again to **Forbes Hill**, where you can swim in the spectacular crescent-shaped bay. Stop for lunch at **La Shante**, a small hotel and club set among the dozen or so gaily painted houses that make up Forbes Hill.

The next and last stop on your drive south is **Williams Town**, a community at the end of the Exumas' world. Here you'll find the church of **St. Mary Magdalene** and the remains of yet another cotton plantation. Only the ruins of the great house and some of the slaves' quarters survive.

From Williams Town it's back to George Town. At the end of the day, you find it hard to believe that your round-trip, after all you saw and did, was less than 35 miles.

Nightlife

 There's a **Fish Fry** every Wednesday evening at the Naval Docks just north of George Town. It's great fun and attracts both the locals and tourists. Fresh snapper, conch fritters, ribs, and plenty of Kalick beer, along with music of the islands, make this a unique experience.

Adventures

■ Sea Kayaking & Sailing

 Sea kayaking is one of the few outdoor adventures that almost anyone, experienced or not, can enjoy. It's offered in several areas of the Bahamas, but nowhere is it as popular as in the Exumas. Here you can spend up to a couple of weeks paddling the open waters between the islands of the chain: long hot days, balmy nights spent under canvas, lots to see and do, good food, and fine company. True, you have to be fairly fit to handle the often strenuous exercise of paddling for several hours at a time. But the sheer vastness of the seascapes, the pristine beaches, and the crystal waters, make this type of experience one-of-a-kind.

There are several outfits that handle sea kayaking expeditions to the Exumas.

Starfish – The Exuma Activity Center, toll-free ☎ 877-398-6222, local 242-336-3033. This outfit offers a variety of outdoor adventures: full- and half-day guided sea kayak trips to caves, shipwrecks, smugglers' hideouts, mangrove rivers, blue holes, and the ruins of former Exuma Governor William Walker's mansion on Crab Cay. In addition, they have more than a dozen five- and seven-day kayak touring trips from November through May. The most popular is the Exuma Classic, with four days and three nights of island-to-island kayak touring, plus three nights lodging, transfers, sailing and bike day trips, for $895 to $995, depending upon your choice of lodging. The six-day, five-night kayak tour is $695, and the week-long "BahamaMamaShip" adventure offers a week of guided day adventures with all meals and houseboat lodging for a group of six people at $5,995. They also have three different eco-tours of the harbor and adjacent islands by motor boat for $25 per person. There's a fleet of Hobie Wave sailboats for rent and instruction is available, for a price, of course. Finally, they offer a day-long, private romantic getaway to a secluded island complete with boat driver, lounge chairs, table, snorkel gear, kayak, camera, mats and a gourmet picnic, all for just $95 per person. www.kayakbahamas.com; e-mail wise@carol.com.

 Late-breaking news from the island tells me that Starfish has just completed the purchase of Exuma Sailing Adventures. See the following listing.

Starfish/Exuma Sailing Adventures, ☎ 877-398-6222, www.exuma-bahamas.com, is offering five- and eight-night sailing expeditions up through the Exuma cays and the Exuma Land & Sea Park. Due to the prevailing winds, these tours are one-way. The boats are 21-foot Sea Pearls, twin sails, 12-inch draught, and they carry two to three people. The sailboats are accompanied by a powerboat, which carries all of the supplies and camping gear. Experienced guides and sailing instructors are on hand. This is a great new adventure opportunity. Check it out – availability and rates – on their website.

Ecosummer, ☎ 800-465-8884, www.ecosummer.com, operates a fleet of Klepper kayaks complete with sailing rigs, offering nine- and 15-day expeditions during February, March and April. The Heart of the Exumas is a nine-day expedition covering some 45 miles between Staniel Cay in the south to Norman's Cay in the north. Most of the trip is spent in the Exuma Land & Sea Park. The itinerary is designed to provide a more leisurely pace than the longer Complete Exumas itinerary. You can expect to paddle, and hopefully sail, an average of seven miles per day. But, as winds in the Bahamas are variable, and often blowing in the wrong direction, you'll get plenty of exercise. Still, the seven miles is usually covered quickly, leaving plenty of time for snorkeling, beachcombing, and exploring. The trip grade for the Heart of the Exumas expedition is level 3, meaning that it demands sustained physical activity. It is designed for those who have less vacation time available and who wish to sample tropical kayaking in the most protected part of the Bahamas.

The Complete Exumas expedition – 15 days – covers a distance of about 100 miles from George Town in the south to Allen's Cay in the north, passing through Exuma Land & Sea Park en route. Each day is a mixture of paddling or sailing between camps and exploring both on land and in the water. Daily distances average about 10 miles, which can take a half-day of paddling, less if the winds are helping you. The expedition also includes paddling in tidal creeks and lagoons, and in and out of the more intricate locations among the cays. Again, there will be plenty of time for snorkeling, beachcombing, and exploring some of the tiny settlements along the way. The trip grade for the Complete Exumas Expedition is level 4, with the potential for long paddling days under weather conditions that might include strong winds and high temperatures. The trip is for those who want to experience the entire Exuma Chain and gain the satisfaction of having completed a seldom-offered kayak opportunity.

You don't need previous experience to go on one of the expeditions, but you do need to be fit and in good physical shape. The kayaks are very seaworthy and easy to handle.

The climate during the three months the expeditions are offered sees daytime temperatures between the mid-70s and the low 80s, while the nights are almost always cool and balmy; rainfall averages less than two inches a month.

Take along your snorkeling mask and fins, casual and outdoor clothes, and a good pair of hiking shoes or boots.

The Heart of the Exumas Expedition is offered seven times between March 1st and April 12th (call for exact dates) and costs $1,595 per person, which includes the services of a fully qualified guide and assistant. All equipment is provided, including folding kayaks, paddles, life jackets, tents, and kitchen/cooking gear. Prices are based on shared occupancy on days one and eight, shuttle bus service between the airport and the hotel, charter flights between Nassau and the Exumas on days two and nine, and all meals from breakfast on day two to breakfast on day nine.

The Complete Exumas Expedition is offered twice during the second half of February each year, and costs $2,295 per person, which includes the services of a fully qualified guide and assistant. All equipment is provided, including folding kayaks, paddles, life jackets, tents, and kitchen/cooking gear. Prices are based on shared occupancy in George Town on day one and in Nassau on day 15, airport transfer in George Town, boat transfer to Nassau on day 14, and shuttle bus service to the airport on day 15, and all meals from breakfast on day two to dinner on day 14.

Ibis Tours of Boynton Beach, FL, ☎ 800-525-9411, e-mail info@ ibistours.com, wwwibistours.com, runs trips in Florida's Everglades as well as the Bahamas. They offer an eight-day kayak trip, including snorkeling and swimming into sea caves. Folding kayaks with sails are used in the Bahamas. Most of this trip is within the Exuma Cays Land & Sea Park. Besides the normal amenities, the price for this tour includes a round-trip charter flight from Nassau to the Exumas, and hotel lodging for the first night plus two hotel meals. $1,595 per person. In 2003, there will be two trips in March and four in April.

Twelve persons is the limit on an Ibis trip, with an average guest-to-guide ratio of 5:1. You'll receive in advance a packing list that identifies what you should bring and what they supply; an itinerary of where and when to meet; a medical information form and an insurance form. The price of an Ibis Tour includes all the meals, the boats, all paddling equipment and all the camping equipment, including tents and sleeping bags. Waterproof storage bags are supplied for all personal gear. They "guarantee" great food on all Ibis Trips and they even have a cookbook in the works. Wine is served with dinner, plus rum punches in the Bahamas.

■ Fishing

As it is on most of the Out Islands, the fishing is spectacular. On the east side of the island chain lies the 6,000-foot drop-off of **Exuma Sound**. Big fish inhabit the waters here. Giant marlin, sailfish, and wahoo have been caught in the Sound in record numbers. On the reefs, the water is clear and shallow, providing a happy hunting ground for snapper, record-breaking grouper and even lobster. For the bonefisherman, there are more wadeable flats in the Exumas than anywhere else in the Out Islands, and there are no crowds to bother you. The bonefish average around four or five pounds, but 10-pounders are not uncommon and you might get lucky and hook something even bigger.

Bonefishing guides, too, are plentiful. The **Peace and Plenty Bonefishing Lodge** has several on its staff and, if you simply ask around, there are plenty of locals who know the area and are willing to serve as guides.

Fishing Tournament

July 4th is the date for the **Annual Bonefish Tournament** at Staniel Cay & Yacht Club. ☎ 242-355-2044 for information and registration.

Fishing Packages

Club Peace and Plenty

Club Peace and Plenty in George Town, ☎ 242-345-5555, www.peaceandplenty.com/resorts/resorts.htm, offers a series of bonefishing packages. The rates are per person, based on double occupancy.

- Three days/two nights: $604
- Four days/three nights: $841
- Five days/four nights: $1,078
- Six day/five nights: $1,318
- Seven days/six nights: $1,552
- An extra night plus fishing is $237 per person
- An extra night with no fishing is $130 per person

Each package includes the following: waterfront location, air-conditioned accommodations; Monday night cocktail party; full days of fishing with an experienced guide; expert instruction for first-timers; transportation to the flats, and to and from the airport; breakfast and dinner daily; boxed lunches on fishing days; boat service to Stocking Island; shuttle between the hotel and the Beach Inn; meal exchange between the hotel and the Beach Inn.

Boat Rentals

Staniel Cay Yacht Club, on Staniel Cay, north of Great Exuma, ☎ 242-355-2044. Fishing charters only from $250 to $650 per day.

Minns Watersports, ☎ 242-336-3483. A 17-foot Boston Whaler rents for $70 per day, or $350 per week. Minns is in downtown George Town on Lake Victoria across from Club Peace & Plenty.

■ Powerboat Adventures

Island World Adventures, Nassau, ☎ 242-363-3333, offers a unique excursion to the northern Exumas. If you have a day to spare, take my advice and book this day-trip; you won't regret it. The adventure begins in Nassau in the early morning – you need to be at the dock by 8:30 am – when you board one of two state-of-the-art, high-speed powerboats. Then, to-

AUTHOR PICK

gether, the two boats speed across the clear waters more than 40 miles to **Saddleback Cay** in the northern Exumas. There you'll wade ashore to relax and unwind on one of the Exumas' many uninhabited islands. Be sure to take along your camera and snorkeling gear. The shallow waters of the coral reef are home to a multitude of colorful marine life, and it's all unspoiled. Here, you're likely to encounter rays, turtles, even dolphins. When lunchtime rolls around, you'll be treated to a meal under the palms and savor some authentic Bahamian cuisine. The palm-thatched roofs and gentle breezes make for a very pleasant dining experience. As the day wears on, you'll reboard the boats and begin the trip back to Paradise Island, stopping along the way at **Leaf Cay**, home to a colony of friendly iguanas. You'll arrive back at the dock around 5 pm. Although the outing is not recommended for children under three, people with acute health problems, or pregnant women, this is one adventure you really shouldn't miss. The cost of the day-trip includes the boat ride, lunch, sodas, water, beer, rum punch, snorkeling, guided tours and pick-up from your hotel.

■ Diving & Snorkeling

They say there are some 365 islands in the Exuma chain. But no one has ever bothered to count them properly. The reefs, blue holes, and drop-offs are teeming with reef and deep water fish and other marine life. With an island and its surrounding beaches and reefs for every day of the year, you'll never lack someplace new to explore. For snorkelers, the Exumas are a wonderland of flats, shallow reefs and beaches. You can snorkel almost anywhere. Just wade out a hundred yards or so, and plunge in.

Best Dive Sites

Pagoda Reef

Pagoda Reef is not far from George Town. The elkhorn coral, leaf and sheet corals here have evolved into a magnificent pagoda-like grotto. The whole formation is populated by a great underwater family of parrotfish, sergeant majors, snappers, angels and crustaceans.

Angelfish Blue Hole

Just outside Elizabeth Harbour, this hole is considered the number one dive site in the Exumas. It is tidal, which creates currents and vortexes in and out of the cave. The idea is to dive the hole at the quiet time between the tides.

 Never dive Angelfish without expert guidance.

Angelfish is a huge aquarium filled with thousands of fish.

Crab Cay Crevasse

Not far from Angelfish, this is another spectacular blue hole. The crescent-shaped opening is just 15 feet below the surface. Here, you can dive to the sandy bottom of the cave, where you'll see crabs, lobsters and anemones.

 We strongly recommend you dive with a guide.

Mystery Cave

Mystery Cave is a network of caverns extending for miles beneath Stocking Island and the surrounding ocean. Starting at a depth of only 15 feet, the cavern system soon drops off to a heart-stopping 100 feet.

 Never dive Mystery Cave without an expert guide.

Dive Operators

Exuma Scuba Adventures, ☎ 242-336-2893, www.exumascuba.com, opened in March of 2000 and is owned and operated by a highly qualified staff from the Small Hope Bay Resort on Andros. They operate out of Club Peace and Plenty in George Town, and fill the gap left when Exuma Fantasea went out business several years ago. They have one instructor and two dive masters, three boats and 20 sets of rental gear. One-tank dives are $45, snorkeling is $15.

Dive/Accommodation Packages

Club Peace and Plenty

Club Peace and Plenty in George Town, ☎ 242-536-2551, offers an eight-day, seven-night package during the period of May 1st to December 15th for $1,099 per person, based on double occupancy; and again from December 16th to April 30th for $1,199 per person, double occupancy. See page 255 for details.

Where to Stay & Eat

Restaurant Price Scale
$ . . . . less than $20 per person
$$ . . . . $20-$50 per person
$$$ . . . . $50+ per person

■ Dining

 $$ Eddie's Edgewater, on Charlotte Street in George Town, is the place for fresh fish. Famous for turtle steak, the restaurant also serves fresh grouper, fried snapper, pea soup and dumplings, and the inevitable peas and rice. ☎ 242-336-2050.

$ Regatta, Queen's Highway, Stevenson, 15 miles north of George Town, is open weekends and in the high season on weekdays as well. You can watch the staff crack the conch, and marvel at Darren's skills with the knife as he chops veggies, fruit and conch. No phone.

$ The Town Café & Bakery, on Main Street, is a great place for breakfast. The fresh-baked donuts and muffins are to die for. The pancakes are terrific and, if you'd like to try the local food, there's boil fish, chicken souse, and Johnny cake. ☎ 242-336-2194.

$$ Sam's Place features a magnificent view of the ocean from an elevated dining room. Great food and a pleasant atmosphere. ☎ 242-336-2579.

$ Kermit's Hilltop Tavern in Rolleville is a bar and restaurant serving lunch and dinner. Fresh fried grouper, minced lobster, conch, curried mutton, and fresh fruit from Kermit's own farm are on the menu. ☎ 242-345-0002.

$$ The Fisherman's Inn in Barraterre is both a night club and a restaurant, featuring an old-world nautical atmosphere. It can be extremely busy. ☎ 242-355-5017.

■ Accommodations

Hotel Meal Plans

- **CP** (Continental Plan) includes a continental breakfast.
- **EP** (European Plan) denotes no meals, although restaurant facilities are available either on the property or nearby.
- **MAP** (Modified American Plan) denotes breakfast and dinner.
- **FAP** (Full American Plan) includes all meals.
- **All-Inc.** (All-Inclusive Plan) includes all meals, beverages (alcoholic and soft), watersports, tennis and golf, if available.

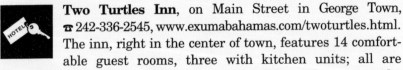

Two Turtles Inn, on Main Street in George Town, ☎ 242-336-2545, www.exumabahamas.com/twoturtles.html. The inn, right in the center of town, features 14 comfortable guest rooms, three with kitchen units; all are air-conditioned. There's also a patio bar shaded by palm trees, and a restaurant where you can sample a variety of Bahamian dishes. The hotel staff will arrange diving, bonefishing, and deep-sea fishing excursions. Bicycles, jeeps and mopeds are available for rent on the premises. The rates start at $88 per night, per person; EP only.

Palms at Three Sisters, Queen's Highway, Mt. Thompson, ☎ 242-358-4040 is right on the ocean. It has 12 air-conditioned rooms and three luxury villas complete with kitchenettes. All rooms have television sets. The dining room offers fresh seafood dinners and a spectacular view of the ocean. The staff can arrange fishing, sailing and diving excursions, and you can go snorkeling among the Three Sisters – three large rocks in the ocean – right off the hotel beach. Rates are around $100 per night; EP only.

Regatta Point, Kid Cove, George Town, ☎ 800-327-0787, www.regattapointbahamas.com. Regatta Point is surrounded on all sides by water. A vacation here is like staying on a private island, but still you're only a few minutes walk from George Town. Each guest apartment is fully equipped with a kitchen, and you'll have use of a skiff that can be tied up at your own private dock. Rates start at $115; EP only.

Club Peace and Plenty, Harbourfront, George Town, ☎ 800-525-2210, www.peaceandplenty.com. The Club has 35 deluxe, air-conditioned rooms, all with tiled floors and private balconies. The restaurant offers fine dining in a candle-lit atmosphere, and a menu featuring both American and traditional Bahamian dishes. There's free ferry service out to the Club's own Stocking Island Beach Club for snorkeling. Windsurfers and Sunfish sailboats are available too. Rates at the Peace and Plenty start at $120 per night; an MAP plan is available for $32 extra.

Coconut Grove Hotel, Queen's Highway, George Town, ☎ 242-336-2659, is an intimate hotel with just 10 guest rooms, all right on the beach. One special suite is perfect for honeymoons or other special occasions. There's a freshwater swimming pool, an outside cocktail bar, and a restaurant where the service is formal but the dress is casual. Rates are $128 per night; MAP will cost you $38 extra.

Peace and Plenty Beach Inn, Harbourfront, George Town, ☎ 242-336-2551, www.peaceandplenty.com. The Beach Inn has 16 deluxe rooms, all with air-conditioning, TVs, refrigerators, and private balconies. The restaurant offers a choice of international or traditional Bahamian cuisine. Tropical drinks from the bar are served around the freshwater swimming pool and on the fishing dock. World-class bonefishing is available. Rates start at $130; MAP is $32 extra.

Staniel Cay Yacht Club, Staniel Cay, ☎ 242-355-2024, www.stanielcay.com. The Yacht Club is in the heart of the island and caters mainly to private pilots, sailors, and vacationers looking for a little peace and quiet. The waters off Staniel Cay provide excellent scuba diving, and the Yacht Club staff will fill your tanks and provide rental scuba gear. The bonefishing is excellent, too. Rates run $195 per night, which includes FAP.

A great new place to stay is **Latitude Exuma Resort**, ☎ 877-398-6222. Located on a private island just a five-minute boat ride from George Town, the resort features one-bedroom waterfront "Casuarina Cottages" overlooking Stocking Island and Elizabeth

Harbour. The units feature exquisite furnishings, a small kitchen, loft, sofa bed or futon, a queen-sized bed, rocking chairs on the porch, dual shower heads in the bathrooms, and terry-cloth bathrobes. There is also a three-bed unit that sleeps nine. There's a bar and grill, a nice beach, and a ferry to Stocking Island. This is the best lodging spot on the Exumas. Rates range from $190 to $240 per day, or $1,200 to $1,400 per week.

Other Islands

Beyond the more well-known Out Islands of the Bahamas, there are many more that are not-so-well-known, just as beautiful, just as inviting, and just as welcoming. They are a little more difficult to get to, but that only makes them more of an adventure. You can spend hours on truly deserted beaches, walk for miles and

never see another soul, fish, dive and snorkel to your heart's content. Package vacations to these islands, with the exception of Long Island and San Salvador, are not available. So you'll need to find a creative travel agent.

With the exception of American Airlines, no major US airline makes scheduled stops at these islands. You can fly into Long Island, usually via Miami, on American, and into the Berry Islands, Long Island, and Cat Island on Island Express out of Fort Lauderdale. But to get to the others you'll need to fly into Nassau via scheduled air, and then onward by Bahamasair, Gulfstream Air or one of the several local air charters.

Another option, one that's worth considering if you have lots of time to spare, is the mail boat. These boats make scheduled runs from Nassau to all of the Out Islands and, for a fee, they'll take you along. If you're truly the adventuresome type, this is the way to go. These little ships, often crowded and noisy, ply the waters between the islands mostly at night and will provide you with an experience you'll remember the rest of your life.

Mail boats leave Nassau, from the docks at the Paradise Island Bridge, for Andros, the Abacos, Eleuthera, the Exumas, Long Island, Cat Island, the Acklins, San Salvador, the Inaguas and others every other week.

The Acklins & Crooked Island

For a remote and tranquil vacation, you might choose a secluded get-away on the Acklins or Crooked Island. Located almost as far south as you can go in the Out Islands, south of the Tropic of Cancer, beyond Long Island and the Exumas, these islands are accessible only by private boat or regularly scheduled flights on Bahamasair.

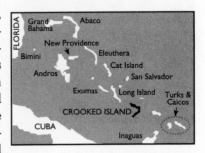

Here you'll discover sunswept shores, scenic coves and hidden bays. On **Crooked Island** there are caves, miles of creeks, tidal flats populated by record tarpon and bonefish. Days on these islands are spent swimming, snorkeling, fishing, visiting tiny churches and historic buildings while you stroll the streets of quaint little towns and villages, such as Snug Corner, Lovely Bay, Delectable Bay Spring Point, Pompey Bay and, on Cat Island, Pittstown Point, Colonel Hill, Landrail Point and Albert Town. In the evening, you'll wander deserted beaches, and enjoy a cool tropical drink as you watch the sun go down in a blaze of glory.

■ History

The history of these islands lies hidden in the mists of time; what's known for sure is that **English** loyalists from Virginia, fleeing the aftermath of the American Revolution, arrived here at the end of the 18th century, bringing with them hundreds of slaves. Soon, more than 40 plantations had been established, but they were short-lived. By 1825, most of them were in ruins, the result of one crop failure after another.

Columbus Was Here

Today, the islands are a quiet little backwater, visited by few, but loved by all that do set foot ashore. Separated from Crooked Island by the Crooked Island Passage, an important shipping route during the early days when sailing ships used it en route to and from the New

World, the Acklins are at the center of the "Columbus-landed-here-first" controversy. These islands entered the debate when *National Geographic* ran an article in 1986, pinpointing Crooked Island as the place where the explorer first set foot in the Bahamas; and the debate will, no doubt, continue.

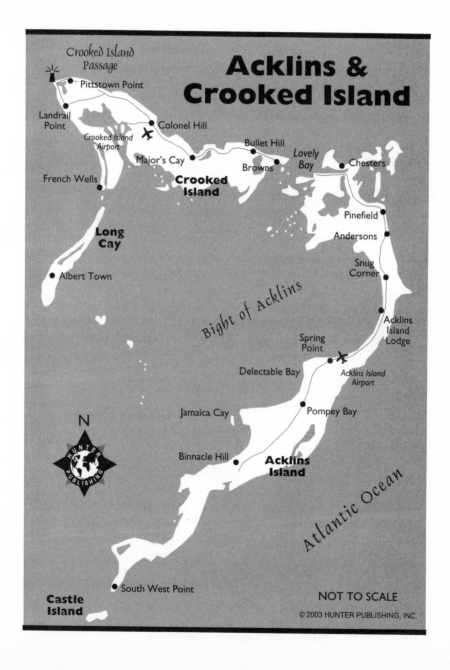

Acklins & Crooked Island

Crooked Island Passage

Pittstown Point

Landrail Point

Crooked Island Airport

Colonel Hill

Major's Cay

Bullet Hill

Browns

Lovely Bay

Chesters

French Wells

Crooked Island

Long Cay

Albert Town

Pinefield

Andersons

Snug Corner

Bight of Acklins

Spring Point

Delectable Bay

Acklins Island Lodge

Acklins Island Airport

N

Jamaica Cay

Pompey Bay

Binnacle Hill

Acklins Island

Atlantic Ocean

South West Point

NOT TO SCALE

© 2003 HUNTER PUBLISHING, INC.

Castle Island

Crooked Island is the hub of activities, such as they are. The island's capital is **Colonel Hill**, a colorful settlement of gaily painted buildings where everyone has a friendly word, and time goes by very slowly. No one's in a hurry here and that, after all, is the essence of a great getaway.

■ Getting There

By Air

From the US, take a regularly scheduled flight into Nassau with a connection to either Colonel Hill or Spring Point. **Bahamasair** flights (☎ 800-222-4262) leave Nassau on Tuesdays and Saturdays at 8:45 am, arriving at 10. Round-trip airfare from Nassau is $168.

By Mail Boat

Lady Matilda leaves Nassau's Potter's Cay Dock weekly for the Acklins, Crooked Island and Mayaguana. The schedule varies according to need and the season. Call the dock master at ☎ 242-393-1064. Sailing time is 15 hours or more, and the voyage is usually overnight. The fares are $65, $70 and $70 respectively.

By Private Boat

There are no marina facilities on Crooked Island or in the Acklins. There are, of course, lots of places where you can drop anchor for the night and pick up supplies – groceries and the like.

*Once you're on the ground and have cleared the small airport building, call your hotel for a ride – ☎ 344-2507 – or grab one of the few **cabs** that may or may not be waiting outside. If you're arriving by mail boat, you may find the telephone is the only option.*

■ Sightseeing

Bird Rock Lighthouse

 If you're a lighthouse enthusiast, you should visit this one. Located on the Crooked Island Passage, it dominates a lonely land- and seascape where the only inhabitants are the gulls and ospreys that squawk and squabble among the rocks where they build their nests.

 The rocky landscape and white lighthouse make this a must for photographers.

Crooked Island Caves

Most of the Out Islands are riddled with caves, and Crooked Island is no different. Many of the caves here are larger than those on other islands: narrow, underground passageways that suddenly open upon vast chambers where shafts of light filter in through holes in the roof. And then there are the bats – harmless enough, but scary even so.

 It's best to explore the caves with a Bahamian guide. Pittstown Point Landing staff will be pleased to arrange this for you. ☎ 242-344-2507.

French Wells

This is one for the environmentalist adventurer. Here, close to the mangroves, is one of the few places in the Bahamas you can watch flamingos in the wild. It is very quiet here. You can almost feel the stillness. The waters are crystal clear – and the fish are fearless. Sit long enough, and you're almost sure to see barracuda, rays and even sharks. Again, the staff at Pittstown Point Landing can arrange a visit.

Marine Farm

Once a British fort built to guard the Crooked Island Passage against marauding Spanish ships and pirates, Marine Farm has long since been abandoned and is now little more than rocks, ruins and rusted cannons. Still, if you have the time, it's well worth a visit to experience a little local history.

The Acklins & Crooked Island

■ Dining

Restaurant Price Scale	
$	less than $20 per person
$$	$20-$50 per person
$$$	$50+ per person

$ In Pittstown, **Ozzie's**, at Pittstown Point Landing, is the place to go. Open from 7 am until 11 pm, they serve three complete meals. Fresh seafood is offered daily, along with a variety of Bahamian dishes. You can even get a picnic basket for a day's outing. ☎ 242-344-2507.

■ Accommodations

Pittstown Point Landings. Just 16 miles from Colonel Hill airport on Crooked Island, this is the premier hotel on the two islands. The hotel has its own airstrip, and the management can arrange for you to be flown in direct from Nassau or Florida. It's an old-world type of establishment where the atmosphere is easy going and quite colonial. The rooms, while a little austere, are comfortable, with nice bathrooms and two double beds. This is a friendly place where you'll soon get to know every member of the staff, as well as the other guests. Speaking of the staff, everyone pitches in: cooks double as waiters, bar tenders double as guides, or might even take you bonefishing. Dress is casual, and rates are reasonable, starting around $100 per night. ☎ 800-752-2322 or 242-344-2507, www.pittstownpointlandings.com. EP, MAP and FAP available.

The Berry Islands

Less than 35 miles to the north of Nassau, close to the fishing grounds on the eastern edge of the Great Bahama Bank, these little-known islands have long been a favorite stop for divers, anglers and yachtsmen. There's not much to them; just 12 square miles of land scattered across a dozen, or so, small cays, most of them privately owned. Small and isolated as the archipelago is, there's plenty for the outdoor en-

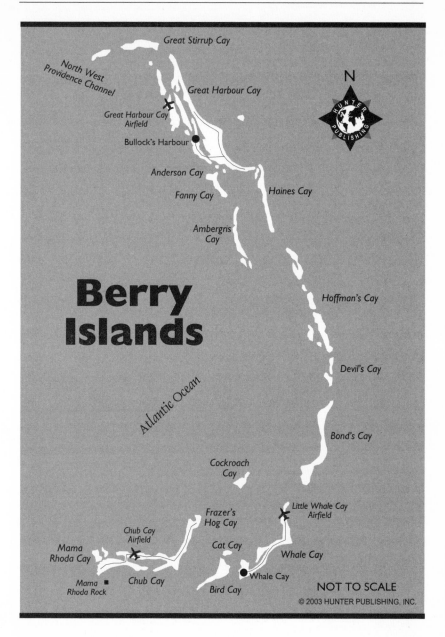

Great Stirrup Cay

North West Providence Channel

Great Harbour Cay

Great Harbour Cay Airfield

Bullock's Harbour

N

Anderson Cay

Fanny Cay

Haines Cay

Ambergris Cay

Berry Islands

Hoffman's Cay

Devil's Cay

Atlantic Ocean

Bond's Cay

Cockroach Cay

Frazer's Hog Cay

Little Whale Cay Airfield

Chub Cay Airfield

Cat Cay

Mama Rhoda Cay

Whale Cay

Mama Rhoda Rock

Chub Cay

Whale Cay

Bird Cay

NOT TO SCALE

© 2003 HUNTER PUBLISHING, INC.

thusiast to see and do. Tiny communities with colorful names – Cockroach Cay, Goat Cay, Hog Cay, Devil's Cay – conjure images of James Bond. Divers can explore the coral reefs off **Mamma Rhoda Rock** and unidentified sunken ships.

Anglers know the Berrys are renowned for championship sport fishing and that they can hunt the "big one" on the Banks, or just off-shore in the deep blue waters to the east. Naturalists can walk the deserted beaches, ply the waters between the islands in a rented boat and perhaps visit the private bird sanctuary on **Bond's Cay**. These islands are perfect for yachtsmen; they lend themselves beautifully to inter-island day-sailing.

The largest of the Berry Islands is **Great Harbour Cay**, where most of the islands' 500 residents live on a narrow strip of land some 10 miles long by only 1½ miles wide.

Chub Cay is the southernmost island in the Berry group. It's a resort island, home to Chub Cay Club, with a 76-slip marina and almost all the modern conveniences you'd expect at a resort in Nassau.

■ Getting There

The Berrys are perhaps the most difficult islands to reach. Your options are limited to charter air, the mail boat and private boat.

By Air

Only private charters serve the Berry Islands. These can be arranged in Nassau or Florida: ☎ 800-688-4752 for information.

From Fort Lauderdale, **Island Express** operates direct flights into Great Harbour Cay. Cost is $200 round-trip. ☎ 954-359-0380 or fax 954-760-9157.

By Mail Boat

Champion II provides service between the Berry Islands and Nassau. The cost of the trip is $30. ☎ 800-688-4752 for information.

By Private Boat

Veteran sailors and yachtsmen will be very familiar with the **Great Harbour Cay Yacht Club and Marina**, a full-service marina with extensive facilities. These include

85 slips, repair facilities, fuel service, laundromat, showers, shops, and a restaurant. The draft at high water is 10 feet; eight feet at low water. The maximum depth is 15 feet. The marina can accommodate boats up to 150 feet long and 70 feet wide. The 30-foot-high bank provides excellent storm protection. You can call for information at ☎ 800-343-7256, fax at 242-367-8115, or call on VHF channel 68.

*You may or may not find a **taxi** at the airport. If not, you'll find local numbers posted. Or you can call your hotel and request a ride.*

■ Adventures on Water

Boat Rentals

Great Harbour Yacht Club & Marina rents small boats and sailboats at rates from $40 per day. ☎ 242-367-8838 or 800-343-7256.

Diving & Snorkeling

While there are a number of excellent diving and snorkeling sites in the Berry Islands, there are no dive operators. You take it as you find it. The barrier reefs are spectacular and unspoiled, ideal for scuba diving: visibility averages over 100 feet. And there are great underwater photo opportunities. Snorkeling is good almost everywhere, but especially so in the shallows off **Chub Cay**.

■ Dining

Restaurant Price Scale
$ . . . . less than $20 per person
$$ . . . . $20-$50 per person
$$$ . . . . $50+ per person

$ Backside Lounge & Disco, Great Harbour Drive, Bullock's Harbour. Open Thursday through Friday, this is a great place for cocktails, dancing and relaxing.

$ The Beach Club. Overlooking the ocean on Great Harbour Drive, Bullock's Harbour, this restaurant is open daily from 7 am until 6 pm for breakfast and lunch.

$ The Tamboo Dinner Club. Located at the Great Harbour Cay Yacht Club, Tamboo is open Wednesday and Saturday for dinner.

$ The Wharf Restaurant and Bar at the Great Harbour Marina is open for breakfast and dinner daily, except Tuesday. It serves local dishes and seafood.

$ White Water Bar & Restaurant. Situated on the causeway into Bullock's Harbour, White Water is open daily for lunch and dinner. Great Bahamian food.

■ Accommodations

Chub Cay Club Resort & Marina. Located on the southernmost island in the Berry group, the resort features beachfront rooms, yacht club rooms, and two- and three-bedroom villas. Amenities include tennis courts, two swimming pools – one for members and one for guests – and two beaches. There's also a full-service dive shop where you can take scuba lessons or guided day-trips to the reefs or wrecks. Guest rooms are comfortable, and most have coffee makers and satellite television. There's a non-member's bar and a fine dining room that serves three meals every day. The fare includes such local delights as peas and rice, grouper and lobster, and not-so-local dishes such as lamb chops and steaks. At night you can while away the hours in the bar, playing pool or dominoes, or dancing. Rates start at $120 per night. EP only. ☎ 800-662-8555 or 242-325-1490, www.chubcay.com.

Great Harbour Marina. Expensive, but well worth it, the accommodations here on Great Harbour Cay border on the luxurious. It offers waterfront townhouses at the marina and beachfront villas on the eastern shore. All are comfortable, with air-conditioning, ceiling fans and fully equipped kitchens. Marina units all have private docks, and daily maid service is provided for all units. Facilities include three restaurants, as many bars, and a couple of small inns. Bicycles and motor scooters are available for rent; diving and snorkeling excursions can be arranged; small boats are also available for rent, as well as larger powerboats and sailboats. There's even a nine-hole golf course. Rates start at $120 per night. EP only. ☎ 800-343-7256 or 242-367-8838, www.greatharbourmarina.com.

Cat Island

Named for a British sea captain, Cat Island is one of the most beautiful in the Bahamas: 50 square miles of tranquility, rolling hills and lush green forests. It's a peaceful retreat of great natural beauty, with a way of life that's quiet and relaxed.

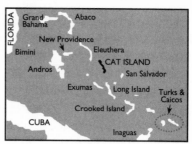

You can enjoy endless miles of wind-blown beaches, explore the **Arawak Indian Caves** near Port Howe, and follow the stations of the cross to the island's highest point, the peak of **Mount Alverina** at 206 feet. At the top is **The Hermitage**, a miniature abbey built by Father Jerome Hawes, by hand, during the early part of the 20th century.

DID YOU KNOW?

During the 17th century, the island was known as San Salvador, the same name as that of the tiny island just to the southeast where, so the story goes, Columbus first landed in 1492.

AUTHOR PICK

Cat Island is not on any list of tourist destinations. It's a distant stop on sailing routes southeast beyond Nassau and Eleuthera. Time goes by slowly; electricity and running water are luxuries. The island's residents make their living farming or fishing, and visitors spend their days quietly: swimming, hiking, visiting the ruins of Colonial plantations, or simply contemplating the great natural beauty of the island.

■ Getting There

By Air

Scheduled service by **Bahamasair** (☎ 800-222-4262) from Nassau to Arthur's Town. The fare is $120 round-trip. Charter service is available to New Bight from Fort Lauderdale, and is provided by **Island Express**, ☎ 954-359-0380; **Air Sunshine**, ☎ 800-327-8900; **Bel Air Transport**, ☎ 954-524-9814. Average charter cost per person is $200.

A 4,600-foot airstrip is within 300 feet of the Hawk's Nest Resort and Marina. Transport to and from the strip can be arranged by calling ☎ 357-7257.

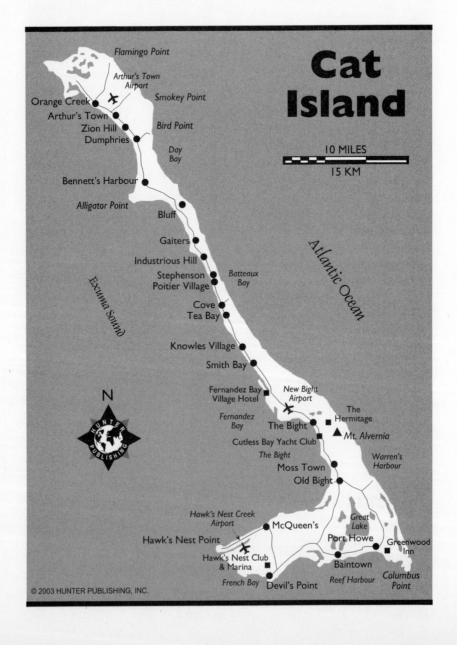

Complimentary transportation to and from the airport is provided by all of the major hotels on the island. Some require advance notice, so it's best to call ahead. Cabs are also available at the airport, and at the dock to meet the mail boats; they will make the run between any and all of the hotels. They are also on call for sightseeing excursions.

By Mail Boat

Cat Island is well served by Nassau's mail boat system. You can leave Potter's Cay dock either on Tuesday or Wednesday, and return either on Friday the same week, or on Monday the week following.

The *North Cat Island Special*, leaves each Wednesday at 1 pm for Cat Island (North and South), Arthur's Town, Bennen's Harbour, Bluff, and Bight, and returns on Friday. Sailing time is 14 hours. The fare is $40.

Sea Hauler leaves each Tuesday at 3 pm for Cat Island (South), Smith's Bay, Bight, Old Bight, and returns on Monday. Sailing time is 12 hours. The fare is $40.

By Private Boat

You can arrive in your own boat and stay at **Hawk's Nest Resort and Marina** (see below).

■ Sightseeing

The Hermitage

Near New Bight, the Hermitage is set atop Mount Alvernia. Mount is, perhaps, a bit of stretch but, at an elevation of 206 feet, it does represent the highest point on the island. The Hermitage is a tiny abbey complete with round tower and cloister, all built of gray native stone by the hand of its founder, Father Jerome Hawes. The little abbey commands an outstanding view of the island, New Bight, and Fernandez Bay away to the north. The seascape as seen from the abbey is spectacular. The

The Hermitage.

pale green shallows glow and sparkle in the sunlight, and the sandy shore is bright white.

From New Bight, take the dirt road, up the rise, through the old stone arch and on along the footpath up the hill. It's a strenuous hike of about 20 minutes, but well worth the effort for the gorgeous views.

The Deveaux Plantation

The Deveaux Plantation, in Port Howe, was once the scene of splendor and luxury. Today, it lies in ruins. This was the home of Colonel Andrew Deveaux, who settled with his family and slaves on Cat Island in the 18th century. It's worth seeing to experience the local history and the spectacular setting.

■ Adventures on Water

Boat Rentals

 Fernandez Bay Village offers guided boat rentals with captain only. Rates are approximately $450 for a half-day and $675 for a full day. ☎ 800-940-1905.

Greenwood Beach Resort. Charters only, from $250 per day for 16-foot reef fishing boats. ☎ 242-342-3053.

Diving & Snorkeling

There are two full-service dive centers on the island. Both offer excursions to the reef, one has night dives and wall diving, and both have equipment rental.

Cat Island Dive Centre

At the Hotel Greenwood Inn. Facilities include equipment rental, PADI instruction, and local ocean dives. Telephone/fax ☎ 242-342-3053.

Hawk's Nest Dive Centre

This facility is at the Hawk's Nest Resort. It is a full-service outfit offering equipment rental, instruction, day and night dive excursions and reef and wall diving. Rates are $45 for a one-tank dive. Snorkel equipment can be rented for $10 per day. ☎ 242-357-7257.

Best Snorkeling Sites

Both the Fernandez Bay Village and the Greenwood Beach Resort participate in the Jean Michel Cousteau "Snorkeling Adventures" program. The best sites are as follows:

Bains Town

An area of the reef with large quantities of sea fans, elk- and staghorns, and brain corals.

Dry Head

A large area of coral reef that includes sea fans, brain and lettuce coral formations, along with schools of grunts and yellowtails.

Greenwood Beach

Adjacent to the resort, this is another section of the reef where you can explore a variety of coral formations.

Guana Keys

The Keys are a chain of reefs, close to a small island you can use for a base, where the water is unusually clear, and fairly shallow to the point where it approaches the drop-off. The marine life here is prolific.

Hazel's Hideaway

An area with lots of soft corals and multitudes of reef fish.

Lump of Limestone

Just a few minutes swim from the beach, this limestone formation is home to a number of large, friendly groupers.

Naked Point

An underwater cave and the home of a variety of marine life, including stone crabs. Lots of fun and an unusual snorkeling experience.

Shipwreck

An old wreck, half-in and half-out of the water. It's an unusual snorkel with lots of marine life, including lobsters, crabs and a variety of multi-colored reef fish.

■ Dining

Restaurant Price Scale	
$	less than $20 per person
$$	$20-$50 per person
$$$	$50+ per person

 $$ The Bluebird Restaurant & Bar, in New Bight, is accessible only by boat. It overlooks the ocean, serves Bahamian dishes incorporating fresh seafood: conch, shrimp, lobster, grouper, etc. The food is good and reasonably priced, starting around $16 for dinner. Open daily except Sunday for breakfast, lunch and dinner. ☎ 242-342-3095.

$$ The Bridge Inn's restaurant is open for breakfast, lunch and dinner. The dining room is clean and attractive and there's a rustic bar where you can enjoy an evening cocktail. The menu is extensive, offering a variety of fresh seafood − steamed grouper, conch, lobster, crab − with garden-fresh vegetables, and peas and rice. ☎ 242-342-3013.

$$$ Fernandez Bay Village's restaurant is open daily for breakfast, lunch and dinner. The menu features Bahamian and international dishes served on the beach terrace. Appetizers and cocktails are available in the evenings before dinner from 7 pm. A reservation is required for dinner. ☎ 242-342-3043.

New Bight, Cat Island.

$$$ The Greenwood Beach Resort's oceanfront restaurant offers outdoor and indoor dining with a menu that features Bahamian and European cuisine along with extensive buffet dinners. ☎ 242-342-3053.

■ Accommodations

The Bridge Inn. Located in The Bight, this is a small, comfortable hotel hideaway. The rooms are spacious. Some have air-conditioning. The food is good, and free round-trip transportation from New Bight airport is provided. Rates start at $60 per night for a room without air-conditioning, and $100 for one with air-conditioning. To get there, you simply fly into New Bight. The hotel will take care of the rest. For reservations and information, ☎ 800-688-4752 or 242-342-3013; fax 242-342-3041.

The Greenwood Beach Resort & Dive Center. This 20-room resort in Port Howe is situated on an eight-mile stretch of pink sand beach. It's an ideal spot for diving and snorkeling – the coral heads are just off-shore from the hotel. All rooms have private baths, king-size beds, and patios. There's a large oceanfront restaurant serving Bahamian and international dishes, and there are beachfront gazebos where you can relax in the shade and enjoy a quiet af-

Fernandez Bay, Cat Island.

ternoon with a good book. The full-service, on-site dive shop on the property can arrange trips for wall and reef diving. Fly into New Bight airport and call the hotel for transportation. Rates are reasonable, starting at $69 off-season; $79 during the peak winter months. ☎ 877-228-7475, 242-342-3053, www.GreenwoodBeachResort.com.

Hawk's Nest Resort & Marina. This resort has its own airstrip which, along with its marina and on-site dive shop, makes it one of the most accessible resorts on Cat Island. Accommodations are limited to just 10 rooms. The rooms are, however, comfortably appointed and, unlike those at most hotels on the island, are air-conditioned. Most rooms have king-size beds. Those that don't have two queen-size beds. Refrigerators are available on request, but there are no TVs in the rooms; satellite TV is available in the lounge. There's a broad sandy beach, just right for relaxing, swimming and shelling, fishing and bird-watching. Bikes and mopeds are available on-site. To get there, fly into Hawk's Nest via charter or private plane, or take Bahamasair into Arthur's Town Airport and call the hotel to make arrangements for transport to the hotel. The rates are on the expensive side, starting at $270 per night. ☎ 800-688-4752 or 242-342-7050, www.hawks-nest.com.

Fernandez Bay Village is a rather remote and rustic resort of nine villas situated on one of the finest stretches of private beach on the island. This small family-run resort specializes in, as they say, "the kind of hospitality you expect when visiting good friends." They do a little better than that, however. The rooms, though rustic, border on the luxurious. The floors are laid with terra-cotta tiles, the walls are made from fieldstone, and the furniture is dark, heavy and opulent. All rooms are cooled by overhead fans, and most have an outdoor garden bath as well as one indoors. All sorts of watersports are available: sailing, water-skiing, snorkeling and fishing. Complimentary bikes are available, too. The food is outstanding, especially the homemade bread,

The beach on Cat Island.

and you can dine outside under the stars. Rates start at $220. ☎ 800-940-1095 or 242-342-3043; fax 242-342-3051, e-mail catisland@fernandezbayvillage.com.

The Inaguas

The most southerly and most remote of the Out Islands, the Inaguas, with fewer than 1,200 inhabitants living on **Great Inagua**, are also the most sparsely populated. Almost all of the locals work for the Morton Salt Company. Very few tourists make it this far out. Those that do are in for a rare experience. The third largest of the islands, this is the Bahamas' answer to the Galapagos Islands. Here is a land where wildlife still reigns over most of the rocky shorelines and uninhabited **Little Inagua** just to the north. This not the place for the casual vacationer in search of

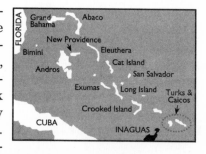

lazy days in the sunshine, nightlife and full-service hotels. If you're an outdoor adventurer, however, this is the place for yu. You can walk for miles along the deserted, rocky coast (sandy beaches are few and far between) and spend long days bird-watching, fishing or bicycling. It's not the easiest place to reach, either. You'll need the services of a creative travel agent.

■ Getting There

You've a couple of options, neither of them very convenient.

By Air

Bahamasair, ☎ 800-433-7300, operates two flights weekly from Nassau during the winter months – Wednesday and Saturday – and three during the summer – Monday, Wednesday and Saturday. The airfare is $180 round-trip.

By Mail Boat

The *Abilin* calls once every two weeks. The sailing time is a whopping 17 hours, but it's a nice ride, most of it overnight. The fair is $70 one-way. ☎ 242-322-7501 for schedules and information.

Taxis meet most incoming scheduled aircraft, and you can call the hotel of your choice to arrange a ride.

■ Sightseeing

Inagua National Park

Covering more than 280 square miles, this is a vast park incorporating inland waters, rocky shoreline, saltwater flats, and large areas of shrubland and jungle. It's here you'll find Inagua's famous **flamingos**: huge flocks of bright pink, long-legged birds that rise and fly, almost as one, from their nesting grounds around **Lake Windsor**. Although the drive from Matthew Town to the National Park campground is only about 20 miles, it takes an hour.

The best time to visit is from early March through the middle of June. This is when the birds are nesting, and you'll be able to get up-close for bird-watching and photography.

Aside from the colonies of flamingos, more than 200 species of birds make their homes in the park. Lake Windsor itself is an unusual sight: the waters are pale pink, due to the salt content. Here and there, wild donkeys can be seen in the distance, but never up close.

Henri Christophe's Treasure

The donkeys were, according to legend, brought to the Inaguas by Henri Cristophe in the early 1800s. Cristophe was a Haitian revolutionary, and something of a rogue. Apparently, his revolution was initially successful, and he had himself crowned king. Then, perhaps as an afterthought, he loaded the Haiti's treasures, mostly gold, on pack animals – donkeys – and headed for the docks. Once there, he loaded everything onto boats, the donkeys included, and sailed away with his loot, finally landing somewhere in the Inaguas. But the story doesn't end there. Cristophe's vast cache of loot lies buried in a cave somewhere on one of the islands, and it's still there, waiting for some lucky adventurer to find it; you, perhaps.

If you want to rough it a little, camp out in one of the park's two rustic cabins. The accommodations are basic, to say the least, but bedding is provided, and there are a couple of fresh-water showers that make life in the outback tolerable. You will need to provide your own food, which you can cook in the park at a specially designated area.

Morton Bahamas Salt Company

Vast mountains of snow-white sodium chloride mark the boundaries of this, the mainstay of Inagua's economy. Beyond the salt lie hundreds of acres of what appear to be ice-bound lakes, something of an enigma in this land where the temperature rarely drops below 70°. But the pink-tinged surface is in fact a thin crust of brine that sparkles and shines in the sunlight, more so at the lakeshore where the

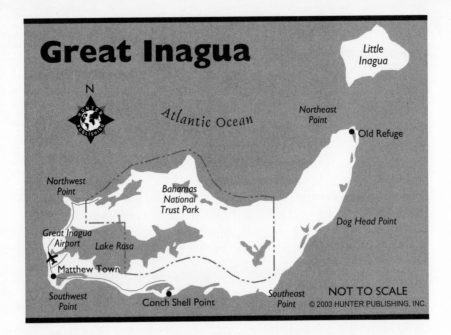

Great Inagua

Little Inagua

N

Atlantic Ocean

Northeast Point

Old Refuge

Northwest Point

Bahamas National Trust Park

Dog Head Point

Great Inagua Airport

Lake Rasa

Matthew Town

Southwest Point

Conch Shell Point

Southeast Point

NOT TO SCALE

© 2003 HUNTER PUBLISHING, INC.

crystals build like the edges of some giant pie crust. The salt produced here is sold around the world to highway departments, fisheries, chemical plants, and the like. If you'd like to visit the plant, take Gregory Street and go north of Matthew Town. But make arrangements beforehand. Call the Bahamas Ministry of Tourism in Nassau for information: ☎ 242-322-7501, fax 242-328-0945.

Matthew Town Lighthouse

Located just beyond the Matthew Town limits, this picturesque lighthouse was erected in 1870 to light the way for ships using the Windward Passage between Inagua and the larger island to the south, Hispaniola, where Haiti and the Dominican Republic are located. It's a lonely spot, fit only for bird-watching, but there's something indefinable about lighthouses that draws people to them. This one is no exception. The climb to the top is a long one and, perhaps, not really worth the effort. The view is of a lonely, rocky shoreline with only Matthew Town to break the monotony of the flat, almost featureless, land- and seascape. Interesting, though, is the machinery that drives the light, and its great fresnel lens.

The Inaguas.

■ Adventures

The Inaguas are not on the list of top dive spots in the Bahamas. Far from it. There is little information available as to dive sites on and around the islands. The waters are crystal clear, but the rocky shoreline is less than inviting.

■ Dining

If you're having breakfast at your hotel, you're in luck. There are not too many places that open for the early meal.

Restaurant Price Scale
$ . . . . less than $20 per person
$$ . . . . $20-$50 per person
$$$ . . . . $50+ per person

$ Tops. This small bar and restaurant on Astwood Street in Matthew Town, is open for lunch and dinner. It's the most popular eatery on the island. The food is traditional Bahamian fare with island vegetables, peas and rice, fried plantain, chicken and fresh seafood – conch, lobster, grouper, etc. The atmosphere is definitely "island home." The tables are set family style, and everyone is friendly and pleased to meet you. No phone.

$$ The Main House. This is the hotel restaurant. Off Gregory Street in Matthew Town, it serves three meals a day. The dining room is small and bright, the tables are dressed with linen cloths, and the food is typically Bahamian. ☎ 242-339-1267.

$ The Cozy Corner serves good, wholesome Bahamian cuisine in a neat little restaurant. The menu includes seafood, plantain and curry. No phone.

■ Accommodations

Great Inagua is better provided with accommodations than you might expect. There are three small hotels/guest houses on the island, all of them fairly inexpensive.

The Main House. This pleasant inn is owned by the Morton Bahama Salt Company. It's a homely place with five air-conditioned rooms, two with private baths, the rest sharing a couple of well-kept modern bathrooms. There's a nice, bright dining room, a comfortable sitting room with satellite TV, a balcony with a view, and a lounge where guests can gather and relax over a drink before dinner. The rate is $50 per night. ☎ 242-339-1267.

AUTHOR PICK

Ford's Inn. This small two-story inn is run by an ex-Detroit policeman and his good lady. Originally from Inagua, Leon Ford spent some 20 years in the Motor City before returning to his homeland. This is one of the best places to stay in the islands. The two-story, block-built inn boasts five brightly decorated rooms. They share modern bathrooms and a comfortable sitting room with satellite TV and a spacious balcony. The only meal they offer is breakfast, but it's served in an atmosphere that rivals the traditional bed & breakfast inns of Europe. The inn is closed March through July. The rate is $50 per night. ☎ 242-339-1277.

Kirk & Eleanor's Inn. This little family-run inn has five guest rooms, three with private baths, two sharing a bath; all are air-conditioned and have TVs. The rate is $80 per night. There is no telephone.

Long Island

Long Island is, well, long. How long is debatable; nobody seems to know, exactly. Some references say it's 60 miles long; others say 70 miles; still others say it's 100 miles long. But if you get hold of a good map, you'll see by the scale that it is a little more than 60 miles from one end to the other, and not more than

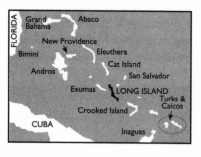

a mile wide; in places, no more than a half-mile wide. It is, however, one of the most scenic of the Out Islands, with starkly contrasting coastlines east and west. On the Atlantic side the coast is a lonely, rocky stretch more reminiscent of New England than the Bahamas. On the Caribbean side, long stretches of sugar-white beach stretch for miles in either direction. They are mostly deserted and rank

AUTHOR PICK

among the best beaches in the world. Best of all, the beach at **Cape Santa Maria** is truly a paradise, a four-mile crescent of pristine white powder that almost encircles a magnificent stretch of turquoise water, and the chances are you'll have it all to yourself. It must be seen to be believed.

The terrain inland is hilly and, here and there, jagged cliffs of coral drop steeply to meet the surging ocean. This is the garden island of the Bahamas. Fertile fields produce a variety of vegetables and local fruits. Beyond the fields, among the hills, the island is riddled with limestone caves and blue holes.

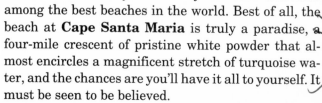

DID YOU KNOW?

Christopher Columbus made Long Island his third stop on passing through the Bahamas in August, 1492. His journals describe the rocky cliffs, isolated beaches and the scent of the flowers, "delicious and sweet." He called the island Fernandina in honor of King Ferdinand of Spain.

This is a must for divers and snorkelers, not to mention those that simply like to spend long lazy days on the beach. There are some 30 sunken shipwrecks within easy distance of the **Stella Maris Resort Club**, the local gathering place for those to whom all-things-wet are important. And, as you might imagine, the sea is the source of wonderful culinary delights, presented as only the Bahamians can.

■ History

During the centuries that followed **Columbus**, Long Island was virtually forgotten, visited only by pirates and freebooters. But the American Revolution changed all that. The years following 1776 saw large numbers of **English loyalists** leaving Virginia and the colonies for new homes all over the Caribbean, and especially the Bahamas.

The Adderleys

The Adderlys fled the American Revolution and settled on Long Island, bringing with them large numbers of slaves. They established a cotton plantation and, for a while at least, prospered. So the story is told, old man Adderley discovered his son was in love with one of his slaves. It's difficult to imagine why the old man was so shocked by his discovery. Liaisons between slaves and their masters were an accepted fact in those days, so one has to wonder exactly what it was that drove the senior Adderley to take his own life. But the event apparently had little effect on his son for the relationship between the two lovers continued. Today, their descendants are still a major part of the population of Long Island. And the ruins of the once-proud Adderley mansion are all that's left of the family's glory days of the early 1800s.

■ Getting There

Getting to Long Island is quite easy but, once again, you will need to enlist the services of a creative travel agent. The main port of entry is **Stella Maris** at the northern end of the island.

By Air

Long Island is served from Fort Lauderdale, Miami and Nassau. You'll need to take a scheduled flight to one of those cities, and then make the local connection. Round-trip airfare from Nassau on **Bahamasair** is $128, and $170 from Miami; flights are scheduled daily. ☎ 800-222-4262.

American Eagle also operates scheduled flights from Miami into Stella Maris. Rates are comparable to Bahamasair. ☎ 800-433-7300.

Island Express serves Long Island out of Fort Lauderdale. Rates are approximately $200 round-trip. ☎ 954-359-0380.

Long Island

By Mail Boat

 The *Sherice M* leaves Potter's Cay Dock in Nassau on Mondays at 5 pm for North Long Island – Salt Pond, Deadman's Cay, and Seymour's – and returns the following Thursday. Sailing time is 15 hours, overnight, and the one-way fare is $45.

The *Abilin* sails from Nassau for Clarence Town on Tuesday at noon and returns the following Saturday. Sailing time is 17 hours and the one-way fare is $65.

See *Mail Boat Schedules*, page 355, for more information.

Vacation Packages

American Airlines FlyAAway Vacations can fit you up with a vacation package for two nights or longer, and from almost any major US and Canadian gateway city. Rates, depending on the city of departure, start at $554 per person, and include an ocean-view room at the Stella Maris Resort Club, round-trip airfare from Miami, and round-trip airport/hotel transfers on Long island.

St. Paul's Anglican Church, Clarence Town.

Long Island.

For more information, call American Eagle, ☎ 800-433-7300, and ask for American FlyAAway Vacations. Visit their website at www.aavacations.com.

The resorts all offer transportation at no charge from and to the airport; just call ahead to make arrangements. Failing that, taxies do meet the mail boats and all incoming scheduled flights from Nassau and the mainland.

■ Sightseeing

The Adderley Plantation

Little is left of this once-stately mansion. The roof-less shells of three buildings, a tall stone chimney, remnants of old stone walls, and large blocks of hand-cut stone scattered here and there belie the opulence of what once was a prosperous and bustling plantation. Even so, it's not difficult to let the imagination wander and conjure images from the past as you wander among the old buildings with their decaying cedar frames and the vegetation, growing wild, threatening to overwhelm what little is left. North of the old house, just a short walk through the undergrowth, is the slave burial ground. You can still see the mounds, though they have all but been reclaimed through neglect and erosion.

Columbus Point

To the north of Stella Maris, near the bridge to Newton's Cay, is a narrow dirt road that leads to Columbus Point. It's an enjoyable walk. It was at the Point that, according to legend, Columbus first set foot on the island in October, 1492. On top of the cliff, with a spectacular view of the ocean, a plaque commemorates the landing.

Conception Island

Northeast of Stella Maris, off the tip of the island, lies tiny Conception Island. It's protected by the Bahamas National Trust as a wildlife sanctuary and is home to many species of wild birds and the endangered green turtle. The island can be reached only by boat, and the surrounding waters offer great diving. Check with the dive center at the Stella Maris Resort Club.

Deadman's Cay Caves

Like to go caving? This is the place for you. Deadman's Cay is close to the center of the island, south of Stella Maris. To get there, rent a car

Stella Maris Resort.

at the Stella Maris Resort Club. Two caves are worthy of note. The first is the Deadman's Cay complex of caves itself. This is an extensive system that's never fully been explored. The other is **Dunmore's Cave**. Used extensively by Arawak Indians in prehistoric times, it later became a refuge and hideaway for pirates. Legend has it that they used to store loot here taken from ships at sea.

Churches

There are several churches on Long Island; all are unique. Three, however, are of special interest. In **Clarence Town**, Father Jerome Hawes, the Catholic missionary who built the Hermitage on Cat Island, was also responsible for two of the town churches, one Anglican, the other Catholic. Both show his inimitable style. If you have the time they are well worth a quick look.

DID YOU KNOW?

*The Spanish Church in **The Bight**, once part of an early Spanish settlement, is the oldest Spanish Church in the Bahamas.*

Simms Post Office & Her Majesty's Prison.

■ Adventures on Water

Diving & Snorkeling

 Locals will tell you that he diving at Long Island is some of the best in the Bahamas. From reef to wreck diving, and shark to wall diving, the island has it all. If you like to stay top-side or in the shallows, the snorkeling opportunities, too, are good. The shallow waters of the reefs on both sides of the island abound with wildlife. Coral formations differ from the Atlantic side, where the waters are more aggressive, to the Caribbean side, where life beneath the ocean is much quieter. The Cousteau Program is available at the Dive Shop, along with an assortment of dive options. You'll find details under *Dive Shop*, page 290.

Best Dive Sites

Grouper Valley

The best time to visit the Valley is in November, when the groupers school in vast numbers. This is a rare opportunity to observe one of nature's wonders. The groupers congregate in vast numbers and seem to hang in the watery sky like an invasion fleet from another world.

Grouper Village

Here in the Village, you'll find six or seven tame groupers that will greet you like old friends. True, they're after a hand-out, but it's fun just the same. Be sure to take along some food for them.

 *Also in the Village, you may be lucky enough to see Brutus, a huge jewfish that weighs in at more than 350 pounds.*

Shark Reef

Shark Reef is one place where you can get up-close with a shark. The reef is a 30-minute boat ride from the Stella Maris Resort Club. The divemasters at the shop will be pleased to arrange a visit.

Ship's Graveyard, Cape Santa Maria

The remains of many a ship lie beneath the waters off Cape Santa Maria. The best site is the wreck of the **MV Comerback**. The ship was sunk in the summer of 1986 to provide a safe and interesting dive for guests of the Stella Maris Resort Club. The 103-foot British freighter lies upright and intact at a depth of 100 feet; the deck is at 65 feet. The hatches, portholes and doors have all been removed to provide safe and easy access to the ship's interior. Visibility, even at maximum depth, is prime; and currents are minimal. There's even a 1975 Ford van in one of the holds. All this makes it an ideal site for the novice diver – under supervision, of course – and for underwater photography.

H.M.S. Southampton

This wreck has only tentatively been identified as the *Southampton*, an English 32-gun frigate under the command of Sir James Yeo that foundered on the reef in November, 1812. All the evidence indicates that the wreck dates from around that time, but a definitive identification has not been made. The wreck lies scattered over a wide area, with only her boilers, engine, propeller shaft, four anchors, three propellers and a pile of rusty anchor chain showing. She offers some rare photographic opportunities.

To visit the Southampton, *you need to make arrangements with Stella Maris Diving,* ☎ *800-426-0466 or 242-338-2053.*

Conception Island Wall

This is a dive for veterans. Not far from the beach, the reef drops away from a depth of about 40 feet into the ocean darkness. If wall diving is for you, this is as good a place as any, and better than some, so the experts say.

Southampton Reef

This is a grand stretch of reef. From shallow waters less than 10 feet deep, descending gently to more than 90 feet at its edge, the reef is a veritable garden of elk and staghorn coral, brain coral and seafans, populated by colorful reef fish.

Rum Cay Wall

Yet another amazing drop-off where the crystal-clear waters at the reef's edge, at a depth of 40 feet, accentuate the feeling of extreme depth as they plunge downward.

Best Snorkeling Sites

 Snorkeling can be done just about any place you can walk into the water, from the beaches at Cape Santa Maria, along the western shore, almost as far south as you can go. Some of the best spots, however, are as follows:

Columbus Harbour

This is where Christopher Columbus first landed on Long Island.

Poseiden Point

The Point is one of the few places in the Bahamas where you can see big tarpon.

Coral Gardens

A reef site with valleys, caves, corals and turtles.

Eagle Ray Reef

A reef where you swim among an amazing variety of coral formations and make friends with a giant grouper.

Flamingo Tongue Reef

This site is home to thousands of colorful reef fish, anemones, crabs and even a large green moray eel.

Rainbow Reef

This reef is famous for its sponges and coral formations.

Rock Pools

A collection of tidal pools where you can observe smaller fish and crabs that inhabit the shallows of the reef.

Watermelon Beach

An easy site just right for the novice snorkeler.

Dive Shop

The single dive shop on the island is at the **Stella Maris Resort Club**. The operator offers full- and half-day scuba diving excursions and participates in the Jean Michel Cousteau snorkeling program. The cost for a basic four-day excursion with up to three dives included, depending on how many people are participating, starts at $75 per person. If you add a specialty dive, such as a shark dive or wall dive, the extra cost is $20 per dive, per person. The cost for a basic half-day dive excursion also depends on the number of people participating; rates vary and are available on request. Snorkeling excursions start at $35 per person and that includes the use of mask, snorkel and fins. ☎ 800-426-0466 or 242-338-2053, fax 954-359-8238, www.stellamaris.resort.com.

Sport Fishing

Long Island is the angler's ultimate destination. The bonefishing here is as good as it gets. Great schools of the silver fish flit this way and that over the flats where the water rarely is deeper than a couple of feet. You can spend hours casting into the schools and, when you hook one of the little demons, you're in for the fight of your life.

 Rarely does the bonefish weigh in at more than 10 or 12 pounds but, pound-for-pound, it's the strongest fighter in the ocean.

A seven-hour reef fishing excursion will put you right on the spot where the best sport bottom fish are found. From the boat, you'll see all that's happening in the water. You can expect to catch barracuda, grouper, yellowtail snapper, horseye jacks, amberjack, king mackerel and tuna.

For the deep-sea angler, charters are available at the Cape Santa Maria Beach Resort, the Stella Maris Resort Club, and the Stella Maris Marina. You can take a seven-hour excursion out into deep waters where the "big ones" lurk: trophy-sized white and blue marlin, kingfish, shark, tuna, grouper, dorado and sailfish.

Boat Rentals

Cape Santa Maria Beach Resort. Guided rentals only, from $250 for seven hours. ☎ 242-355-2044, www.capesantamaria.com.

Stella Maris Resort Club. Charter boats with guide only, starting at $200 per day. ☎ 800-426-0466, www.stellamarisresort.com.

■ Dining

 There are several nice restaurants on the island, one each at Cape Santa Maria Beach Resort and Stella Maris Resort Club, the others in Stella Maris. The cuisine is varied, including international and European fare, as well as Bahamian dishes.

Restaurant Price Scale	
$	less than $20 per person
$$	$20-$50 per person
$$$	$50+ per person

$$$ Cape Santa Maria. This restaurant is part of the resort complex and features a full-service bar where you can enjoy a cocktail before dinner. Open for breakfast, lunch and dinner daily, it's best to make a reservation, especially in the high season. The menu includes continental, American and local dishes, as well as a wide range of fresh seafood dishes such as lobster, grouper and conch. A fine selection of imported wines is also available. ☎ 242-338-5273.

$$ Conchy's. Located in the Stella Maris shopping district, Conchy's is open for lunch and dinner and offers a choice of indoor or patio dining. The menu is mostly Bahamian and the food is good. Reservations for dinner are preferred. No phone, VHF channel 16 only.

$$ Salty's is in the Stella Maris Marina main building. If you're an angler, the staff will be happy to prepare and serve your catch. The menu includes Bahamian and American dishes, and the restaurant is open for breakfast, lunch and dinner weekdays only. Reservations are required for dinner. No phone, VHF channel 16 only.

$$ Stella Maris Resort Club Dining Room and Garden serves lots of fresh seafood. American, Bahamian and European dishes are offered for dinner, along with full breakfasts and lunches. Specialties include patio cookouts, moonlight dinner cruises, a cave party, and the weekly Bahamian night. You must make a reservation for dinner. ☎ 242-338-2051.

$$ The Tennis Club. Set on the hillside in Stella Maris, the Club is open only for dinner. The menu is European, and you have a choice of indoor or outdoor dining; both options offer spectacular ocean views. ☎ 242-336-2106.

■ Accommodations

Cape Santa Maria Beach Resort. This resort has a fabulous, crescent-shaped stretch of beach. The resort itself is small and exclusive. Accommodations consist of one- and two-bedroom beachfront cottages. Each is air-conditioned and tastefully decorated, with cool marble floors and comfortable furniture. There are no telephones, radios or televisions in the rooms; the emphasis is on uncomplicated luxury and stress-free living. Amenities for guests include use of a small catamaran, Sunfish, sailboards, snorkeling gear, and bicycles. Rates start at $195 per night in the off-season, and go up from there. ☎ 800-663-7090, fax 242-338-6013, www.capesantamaria.com, e-mail obmg@pinc.com.

Stella Maris Resort Club. Set in the middle of a garden estate, just a few steps from the beach, this resort has a lot to offer. The full-service dive shop is the only one on the island, and you can go wreck diving at more than 30 locations. For the angler, there's deep-sea, bone, and reef fishing. The club even has its own guest air service. Accommodations range from one-bedroom apartments to two- and four-bedroom villas and bungalows, all with ocean views, refrigerators and ceiling fans; every room is air-conditioned. Rates start at $100 for a single room ($120 for a double) in the off-season (May through August) and go up from there. American Airlines Vacations arranges all sorts of air-inclusive packages with the resort. ☎ 800-426-0466, fax 242-338-2052, www.stellamarisresort.com, e-mail smrc@stellamarisresort.com.

San Salvador

Northeast of Long Island, on the outer reaches of the Great Bahama Bank, lie two small islands, San Salvador and Rum Cay. They are just a couple of dots on the map. Fewer than 600 people live on San Salvador, and even fewer on Rum Cay. San Salvador is six miles wide and 12 miles long. It's a strange place

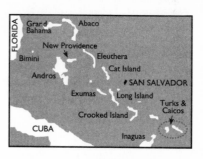

where there's almost as much water inland as there is *terra firma* – brackish lakes joined one to the other by narrow, man-made waterways.

The island's one and only sizable community is **Cockburn Town** (pronounced "Coburn"). Named for Sir Francis Cockburn, Royal Governor of the Bahamas from 1837 until 1844, it's the capital of San Salvador and Rum Cay, its smaller, sister island just to the west.

■ History

They say it was here, in 1492, that Christopher Columbus first set foot ashore in the New World. Did he? There's a certain amount of evidence to support the theory, but some at National Geographic *might beg to differ. Their choice is an island 65 miles farther south, Samana Cay.*

At the time when Columbus made his historic landing, many of the islands, San Salvador included, were inhabited by **Lucayan Indians**. The explorers, and those that followed, quickly enslaved the Indians, shipped them out, and worked them to death. As an added bonus, they introduced the luckless Lucayans to a whole range of new diseases against which they had no defense. And so, by the mid-1500s, the Lucayans had been exterminated.

Today, once a year, on the weekend closest to October 12, visitors converge on the island for the **Columbus Day** celebrations. There's always plenty to eat, dancing in the streets, and lots of fun in the sun. If you can make it, this is a good time to visit.

John Watling

An extraordinarily bloodthirsty, but pious, English pirate, John Watling made San Salvador his base of operations during the latter part of the 17th century. In fact, for many years, San Salvador was known as Watling's Island. It was renamed only in 1926, thanks mainly to the efforts of Father Chrysostome Schreiner, a Catholic missionary who lived here until his death in 1928. The impressive ruins of Watling's Castle, at Southwest Point, are all that remain of what is reputed to be the pirate's home. Archaeologists, however, say the ruins are not that old, dating only from the early 19th century. Stories of buried treasure on the island abound, as they do throughout the Out Islands. As to John Watling, he came to sticky end, like most of his contemporaries – at the end of a rope.

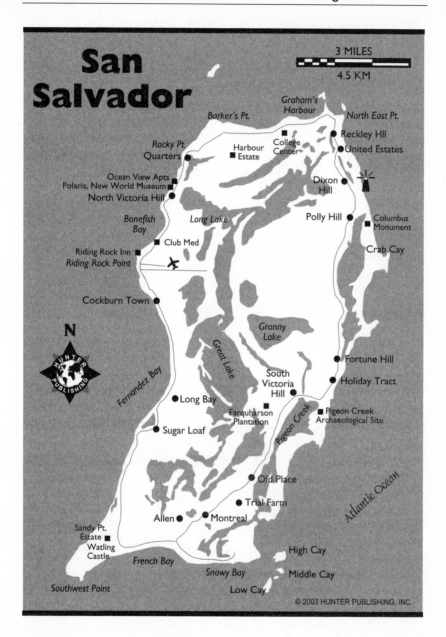

■ Getting There

By Air

Island Express, ☎ 954-359-0380, offers service from Fort Lauderdale and **Bahamasair, ☎** 800-222-4262, provides scheduled air service daily between Nassau and Cockburn

Town – the round-trip fare is $12. **Riding Rock Inn** operates a charter air service from Fort Lauderdale on Saturdays only. Flights depart from Fort Lauderdale at 10 am and leave the island at 12:30 pm. Round-trip fare, $289. ☎ 800-272-1492.

By Mail Boat

 Your other option is to take the mail boat. The *Lady Frances* leaves Potter's Cay Dock in Nassau weekly, on Tuesday, at 6 pm and makes the 12-hour trip overnight. She returns on Friday, which means you could pre-book two nights accommodations at the Riding Rock Inn, spend a couple of days enjoying the sights and sounds of the island, then return to Nassau and finish your vacation. The fare is $80 round-trip. Call the dock master at ☎ 242-393-1064.

By Private Boat

 Riding Rock Inn & Marina, ☎ 800-359-8254, near Cockburn Town, is the main port of entry and maintains seven slips with a maximum depth of 12 feet; there are no width restrictions. There's also 415 feet of docking wall where visiting boats can stock up on fuel, water, ice and off-site groceries. Sailors have access to the Inn's restaurant, showers, accommodations and laundry. The VHF frequency is 16.

San Salvador basket maker.

Package Vacations

Only two operators offer vacation packages on San Salvador: one is Club Med (☎ 800-932-2582, www.clubmed.com), the other is locally operated by the Riding Rock Inn (☎ 800-272-1492, www.ridingrock.com). A good travel agent should also be able to put something together for you.

*If you arrive on a Club Med or Riding Rock Inn package, someone will meet, greet and transfer you to the resort. If you arrive by scheduled air or private charter from Nassau or the mainland, you'll need a **taxi**. These are usually available at the airport. Most drivers depend heavily upon arriving and departing flights for a major portion of their income. The same goes if you arrive by mail boat. If drivers are not ready and waiting, they're only a phone call away; ask at the harbour master's office. If all else fails, call your resort and they'll arrange transport for you; Riding Rock Inn is quite close to the airport, so you should experience no difficulties.*

■ Sightseeing

Small and isolated as it is, there's plenty to see and do on San Salvador. While many of the sites are within easy walking distance of both Club Med and Riding Rock Inn, you'll need a car to see all of the island. Your hotel staff will be pleased to arrange one for you. An even better option would be to rent a bike or moped for a couple of days, then head in one direction one day, the other the next day. Make arrangements with your hotel to supply picnic lunches; there are plenty of places along the way to stop and enjoy them. Also, be sure to take along plenty to drink and something to snack on.

The main road around the island is the Queen's Highway – 35 miles of white road. Although the word "highway" is sometimes a bit of a stretch, it is well-maintained and provides a fairly smooth ride. Side roads branching off the highway are neither marked nor always easy to negotiate, especially on a bike or moped. Sometimes they lead to a deserted sandy beach where you can enjoy a swim, snorkel or picnic. Sometimes it's a rocky escarpment with a seascape, ideal for bird watching and nature photography. Often, it's an inland lake, quiet

San Salvador

and mysterious, surrounded by palms and seagrass. Sometimes they just end.

On a small island such as this, it's difficult to imagine getting lost. But, with none of the roads marked, not even the highway, you can become disoriented. After a while, all roads seem to lead northward. If you do get lost, ask a local for help.

Cockburn Town

Although it's the capital of San Salvador, Cockburn Town (pronounced "Coburn") is one of the smallest communities in the Out Islands, and definitely old-world Bahamian. Two miles south of Riding Rock Inn and 2½ miles south of Club Med, it's little more than a collection of clapboard and cinder block houses. Most of the sights are on or close to Fifth Avenue, just across the street from the dock. It's here you'll land if you decide to visit the island via mail boat. Aside from the **Public Library**, which stands on the corner of Fifth Avenue and Queen's Highway, there's a pub, the **Ocean View Club**, where you can drop in for a cold beer, even breakfast or lunch. The **San Salvador Gift Shop** is the place to stock up on film, candy, local crafts, books and all sorts of other odds and ends, including newspapers (sometimes a day old). The **Hanover Square Club** is a bar run by Marcus Jones, a friendly and well-traveled host. His wife, Faith, runs the **Three Ships Restaurant** just across the street. The food is good, reasonably priced, and decidedly Bahamian. In fact, Faith is a talented cook: her cracked conch, peas and rice, and fried grouper have made her something of a celebrity among the island-hopping, sailing fraternity. If you want to eat dinner, you'll need to make a reservation; she only cooks to order. ☎ 331-2787.

There are a couple of churches in Cockburn Town, both of which are worth a visit: **St. Augustine's Anglican Church** and the **Holy Savior Catholic Church**, famous for its image of Christopher Columbus above its entrance. The **San Salvador Museum**, next door to Holy Savior, once was the island jail. Today, it houses a collection of artifacts that interpret the history of San Salvador from pre-historic through Colonial times to the present day. If you want to visit, call in advance. ☎ 331-2676.

Sandy Point

Sandy Point is at the extreme southern end of the island, about six miles south of Cockburn Town, eight miles from Riding Rock Inn, and 8½ miles from Club Med. Here you'll find Watling's Castle, Lookout Tower, and Dripping Rock Cave.

Take the Queen's Highway south from Cockburn Town and go six miles to Mile Marker 9. This will put you very close to Watling's Castle.

Watling's Castle

There's little left of the one-time thriving plantation that bears the name of one the most bloodthirsty buccaneers in the history of piracy. Watling, for whom the island was once named, is said to have lived here during the 17th century. It's doubtful, however, that any of the structures now in ruins were there during his tenancy. They date from the early 19th century and were probably built by Loyalist refugees fleeing the aftermath of the American Revolutionary War.

Wrecking
Aside from his terrorist activities on the high seas, Watling engaged in another nefarious activity: wrecking. He and his men would lure passing ships onto the rocks by flashing lights, board the doomed vessels, slaughter the survivors and then pick the wreck clean. Not a nice character.

Today, nothing is left that can be attributed to Watling. The plantation, however, thrived well into the 20th century. In the early days it was worked by slaves. The remains of the slave quarters can still be seen in the undergrowth that is slowly reclaiming the land upon which they stood.

Lookout Tower

Also once a part of the Watling's Castle Estate, the old tower is now reached via the road to the west of the estate. It was used to watch for ships bringing supplies from Nassau. One can't help but wonder, though, if this might have been the spot from which Watling conducted his wrecking enterprise.

Dripping Rock Cave

At Sandy Point itself, Dripping Rock is a limestone cavern surrounded by fruit trees. There's a fresh-water well inside the cave, and a secluded beach just to the north. It's an ideal spot for snorkeling or a romantic picnic.

Graham's Harbour

On October 12 each year, Graham's Harbour plays host to the **Discovery Day** celebrations. Everyone gets together for a grand time: boat races, dancing, kite flying and picnicking.

DID YOU KNOW?

The huge natural harbor located on the northernmost tip of the island is said to have inspired Columbus to comment that it was big enough to take "all the ships in Christendom."

There's a nice beach; the waters are calm most of the time, making it the ideal spot for an afternoon picnic.

Father Schreiner's Grave

From Graham's Harbour, take the rocky path to Father Schreiner's Grave. This was the man who was responsible for changing the island's name from Watling's Island to San Salvador. He is also responsible for the image of Columbus on Holy Savior Catholic Church in Cockburn Town. Father Schreiner died in the church in 1928. Of special interest is the circular stone block next to the grave; it's thought to have been either a slave whipping post or an auction block.

North Victoria Hill

North Victoria Hill is a small community on the coast a couple of miles north of the Riding Rock Inn and Bonefish Bay. Its main claim to fame is that it's the home of Ruth Durlacher Wolper, widow of movie producer David Wolper. Her beachfront estate is where you'll find the New World Museum.

New World Museum

This relatively small museum houses the Wolpers' private collection of New World relics that help to interpret the history of the islands and their Spanish occupation, including pre-Columbian and Native American artifacts, and pieces of Spanish origin that date to the late 15th century. The museum is within walking distance of Club Med and the Riding Rock Inn. It's open during daylight hours every day and is free. The walk and the museum, along with a visit to the beach, make a very pleasant afternoon.

The Columbus Monuments

There are several permanent monuments that commemorate Columbus' first landings in 1492. He is said to have come ashore at all four. Whether or not he did so is debatable. Today, the monuments present a unique opportunity for exploration. It's doubtful that you could visit them all in a single day, but a couple of afternoons should see the job through. The first and best known is the much-photographed **white cross** that stands on the beach near Mile Marker 6 on the Queen's Highway south of Cockburn Town.

A **second monument**, erected in 1951 by the Tappan gas company, is near Mile Marker 5. The **third monument** lies close by somewhere on the ocean floor; you'll need your snorkeling gear to find it. The **fourth monument** was erected on the eastern shore of the island, close to Mile Marker 25, by the *Chicago Herald* in 1891. The Chicago monument is not easy to find. If you like to explore, however, the search can be quite entertaining. Take along your swimming and snorkeling gear, lots to drink, sunblock, and allow a full afternoon for the excursion. Go to Mile Marker 24 on the Queen's Highway. From there take the side road to **East Beach**, a great snorkeling spot. When you reach the beach, park your vehicle and walk two miles south along the beach and be on the lookout for a path leading off the beach to the right. From there it's a short walk along the path through lush green vegetation to the old limestone monument. This trip also presents a good opportunity to visit the Dixon Hill Lighthouse.

Dixon Hill Lighthouse.

Dixon Hill Lighthouse

Built in 1856, Dixon Hill is a traditional lighthouse in every sense of the word. Its light, more than 160 feet above sea level, is the highest point on the island. The snow-white tower stands on a limestone plateau, and the view from the top is spectacular. Far into the distance, the sea, land and

San Salvador's East Coast.

lake are laid out in sharp relief. The sea to the east stretches endlessly, starting as the palest green in-shore and changing to the deepest indigo of the ocean out beyond the reef to the horizon. The light itself is one of only a few kerosene-fueled, hand-operated lamps left in the world. To make the climb to the top you'll need to be in good shape. Once there you can view the lamp itself. You'll be amazed how small it is. Small or not, it does the job. Twice a minute it sends out a 400,000 candle-power beam of light that can be seen more than 19 miles at sea.

■ Adventures on Foot

Walking & Hiking

 San Salvador is a great place for hikers. From Cockburn Town, Club Med or Riding Rock Inn, set off in any direction. Take your time and explore the sights and beaches along the way. Once you've seen the local area, rent a car or moped and head to the extreme ends of the island. Park your vehicle, and set out again on foot.

WORD TO THE WISE

Be sure to take along plenty to drink. There's little available on the outer reaches of the island.

Even with such a tiny population, San Salvador's roads are not quite as deserted as you might imagine. You can go long periods without seeing a soul, but you can also count on a friendly face to appear just when you need it most. The gently rolling terrain, dusty roads and narrow trails lined with a profusion of local flora, and the little, colorful communities, all make for a delightful walking adventure.

■ Adventures on Water

Diving & Snorkeling

 San Salvador is one of the most exciting diving locations in the Bahamas. It's doubtful that there's a comparable diversity of locations anywhere other than the Cayman Islands or Bonaire. Visibility is from 100 to 200 feet, currents are minimal and, whether you're an experienced diver or just learning, there something here for you. For experienced divers, the reef wall, on the leeward side, starts at a depth of less than 40 feet and runs more than 12 miles from one end of the island to the other.

The Riding Rock Inn participates in Jean Michel Cousteau's "Snorkeling Adventures" program, which includes 10 sites, one of them a shipwreck.

Best Dive Sites

Most of the sites involve the reef that runs the entire length of the leeward side of the island. Veteran divers will tell you, it's a rare day that the reef doesn't yield some new and rare experience. Some of the best-known sites are listed below.

Devil's Claw

This site includes three large craters, side by side, that start at a depth of 45 feet, then descend fairly slowly to 80 feet, before dropping off into the darkness. Lots of small marine life inhabit the crevices in the crater walls, while larger fish such as groupers, barracudas and sharks can be seen lurking in the deeper waters.

Frascate

The *Frascate* was a German-built English freighter that ran aground in 1902 while steaming south from New York to Jamaica. Built in 1886, she measured some 260 feet by 35 feet. Her bones lie in shallow waters off Riding Rock Point, and are a favorite spot for beginning divers, and snorkelers too. She lies scattered across a wide area in 15 to 20 feet of water. The ocean floor is sandy and the visibility is usually 100 to 150 feet. The wreck is home to all sorts of marine life, including a large green moray eel that lives in her boiler. The boiler and stern section are excellent for underwater photography.

The Hump

This is a fun dive suitable for both beginner and veteran divers. It's a shallow reef dive with the coral heads starting less than 15 feet from the surface to a maximum depth of 40 feet. The hump itself is an underwater hillock some 80 feet long, 40 feet wide, and 20 feet high, covered in coral of various types. It's a microcosm of the greater reef itself. There are angels, clowns, sergeant majors, crabs, lobsters, morays, snappers, groupers, parrotfish, anemones, octopus, and shrimp; even the odd barracuda has been known to drop by.

Vicky's Reef

This is really a wall dive. From 40 feet at the edge of the reef, the wall drops away. This is not a dive for the fainthearted. At 60 feet the reef is undercut. Here, the coral heads are at their best. It's also home to moray eels, yellow stingrays, grouper and snappers. If you are not subject to vertigo (the drop-off is alarming!), this is a fabulous site.

Best Snorkeling Sites

East Beach

 From Crab Cay almost to Graham's Harbour, there's a deserted, six-mile stretch of beach that reminds one of the Outer Banks off North Carolina. With waving seagrass, soft white sand and sea the color of Colombian emeralds, it's an ideal snorkeling site. Visibility stretches well beyond 150 feet, and the coral formations teem with wildlife. Take along something to shield you from the sun; there's no shade along the entire length of the beach.

Elkhorn Gardens

A reef site where the main feature is the extensive growths of elk and staghorn coral, along with several acres of turtle grass. Lots of marine life.

The Flower Gardens

An area of the reef with large coral heads, caves, and ledges. You can snorkel down among the heads and get up close with the reef creatures.

The Movie Caves

This nice snorkeling site is close to where Columbus is thought to have first set foot ashore in 1492.

Natural Bridges

This is a fun site, with lots of natural bridge formations to explore and swim through.

The Rookery

A great site for shellfish, especially conch.

Snapshot Reef

This is one of the most popular snorkeling sites on San Salvador. Here you can enjoy the best of life on the reef. The site is home to millions of sea creatures, most too small to see. The reef fish are friendly, and will take time out from their daily chores to meet and greet.

Staghorn Reef

Very similar to Snapshot Reef. Life on the reef is full of fun and danger, for the local inhabitants, of course.

Also, see **The Hump** and **Frascate** above under *Best Dive Sites*.

Dive Operator

Guanahani Divers Ltd. are based at the Riding Rock Inn and Marina. They operate three dive boats, each with a capacity for six divers. Certified instruction, equipment rental, underwater camera rental and instruction, and one-day film processing are all available. You can also take a course in underwater photography and videography. They offer three boat dives daily, and a night dive once a week. Dive packages are available through the Inn. Rates are $45 for a one-tank dive. The beginner's one-day certification course is $105 and full PADI certification is $400. For more dive information, and for dive-inclusive vacation packages, ☎ 800-272-1492 or 242-331-2631.

■ Dining

As you might imagine, your dining options are pretty much limited to the particular resort where you're staying, with this exception: Club Med visitors can dine out at the Riding Rock Inn restaurant.

Restaurant Price Scale	
$	less than $20 per person
$$	$20-$50 per person
$$$	$50+ per person

San Salvador

$$ The Riding Rock Inn's oceanfront restaurant in Cockburn Town is open daily for breakfast from 7:30 am until 9:30 am, for lunch from 12:30 pm until 2:30 pm, and for dinner from 6:30 pm until 9:30. The menu includes American, European and Bahamian cuisine. The specialty of the house – conch chowder and bread – is served daily for lunch. In the evening, you can enjoy a cocktail before dinner out on the oceanfront terrace of the inn's **Driftwood Bar**. Reservations are required. ☎ 242-331-2631.

AUTHOR PICK

Also in Cockburn Town, you can eat breakfast and lunch at the **$ Ocean View Club**, or you can eat breakfast lunch or dinner at the **$ Three Ships**. The Three Ships is owned by Faith Jones, a lady with the magic touch where cooking is concerned. She cooks only to order, so you'll need to make a reservation, but her cracked conch, fried grouper, and peas and rice are to die for. ☎ 242-331-2787.

■ Accommodations

As previously mentioned, accommodations on San Salvador are quite limited. Club Med is, of course, the best resort on the island. Then there's a small inn/hotel comprising three cottages and little else. Finally, there's the Riding Rock Inn, a moderately priced, comfortable inn in Cockburn Town.

Riding Rock Inn Resort & Marina. This small resort is dedicated to divers and diving. There is a full-service dive shop on the premises and guided dives, instruction, and equipment rental are all offered.

Guest rooms – 30 oceanfront rooms and 12 standard rooms – are located along the shore. All are air-conditioned, with cable television, telephones, ceiling fans, patio or balcony, chaises and refrigerators. The furnishing are rather plain, but functional. Unfortunately, time and tides take their toll on most small island hotels and motels, and this one is no exception. Although maintenance work on the buildings and rooms is ongoing, there's always that little something that can give cause for complaint. On the whole, this resort offers real value for money, but make allowances for its remote location and exposure to the elements. There are tennis courts and a pool, with plenty of room and furniture for lounging. Rental bikes, mopeds and cars are available on-site. The beach is a 50-yard walk from the hotel.

The dining room is clean, the service prompt and friendly. The menu features all of the popular Bahamian dishes – conch, fresh fish, lobster, peas and rice, even turtle – along with American and European cuisine. The home-baked bread alone is worth the trip. The **Driftwood Bar** is the watering hole on the island. Its oceanfront deck is a great place to enjoy a beer or tropical drink after a long day out on the water. The atmosphere is lively and friendly and the locals will make you welcome. Wednesday night is live music night; Friday night is when most of the locals drop in to round off the week.

Riding Rock Inn.

San Salvador

Rates start at $135 per night for a deluxe oceanfront room, and $105 per night for a standard poolside room; both are based on double occupancy.

The hotel runs its own charter air service from Fort Lauderdale on Saturdays. Better yet, they also offer **packages**: some specifically for divers, some for those who just want a vacation far away from the hustle and bustle of life in the city. An all-inclusive dive package – with round-trip air fare from Fort Lauderdale, three dives per day for six days, round-trip airport/hotel transfers, seven nights accommodations, all meals and gratuities (alcoholic beverages are not included) – costs $1,526 with a deluxe oceanfront room, or $1,400 with a standard poolside room.

For non-divers the package includes all the above except the dives. The seven-night all-inclusive package with a deluxe oceanfront room costs $1,200, and the same package with a standard poolside room costs $1,099. ☎ 800-272-1492, www.ridingrock.com.

Club Med Columbus Isle. Club Med has a reputation for service and quality and their Columbus Isle resort more than lives up to it. Billed as one of their "finest" and most exotic locations, it certainly has a lot to offer. Situated right on one of the best stretches of beach, it's a tropical village of gaily painted Bahamian cottages built very much with the local ecology in mind. Narrow footpaths lead to all corners of the resort to ensure walkers don't disturb or damage the rolling dunes and vegetation. The public access rooms house a wonderful collection of art and artifacts brought in from around the world: Asia, the islands of the Pacific, South America, Turkey, Thailand, India and Africa.

 Although this particular location is not one of Club Med's designated family villages, kids of all ages are welcome, and there is plenty for them to do.

The guest rooms are tastefully and comfortably furnished and decorated with international handicrafts. All are air-conditioned, have televisions, telephones, safes, refrigerators and hair dryers. Each has its own private balcony or patio, private bathroom, and shower with desalinated water. Some offer spectacular views of the ocean, others look out over the gardens; each has a character all its own.

WORD TO THE WISE *Because the cottages are situated along the beach, some are quite a long walk from the public rooms, dining rooms and facilities.*

The resort boasts three restaurants and a spa where you can have a wonderful full-body overhaul. There are tennis courts, three of which are lighted, and a fitness center.

As at all Club Med resorts, the emphasis here is on organized activities. If you want to get involved, and the powers that be will do their best to make sure you do, there's aerobics, bocce ball, deep-sea fishing, horseback riding, sea kayaking, ping pong, sailing, scuba diving, snorkeling, softball, soccer, swimming, tennis, volleyball, basketball, water exercises, water-skiing and windsurfing – more to do than you could possibly manage in a single week. And, as if all that's not enough, you can take a day excursion to Nassau for shopping, a snorkeling day-trip that includes a beach picnic lunch and a speedboat ride, or a sunset cruise.

The resort also features one of Club Med's exclusive **Dedicated Dive Centers**. All this really means is that it's a full-service dive center where everything is available, from guided dives to rental equipment. The Club Med Dive Center offers up to six days of diving per package, up to two boat dives per day, up to three dives per day, one night dive per week, snacks on board the boat and, if required, the supervision of a Club Med guide. Diving does carry an extra charge over and above the regular package charge, in this case $160 per person per week, and that includes two dives daily and one night dive.

Club Med packages usually start and end on Saturdays. Rates begin at $1,499 in the off-season (August 29 through December 12), $1,699 in the high season. The rate includes airfare from Boston, Los Angeles, New York, San Francisco and Washington, DC. You can fly out of other major cities, but air add-ons will raise the base rate accordingly. If you've not been to a Club Med resort before, you will be required to pay a one-time $50-per-person initiation fee, and an annual membership fee of $30 per family. You can have your travel agent make arrangements for you – probably the most painless way to do it – or you can book the trip yourself: ☎ 800-CLUBMED, www.clubmed.com.

Rum Cay

This tiny island to the west of San Salvador has a population of less than 150. It's a pleasant, though remote, spot on the map, accessible only by private boat and mail boat. Unless you're a sailor with a boat of your own upon which you can live while you're there, Rum Cay is not the place for an extended vacation. You could visit by mail boat, but that would mean a stay on the island of slightly more than two days, and the only hotel was, at the time of writing, closed indefinitely.

Ecologists will find Rum Cay to be something special. Completely unspoiled, and just as it must have been when Christopher Columbus first set foot on San Salvador, it's a microcosm of the islands: gently rolling hills, deserted beaches, limestone caves, deserted farms, salt ponds, and seas where the visibility underwater approaches 200 feet.

If you do decide to come here, be sure to visit **Port Nelson**. It's a friendly little place where you're sure of a warm welcome, and the opportunity to stock up on supplies. The town is reminiscent of those featured in movies of a type that were made only in the late 1940s and early 1950s; *Donovan's Reef*, starring John Wayne, and *The Coral Reef*, starring Gilbert Roland, are two that come to mind. There are a couple of places to eat where you can sample good food made only as the locals can.

San Salvador

There are no phones on the island – islanders communicate by VHF. If you've been at sea for awhile, you'll probably want to hike. You can leave your boat at anchor, take to the road, and walk to the far side of the island, where you will find a beautiful beach. You can do the whole island in a single day. Bikes and cars are available for rent in Port Nelson.

Turks & Caicos Islands

Mention these islands to almost anyone and you're likely to receive, at the very least, a couple of raised eyebrows and a query: "Who? What? Where?"

Very few casual travelers have heard of the tiny group of islands that lie just to the south and east of the Bahamas, and just to the north of the island of Hispaniola (Haiti and The Dominican Republic) on the upper reaches of the Caribbean. But gradually the word is getting out. These little islands are a rare undiscovered, unspoiled paradise.

The Turks and Caicos comprise two groups. A half-dozen small islands to the south and east of the Bahamian archipelago make up the Turks, of which **Grand Turk** and **Salt Cay** are the ports of entry. To the west and north are the larger islands of the Caicos group, for which **Providenciales** (locally known as Provo) is the port of entry, and the islands' center of tourism.

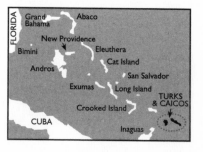

Turks & Caicos

History

Those who claim to know these things assert that it was in these islands that Christopher Columbus first made landfall, not on San Salvador in the Bahamas. Several prominent historians have made the case for Grand Turk. What is known is that Columbus's flag ship, *Santa Maria*, sank in local waters just to the south of the island group on Christmas night, 1492.

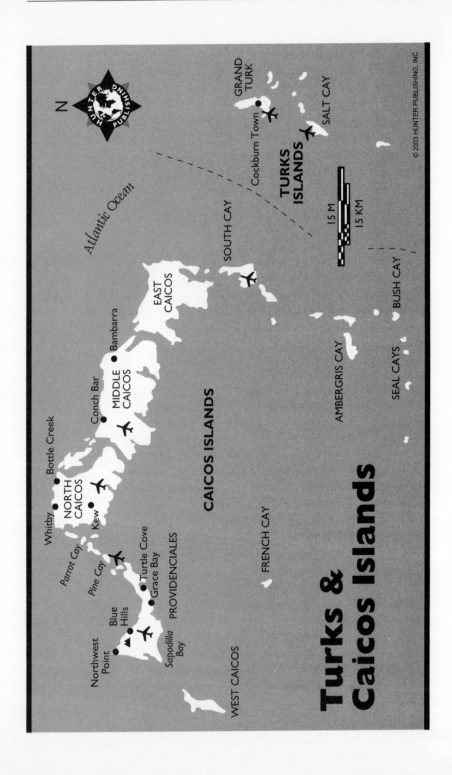

Turks &
Caicos Islands

Back then, the Turks and Caicos Islands were inhabited by **Arawak Indians**, as were most of the islands in the Bahamian archipelago, and it would have been these people that Columbus first set eyes upon. These islands, because of their isolated location, don't have the kind of extended history that most of the other islands do, but they can boast of a moment or two. For instance, they were home to The Brothers of the Coast, a band of pirates who preyed upon the Spanish treasure ships that plied the waters between Hispaniola and Spain. The islands are a maze of tiny, hidden coves and bays from which the marauders could hit and run.

The native Arawak Indians were, unfortunately, situated a little too close to Spanish interests. It wasn't many years after the Spanish had established themselves on Hispaniola just to the south when they became an instant source of slave labor, and it wasn't too much longer before the Indians had been eradicated from the Turks and Caicos Islands completely; they ended their days, and their race, in the Spanish mines on Hispaniola.

Following the demise of the Arawaks, the islands lay uninhabited for almost 100 years. Then, in 1678, adventurers from **Bermuda** discovered the islands were a rich source of salt, and they moved in, at least for a while. In 1710 they were driven off by the **Spanish**, who thought they owned everything west of Portugal. But the Bermudans were tenacious, if nothing else, and they soon returned, only to suffer more attacks, not only from Spain but from France as well. This time, however, they had help: English loyalists who had fled the American Revolution joined them on the islands and, for a while at least, they managed to hold on to their positions. But, in the end, it was all for naught. Their neighbors to the north in the Bahamas took the islands under their wing, and the Bermudan occupation ended in 1799.

For almost 50 years the islands bowed to the Bahamian government to the north. The government did little for the islanders but collect taxes and send a mail boat once or twice a year, so they decided there was little advantage to the association between them and the Bahamas. The two agreed to separate, and the Turks and Caicos Islands became a part of **Jamaica**; yes, Jamaica. This association lasted from 1848 until 1962, when Jamaica became independent from Great Britain. This left the island group one of the few remaining British Crown colonies, and it remains so even today – a quiet little British backwater where little ever happens, the food is good, the atmosphere serene, and the islanders live out their lives, for the most-part, in contentment.

Turks & Caicos

The Islands Today

These islands are not for those vacationers who are looking for the high life, nightlife or wild times under the sun. But if you're looking for a week or so of sun, sand and relaxation, or if you're looking for some fine offshore fishing, or scuba diving, then the Turks and Caicos might be just the place for you.

Comprised of about 40 small islands and cays, the Turks and Caicos Islands are ecologically pure. The waters are unpolluted; the beaches are clean and pristine; the population is friendly and outgoing. The only problem might be a lack of what most Europeans, and all Americans, regard as basic creature comforts. Many of the smaller hotels and guest houses lack air-conditioning; in-room phones are the exception rather than the norm; refrigerators, where available, are often old and noisy; in-room televisions are also in short supply; and it's not advisable to drink the water – buy bottled water where you can. All this might sound a little off-putting, but don't let it be. The pros far outweigh the cons. The lack of air-conditioning should not present too much of a problem. Cool ocean breezes in the evenings and ever-present ceiling fans keep the guest rooms relatively cool and comfortable. And who needs a television or telephone anyway? If these items are a priority for you, you need to go somewhere a little less remote. Remember: when in Rome....

The climate here is as close to perfect, at least for me, as you can get. The average mean temperature is around 80°, falling to about 70° at night. The rainfall averages 21 to 22 inches per year, with the rainy season arriving in the late spring and continuing on into summer – May through August. The Turks and Caicos sometimes suffer in the hurricane season, June through November. More often than not, however, hurricanes skirt the Bahamian archipelago, doing little more damage than dumping a lot of water on the islands.

These islands offer excellent diving and deep-sea fishing. For the beachcomber, there are acres of pristine coral sand, much of it deserted. There are almost 230 miles of beaches. The coral reefs upon which these islands sit are home to a vast undersea population of colorful marine life, most of it friendly and inquisitive.

The reef system, more than 200 miles long and 65 miles wide, offers opportunities for divers and snorkelers at all experience levels. There are coral flats at depths varying from a couple of feet to more than 20 feet where a vibrant fish community will provide endless hours of fun under the sea. There are ledges and walls where the depths plunge hundreds of feet offering more experienced divers a variety of choices to explore one of the last unspoiled reef systems in the western hemisphere. There are wrecks, some only recently discovered and still on the secret list. Some were discovered long ago, but still make for an exciting morning or afternoon of exploration.

Getting There

If you don't own a private, sea-going vessel, your only option is to fly in, and even then your choices are limited.

American Airlines offers the best schedule from the US mainland, with flights from Miami, Boston and New York. They offer three flights daily into Provo from Miami at 10:50 am, 1:15 pm and 5:10 pm. Return flights leave for Miami each day at 7:50 am, 1:46 pm and 3:52 pm. It's easy for you to make connections flying into Miami from almost anywhere in the continental United States; the same applies if you are inbound from Provo. Round-trip rates range from a low of $239 to upwards of $500, depending on how far in advance you book. Flight time is about an 1½ hours each way. ☎ 800-433-7300, www.aa.com.

Air Canada flies to Provo from Toronto, with fares from $600 round-trip. ☎ 888-247-2262.

Bahamasair offers limited service from Nassau to Providenciales on Tuesdays, Thursdays and Sundays. Fares start at $366, round-trip. ☎ 800-222-4262, www.bahamasair.com.

Delta Airlines now has weekly non-stop service from Atlanta for $500 round-trip, and **US Airways** began flights from Charlotte in November, 2002.

Service from Provo to the other major islands in the Turks and Caicos group is provided by **Turks and Caicos Airways, ☎** 649-946-4255.

Turks & Caicos

Getting Around

 You have to make getting around these islands part of the experience. Only in Provo can you expect anything approaching what you're used to. Rental cars are available in Provo, as are taxis. On any of the other islands, you'll have to improvize.

At the main airports – **Provo**, **Grand Turk** and **South Caicos** – taxis are readily available to take you to and from the hotels. Taxi drivers are for the most-part friendly and willing to do whatever it takes to make you and yours happy. Rates between the airports and hotels are usually fixed, on the spot, and most drivers will be willing to come and pick you up at your hotel and take you to some deserted beach, either of your choosing or theirs. They are knowledgeable and helpful; take advantage of them.

Practical Concerns

BANKING: There are branches of most major banks in Providenciales, and you'll even find an ATM or two. On the other islands banks are few and far between so you'll need travelers checks or cash.

CLIMATE: The average monthly temperature is 80°. The annual rainfall is 21 inches. The temperature of the ocean ranges from 71° to 80°. Hurricane season runs from June through November.

CREDIT CARDS: Most of the major hotels and a few restaurants take American Express, Mastercard and Visa. On the smaller islands, cash is king; don't get caught short.

CURRENCY: The US dollar is the currency of the Turks and Caicos.

CUSTOMS: You may bring in one quart of liquor, 200 cigarettes or 50 cigars or eight ounces of tobacco duty free. You may not bring in spear guns of any description, nor firearms without a permit. Import illegal drugs, get caught, and you can expect a heavy fine and a long stay at government expense.

DEPARTURE TAX: At the time of writing the departure tax was $15.

DRESS: For the most part, casual dress is the order of the day. Ladies might want to take along a cocktail dress for a special evening, and men a dress shirt and a tie. I don't know of any place where a jacket is required.

DRUGSTORES: Help is available at island clinics (see *Medical*, below), and at the **Providenciales Health Center** (☎ 649-941-3000). However, it's best to take what you need with you.

ELECTRICITY: 120 volts throughout the islands. American appliances will work; Europeans will need to bring along an adaptor.

ENTRY REQUIREMENTS: US and Canadian citizens must have a passport, or a birth certificate plus a photo ID, and a return or on-going ticket. Citizens from Great Britain, Ireland, Caribbean Countries of The British Commonwealth, and of the European Community must have a current passport. All other visitors must have a visa as well as a current passport.

HOTEL TAX: The island government collects an 8% hotel/inn/guesthouse tax. You'll find it added to your bill.

MEDICAL: What is available is quite good. The islands are served by three medical doctors with qualified staff. There is a small but well-run hospital on Grand Turk (**Grand Turk Hospital**, ☎ 649-946-2040), complete with OR, path lab, and X-ray facility. There is a Health Center in Providenciales at Leeward Highway and Airport Road, ☎ 649-941-3000. There is a medical clinic on South Caicos, ☎ 649-946-3216; one on Middle Caicos, ☎ 649-946-61454; and another on North Caicos, ☎ 649-946-7194. The islands are also served by a dentist, who can be contacted at the Providenciales Health Center.

POST OFFICES: There are post offices on Grand Turk, ☎ 649-946-1334, and Providenciales, ☎ 649-946-4676, and there are sub-post offices on many of the smaller islands. Hours are from 8 am to noon and 2 to 4 pm, Monday through Thursday, and on Friday from 8 am to 3:30 pm.

SAFETY: You have very little to fear as far as personal safety is concerned; violent crime on these islands is virtually nonexistent. But petty theft is a possibility. Don't leave valuables lying around in hotel rooms, in cars or on the beach.

TELEPHONES: The system on the islands still leaves a lot to be desired, but is improving rapidly. Incoming calls don't seem to be a problem. Outgoing direct dialed calls? They're still working on that one. Cell phones? Best leave yours at home.

TIME ZONE: The Turks and Caicos Islands are in the Eastern US Time Zone; daylight saving time is observed.

TIPPING: As with most countries that have been or still are under British influence, tipping is generally taken care of for you. You need to give your taxi driver a tip, about 10%, but almost all hotels and restaurants add a 15% gratuity to your bill. I think that should cover it. Unfortunately, some hotel and restaurant staff members seem to think otherwise. So if you think someone deserves a little extra, go ahead and give it.

TOURIST INFORMATION: The Turks and Caicos Information Office, Front Street, Cockburn Town, Grand Turk, BWI, is open Monday through Friday from 8 am until 5 pm. ☎ 800-241-0824 or 649-946-2322. www.turksandcaicostourism.com.

WATER: Some hotels provide good drinking water (be sure to ask), but it's not a good idea to drink the tap water anywhere else on the islands or brush your teeth with it, nor is it wise to take drinks with ice made from tap water. Bottled water is readily available almost everywhere.

Providenciales

Provo is the most developed of the islands in the group. It lies on the western end of the Turks and Caicos; only West Caicos lies beyond its most westerly Bonefish Point. Provo is where most of the tourists come, which means it has hotels. And it's the only island with an airport capable of handling wide-bodied jets. Those traveling onward to the other islands must do so by way of the national airline, **Turks and Caicos Airways**, ☎ 649-946-4255. Provo is basically a peaceful little island some 15 miles long by about eight miles at its widest point. It's a land of gently undulating hills where the sea grapes and

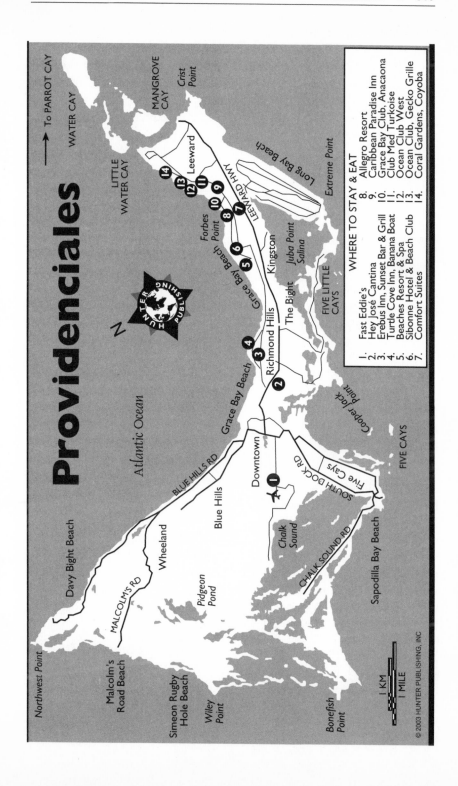

Providenciales

Northwest Point

Davy Bight Beach

Atlantic Ocean

To PARROT CAY

WATER CAY

MANGROVE CAY

Crist Point

LITTLE WATER CAY

Leeward

Long Bay Beach

Extreme Point

Forbes Point

LEEWARD HWY

Grace Bay Beach

Grace Bay Beach

Richmond Hills

The Bight

Kingston

Juba Point Salina

FIVE LITTLE CAYS

BLUE HILLS RD

Wheeland

Blue Hills

Pidgeon Pond

MALCOLM'S RD

Malcolm's Road Beach

Simeon Rugby Hole Beach

Wiley Point

Bonefish Point

Downtown

Chalk Sound

Cooper Jack Point

SOUTH DOCK RD

Five Cays

FIVE CAYS

CHALK SOUND RD

Sapodilla Bay Beach

HUNTER PUBLISHING

N

WHERE TO STAY & EAT

1. Fast Eddie's
2. Hey José Cantina
3. Erebus Inn, Sunset Bar & Grill
4. Turtle Cove Inn, Banana Boat
5. Beaches Resort & Spa
6. Sibonne Hotel & Beach Club
7. Comfort Suites
8. Allegro Resort
9. Caribbean Paradise Inn
10. Grace Bay Club, Anacaona
11. Club Med Turkoise
12. Ocean Club West
13. Ocean Club, Gecko Grille
14. Coral Gardens, Coyoba

1 KM
1 MILE

© 2003 HUNTER PUBLISHING, INC

casuarinas grow. Roads and trails – some paved, some not – meander all over the island. If you're the outdoor type, and fairly fit, you should rent a bicycle. Try **Provo Fun Cycles, Autos & Scooters** at Ports of Call, Grace Bay Road, Provo, ☎ 649-946-5868. Cost is $15 per day. You can make it to almost every point of interest, and all of the beaches, in a couple of hours of fairly stiff pedaling. As to the hotels and resorts, some of the best known companies are already represented, and you can bet the rest have plans already on the drawing board.

■ The Beaches

 Wherever you might be on Provo you're not very far from one its beaches. There are more than 12 miles of pristine white along Provo's northern shore: **Grace Bay Beach** stretches from Leeward-Going-Through Point westward past Richmond Hills almost to Tom Foot Rock and Northwest Point, where you'll find another spectacular stretch of sand called **Davy Bight Beach**. Grace Bay Beach is considered Provo's finest.

 If you have kids with you, this is where you should stay. There are endless shallows, no rocks and an ocean that's crystal clear, where gentle rollers swish across flats. There are no public restrooms on the beaches. You'll need to head to one of the nearby bars or restaurants.

Along the western shore of Provo you'll find two more beautiful beaches. **Malcolm's Road Beach** is reached by traveling west along Malcolm's Road from downtown Provo. A little south of there is **Simeon Rigby Hole Beach**, not quite so easily reached as its more northerly neighbor, but well worth the hike south. Both beaches are areas of great natural beauty. The snorkeling is good, the sand beyond description and, for the most part, you can expect to have them almost to yourself. Again, there are no public facilities on either of these two beaches, and no cafés or bars.

On the south shore are two more grand beaches. **Long Bay Beach** runs westward from Stubbs Cove to Extreme Point. Then there's Sapodilla Bay Beach to the southwest. Both are nice, though not quite in the same class as Grace Bay, but both have well-protected waters where the kids can splash about and you won't have to worry about them being swept away by rough waves. Sapodilla is exceptionally kid-friendly; the waters are clear and the shallows extend outward from the sandy shore more than 100 feet.

■ Adventures

Snorkeling

Snorkeling is something you can do off any of the beaches scattered around the island. The waters are gentle and lend themselves to shallow water exploration. The undersea life is colorful and fascinating. The real danger here is not underwater predators, but long exposure to the sun. The waters enhance the effects of its rays, and you can easily end up with a nasty burn. Take plenty of sunblock, SPF 15 or better.

If you're looking for something different, a real adventure, you might like to give a company called **Ocean Outback** a call, ☎ 649-941-5810; www.provo.net/oceanoutback. They offer day-long snorkeling adventures aboard a 70-foot cruiser to one or more of the neighboring uninhabited islands. A full-day trip – 9 am to 4 pm – costs $85 per person, and includes the use of snorkeling gear, a beach umbrella, picnic lunch and cold drinks – a great value. A second company, **Tao**, ☎ 649-946-5040, specializes in sunset cruises, but more and more they too are offering snorkeling cruises to the outer islands. Rates start at around $80 per person, which includes snorkeling gear and lunch.

Scuba Diving

The Turks and Caicos have fine scuba diving. The waters are crystal clear. The undersea life is colorful and exotic. Provo is unique among the islands. In fact, the late Jacques Cousteau proclaimed it one of the 10 best dive sites in the world. The reef runs the entire 17 miles of the island's north coast. Northwest Point is a premier wall dive with a vertical drop of some 7,000 feet. On Provo itself, there are a number of companies that can cater to almost every need. A single dive will probably cost you $50. A two-tank dive runs around $75. PADI open water certification costs about $350.

Art Pickering's Provo Turtle Divers, PO Box 219, Providenciales, Turks and Caicos, BWI, ☎ 800-833-1341, www.provoturtledivers.com.

Providenciales

Big Blue, at Leeward Marina, Providenciales, Turks and Caicos, BWI, ☎ 649-946-5034.

Caicos Adventures, at Turtle Cove Marina, Providenciales, Turks and Caicos, BWI, ☎ 800-513-5822, www.caicosadventures.tc.

Dive Provo, at the Allegro Resort, Grace Bay, Providenciales, Turks and Caicos, BWI, ☎ 800-234-7768, www.diveprovo.com.

Sport Fishing

 Provo is great for the sport-fishing enthusiast. Deep-sea fishing is expensive, but exciting. You can hunt marlin, kingfish, wahoo, tuna, shark, and more. Better yet, you will find some excellent bone-fishing flats. Most guides will provide tackle, bait and soft drinks. The cost averages $400 per half-day or $650 per full day.

Silver Deep, at the Turtle Cove Marina, Providenciales, Turks and Caicos, BWI, ☎ 649-946-5612.

J&B Tours, at Leeward Marina, Providenciales, Turks and Caicos, BWI, ☎ 649-946-5047.

Sakitumi Charters, Providenciales, Turks and Caicos, BWI, ☎ 649-946-4065.

Eco Tours

 Ocean Outback is an outfit somewhat similar to East End Adventures described in the Grand Bahamas section. Just you and one other person of your choice leave in the early morning for Silly Cay, one of Provo's best-kept secrets – so secret, in fact, that the company guarantees you'll have it all to yourself. The day-trip costs $95 per person, or you can overnight in a tent for only $115 – dinner and breakfast included. You can even spend the night in a stateroom on board a 70-foot yacht. The company also offers what they term "The Ultimate Getaway." The cost for the day-long trip is just $79 – a bargain – and includes pickup at your hotel, snorkeling, breakfast, lunch, and all you can drink. Visit the website for a list of the company's tours and adventures, or ☎ 649-941-5810; www.provo.net/oceanoutback.

J&B Tours, at Leeward Marina, ☎ 649-946-5047, offers a variety of options from snorkeling to deep-sea fishing to an Island Exploration tour, which includes a look at Provo's historic and scenic sites, as well as an opportunity to snorkel over the wreck of the *Merifax*. A picnic lunch is included in the cost and the drinks are free. Cost per adult is $119, kids go for $69. A great value.

Little Water Cay is a rocky islet off Provo. Not unique as far as little islands go, except for the **iguanas**; there are some 2,000 of them on the island. They are friendly critters and come to meet the boats bringing visitors. They are, of course, protected. The **Little Water Cay Nature Trail Program** was instituted to facilitate this. It consists of a series of boardwalks that lead into the interior of the island where you can observe the iguanas without disturbing them. There are also several observation towers high enough for you to get a real look at the habitat. You can visit on your own, in a rental boat, or take a guided tour with J&B Tours at Leeward Marina, ☎ 649-946-5047. The cost is $30 per person.

Sky Diving

Yes, you can do it here on Provo. Contact **Rainbow Flyers**, ☎ 649-946-4201. Even the inexperienced can have a go, strapped in a double harness with an experienced skydiver.

■ Dining

Restaurant Price Scale
$ . . . . less than $20 per person
$$ . . . . $20-$50 per person
$$$ . . . . $50+ per person

 $$ Anacaona, at Grace Bay Club. Elegant, international and Bahamian cuisine, is served at lunch and dinner. Reservations are recommended. It has great salads, lobster, lamb, and the house specialty desert: crème brulée topped with peaches. Open daily for lunch from noon to 3 pm, and for dinner from 7 pm until 9. ☎ 649-946-5050.

$ Banana Boat Restaurant, at Turtle Cove Marina, is one of the most popular eateries on Provo. The cuisine is said to be international; that might be a bit of a stretch but, if you like your food plain and simple, this is the place for you. T-bone steaks, fresh fish, lobster and tuna salads, and my favorite: conch salad. The restaurant overlooks the marina. Recommended. ☎ 649-941-5706.

$ Hey Jose Cantina, Central Square, Leeward Highway. I had to include this one. It serves tongue-in-cheek Mexican food, but it's good, with chicken dishes, steaks, burritos, chimichangas, tacos, quesadillas, even pizza. Good value for money. Open Monday through Saturday from noon until 10 pm. ☎ 649-946-4812.

$$ Sunset Bar and Grill, Erebus Inn, Turtle Cove. Run by a couple from Canada, this restaurant offers a variety of French and international cuisine. Specialties include boeuf bourguignonne and roast lamb. The lunch menu includes pizza and burgers. You can dine indoors or out, depending upon the weather. Not expensive compared to some, but the food is excellent and views over Grace Bay are, alone, worth the visit. ☎ 649-946-4240.

$ Fast Eddie's, on Airport Road, is a neat place where Americans can find the food they like best: burgers, fries, steaks and apple pie, along with a variety of Bahamian dishes that include fresh fish, pork and conch. No alcohol and no credit cards. Recommended.

■ Accommodations

With rare exceptions, hotel standards in the Bahamas are not what you'd expect on the US mainland, or in Europe. Because almost everything must be imported, and is thus expensive, there is a tendency to put off until tomorrow what should be done today. Hotels that might have been considered upscale five years ago can quickly become slightly seedy as time and weather take their toll. Don't expect too much in the Turks and Caicos; a little inconvenience should not spoil an otherwise wonderful experience. All prices shown are per unit, unless otherwise indicated.

Hotel Meal Plans

- **CP** (Continental Plan) includes a continental breakfast.
- **EP** (European Plan) denotes no meals, although restaurant facilities are available either on the property or nearby.
- **MAP** (Modified American Plan) denotes breakfast and dinner.
- **FAP** (Full American Plan) includes all meals.
- **All-Inc.** (All-Inclusive Plan) includes all meals, beverages (alcoholic and soft), watersports, tennis and golf, if available.

Allegro Turks & Caicos and Casino. This is one of the most expensive resorts on the island, one of a chain of all-inclusive luxury hotels based in the Dominican Republic. The best feature is its more than 900 feet on Grace Bay's top beach. Then there are the beautifully landscaped gardens, a large pool, and cool, quiet public rooms and reception areas. The guest rooms, centered around the pool and sundeck, are all air-conditioned, have ceiling fans, tiled floors, rattan furniture, oversized bathrooms, and either patios or balconies, all with ocean views. It's very much a family-oriented resort with a good mix of people from all age groups; the kids will like the "Kids on Vacation Club." There are several dining areas – one all-purpose restaurant, two open for dinner only, and a couple of cafés. You'll need to make a reservation for dinner. All of your food and beverages, along with entertainment, non-mechanized watersports, snorkeling, kayaking, and windsurfing, are free. Well, not free exactly, since it's all included in the price of the vacation. **The American Casino**, the only one in the Turks & Caicos, is open for slot machines from 6 pm to 1 am, and table games run from 8 pm to 1 am. PO Box 205 Grace Bay, Providenciales, Turks and Caicos, BWI, ☎ 800-858-2258; www.allegroresorts.com. All-inclusive, from $200 per night per person.

Club Med Turkoise. I've always had a soft spot for Club Med. Set on 70 acres of the eastern part of Grace Bay, this is one of Club Med's most popular establishments. It's one of the oldest resorts on the island, and one of the best. As always with Club Med, the atmosphere and accommodations are laid back, the emphasis being on rest and relaxation, rather than luxury and sophistication. The rooms are simply furnished, some with twin beds, some with kings. All have air-conditioning. There are tennis courts, a dive center, and a large pool. Meals are included in the cost, but beverages are not. Week-long only vacation packages are available from a variety of US and European gateways. Not a family destination: adults only. Grace Bay, Providenciales, Turks and Caicos, BWI, ☎ 800-CLUBMED; www.clubmed.com. FAP from $1,050 to $1,950 per person, weekly.

The Mansions. This is a private condominium complex, quite upscale, where you can, if you're lucky, rent direct from an owner. The minimum stay is one week. Not a family-oriented destination: no children under 12. Grace Bay, Providenciales, Turks and Caicos, BWI, ☎ 649-946-5863. From $650 to $850 per week.

Crystal Bay Resorts. This is another upscale condominium complex, with more than 160 deluxe units on 98 acres at the northwestern end of the island. Almost all are available for rent. Choose from one-, two- or three-bedrooms, and there are some junior suites. Facilities include a restaurant, bar, two freshwater pools, and a Jacuzzi. The guest units are luxuriously appointed, air-conditioned, and comfortable. PO Box 101, Providenciales, Turks and Caicos, BWI, ☎ 649-941-5555; www.crystalbay.tc. From $225 to $520.

Grace Bay Club. Arguably the best destination in the Turks and Caicos, this Swiss-owned resort is certainly sitting on the best stretch of beach of Grace Bay. They've spared no expense here. More than 200 palm trees were brought in from Florida, and what used to be five acres of arid scrubland is now a series of beautifully landscaped gardens and fountains. Inside, the public areas are quiet, but luxuriously appointed. The complex is designed to emulate a Spanish village. And there are only 21 suites, ranging in size from junior to three-bedroom units. These are tastefully decorated, mostly in white, with fine furnishings and artworks. Beds are king-size, carpets and rugs are Indian, tables and armoires are from Mexico. All of the suites have kitchens with washers and dryers. They are outfitted with 27-inch flat-screen TVs, DVD players and CD players. The bathrooms are all spacious and well-appointed. There is only one restaurant at the resort, the open-air, oceanfront **Anacaona**. The atmosphere there is upbeat, the service is top notch, and the food is beyond reproach, with a variety of French and Caribbean cuisine – everything from lobster to lamb. Very expensive, but highly recommended. A member of Small Luxury Hotels. PO Box 128, Grace Bay, Providenciales, Turks and Caicos, BWI, ☎ 800-946-5757; www.gracebayclub.com. From $395 to $1,395.

Coral Gardens. Situated on Whitehouse Reef, this upscale resort is set in an expanse of tropical greenery and color. The three-story hotel exudes an atmosphere of elegance and grace. The condominium-style guest suites are spacious and tastefully furnished, air-conditioned, with king-size beds and large windows. Each has a patio that overlooks the pool and gardens. Each has a fully equipped kitchen. The bathrooms are large and cool. Facilities include two pools, the **Coyoba** restaurant – elegant, great food, good service – and, of course, the beach and its adjacent reef complex, which provides one of the finest snorkeling opportunities on the island. It's expensive, but worth the money. PO Box 281, Penn's Road, Grace Bay, Providenciales, Turks and Caicos, BWI, ☎ 800-532-8536; www.coralgardens.com. From $135 to $600.

Beaches Turks and Caicos Resort and Spa. Part of the Sandals group of companies, and almost as upscale and expensive. Beaches is, however, much more family-oriented. The $30 million complex is situated on one of the nicest sections of Grace Bay Beach. The guest rooms are more like cottages than rooms, and each is furnished and decorated to match the expensive rates. All are fully air-conditioned, have either two double or one king-size bed, and all have panoramic views of the ocean. Some even have kitchenettes. Villa suites even have two bathrooms. The resort offers plenty to see and do – they have to justify the cost – and there are all the usual facilities you might expect in an upscale resort, and more: fitness center, pool, swim-up bar, in-room massage. Ladies will find the spa especially appealing. As I said, very expensive, but worth it. Lower Bight Rd, PO Box 186, Providenciales, Turks and Caicos, BWI, ☎ 800-BEACHES; www.beaches.com. All-inclusive from $600 to $1,200.

Parrot Cay Resort. This one is a class act, and it's very expensive. Located on an isolated private island north of Provo, the resort complex is a collection of 10 pastel-colored buildings in which the luxury guest rooms are located. Each has a private terrace (not just a balcony, you'll notice) or veranda, and a large, cool bathroom. Rooms are decorated in white with dark wood trim. The furniture includes four-poster beds, complete with mosquito nets (just decorative, not necessary), and each is fully air-conditioned. All meals, beverages, and most activities are included in the rates. The food and drink are just about as good as it gets in an all-inclusive resort. Facilities include what is claimed to be the largest swimming pool in the Turks and Caicos, along with a whole range of watersports that include Hobie Cats, windsurfing, canoes and water skiing. There's also a very upscale spa – at an extra cost – which has three pavilions, complete with treatment salons where you can partake of a range of Eastern healing and rejuvenating therapies, from meditation to yoga. Bone fishing can be arranged. Finally, there's the beach: it's one of the best, really. PO Box 164, Parrot Cay, Providenciales, Turks and Caicos, BWI, ☎ 877-754-0726; www.parrot-cay.com. All-inclusive from $500 to $1,650.

Ocean Club. This is another condominium resort on Grace Bay Beach. The units here are for sale or, and this is what interests us most, for rent. There are some 86 units ranging in size from one-bedroom to three-bedroom deluxe suites. All have ocean views, large bathrooms, air-conditioning, and kitchens of one sort or another. The resort is a series of buildings built around landscaped gardens and a courtyard. The resort does have a restaurant that serves "international" cuisine, and there's a cabana bar. **Art Pickering's Provo Turtle Divers** – see page 321 – is located just next door in an annex. Dive classes are available through the hotel. Expensive, but nice. PO Box 240, Grace Bay, Providenciales, Turks and Caicos, BWI, ☎ 800-457-8787; www.oceanclubresorts.com. From $180 to $910.

Ocean Club West. This is the sister complex to the Ocean Club described above. It, too, is situated on the shores of Grace Bay and its splendid beach. The ambiance here is a little more casual, with an assortment of one-, two- and three-bedroom suites to choose from. All are air-conditioned, have TVs, refrigerators, and safes, along with the usual amenities such as hairdryers and irons. Still expensive, but not quite as costly as its mate to the east. PO Box 640, Grace Bay Beach, Providenciales, Turks and Caicos, BWI, ☎ 800-457-8787; www.oceanclubresorts.com. From $180 to $550.

Turtle Cove Inn. Now we're moving on to the less expensive opportunities. This is a two-story hotel built around a large, freshwater swimming pool. It's rather a simple affair, but clean and inviting. The rooms are comfortably furnished and provide views over either the pool or the marina, which is just a few yards away. All rooms are air-conditioned, and the bathrooms, though adequate, are a little on the small side. Poolside, you'll find the **Tiki Hut Cabana and Grill**. The other on-site restaurant is the **Terrace**, but it's open only for dinner; reservations are recommended. No beach, I'm afraid, but a shuttle runs throughout the day between the hotel and the beach. Inexpensive and recommended. Turtle Cove Marina, Suzie Turn Rd., Providenciales, Turks and Caicos, BWI, ☎ 800-887-0477; www.provo.net/turtlecoveinn. EP $142.

Caribbean Paradise Inn. Another moderately priced resort – actually more of an inn. The hotel overlooks Grace Bay and it's small and intimate; only 16 guest rooms, all fully air-conditioned and comfortably furnished. The bathrooms are small, with shower stalls only. All rooms also have mini-bars and TVs. There is a pool, but no on-site restaurant. Clean and nice, but a bit on the sparse side. PO Box 673, Grace Bay, Providenciales, Turks and Caicos, BWI, ☎ 649-946-5020; www.paradise.tc. EP from $129.

Comfort Suites Turks and Caicos. Try this hotel and you'll think you're back home, or at least in Florida. Typical of Comfort Inn/Suites chain, this is a traditional American-style hotel. All rooms are built and furnished to spec, with air-conditioning, king or double beds, bathrooms and a TV, along with a coffee maker, refrigerator, and a hairdryer. Some of the rooms have balconies, although the only ocean views available are at the outer ends of the units. PO Box 590, Grace

Bay, Providenciales, Turks and Caicos, BWI, ☎ 888-678-3483; www.comfortsuitestci.com. EP from $135.

Erebus Inn. Built in the early 1960s, before the tourist boom began, this is Provo's veteran inn. It looks down on Turtle Cove from its location on the cliffs. It only has 25 guest rooms, all of which have been renovated several times in an effort to stay up with the big boys on Grace Bay. The air-conditioned guest rooms are decorated in pastel colors, the furnishings are comfortable. Some of the units are small cottages apart from the main building. There are two pools, a restaurant, bar, two tennis courts, a dive shop, and a health club. It's a cozy little inn and, if you can live with the lack of glitz and newness found in most other hotels on the bay, I think you'll find it a pleasant experience; it's cheap, too. PO Box 238, Turtle Cove, Providenciales, Turks and Caicos, BWI, ☎ 649-946-4240, www.miramarresort.tc. EP from $100.

Sibonné Boutique Hotel. This rather pleasant West Indian-style resort is, perhaps, just what the doctor ordered if you're looking for a getaway from the stress and hubbub of the city. There are only 25 units in this laid-back seaside destination. It's quiet, though lacking in many of the amenities of the larger hotels and resorts on the bay. Guest rooms are all air-conditioned, have ceiling fans, and TVs, and that's about all. The bathrooms are small, with shower stalls only. There is an on-site restaurant, a pool, and a bar. The restaurant has big picture windows with ocean views, making it a very pleasant place for an intimate dinner; the food's not bad either. The hotel is within easy walking distance of the Allegro Resort, so you can eat there too – and spend some in the casino. PO Box 144, Grace Bay, Providenciales, Turks and Caicos, BWI, ☎ 800-528-1905, www.sibonne.com. EP from $210.

Grand Turk

Grand Turk is where the government of the tiny island group has its headquarters. It's also the location of the capitol city, Cockburn Town. Cockburn, by the way, is pronounced "Coburn." This town of 3,500 is a happening place. Grand Turk is not top of the list as far as tourism is concerned, but it is a little less expensive than its more popular neighbor, Providenciales. The island itself has little going for it. It does have some fine beaches and the snorkeling is good, but it lacks aesthetic appeal. There is no lush tropical vegetation here, few colorful plants and flowers, and the prevailing breezes that blow constantly across the landscape give the island a somewhat windswept look. Still, there are bargains to be found on Grand Turk, so you might want to consider the island when making your plans.

■ Getting Around

There's not too much to getting around on Grand Turk. Taxis are available – check with your hotel. The fare from the airport to all hotels in and around Provo is $15. There's also a bus service, which is a bit of an adventure: will it or won't it? If you want to rent a car, you can do that too for about $50 per day. Contact **Dutchie's Car Rental**, ☎ 649-946-2244. You can also rent bicycles at some of the hotels for about $10; cheaper if you rent by the week. Then, if all else fails, you can reach most places of note on foot.

■ Banking

Banks are always the best places to cash traveler's checks. The exchange rates are better. Most are on Front Street. **Bank of Nova Scotia**, Front Street, ☎ 649-946-2831. **Barclays Bank** (great for visitors from the UK), Front Street, ☎ 649-946-2506.

■ Information

Turks and Caicos Information Office, Front Street, Cockburn Town, Grand Turk, BWI, ☎ 800-241-0824; local 649-946-2322.

■ Cockburn Town

The biggest little town south of Nassau, Cockburn Town is the Capitol of Turks and Caicos, though it's difficult to believe, when you

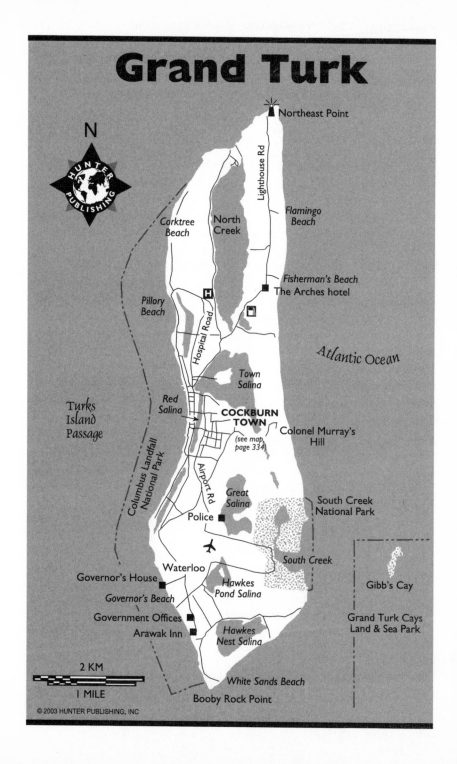

Grand Turk

N

Northeast Point

Lighthouse Rd

Corktree
Beach

North
Creek

Flamingo
Beach

Fisherman's Beach
The Arches hotel

Pillory
Beach

Hospital Road

Atlantic Ocean

Town
Salina

Red
Salina

**COCKBURN
TOWN**

Colonel Murray's
Hill

Turks
Island
Passage

(see map,
page 334)

Columbus Landfall
National Park

Airport Rd

Great
Salina

South Creek
National Park

Police

South Creek

Governor's House

Waterloo

Hawkes
Pond Salina

Gibb's Cay

Governor's Beach

Government Offices

Arawak Inn

Hawkes
Nest Salina

Grand Turk Cays
Land & Sea Park

2 KM

1 MILE

White Sands Beach

Booby Rock Point

© 2003 HUNTER PUBLISHING, INC

Grand Turk

stand on one of its two dusty main streets. It's an old world town with white painted colonial style buildings reminiscent of those you find on the island of Bermuda. One gets a feeling that Humphrey Bogart will, any minute, walk around the next corner with Lauren Bacall on his arm. This intriguing place is well worth a visit if you have time.

■ Sightseeing

Turks & Caicos National Museum. Housed in an historic building constructed out of old ships' timbers from shipwrecks, this could be considered the highlight of a visit to Grand Turk. It's a catalog of the history of the tiny island group, and you'll find many unique and interesting artifacts on display. For instance, some 50% of the museum's displays are centered around the remains of the wreck of Molasses Reef. That's where the Spanish caravel, name unknown, was found. It sank off Grand Turk sometime prior to 1513, making it the oldest known shipwreck in the Americas. When the wreck was first discovered, it was thought to be the wreck of one of Christopher Columbus' ships, the *Pinta*, but this was not the case. It seems there's no evidence that the *Pinta* ever returned to Grand Turk. Today, little is left of the hull of the wreck, but what remains is on display, along with artifacts from the wreck. There are also some pre-Columbian artifacts, including a whole room dedicated to the Taino culture, with a Taino paddle dated to around 1100 AD. Open 9 am until 4 pm weekdays, and 9 am until 1 pm on Saturdays. Tours of the museum are conducted weekdays at 2 pm. Admission is $5 for adults, 50¢ for students. It's located in Guinep House, Front Street, Cockburn Town. ☎ 649-946-2160.

■ Adventures

Snorkeling & Diving

Diving around Grand Turk is exceptional, ranging from shallow reef tops to tunnels. Listed below you'll find several dive operators. Single-tank dives range upward from $35.

Blue Water Divers, at the Salt Raker Inn, Grand Turk, Turks and Caicos, BWI, ☎ 649-946-2260.

Oasis Divers, Duke Street, Grand Turk, Turks and Caicos, BWI, ☎ 800-892-3995.

Whale Watching

 One of the more spectacular opportunities offered on Grand Turk is whale watching. Every year, from January through April, more than 2,500 humpback whales come to breed in the warm waters to the south and east of Salt Cay. They pass through the 22-mile-wide passage between the islands. Here, for more than three months, the great mammals gather to mate and give birth. Humpbacks grow to more than 40 feet long. You can see the great beasts breaching from the shores of Grand Turk and Salt Cay. Better yet, take a trip with Oasis Divers, for $45. Be sure to take along a camera and plenty of film.

■ Dining

Restaurant Price Scale
$ . . . . less than $20 per person
$$ . . . . $20-$50 per person
$$$ . . . . $50+ per person

 $$ Calico Jack's, on Duke Street, is the oldest and busiest inn on Grand Turk. The cuisine claims to be international and, for the most part, it is, with grilled steaks, chicken, fresh fish, and all served in generous portions. There's also a busy bar open from early afternoon until after midnight. The restaurant is open for breakfast, lunch and dinner from 7 am until 10 pm. It's best to make a reservation for dinner. ☎ 649-946-2466.

$ to $$ The Secret Garden, at the Salt Raker Inn, is open most of the day and early evening for breakfast, lunch and dinner. Breakfast (the full English heart attack with eggs, bacon, sausage, fried tomato, and fried bread) and lunch are casual affairs, except for a couple of nights a week when the dinner menu includes lobster, steaks, and fresh fish cooked in a variety of ways. Dessert (apple or cherry pie with ice cream) is also worth a mention. Open from 7:15 am until 9 pm. Reservations for dinner a must. ☎ 649-946-2260.

$ to $$ The Water's Edge, on Duke Street, is all character and atmosphere. The menu is basically Bahamian, but the offerings cover a much wider spectrum. There is, of course, the inevitable conch (good job, too) cooked and served a variety of ways, including curried, along

Cockburn Town

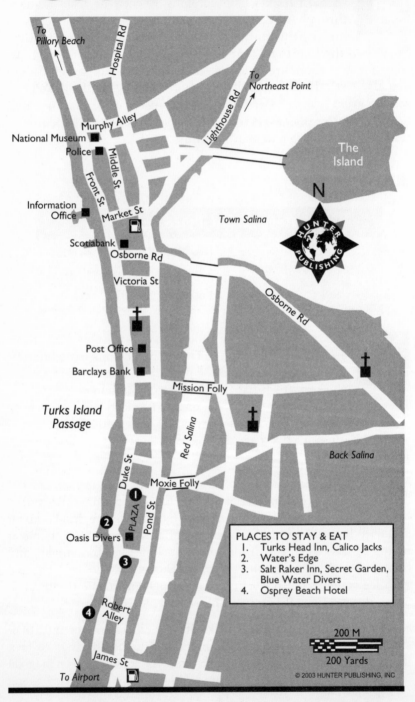

To Pillory Beach

Hospital Rd

To Northeast Point

Murphy Alley

Lighthouse Rd

National Museum

The Island

Police

Middle St

N

Front St

Information Office

Market St

Town Salina

HUNTER PUBLISHING

Scotiabank

Osborne Rd

Victoria St

Osborne Rd

Post Office

Barclays Bank

Mission Folly

Turks Island Passage

Red Salina

Back Salina

Duke St

Moxie Folly

Pond St

PLAZA

Oasis Divers

Robert Alley

James St

To Airport

PLACES TO STAY & EAT
1. Turks Head Inn, Calico Jacks
2. Water's Edge
3. Salt Raker Inn, Secret Garden, Blue Water Divers
4. Osprey Beach Hotel

200 M

200 Yards

© 2003 HUNTER PUBLISHING, INC

with an assortment of steaks, fresh fish and chicken dishes. You can even get an order of buffalo wings, a pizza, all-you-can-eat pasta, and, believe it or not Tex-Mex. Open from noon until 11 pm for lunch and dinner. No need to make a reservation. ☎ 649-946-1680.

■ Accommodations

Hotel Meal Plans

- **CP** (Continental Plan) includes a continental breakfast.
- **EP** (European Plan) denotes no meals, although restaurant facilities are available either on the property or nearby.
- **MAP** (Modified American Plan) denotes breakfast and dinner.
- **FAP** (Full American Plan) includes all meals.
- **All-Inc.** (All-Inclusive Plan) includes all meals, beverages (alcoholic and soft), watersports, tennis and golf, if available.

 Accommodations on Grand Turk, even though the island is the seat of government, are not as modern as they are on Provo, nor are the amenities as extensive. Many hotels and guest houses are not air-conditioned, few have in-room TVs or telephones, and the plumbing can often be a thing mystery and magic. Still, most place are clean and well run, if a little run-down. Those that follow can be relied upon to fulfill most needs, and provide a little old-world charm as well; just don't expect too much. All prices shown are per unit, unless otherwise indicated.

The Arches is a small, modern hotel set on a ridge where you can enjoy some spectacular ocean views. There are just 24 guest units, all air-conditioned, with cable TV and kitchenettes. It's a bit expensive, but nice. Lighthouse Road, PO Box 226, Grand Turk, Turks and Caicos, BWI, ☎ 649-946-2941. EP from $150.

Arawak Inn and Beach Club is two miles south of town. This little resort has 16 suites, all with kitchens. Suites are air-conditioned and can sleep up to four people. There's a nice freshwater pool and a beach bar were you can enjoy a meal. Dive packages and horseback riding are available too. PO Box 190, Cockburn Town, Grand Turk, Turks and Caicos, BWI, ☎ 649-946-2277. Weekly per person from $580.

Osprey Beach Hotel is pretty basic. All of the 16 guest units over-look the ocean. It's a bit run-down, but passable, if you don't mind roughing it a little. Clean, inexpensive. Duke Street, PO Box 42, Grand Turk, Turks and Caicos, BWI, ☎ 649-946-1453. EP from $95.

Salt Raker Inn is a real charmer. There are just 13 guest units, all of them air-conditioned, and all individually decorated. Some have ocean views, some overlook the gardens. Some have TVs and tele-phones, all have ceiling fans and refrigerators. Upstairs units have balconies with hammocks: nice. There's even a restaurant. Inexpen-sive. Duke Street, PO Box 1, Grand Turk, Turks and Caicos, BWI, ☎ 649-946-2260. EP from $75.

Salt Cay Sunset House. Close to the beach, this is the oldest bed & breakfast inn on the Turks and Caicos. Built by a shipwright in 1832, it became the home of one of the island's salt barons. Today, after years of renovations and restoration, the old house provides for a very pleasant and unique vacation. There are just three guest rooms, each with its own bathroom and comfortably furnished. Amenities are few, but the views far and away make up for the lack of creature comforts. There are ceiling fans in each of the three guest rooms, but no phones and no TVs. There is a TV in the one of the public rooms, and there's a café, a laundry, and a picnic area. Fabulous panoramic views can be seen from the patio and outdoor dining area. Rooms are very reason-ably priced, from $35. Salt Cay Sunset House, Balfour Town, Grand Turk, Turks and Caicos, BWI, ☎ 649-946-6942.

Turks Head Inn. This old inn, circa 1869, oozes atmosphere. There are just eight guest rooms, all recently renovated and furnished with antique reproductions. Satellite TV is a bonus, as are the telephones, if you consider such luxuries an essential. Some of the downstairs rooms have their own gardens, and the upstairs rooms have balco-nies. Best of all, it's inexpensive. Duke Street, PO Box 58, Grand Turk, Turks and Caicos, BWI, ☎ 649-946-2466. From $65.

North Caicos

The northernmost island in the group, this is a remote spot. It's a green little island most of the year, due to the fact that it receives more rainfall than the other islands. It's a land of deserted beaches, sparse population, primitive lodgings, basic catering and, above all, seclusion. It has great white stretches of sand where you can wander

North Caicos

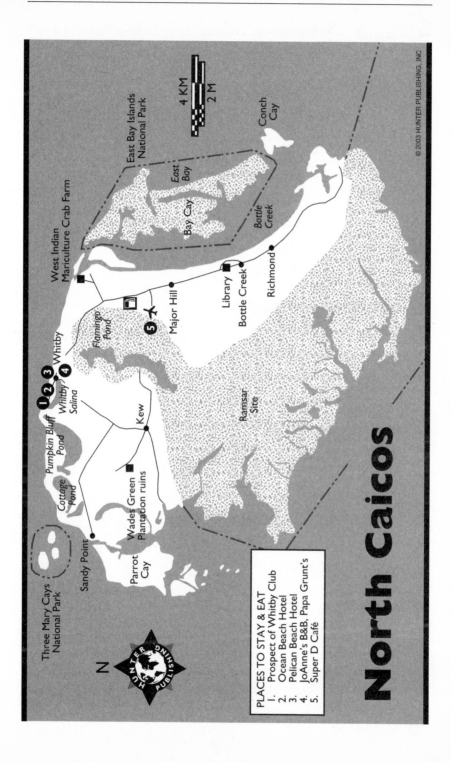

© 2003 HUNTER PUBLISHING, INC.

East Bay Islands
National Park

4 KM
2 M

Conch
Cay

East
Bay

Bay Cay

Bottle
Creek

West Indian
Mariculture Crab Farm

Library
Bottle Creek
Richmond

Major Hill

Flamingo
Pond

Whitby

Whitby /
Salina

Pumpkin Bluff
Pond

Kew

Ramsar
Site

Cottage
Pond

Wades Green
Plantation ruins

Sandy Point

Parrot
Cay

Three Mary Cays
National Park

N

PLACES TO STAY & EAT
1.   Prospect of Whitby Club
2.   Ocean Beach Hotel
3.   Pelican Beach Hotel
4.   JoAnne's B&B, Papa Grunt's
5.   Super D Café

North Caicos

for hours, never setting eyes on another human being. The waters off the island are a snorkeler's and scuba diver's paradise. The ocean teems with colorful life, and the corals lie undisturbed, as they have for thousands of years. You can visit the flamingos at Flamingo Pond, observing them in their own environment. You can snorkel the shallow waters of the barrier reef, and fish the ocean for such prizes as marlin, kingfish, wahoo, tuna, shark, and more. There's also bone fishing. How long this little section of paradise will remain undiscovered is anybody's guess.

■ Getting There

The only way in, unless you own a boat, is by **Turks and Caicos Airways** from Provo, less than 10 minutes away by air. ☎ 649-946-4255.

■ Getting Around

Either rent a bike at **Whitby Plaza**, at the Prospect of Whitby Club, for about $15 a day, ☎ 649-946-7301, or pick up a taxi at the airport.

■ Sightseeing

 Cottage Pond is a large blue hole and only one of a number of ponds and lakes at the northwest end of the island. It's an area of natural beauty alive with birds, including several species of ducks, grebes and other wading waterfowl.

Nearby **Flamingo Pond** is home to flock of wild flamingos, one of only a couple in the entire Bahamian archipelago. It's well worth a visit.

Other ponds and wildlife areas include **Bellfield Landing Pond**, **Dick Hill Creek**, and **Pumpkin Bluff Pond**. Spend a day hiking or bicycling around them all. Be sure to take along plenty of water, sunscreen and a snack.

East Bay Islands National Park encompasses several small islets off the northeast coast of the main island. Three other cays, to the northwest, make up **Three Mary Cays National Park**. These two park systems offer many unique experiences: there are vast bone fish flats, another flamingo sanctuary, excellent snorkeling, and numerous opportunities for wildlife watching. Again, take along water, sunscreen, and a snack.

On the far western shore of the island is **Sandy Point**, a tiny settlement beyond the salt flats where there is yet another colony of flamingos. It's an excellent place for snorkeling and wandering the lonely beaches.

The western side of the island, as you'll see from the map, is a vast stretch of salt marshland and tidal wetlands know as the **Ramsar Site**. This is one of last great, undisturbed wetlands in the Western Hemisphere. It's a world of waterfowl, vast bonefish flats, lobster beds, conch flats, and meandering creeks and streams full of bonefish. If you can find someone to guide you, it would be a shame to miss such an opportunity. Make enquiries at your hotel.

West Indian Mariculture Crab Farm, on the northeast shore, ☎ 649-0946-7213, is a commercial crab farming operation, but you can visit and see how such a venture works, how they breed and grow crabs, maybe even take a boat tour.

■ The Beaches

Whitby Beach lies to the northeast. Then there's **Pumpkin Bluff**, **Bluff Beach**, and **Horsestable Beach** farther to the north and west. All deserted, all fabulous, and all littered with shells and sand dollars.

■ Dining

Restaurant Price Scale
$ . . . . less than $20 per person
$$ . . . . $20-$50 per person
$$$ . . . . $50+ per person

$ Papa Grunt's Seafood Restaurant. The cuisine is American and West Indian, and the food is excellent. The menu includes such delights as conch salad, cracked conch, steamed conch and conch fritters. Fresh fish is also a mainstay of the menu, as is chicken in a variety of forms. Those with a hankering for American goodies can enjoy pizza, steaks, lobster, and even banana splits. Open daily from 7 am until 7 pm, but you'll need to make a reservation for dinner. ☎ 649-946-7301.

$ The Super D Café, at the airport, offers West Indian goodies, including conch and a variety of chicken dishes. ☎ 649-946-7528.

There are restaurants and cafés at the **Pelican Beach**, **Ocean Beach**, and **Prospect of Whitby Hotels**, all open to the public (see below). Reservations are probably a good idea if you want dinner, but most will fit you in for lunch.

■ Accommodations

All prices shown are per unit, unless otherwise indicated.

Club Vacanze/Prospect of Whitby caters mainly to an Italian clientele. There are 23 air-conditioned rooms and four suites. All have tiled floors, rattan furniture, two double beds, a small refrigerator, and a telephone. There's a TV lounge, sun deck, and a pool. Diving, snorkeling, and kayaking are all available through the hotel. It's an all-inclusive resort. Whitby, North Caicos, Turks and Caicos, BWI, ☎ 649-946-7119. All-inclusive from $350.

Pelican Beach Hotel has no frills, but it's clean and functional. There are 12 guest rooms and two suites, all with ocean views, tile floors and patios, small bathrooms. No TV or telephones. There's a bar and snack lunches are available. There's also a dining room where Bahamian-style meals are available . North Caicos, Turks and Caicos, BWI, ☎ 649-946-7386. Rates from $100.

JoAnne's Bed & Breakfast is a very basic, hodge-podge B&B with two rooms that share a bathroom, and six more sort of pre-fabricated affairs, all with hand-made furniture. There's also a two-bedroom villa and a two-bedroom apartment. The owner, JoAnne, is an expatriate originally from Michigan. It's a fun kind of place, and relatively inexpensive. Whitby Beach, North Caicos, Turks and Caicos, BWI, ☎ 649-946-7184. From $70.

Ocean Beach Hotel is a small, intimate hotel with 10 guest units, some two-bedroom, some three-bedroom. All have ocean views, ceiling fans, bamboo furniture and fully equipped kitchens. There's an on-site restaurant and a bar. It's a bit pricey, but kids stay free. Whitby, North Caicos, Turks and Caicos, BWI, ☎ 649-946-7113. From $110.

Middle Caicos

Covering some 48 square miles, Middle Caicos is the largest island in the Caicos group and, with a population of only 300, it's also the least developed. But it's one of the most interesting of the islands – at least, as far as historians and archeologists are concerned. There are 38 pre-Columbian Lucayan Indian sites on the island. The locals are welcoming and love to see visitors. This wild and remote land has towering limestone cliffs and undiscovered stretches of white, sandy shore. There are huge caves in the limestone with crystal clear lakes, stalagmites and stalactites, to explore. The islanders live in three tiny communities – **Conch Bar**, **Lorimers** and **Bambarra**, each barely more than collections of small, primitive dwellings – and there are a number of run-down, outlying farms. To enjoy a vacation here you'll need to be able to leave everything behind. There's rarely an in-room TV, and telephones are few and far between. Very few home comforts are available, and restaurants, what few there are, offer little more than the basics. What you can expect, though, are some fine beaches, a getaway beyond your imagination, and quiet times under blue skies and a hot, tropical sun.

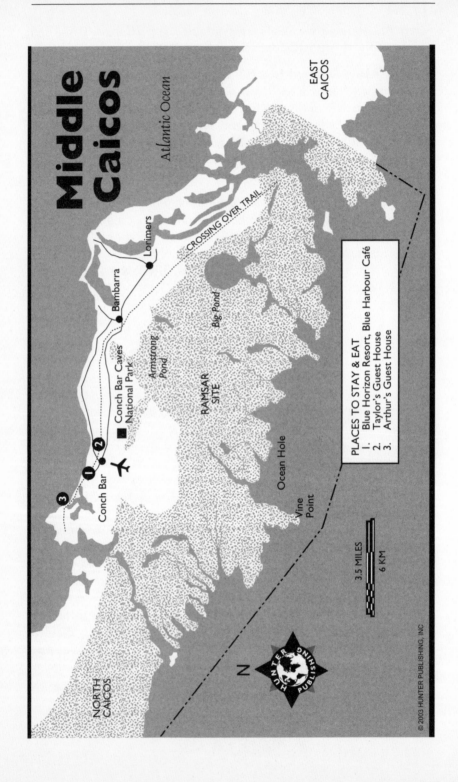

Middle Caicos

Atlantic Ocean

EAST CAICOS

Lorimers

Bambarra

CROSSING OVER TRAIL

Conch Bar Caves National Park

Armstrong Pond

Big Pond

RAMSAR SITE

Conch Bar

Ocean Hole

Vine Point

NORTH CAICOS

PLACES TO STAY & EAT
1. Blue Horizon Resort, Blue Harbour Café
2. Taylor's Guest House
3. Arthur's Guest House

3.5 MILES
6 KM

N

HUNTER PUBLISHING

© 2003 HUNTER PUBLISHING, INC

■ Getting There

The easiest way to get here is to fly onto the island from Provo. You can day-trip the island by way of **Turks and Caicos Airways** (☎ 649-946-2455), which operates a fairly reliable schedule, several times a day, and the fare is only $35 one-way. If you have a private boat with a shallow draft, you can go by sea and enjoy spectacular views of one of the most rugged shorelines in the group. Other than that, you might like to take a tour from Provo with **J&B Tours**, ☎ 649-946-5047, or **Silver Deep Tours**, ☎ 649-946-5612, for about $135 per person.

■ Adventures

The Middle Caicos Reserve & Trail System

 This is a vast nature park incorporating many miles of deserted beach, silent freshwater lakes, and extensive pine forests, all connected by more than 10 miles of trails. The reserve is a part of the Turks and Caicos National Trust and the Ramsar Site, described on page 339. The trail leads past the ruins of a number of old cotton plantations, remnants of Loyalist times, until it joins with the **Crossing Over Trail** that leads to North Caicos. If you're into hiking, you'll want to give this trail a try; be sure to take plenty of water and sunscreen; the round-trip is a long one, and there are no facilities along the way.

Conch Bar Caves National Park

 More than 15 miles of underground, limestone caves, some with large lakes, some with stalagmites and stalactites, make up this unique national park just southeast of the tiny community of Conch Bar. Some are huge, cathedral-like structures, and most are inhabited by colonies of bats – if you have an aversion to the little critters, you might want to give this one a miss. If not, you should visit. The caves are also home to a colony of huge white owls, a rare sight in themselves, should you be lucky enough to see them.

Fishing & Snorkeling

 Call **Cardinal Arthur** in Conch Bar – ☎ 649-946-6107 – for bone fishing, reef fishing and snorkeling outings.

■ Dining

Restaurant Price Scale	
$	less than $20 per person
$$	$20-$50 per person
$$$	$50+ per person

 $ The Blue Harbour Café, at the Blue Horizon Resort, is open for lunch and dinner, but you must make a reservation. ☎ 649-946-6141.

$ Annie Taylor. She does the cooking for Maria at Taylor's Guest House. Just give her a call (☎ 649-946-6117) and she'll provide you with the best of local cuisine, almost for a song: fresh fish, conch in variety of forms, and chicken. If you're looking for local color, this is where you'll find it, and then some.

■ Accommodations

 Accommodations on Middle Caicos are few and far between. What's there is quite basic, with few amenities, and bordering on the primitive, but worthwhile experiences nonetheless. Here's your chance to get to know the islanders for what they really are, warm, welcoming, and extremely hospitable. All prices shown are per unit, unless otherwise indicated.

Arthur's Guest House is a very small, family-run, bed & breakfast inn with two small guest rooms. Both have TVs and small kitchens, but no telephones. It's run by a very hospitable couple, Stacia and Adolphus Arther, who do their very best to make sure your stay is a happy one. It's inexpensive, short on facilities, but comfortable.

Conch Bar, Middle Caicos, Turks and Caicos, BWI, ☎ 649-946-6112. From $60. No credit cards.

Blue Horizon Resort is the best place to stay on Middle Caicos. This five-unit cottage complex is run by a couple from Florida, the Witts, who decided that life on the mainland was something they didn't want anymore. With that in mind, they found this secluded little "resort" and made it their own. They, too, will go out of their way to make sure that all of your vacation needs are met. The five cottages are brightly painted and furnished. Each has a full kitchen – evening meals are available in the dining room on request – and a small bathroom. One or two units are air-conditioned – make a request when you book – and a few have TVs. All are equipped with ceiling fans, but none have phones. A bit pricey, but nice. Mudjin Harbour, Middle Caicos, Turks and Caicos, BWI, ☎ 649-946-6141. From $150.

Taylor's Guest House is owned and run by Maria Taylor. This guest house offers only the basics. Three of the four rooms share a single bathroom; the other has its own. There's a single TV on the property, and there are no in-room phones. The beach is a short walk away. Maria is very congenial, though, and will to do her best to make your stay an enjoyable one. She can arrange local trips (snorkeling, etc.), and will provide meals on request. It's cheap, and very basic. Conch Bar, Middle Caicos, Turks and Caicos, BWI, ☎ 649-946-6161. From $55. No credit cards.

South Caicos

South Caicos is the smallest and easternmost of the Caicos group. Until the end of the 19th century, it was the most productive of the islands, due to its vast salt flats. The shallow waters to the west of the island – Stoke Bank and Caicos Bank – provide some of the best bone fishing in the entire Bahamian archipelago. Experienced scuba divers will tell you that the reef east of South Caicos offers unprecedented opportunities. The reef runs north and south the entire length of the island. There are coral gardens, walls, trenches, and the reef teems with underwater life: rays, sharks, morays, lobster, angels, and the list goes on.

Cockburn Harbour is the only settlement on the island, an eclectic collection of shacks, modern houses and run-down colonial buildings that give evidence of better days. Here, most of the population lives and works. Fishing and conch and lobster farming have long been the only source of income for the islanders, but the lobsters have been over-fished and the industry is now in serious decline. Things are not good on South Caicos, and it shows on the faces of the people. Better times, though, might be just around the corner. There's been some talk lately of plans to build a large resort here and residents are hopeful it will come to fruition. As it is, accommodations on the island are sparse indeed.

■ Getting There

Once again, **Turks and Caicos Airways**, flying from Provo, ☎ 649-946-2455, is the only practical way for vacationers to visit the island.

■ Getting Around

Some of the islanders make their living by using their cars as taxis. You'll find several waiting for you at the airport. Most will be only too pleased to take you on a tour.

■ Adventures

There's not too much, I'm afraid, but if you love nature and the great outdoors, a trek along **Salt Rock Hills** offers some spectacular views. To the west is Belle Sound and tiny Horse Cay, no more than a rock jutting out of the ocean; to the east is the Turks Island Passage.

Fishing

 Call **Julius Jennings**, ☎ 649-946-3444. I hear that he's the man – the guide – who knows all the secrets of where to fish on Belle Sound.

Diving

 South Caicos Ocean Haven, ☎ 649-946-3444, is a full-service dive center offering three dives a day (no certification courses).

■ Dining

 $$ South Caicos Ocean Haven, in the dining room at the hotel on West Street in Cockburn Harbour, ☎ 694-946-3444. They have local cuisine, good wholesome food from set menus that feature fresh fish and shellfish. Reservations required for those not staying at the hotel.

$ Murial's Restaurant, Graham Street, Cockburn Harbour, ☎ 694-946-3535, serves island food as the locals like it. Fish, conch, stews. No frills.

$ Dora's Restaurant, at the airport, ☎ 694-946-3247, has fresh fish and shellfish. The lobster sandwich is their specialty.

■ Accommodations

 All prices shown are per unit, unless otherwise indicated.

South Caicos Ocean Heaven. If you're seeking an air-conditioned place, this is it. There are 22 rooms, all air-conditioned, with a small bathroom, ceiling fan, bed, and a few more pieces of furniture. Not a luxury retreat, but it's clean and fairly comfortable. There are also a couple of villas, each with four guest units; none of these is air-conditioned. Bicycles are available, along with sea kayaks and snorkeling gear. The "resort" is also the island's dive operator. West St., Cockburn Harbour, South Caicos, Turks and Caicos, BWI, ☎ 649-946-3444. Meals-included, from $100.

Mae's Bed & Breakfast, on Tucker's Hill, is run by one of the nicest little old ladies you're ever likely to meet. She offers three clean, comfortably furnished guest rooms and a great breakfast for around $70. She will cook lunch and dinner on request. Mae's is very pleasant, with nice views and great hospitality. ☎ 649-946-3207.

At a Glance

Airlines Serving the Islands

■ Airline Telephone Numbers

Air Canada:............. ☎ 888-247-2262

Air Sunshine: .... ☎ 800-327-8900, fax 954-359-8211

American Airlines: ...... ☎ 800-433-7300

Bahamasair: .... ☎ 800-222-4262, fax 305-593-6246

Bel Air Transport: ...... ☎ 954-524-9814, fax 954-524-0115

Delta: .... ☎ 800-221-1212

Gulfstream (Continental): ☎ 800-231-0856

Island Air Charters: ..... ☎ 800-444-9904, fax 954-760-9157

Island Express:......... ☎ 954-359-0380, fax 954-359-7944

Lynx Air: .... ☎ 954-491-7576, fax 954-491-8361

Major Air: .... ☎ 242-352-5778, fax 242-352-5788

Pan Am Air Bridge:...... ☎ 800-424-2557, fax 305-371-3259

Sandpiper Air: .... ☎ 242-328-7591, fax 242-328-5069

Twin Air: .... ☎ 954-359-8266, fax 954-359-8271

USAirways Express: ..... ☎ 800-622-1015

Package Operators

American Airlines Vacations: ☎ 800-321-2121,
www.aavacations.com.

Air Jamaica Vacations: (phone number available only to travel
agents), www.airjamaicavacations.com.

Apple Vacations: www.applevacations.com.

British Airways Vacations: ☎ 800-AIRWAYS,
www.britishairways.com.

Classic Custom Vacations: sold only through travel agents, but
you can visit their website at www.classicvacations.com.

Delta Vacations: ☎ 800-872-7786, www.deltavacations.com.

USAir Vacations: ☎ 800-455-0123, www.usairvacations.com.

Vacation Express: ☎ 800-309-4717, www.vacationexpress.com.

Travel Impressions: www.travelimpressions.com (book through
travel agents only).

Charter Airlines - Islands of the Bahamas

Cherokee Air: . . . . ☎ 242-367-2089, fax 242-367-2530

Cleare Air: . . . . ☎ 242-377-0341, fax 242-377-3296

Congo Air: . . . . ☎ 242-377-7413, fax 242-377-7413

Charter Airlines - Florida

Air Charter One: . . . . ☎ 800-538-5433, fax 561-750-6111

Dolphin Atlantic Airlines: ☎ 800-353-8010, fax 954-359-8009

Trans-Caribbean Air: . . . ☎ 888-239-2929, fax 954-434-2171

Resort Charter Airlines

Deep Water Cay Club: . . . ☎ 954-359-0488, fax 954-359-9488

Fernandez Bay Village, Cat Island: ☎ 800-9490-1905
fax 954-474-4864

Great Harbour Cay, Berry Islands: ☎ 800-343-7256

Greenwood Beach Resort, Cat Island: ☎ 242-342-3053

Hawk's Nest Club, Cat Island: ☎ 242-357-7257

Riding Rock Inn, San Salvador: ☎ 800-272-1492

Small Hope Bay Lodge, Andros: ☎ 800-223-6961

Stella Maris Resort, Long Island: ☎ 800-426-0466

Getting There

■ Nassau/New Providence

Many direct flights are available, as follows: **Air Jamaica** flies from Newark and Philadelphia; **American Eagle**, from Fort Lauderdale, Miami, Orlando and Tampa; **Bahamasair**, from Fort Lauderdale, Miami and Orlando; **British Airways**, from London; **Comair**, from Cincinnati; **Continental**, from Fort Lauderdale, Miami and West Palm Beach; **Delta**, from NY/Laguardia, Boston and Atlanta; **US Airways**, from Philadelphia, NY/Laguardia and Cleveland.

■ Freeport/Grand Bahama

Direct flights include: **AirTran**, from Atlanta; **American Eagle**, from Miami and Fort Lauderdale; **Bahamasair**, from Miami; **Continental**, from Miami, Fort Lauderdale and West Palm Beach; **TWA**, from NY/JFK.

Getting to Abaco		
Airport	**From**	**Airline**
Marsh Harbour	Ft. Lauderdale	Island Express, Gulfstream, Air Sunshine, Bel Air Transport
	Miami	American Eagle, Gulfstream
	Orlando	USAirways Express

	Freeport	Major Air
	Nassau	Bahamasair
Treasure Cay	Ft. Lauderdale	Island Express, Air Sunshine, Twin Air, Gulfstream
	Miami	Gulfstream
	Orlando	USAirways Express
	West Palm Beach	USAirways Express
	Freeport	Major Air
	Nassau	Bahamasair

Getting to Andros

Airport	From	Airline
Andros Town	Ft. Lauderdale	Island Express
	Freeport	Major Air
	Nassau	Bahamasair
Congo Town	Ft. Lauderdale	Island Express, Lynx Air
	Freeport	Freeport
	Nassau	Bahamasair
Mangrove Cay	Ft. Lauderdale	Island Express
	Freeport	Major Air
	Nassau	Bahamasair
San Andros	Ft. Lauderdale	Island Express
	Freeport	Major Air
	Nassau	Bahamasair

Getting to the Berry Islands

Airport	From	Airline
Great Harbour Cay	Ft. Lauderdale	Island Express

Getting to Bimini

Airport	From	Airline
North Bimini	Ft. Lauderdale	Pan Am Air Bridge
	Watson Island, Miami	Pan Am Air Bridge
	Paradise Island	Pan Am Air Bridge
South Bimini	Ft. Lauderdale	Island Air Charters

Getting to Cat Island

Airport	From	Airline
Arthur's Town	Nassau	Bahamasair
New Bight	Ft. Lauderdale	Island Express
	Nassau	Bahamasair

Getting to Crooked Island

Airport	From	Airline
Crooked Island	Nassau	Bahamasair

Getting to Eleuthera

Airport	From	Airline
Governor's Harbour	Ft. Lauderdale	USAirways Express, Air Sunshine, Bel Air Transport
	Miami	American Eagle

Airlines

	Freeport	Major Air
	Nassau	Bahamasair
North Eleuthera	Ft. Lauderdale	Gulfstream, USAirways Express
	Freeport	Major Air
	Nassau	Bahamasair, Sandpiper Air
Rock Sound	Ft. Lauderdale	Island Express
	Freeport	Major Air
	Nassau	Bahamasair

Getting to Exuma

Airport	From	Airline
George Town	Ft. Lauderdale	Island Express, Air Sunshine, Lynx Air
	Miami	American Eagle, Bahamasair
	Freeport	Major Air
	Nassau	Bahamasair
Staniel Cay	Ft. Lauderdale	Island Express

Getting to Long Island

Airport	From	Airline
Stella Maris	Ft. Lauderdale	Island Express, Bel Air Transport
	Miami	American Eagle
	Nassau	Bahamasair

Getting to San Salvador		
Airport	**From**	**Airline**
San Salvador	Ft. Lauderdale	Air Sunshine
	Miami	Bahamasair
	Nassau	Bahamasair

Getting to the Turks & Caicos		
Airport	**From**	**Airline**
Provo	Miami	American Airlines
	Atlanta	Delta
	Toronto	Air Canada
	Nassau	Bahamasair

Mail Boat Schedules

The following schedules and one-way fares were current at the time of writing but are subject to change without notice. Mail boats leave Potter's Cay, Paradise Island bridge, in Nassau, weekly.

To	**Route**	**Times & Fares**
Abaco	Marsh Harbour, Treasure Cay, Green Turtle Cay, Hope Town	*Miz Desa* leaves Tuesday at 5 pm and returns on Thursday at 7 pm. Sailing time is 12 hours. The fare is $45.

Mail Boats

	Sandy Point, Moore's Island, Bullock Harbour	*Champion II* leaves Tuesday at 8 pm and returns on Thursday at 10 am. Sailing time is 11 hours. The fare is $30.
Acklins, Crooked Island & Mayaguana		*Lady Matilda*, schedule varies, ☎ 242-393-1064. Sailing time is upwards of 15 hours. The fare is $65, $70 and $70 respectively.
Central Andros	Fresh Creek, Stafford Creek, Blanket Sound, Staniard Creek, Behring Point	*Lady D.* leaves Tuesday at 12 noon and returns on Sunday. Sailing time is five hours. The fare is $30.
North Andros	Nicholl's Town, Majestic Point, Morgan's Bluff	*Lisa J. II* leaves Wednesday at 3:30 pm and returns on Tuesday at 12 noon. Sailing time is five hours. The fare is $30. *Lady Margo*, leaves Wednesday at 2 am and returns on Sunday at 5 pm. Sailing time is five hours. The fare is $30. *Challenger.* ☎ 242-393-1064 for schedule. Sailing time is five hours. The fare is $30.

South Andros	Kemp's Bay, Bluff, Long Bay Cay, Driggs Hill, Congo Town	*Captain Moxey* leaves Monday at 11 pm and returns on Wednesday at 11 pm. Sailing time is 3½ hours. The fare is $30. *Delmar L.* leaves Thursday at 10 pm and returns on Monday at 5 am. Sailing time is seven hours. The fare is $30.
Bimini & Cat Cay		*Bimini Mack.* Schedule varies. ☎ 242-393-1064. Sailing time is 12 hours. The fare is $45.
Berry Islands		*Mangrove Cay Express* leaves Nassau Thursday at 10 pm. Return arrives 7-9 am on Sundays. Fare is $30.
Cat Island, North & South	Arthur's Town, Bennen's Harbour, Bluff, Bight	*North Cat Island Special* leaves Wednesday at 1 pm and returns on Friday. Sailing time is 14 hours. The fare is $40.
Cat Island, South	Smith's Bay, Bight, Old Bight	*Sea Hauler* leaves Tuesday at 3 pm and returns on Monday. Sailing time is 12 hours. The fare is $40.
Eleuthera	Rock Sound, Davis Harbour, South Eleuthera	*Bahamas Daybreak III* leaves Monday at 5 pm and returns on Tuesday at 10 pm. Sailing time is five hours. The fare is $20.

Mail Boats

	Governor's Harbour & Spanish Wells	*Eleuthera Express* leaves Monday at 7 pm and returns on Tuesday at 8 pm. She also leaves on Thursday at 7 am and returns on Sunday. Sailing time is five hours. The fare is $20.
The Exumas	Ragged Island, Exuma Cays, Barraterre, Staniel Point, Black Point, Farmer's Cay	*Ettienne & Cephas* leaves Tuesday at 2 pm. ☎ 242-393-1064 for return. Sailing time is 21 hours. The fare is $50.
	George Town	*Grand Master* leaves Tuesday at 2 pm and returns on Friday at 7 am. Sailing time is 12 hours. The fare is $40.
Grand Bahama	Freeport	*Marcella III* leaves Wednesday at 4 pm and returns on Saturday at 7 pm. Sailing time is 12 hours. The fare is $45.
Inagua		*Abilin* leaves Tuesday at 12 noon and returns on Saturday (time varies). Sailing time is 17 hours. The fare is $70.
Long Island	Clarence Town	*Abilin* leaves Tuesday at 12 noon and returns on Saturday (time varies). Sailing time is 17 hours. The fare is $65.

North Long Island	Salt Pond, Deadman's Cay, Seymours	*Sherice M* leaves Monday at 5 pm and returns on Thursday (time varies). Sailing time is 15 hours. The fare is $45.
Mangrove Cay	Cargill Creek, Bowen Sound	*Lady Gloria* leaves Tuesday at 8 pm and returns on Thursday at 10 am. Sailing time is five hours. The fare is $30.
	Hatchet Bay	*Captain Fox* leaves Friday at 12 noon and returns on Wednesday at 4 pm. Sailing time is six hours. The fare is $25.
San Salvador	United Estates, Rum Cay, Cockburn Town	*Lady Francis* leaves Tuesday at 6 pm and returns on Friday. Sailing time is 12 hours. The fare is $40.

Other Sailings

Mail boats also leave Nassau at unscheduled times. You can find out when and for which destinations by calling ☎ 242-393-1064.

Fishing Guides

■ Abaco

Will Key, Marsh Harbour, ☎ 242-266-0059.

Robert Lowe, Hope Town, ☎ 242-366-0266.

Maitland Lowe, Hope Town, ☎ 242-366-0004.

Truman Major, Hope Town, ☎ 242-366-0101.

Creswell Archer, Marsh Harbour, ☎ 242-367-4000.

Orthnell Russell, Treasure Cay. ☎ 242-367-2570 or 242-365-0125.

The King Fish II, Treasure Cay, ☎ 242-367-2570.

Lincoln Jones, Green Turtle Cay, ☎ 242-365-4223.

Joe Sawyer, Green Turtle Cay, ☎ 242-365-4173.

Trevor Sawyer, Cherokee, ☎ 242-366-2065.

■ Andros

Cargill Creek Lodge, Cargill Creek, ☎ 242-368-5129.

Andros Island Bone Fishing Club,
Cargill Creek, ☎ 242-368-5167.

Nottages Cottages, Behring Point, ☎ 242-368-4293.

■ Bimini

The Bimini Big Game Fishing Club, Alice Town, ☎ 242-347-2391.

The Bimini Blue Water Resort & Marina, Alice Town, ☎ 242-347-3166.

The Bimini Reef Club & Marina, South Bimini, ☎ 05-359-9449.

The Sea Crest Hotel & Marina, Alice Town, ☎ 242-347-3071.

Weech's Dock, Alice Town, ☎ 242-347-2028.

■ Eleuthera

Coral Sands Hotel, Harbour Island, ☎ 800-333-2368.

The Cotton Bay Club, Rock Sound, ☎ 800-221-4542.

Valentines Inn & Yacht Club, Harbour Island, ☎ 242-333-2080.

Spanish Wells Yacht Haven, Spanish Wells, ☎ 242-333-4255.

Spanish Wells Marina, Spanish Wells, ☎ 242-333-4122.

Hatchet Bay Marina, Hatchet Bay, ☎ 242-332-0186.

Harbour Island Club & Marina, Harbour Island, ☎ 242-333-2427.

■ Exuma

Club Peace and Plenty, George Town, ☎ 242-345-5555.

■ Grand Bahama

Captain Ted Been, Freeport, ☎ 242-352-2797.

Captain Tony Cooper, Freeport, ☎ 242-352-6782.

Captain Steve Hollingsworth, Freeport, ☎ 242-352-2050.

Captain Elon "Sonny" Martin, Freeport, ☎ 242-352-6835.

Captain John Roberts, Freeport, ☎ 242-352-7915.

Captain Doug Silvera, Port Lucaya, ☎ 242-373-8446.

■ New Providence

Brown's Charters, Nassau, ☎ 242-324-1215,

Captain Arthur Moxey, Nassau, ☎ 242-361-3527.

Captain Mike Russell, Nassau, ☎ 242-322-8148.

Born Free Charter Service, Nassau, ☎ 242-363-2003.

■ Turks & Caicos

Providenciales

Silver Deep at the Turtle Cove Marina, Providenciales, ☎ 649-946-5612.

J&B Tours, at Leeward Marina, Providenciales, ☎ 649-946-5047.

Sakitumi Charters, Providenciales, ☎ 649-946-4065.

Grand Turk

Duchie's, Airport Road, Grand Turk, ☎ 649-946-2244.

Fishing Guides

Dive Operators

■ Abaco

Brendal's Dive Shop International, Green Turtle Cay, ☎ 800-780-9941, www.brendal.com.

Dive Abaco, Marsh Harbour, ☎ 800-247-5338, fax 242-367-2787, www.diveabaco.com.

Dive Odyssea, Great Abaco Beach Resort, Marsh Harbour, ☎ 800-468-4799.

The Hope Town Dive Shop, Hope Town, ☎ 242-366-0029.

Walker's Cay Undersea Adventures, PO Box 21766, Ft. Lauderdale, FL 33335, ☎ 800-327-8150, www.nealwatson.com/Walkers/WalkersTransportation.html.

■ Andros

Small Hope Bay Lodge, PO Box 21667, Ft. Lauderdale, FL 33335, ☎ 800-223-6961, www.smallhope.com.

■ Bimini

Bimini Big Game Fishing Club, Alice Town, North Bimini, ☎ 242-347-3391.

Bill and Nowdla Keefe's Bimini Undersea Adventures, PO Box 21766, Ft. Lauderdale, FL 33335, ☎ 800-348-4644, www.biminiundersea.com.

■ Eleuthera

The Romora Bay Club Dive Shop, Harbour Island, ☎ 242-333-2323.

Valentine's Dive Center, Harbour Island, ☎ 800-383-6480, www.valentinesdive.com.

■ Exuma

The Club Peace and Plenty, George Town, ☎ 242-345-5555, www.peaceandplenty.com.

Exuma Fantasea, George Town, ☎ 800-760-0700.

Staniel Cay Yacht Club, Staniel Cay, ☎ 242-355-2011, www.stanielcay.com.

■ Grand Bahama

Under Water Explorers Society (UNEXSO), PO Box 22878, Ft. Lauderdale, FL 33335, ☎ 800-992-DIVE, 242-373-1244, www.underwater-explorers-society.visit-the-bahamas.com.

Xanadu Undersea Adventures, PO Box 21766, Ft. Lauderdale, FL 33335, ☎ 800-327-8150, 242-352-3811, www.xanadudive.com.

Deep Water Cay Club, Grand Bahama, ☎ 242-359-4831, www.deepwatercay.com.

Sunn Odyssey Divers, Freeport, ☎ 242-373-1444, www.sunnodysseydivers.com.

■ New Providence

Bahama Divers, Box 21584, Ft. Lauderdale, FL 33335 ☎ 800-398-DIVE, www.bahamadivers.com.

Custom Aquatics, Box CB-12730, Nassau, ☎ 242-362-1492, www.divecustomaquatics.com.

Dive Dive Dive, 1323 SE 17th St., Ft. Lauderdale, FL 33316, ☎ 800-368-3483, www.divedivedive.com.

Diver's Haven, PO Box N1658, Nassau, ☎ 242-393-0869, www.divershaven.com.

The Nassau Scuba Centre, Box 21766, Ft. Lauderdale, FL 33335, ☎ 800-327-8150, www.nassau-scuba-centre.com.

Stuart Cove's Dive South Ocean, PO Box CB-11697, Nassau, ☎ 800-879-9832, www.stuartcove.com.

Sun Divers, PO Box N-10728, Nassau, ☎ 242-325-8927.

Sunskiff Divers, PO Box N-142, Nassau, ☎ 800-331-5884.

■ Turks & Caicos Islands

Providenciales

Art Pickering's Provo Turtle Divers, PO Box 219, Providenciales, ☎ 800-833-1341, www.provoturtledivers.com.

Big Blue, at Leeward Marina, Providenciales, ☎ 649-946-5034.

Caicos Adventures, at Turtle Cove Marina, Providenciales, ☎ 800-513-5822, www.caicosadventures.tc.

Dive Provo, at the Resort, Grace Bay, Providenciales, ☎ 800-234-7768, www.diveprovo.com.

Grand Turk

Blue Water Divers, at the Salt Raker Inn, Grand Turk, ☎ 649-946-2260, www.grandturkscuba.com.

Oasis Divers, Duke Street, Grand Turk, ☎ 800-892-3995, www.oasisdivers.com.

Accommodations

Many of these hotels have websites as well. To find them quickly, go to the search engine, www.google.com, and type in the hotel name. If it has a website, the address will come up.

Hotel Meal Plans

- **CP** (Continental Plan) includes a continental breakfast.
- **EP** (European Plan) denotes no meals, although restaurant facilities are available either on the property or nearby.
- **MAP** (Modified American Plan) denotes breakfast and dinner.
- **FAP** (Full American Plan) includes all meals.
- **All-Inc.** (All-Inclusive Plan) includes all meals, beverages (alcoholic and soft), watersports, tennis and golf, if available.

■ The Abacos

The Abaco Inn, Elbow Cay, ☎ 800-468-8799, $120, MAP $33 extra.

The Bluff House Club & Marina, Green Turtle Cay, ☎ 242-365-4247, $90, MAP is $34 extra.

The Club Soleil, Hope Town Marina, ☎ 242-366-0003, $115, MAP $32 extra.

The Conch Inn, Marsh Harbour, ☎ 242-367-4000, $85 EP only.

The Great Abaco Beach Hotel, Marsh Harbour, ☎ 800-468-4799, $165 EP only.

The Green Turtle Club, Green Turtle Cay, ☎ 242-365-4271, $165, MAP $36 extra.

The Guana Beach Resort, Great Guana Cay, ☎ 242-367-3590, $140, MAP $35 extra.

Hope Town Harbour Lodge, Elbow Cay, ☎ 800-316-7844, $100, MAP is $33 extra.

Hope Town Hideaways, Elbow Cay, ☎ 242-366-0224, $140 EP only.

The Inn at Spanish Cay, Spanish Cay, ☎ 800-688-4725, $180 EP only.

Island Breezes Motel, Marsh Harbour, ☎ 242-367-3776, $75 EP only.

The New Plymouth Inn, Green Turtle Cay, ☎ 242-365-4161, $120, includes MAP.

Pelican Beach Villas, Marsh Harbour Marina, ☎ 800-642-7268, $145 EP only.

Schooner's Landing, Man-O-War Cay, ☎ 242-365-6072, $150 EP only.

The Sea Spray Resort & Villas, Elbow Cay, ☎ 242-366-0065, $150 EP only.

The Tangelo Hotel, in Wood Cay, ☎ 242-359-6536, $66 EP.

Walker's Cay Hotel & Marina, Walker's Cay, ☎ 800-432-2092, $125, MAP $32-50 extra.

■ Andros

Andros Island Bone Fishing Club, Cargill Creek, ☎ 242-329-5167, call for rates, EP only.

Cargill Creek Lodge, Cargill Creek, ☎ 800-533-4353, $275, includes all meals and unlimited fishing.

The Chickcharnies Hotel, Fresh Creek, ☎ 242-368-2025, $50, EP, no credit cards.

Emerald Palms by the Sea, Driggs Hill, ☎ 800-688-4752, $90, MAP $40 extra.

Green Willows Inn, Nicholl's Town, ☎ 242-329-2515, $65, EP only, includes taxes.

Longley's Guest House, Lisbon Cay, $60, EP only.

Mangrove Cay Cottages, Mangrove Cay, ☎ 242-3680, $88 MAP and EP.

Moxey's Guest House, Mangrove Cay, ☎ 242-329-4159, $60 EP, FAP.

Small Hope Bay Lodge, Fresh Creek, ☎ 800-223-6961, $150 per person per night, meals and activities included.

■ Bimini

Bimini Big Game Fishing Club, Alice Town, ☎ 800-327-4149, $150 EP.

Bimini Blue Water Resort, Alice Town, ☎ 242-347-2166, $100 EP.

The Compleat Angler Hotel, Alice Town, ☎ 242-347-3122, $85 EP.

Sea Crest Hotel, Alice Town, ☎ 242-347-2071, $90 EP.

■ Eleuthera

Cambridge Villas, Gregory Town, ☎ 242-335-5080, $55, MAP $25 extra.

Coral Sands Hotel, Romora Bay on Harbour Island, ☎ 800-333-2368, $160 MAP and EP available.

The Cotton Bay Club, Rock Sound, ☎ 800-221-4542, $180 MAP and EP available.

The Cove-Eleuthera, Gregory Town, ☎ 800-552-5960, $110, MAP $38 extra.

Hilton's Haven, Tarpum Bay, ☎ 242-334-4231, $55, MAP $30 extra.

Laughing Bird Apartments, Governor's Harbour, ☎ 242-332-2012, $70 EP only.

Palm Tree Villas, Governor's Harbour, ☎ 242-332-2002, $105 EP only.

Palmetto Shores Villas, South Palmetto Point, ☎ 242-332-1305, $100 EP only.

Pink Sands, Harbour Island, ☎ 800-OUTPOST, $300, MAP $55 extra.

The Rainbow Inn, Hatchet Bay, ☎ 242-335-0294, $90, MAP $30 extra.

The Romora Bay Club, Harbour Island, ☎ 800-327-8286, $160, MAP $38 extra.

The Runaway Hill Club, Harbour Island, ☎ 800-728-9803, $125, MAP $40 extra.

Unique Village, North Palmetto Point, ☎ 242-332-1830, $90, MAP $35 extra.

Valentines Inn & Yacht Club, Harbour Island, ☎ 242-333-2080, $125, MAP and EP available.

◾ The Exumas

Club Peace and Plenty, George Town, ☎ 800-525-2210, $120, MAP $32 extra.

Coconut Grove Hotel, George Town, ☎ 242-336-2659, $128, MAP $38 extra.

Latitude Exuma Resort, ☎ 877-398-6222, George Town, Exuma, from $190.

Palms at Three Sisters, Mt. Thompson, ☎ 242-358-4040, $100 EP only.

Peace and Plenty Beach Inn, George Town, ☎ 242-336-2551, $130, MAP $32 extra.

Regatta Point, George Town, ☎ 800-327-0787, $115 EP only.

Staniel Cay Yacht Club, Staniel Cay, ☎ 242-355-2024, $195, includes FAP.

Two Turtles Inn, George Town, ☎ 242-336-2545, $88 EP only.

■ Grand Bahama

Castaways Resort, Box 2629, Freeport, ☎ 242-352-6682, $75 EP.

Coral Beach Hotel, Box F-2468, Freeport, ☎ 242-373-2468, $75 EP.

Club Fortuna Beach Resort, Freeport, ☎ 800-847-4502, $240 EP.

Deep Water Cay Club, Box 40039, Freeport, ☎ 242-353-3073, $350 per night for a minimum of three nights.

The Oasis, The Mall at Sunrise Highway, Freeport, Bahamas. ☎ 800-545-1300. Rates from $118 through $350.

Our Lucaya, PO Box F-42500, Royal Palm Way, Lucaya, Grand Bahamas. ☎ 800-LUCAYAN. Rates from $155 through $490.

Port Lucaya Resort & Yacht Club, Box F-2452, Freeport, ☎ 800-LUCAYA-1, $95 EP.

Running Mon Marina & Resort, Box F-2663, Freeport, ☎ 242-352-6834, $90 EP.

Xanadu Beach Resort & Marina, Box F-2438, Freeport, ☎ 242-352-6782, $140 EP.

■ Nassau-New Providence

The Atlantis on Paradise Island, Box N-4777, Nassau, ☎ 800-321-3000, $170 EP.

The Bay View Village, Box SS-6308, Nassau, ☎ 800-757-1357, $165 EP.

Breezes, Cable Beach, ☎ 242-327-8231, $200 all-inclusive.

British Colonial Hilton, Box N-7148, ☎ 800-445-8667, $150 EP.

The Buena Vista Hotel, Box N-564, Nassau, ☎ 242-322-2811, $95 EP.

Casuarina's of Cable Beach, Box N-4016, ☎ 800-325-2525, $105 EP.

The Comfort Suites, Box SS-6202, Nassau, ☎ 800-228-5150, $150 EP.

Club Med, Box N-7137, Nassau, ☎ 800-CLUBMED. Call for rates.

Club Land'Or, Box SS-6429, Nassau, ☎ 800-363-2400, $230 EP.

Dillet's Guest House, Dunmore Avenue and Strachen Street, Nassau, ☎ 242-325-1133, $50 EP.

The El Greco Hotel, Box N-4187, Nassau, ☎ 242-325-1121, $100 EP.

The Grand Central Hotel, Box N-4084, Nassau, ☎ 242-322-8356, $95 EP.

The Graycliff Hotel, Box N-10246, ☎ 242-322-2796, Nassau, $170 EP.

Holiday Inn Junkanoo Beach Hotel, Box N-236, Nassau, ☎ 800-465-4329, $70 to $100.

Holiday Inn Sunspree, Paradise Island, Box SS-6249, Nassau, ☎ 800-331-6471, $180 to $225.

Nassau Beach Hotel, Cable Beach, ☎ 800-627-7282, $125 EP.

Nassau Marriott Resort & Crystal Palace Casino, Cable Beach, ☎ 800-222-7466, $225 EP.

The Nassau Harbour Club Hotel & Marina, Box SS-5755, Nassau, ☎ 242-393-0771, $90 EP.

Ocean Club Golf & Tennis Resort, Box N-4777, Nassau, ☎ 800-321-3000, $280 EP.

The Ocean Spray Hotel, Box N-3035, Nassau, ☎ 800-327-0787, $90 EP.

The Orange Hill Beach Inn, Box N-8583, Nassau, ☎ 800-327-0787, $90 EP.

Paradise Island Fun Club, Box SS-6249, Nassau, ☎ 800-952-2426, $200 EP.

The Parliament Inn, Box N-4138, Nassau, ☎ 800-327-0787, $70 EP.

The Parthenon Hotel, Box N-4930, Nassau, ☎ 242-322-2643, $65 EP.

The Pink House, Box N-1986, Nassau, ☎ 800-363-3363, $90 EP.

Pirate's Cove, Box 6214, Nassau, ☎ 800-HOLIDAY, $200 EP.

The Radisson Cable Beach Casino & Golf Resort, ☎ 800-333-3333, $180 EP.

Sandals, Cable Beach, ☎ 800-SANDALS, $200 all-inclusive.

Sheraton Grand Resort, Paradise Island, Box SS-6307, Nassau, ☎ 800-782-9488, $215 EP.

The South Ocean Golf & Beach Resort, 808 Adelaide Drive, ☎ 800-228-9898, $140 EP.

Sunrise Beach Club & Villas, Box SS-6519, Nassau, ☎ 800-363-2250, $185 EP.

Villas in Paradise, Box SS-6379, Nassau, ☎ 242-363-2250, $140 EP.

■ Turks & Caicos

Grand Turk

Arawak Inn and Beach Club, PO Box 190 Cockburn Town, Grand Turk, ☎ 649-946-2277. Weekly from $550.

The Arches, PO Box 226, Grand Turk, ☎ 649-946-2941. From $150.

Mount Pleasant Guest House, Grand Turk, ☎ 649-946-6927. From $85.

Osprey Beach Hotel, Duke Street, PO Box 42, Grand Turk, ☎ 649-946-1453, EP $95.

Pirate's Hidaway B&B, Grand Turk, ☎ 649-946-6909, $85.

Salt Cay Sunset House, Balfour Town, Grand Turk, ☎ 649-946-6942. From $35.

Salt Raker Inn, Duke Street, PO Box 1, Grand Turk, ☎ 649-946-2260, EP $75.

Turks Head Inn, Duke Street, PO Box 58, Grand Turk, ☎ 649-946-2466. From $65.

North Caicos

Club Vacanze/Prospect of Whitby Hotel, Whitby, North Caicos, ☎ 649-946-7119. All-inclusive from $350.

JoAnne's Bed & Breakfast, Whitby Beach, North Caicos, ☎ 649-946-7184. From $70.

Ocean Beach Hotel, Whitby, North Caicos, ☎ 649-946-7113. From $110.

Pelican Beach Hotel, North Caicos, ☎ 649-946-7386, EP $125.

Middle Caicos

Arthur's Guest House, Conch Bar, Middle Caicos, ☎ 649-946-6112, EP $60. No credit cards.

Blue Horizon Resort, Mudjin Harbour, Middle Caicos, ☎ 649-946-6141, EP $175.

Taylor's Guest House, Conch Bar, Middle Caicos, ☎ 649-946-6161, EP $55. No credit cards.

South Caicos

Mae's Bed & Breakfast, Tucker's Hill, South Caicos, ☎ 649-946-3207. B&B from $70.

South Caicos Ocean Heaven, West St. Cockburn Harbour, South Caicos, ☎ 649-946-3444. Meals-included, from $100.

Providenciales

Allegro Turks & Caicos and Casino, Grace Bay, Providenciales, ☎ 800-858-2258. All-inclusive from $200.

Beaches Turks and Caicos Resort and Spa, Providenciales, ☎ 800-BEACHES. All-inclusive from $600 to $1,200.

Caribbean Paradise Inn, Grace Bay, Providenciales, ☎ 649-946-5020, EP $165.

Club Med Turkoise, Grace Bay, Providenciales, ☎ 800-CLUBMED. FAP from $1,050 to $1,950 per person weekly.

Comfort Suites Turks and Caicos, Grace Bay, Providenciales, ☎ 888-678-3483, EP $150.

Coral Gardens, Grace Bay, Providenciales, ☎ 800-532-8536. From $135 to $600.

Crystal Bay Resorts, Grace Bay, Providenciales, ☎ 649-941-5555. From $225 to $520.

Erebus Inn, Turtle Cove, Providenciales, ☎ 649-946-4240, EP $120.

Grace Bay Club, Grace Bay, Providenciales, ☎ 800-946-5757. From $395 to $1,395.

The Mansions, Grace Bay, Providenciales, ☎ 649-946-5863. From $650 to $850.

Ocean Club, Grace Bay, Providenciales, ☎ 800-457-8787. From $180 to $850.

Ocean Club West, Grace Bay, Providenciales, ☎ 800-457-8787. From $180 to $550.

Parrot Cay Resort, Parrot Cay, Providenciales, ☎ 877-754-0726. All-inclusive from $500 to $1,650.

Point Grace, Grace Bay, Providenciales, ☎ 888-682-3705. From $345 to $1,175.

The Sands at Grace Bay, Grace Bay, Providenciales, ☎ 877-77SANDS. From $155 to $575.

Sibonne Hotel & Beach Club, Grace Bay, Providenciales, ☎ 800-528-1905, EP $2.

Turtle Cove Inn, Turtle Cove Marina, Suzie Turn Rd., Providenciales, ☎ 800-887-0477, EP $142.

Index

Index

Adventure Guides
from Hunter Publishing

"These useful guides are highly recommended." *Library Journal*

ALASKA HIGHWAY

3rd Edition, Ed & Lynn Readicker-Henderson
"A comprehensive guide.... Plenty of background
history and extensive bibliography."
(*Travel Reference Library on-line*)
Travels the fascinating highway that passes
settlements of the Tlingit and the Haida Indi-
ans, with stops at Anchorage, Tok, Skagway,
Valdez, Denali National Park and more.
Sidetrips and attractions en route, plus details
on all other approaches – the Alaska Marine
Hwy, Klondike Hwy, Top-of-the-World Hwy.
Color photos. 420 pp, $17.95, 1-58843-117-7

BELIZE

5th Edition, Vivien Lougheed
Extensive coverage of the country's political,
social and economic history, along with the
plant and animal life. Encouraging you to min-
gle with the locals, the author entices you with
descriptions of local dishes and festivals.
Maps, color photos.
480 pp, $18.95, 1-58843-289-0

CANADA'S ATLANTIC
PROVINCES

2nd Edition, Barbara & Stillman Rogers
Pristine waters, rugged slopes, breathtaking
seascapes, remote wilderness, sophisticated cities, and quaint, historic towns. Year-round adventures on the Fundy Coast, Acadian
Peninsula, fjords of Gros Morne, Viking Trail &
Vineland, Saint John River, Lord Baltimore's
lost colony. Color photos.
632 pp, $21.95, 1-58843-264-5

THE CAYMAN ISLANDS

2nd Edition, Paris Permenter & John Bigley
The only comprehensive guidebook to Grand
Cayman, Cayman Brac and Little Cayman. En-
cyclopedic listings of dive/snorkel operators,
along with the best dive sites. Enjoy nighttime
pony rides on a glorious beach, visit the turtle
farms, prepare to get wet at staggering blow-
holes or just laze on a white sand beach. Color
photos. 256 pp, $16.95, 1-55650-915-4

THE INSIDE PASSAGE
& COASTAL ALASKA

4th Edition, Lynn & Ed Readicker-Henderson
"A highly useful book." (*Travel Books Review*)
Using the Alaska Marine Highway to visit
Ketchikan, Bellingham, the Aleutians, Kodiak,
Seldovia, Valdez, Seward, Homer, Cordova,
Prince of Wales Island, Juneau, Gustavas,
Sitka, Haines, Skagway. Glacier Bay, Tenakee.
US and Canadian gateway cities profiled.
460 pp, $17.95, 1-58843-288-2

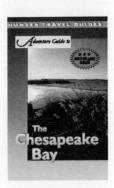

THE CHESAPEAKE BAY

Barbara & Stillman Rogers
One of the most visited regions in the US, including Maryland, Washington DC and Virginia's Eastern Shore. Fishing, paddling,
walking, cycling, skiing, riding are some of the
ways to enjoy this area. The authors tell you
about the best shopping, restaurants and hotels,
along with all other information you will need.
496 pp, $18.95, 1-55650-889-1

COSTA RICA

4th Edition, Bruce & June Conord
Incredible detail on culture, history, plant life,
animals, where to stay & eat, as well as the
practicalities of travel here. Firsthand advice on
travel in the country's various environments –
the mountains, jungle, beach and cities.
360 pp, $17.95, 1-58843-290-4

EXPLORE THE DOMINICAN REPUBLIC

3rd Edition, Harry S. Pariser
Virgin beaches, 16th-century Spanish ruins, the Caribbean's highest mountain, exotic wildlife, vast forests. Visit Santa Domingo, revel in Sosúa's European sophistication or explore the Samaná Peninsula's jungle. Color.
352 pp, $16.95, 1-55650-814-X

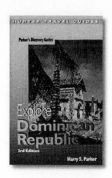

FLORIDA KEYS & EVERGLADES

2nd Edition, Joyce & Jon Huber
"... vastly informative, absolutely user-friendly, chock full of information...." (Dr. Susan Cropper)
"... practical & easy to use." (*Wilderness Southeast*)
Canoe trails, airboat rides, nature hikes, Key West, diving, sailing, fishing. Color.
224 pp, $14.95, 1-55650-745-3

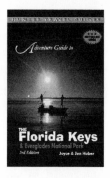

PUERTO RICO

4th Edition, Kurt Pitzer & Tara Stevens
Visit the land of sizzling salsa music, Spanish ruins and tropical rainforest. Explore archaeological sites and preserves. Old San Juan, El Yunque, the Caribbean National Forest, Mona Island – these are but a few of the attractions. Practical travel advice, including how to use the local buses and travel safety. Island culture, history, religion. Color photos.
432 pp, $18.95, 1-58843-116-9

THE VIRGIN ISLANDS

5th Edition, Lynne Sullivan
A guide to all the settlements, nature preserves, wilderness areas and sandy beaches that grace these islands: St. Thomas, St. John, St. Croix, Tortola, Virgin Gorda and Jost Van Dyke. Town walking tours, museums, great places to eat, charming guesthouses and resorts – it's all in this guide. Color photos.
320 pp, $17.95, 1-55650-907-3

THE YUCATAN including Cancún & Cozumel

2nd Edition, Bruce & June Conord
"... Honest evaluations. This book is the
one not to leave home without." (*Time Off
Magazine*)
"... opens the doors to our enchanted
Yucatán." (Mexico Ministry of Tourism)
Maya ruins, Spanish splendor. Deserted
beaches, festivals, culinary delights.

Other Adventure Guides include: *Anguilla, Antigua, St. Barts, St. Kitts
& St. Martin; Aruba, Bonaire & Curacao; The Bahamas; Bermuda; The
Georgia & Carolina Coasts; Jamaica; The Pacific Northwest; New
Brunswick & Prince Edward Island* and many more. Send for our com-
plete catalog. All Hunter titles are available at bookstores nationwide.

We Love to Get Mail

This book has been carefully researched to bring you current, accurate
information. But no place is unchanging. We welcome your comments
for future editions. Please write us at: Hunter Publishing, 130 Campus
Drive, Edison NJ 08818, or e-mail your comments to comments@
hunterpublishing.com.